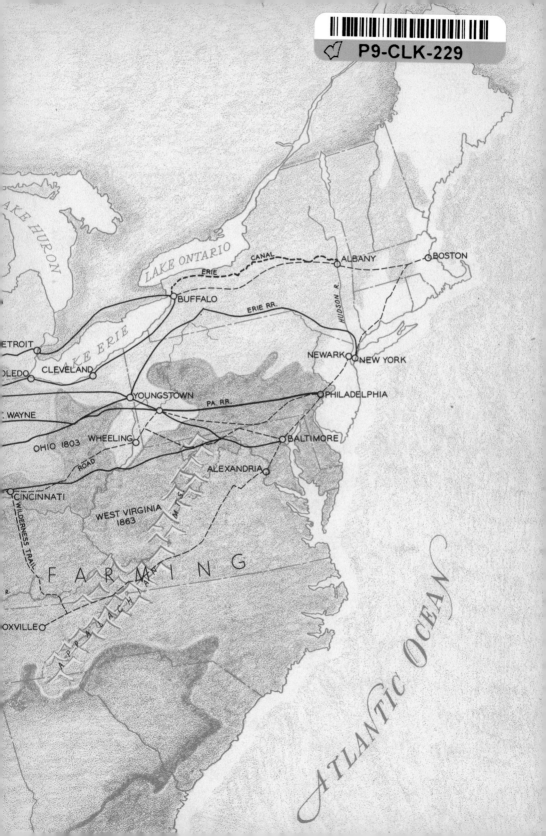

LAKE HURON

LAKE ONTARIO

ERIE   CANAL   ALBANY   BOSTON

BUFFALO

ERIE RR.

LAKE ERIE

HUDSON R.

DETROIT

NEWARK   NEW YORK

OLEDO   CLEVELAND

YOUNGSTOWN   PA. RR.   PHILADELPHIA

. WAYNE

OHIO 1803   WHEELING   BALTIMORE

ROAD

ALEXANDRIA

CINCINNATI

WEST VIRGINIA
1863

F A R M I N G

WILDERNESS TRAIL

APPALACHIAN MTS.

OXVILLE

ATLANTIC OCEAN

BY GRAHAM HUTTON

MIDWEST AT NOON

UNIVERSITY OF CHICAGO PRESS · CHICAGO

University of Chicago Press · Chicago 37

AUTHOR'S FOREWORD

IN THE MIDDLE OF THE JOURNEY OF MY LIFE AND BY THE ACCIDENT OF war, I came to live in the Middle West. It was the region of America which I had always liked best, where I felt and was made to feel most at home, and where I spent the most absorbing, interesting, and happy years of a not uneventful life. The longer I lived there, the more I became convinced that the Midwest and its people were largely unknown, widely misinterpreted, and greatly misunderstood. I also came to believe that the Midwest today was not what it had been and what American folklore makes it out to be. I felt it had altered and was altering profoundly and very rapidly. I felt all this strongly enough to write the book which follows.

It is not just another book by a foreigner about America. If it were, a better excuse would be needed for adding to the thousand or more written by foreigners about the American Republic since 1815. It is about a region of the United States, the people who live in it, their institutions and their characteristics; and even on this geographically limited subject it is not exhaustive. There are great gaps in it, simply because I did not feel qualified to try to fill them. It cannot claim to be either "scientific" or definitive, because it is only a personal record of what struck an Englishman most about the region in which he has spent five of the last eight years. To that extent, what he has written is obviously as much a revelation of his own background and makeup as it is of his chosen subject.

It surprised me back in the thirties, when I first spent some months in, and became fascinated by, the Midwest, that in libraries to which I went for knowledge of that vital and vigorous territory there were few books by Americans, or indeed by anyone else, that told all about the region, its history, and its way of life. Bryce intended to write a separate study of the Great West, but he never got around to it. A Bryce is needed today more than ever to tackle so vast and absorbing a task. Americans of all kinds are forever speaking of the Midwest and its attitude to this or that problem; it always looms large in discussions about politics or policies; and for the last thirty years the entire civilized world has been talking about it.

But try to find out what it is. Ask what states it comprises. See if you can discover one book which will tell you all about its origins, its changing nature during an amazing development, what it has come to be today, and why it is as it is. You will find, like me, that you will have to go to many books and writings. You soon lose the shape of the forest in a maze of different trees, to say nothing of scrub and tall grasses. There is an embarrassing wealth of detail scattered through hundreds of valuable volumes; but the "altogetherness," *das verbindende Etwas*, the something that links it all up and makes it *the* Midwest, will escape you. And if you unexpectedly live and travel in the Midwest for some years, you will feel more certain every day that the Midwest "has something" that makes it what it is, that makes it "tick" as the Midwest. But in the end your own opinion what that something is will probably be as valid as that of the few, the very few, pundits.

As I observed and read more and more, I decided to write merely my own impressions of the Midwest as it was, as it is, and as it yet may be. Here is the result. No one knows its shortcomings, its superficialities, its gaps, its screaming silences, and its probable errors better than the author. But all this may serve a purpose: namely, to provoke, annoy, or stimulate sufficiently to get the proper study of the Midwest written at last. And as to errors of fact or emphasis: the important point, as I see it, is that I have gained these impressions over a period of years, both in peace and in war. I do not mean to say here that the Midwest was, or is, or will be this or that. What I do say is that it so appeared to a stranger in the land, one as free of an American's bias or prejudices as he could possibly be. (The Englishman's bias will inevitably appear as you read on!) Impressions are frequently false. But, as the ancient Greek philosophers noted, men and nations do not act upon facts or truth; they act upon what they believe are facts and truth—and that is often quite another thing.

Anyone who writes of another country than his own tempts Providence and leads with his chin. Despite his intentions, he is not writing just for one public. He will be judged by the people of whom he writes as well as by his own people. He must have a basis or a yardstick for comparisons and contrasts; and he will naturally tend to choose those he knows best, which are those of his own land. Thus he will tread upon corns.

In the whole realm of such literature there is nothing more dangerous than for an Englishman to write about America and Americans. The trail is strewn with the literary skeletons of Englishmen who hazarded it. (Bryce got through brilliantly; and my friend Denis Brogan has succeeded, thanks, in part perhaps, to his self-advertised lack of one drop of *English* blood.) The obvious similarities of language, habit, and way of life mask differences between Americans and Englishmen as numerous and profound as any which distinguish Americans from, say, Frenchmen, Spaniards, Chinese, Germans, and Hollanders—from all of whom have recently come books on America at which no American takes umbrage. On the other hand, if one English voice—and I mean English, not Welsh or Scotch or Irish—be raised in what may be taken as doubt or criticism about things American, the heavens are like to fall. That is not, as poor Mrs. Trollope wrongly said over a century ago, because Americans shiver in the chill wind of criticism; it is because they will accept criticism from everyone except the English. For that I can think of many explanations. One, at least, is that Americans respect—perhaps even love—the English more than they do others but do not care to confess it. Who knows?

But there it is; almost the only unfavorable public comment in America on the young French aristocrat De Tocqueville's book, *Democracy in America*, was Senator Thomas Hart Benton's remark to Van Buren that De Tocqueville "must have kept bad company when in the United States." Yet the list of English writers who did not escape so easily and unscathed is enormous and includes the favored and favorable Bryce. Perhaps they reached out too far toward the Ark of the American Covenant. Perhaps they were supercilious or ill-mannered, which is the same thing. Well, good manners *when abroad* are no more the distinguishing characteristic of the English than of other nations. All people are seen at their best when seen at home. However it be, I hope I shall be thought to have "kept bad company" when in the Midwest if my observations wound or annoy; it is a most charitable excuse, though my only claim to benefit from it is that I intend no hurt, no annoyance. I think every American will find himself believing that if, as I hope, he reads to the end of the book. And if he does not, let him re-read Emerson's *English Traits*. He will find how much alike are the midwesterners of today and the Britishers of yesterday.

Another point: of all foreigners visiting America, naturally those who wrote about it were, according to the standards of their own countries, the most cultivated or educated—two terms which in the eighteenth century meant the same thing, but which our educational systems have not yet succeeded in reintegrating. So these foreign writers naturally tended to compare and contrast the life of *all* Americans with the life of only their own class or group. They tended, with few and notable exceptions, to compare the mass in America with the minority at home.

Few, indeed, were those who made the only valid comparisons: those of like with like, equivalent with equivalent. Bryce was perhaps the best observer of things American in this respect, though he did not, as he intended, make a study of the Midwest. I have tried to follow his course and, in any case, not to lean unduly upon any comparisons. For this and other reasons I have forborne from statistics except where I thought it necessary. The old quip is still true—that figures do not lie but liars figure. There are many books in which a wealth of statistics about the Midwest can be found; but, again, among all those trees you lose the shape of the forest. I have undergone that experience and will spare the reader.

Of course, the book runs the risk of seeming contradictory here and there. How could it be otherwise? The Midwest lies within the longitude and latitude of extremes, in a country of the most striking extremes in the world. It is a region bounded by parallels of paradox. "Do I contradict myself? Very well, then, I contradict myself."

A last but important point: writing about the Midwest, or about any region of any country, necessitates knowledge of other countries and of the other regions of America and of the entire United States. I can fairly claim that. I have worked and lived in six European countries and visited, for my work, all save Russia. Maine and Washington, separated by the width of the continent, are the only American states which I have never visited. In the other forty-six and in the District of Columbia, I have spent weeks or months or years. I have traveled by horse and buggy, automobile, bus, train, airplane, river, Great Lakes steamer, bicycle, shanks' mare, skis, and horse and sled. My automobile was fixed so that I could let down the front seat and use it as a caravan; in it I traveled more than a score of thousand miles. That was in the thirties, and since then I have traveled over a hundred thousand miles in the Midwest.

I have had the great and informative pleasure, which must surely befall every traveler in this great and hospitable country, of finding the most courteous, congenial, friendly, and diverting casual acquaintances and traveling companions: businessmen, mechanics, Mexicans of the Southwest, newspapermen, Negroes, cops, sheriffs, farmers, lawyers, welders, and very many children. There has not been one unpleasant experience in my journeyings. The number of hotels in which I have stayed passes account; but I have been singularly fortunate in the number of homes—homes, not houses—in which I have been lodged as a stranger, only to leave as a friend. I have never lost a dime or anything else—not even my English accent! I have never met with anything but kindness, helpfulness, and a generosity beyond the bounds of imagination. Yet I was always and everywhere unmistakably English. This exemplifies the unwritten law of all America, which is more uniformly observed than many laws on American statute books: namely, that of goodness to the stranger.

So if I write about the Midwest alone, it does not imply that the qualities I mention here are peculiar to that region. I am writing about much more than the *unique* characteristics or ways of life in the Midwest. I am trying to tell of the Midwest as I saw it and as I lived in it, as a temporary part of it, just as the Midwest itself is a part of the all-American team. To the reader I leave, as I must, the decision how much of this or that is "just plain American" and how much is more, or less, American; more, or less, peculiar to the Midwest. I shall try to help him here and there: but no more.

This book makes no pretensions to scholarship. It was conceived and written with too much enthusiasm over the subject for that! It was written to make people think a little more of, and about, the Midwest. If it makes others write more about the Midwest, it will have justified itself.

To attempt to thank here the hundreds of friends whose wise counsel and constant kindness prompted and helped me to write this book is, alas, impossible. I comfort myself with the assurance that they know their names are comprised in the dedication. But I owe a special debt of gratitude and appreciation to the Trustees and Librarian of that remarkable institution, the Newberry Library of Chicago, who made it possible for me to write this book in most congenial surroundings. I am honored, indeed, to be numbered among the Newberry Fellows. They are achieving much, and will achieve even more, in the interpretation of the life and culture of the Midwest. My great appreciation of the staff of the Library should be recorded here. I am grateful to my secretary, Priscilla Thomas, and to Doris Force Flowers of the University of Chicago Press, for their patient and efficient labor in preparing the manuscript. Last, but not least, I want to record my thanks for the understanding co-operation of the University of Chicago Press, with which it has been nothing but a pleasure to be associated.

Chicago
December 1945

CONTENTS

I. "A COUNTRY OF EXTREMES"
Page 1

II. "FRONTIER INFLUENCE"
Page 19

III. "UNCONSIDERED EARTH"
Page 52

IV. "THE CITIES RISE"
Page 96

V. FOLK AND WAYS
Page 163

VI. THE CULT OF THE AVERAGE
Page 246

VII. IDEAS, INCORPORATED
Page 265

VIII. "WE, THE PEOPLE"
Page 285

IX. AFTERNOON
Page 322

INDEX
Page 345

I. "A COUNTRY OF EXTREMES"

A country of extremes .... nothing can be praised in it without damning exceptions, and nothing denounced without salvos of cordial praise.—EMERSON, on England, in *English Traits* (1856).

THE IMPORTANCE OF THE REGION IN NATIONAL LIFE IS GREATER TODAY than we realize. Germany and Italy were made into nation-states only within living memory. Accordingly, the influence of regions looms larger beneath their national surface than we think; for example, Prussia, the Rhineland, Lombardy, Piedmont, the two Sicilies. The role of Great Russia in the making of the czarist and Soviet Russian empires is another instance.

As soon as we turn our eyes to the regions and nations of the New World, however, we encounter an entirely different set of factors: different historically, geographically, economically, and politically. Before Columbus, the vast New World was remarkably thinly populated. America was really a brave new world to the white man. The white man has been there only four and a half centuries, of which the first two hundred or two hundred and fifty years were spent in slow and simple colonization. This colonial pattern, impressed (except in Mexico) mainly on the coastal areas, lasted until a little more than a hundred and fifty years ago. Then it was suddenly and violently torn to shreds by revolutions which successfully laid the foundations for, but did not fully create, the American nations of today.

1

In none of these young nation-states of the New World have its original regions or regional characteristics been as obscured or obliterated as in the nations of the Old World. In the leading American countries, mainly because of their newness and vastness and because of their resulting federal principle of government, federalism and regionalism constantly interacted and are today still interacting—perhaps more than ever and certainly over a wider field of issues and subjects.

Indeed, it was not until our own day, and still first (be it noted) in Europe, that central governments became so harassed by demands for central solutions of the resulting social and economic problems that they and their experts began to think of regions, regional life, and decentralization into regional administration again—after a lapse of centuries. Our technique, our inventions, have made national life so complex that it almost defies the wits of men to run a nation at all—let alone run it well!

All the nations of the New World had to undergo in varying degrees the strains and stresses of the industrial revolution. They were, and are still, tackling three great problems simultaneously which in the leading European nations had come to the fore gradually and in succession through centuries. And they were, and are, tackling them virtually in little more than a lifetime.

They were first building modern, united nations out of vast stretches of an almost virgin continent. Secondly, they were rapidly endowing their young countries with the modern apparatus of production and communication which came from the more gradual European process of the industrial revolution. And, thirdly, they were equally rapidly having to develop *and modify*, as they went on tackling the first two problems, their domestic systems of government and civil administration—political, economic, and administrative.

But it is much more interesting to a European observer today to see the same internal stresses and struggles, which have for a longer time vexed the leading European nations (as the full implications of industrialization and technique were first borne in on European peoples), becoming a grievous problem to Americans in their various American countries: from Canada to Argentina. In all of them, true to type, the parties and people, striving for a solution, think back to the foundations of their form of government and to their beginnings as independent nations. They speak, again, either for stronger powers at the center or for decentralization and for "a regional solution."

2

This book is about the life of a very big region of a very big country. In its influence on its own country and the world it is perhaps the most important single region in the New World. It does not follow, therefore, that, because we look at this one region of one country, we are turning our backs on the world. The development of the American Midwest and its life today—that is, the way it met and still meets its problems—was and still is a record, writ large in that region, of the impact of influences from outside itself and of the reaction of its people to those influences. The influences came mainly from outside, as I say; but the reactions, the response to the challenge, came from the people themselves who made and still make the Midwest. And it is by their responses to the unforeseeable that men, and nations, survive or perish and are judged.

One night in 1944 a dozen of us met for dinner in Chicago to determine for our own satisfaction how one could best describe the Midwest. We were geographers, historians, sociologists, novelists, economists, and political scientists; we came from six states of the Union; we were tolerably well read in the subject beforehand; but we separated, after five hours, "faint yet pursuing." Each, like the blind men describing their first contact with the elephant, was convinced that his particular definition was alone valid. All agreed that there was an elephant. All of us agreed that there was a Midwest. Beyond that, agreement ceased. The region was defined by history, by zones of agriculture, by the dispersion of types of architecture, by the distribution of forms of local government, by political boundaries, by settlements and migrations of peoples, and so on.

One thing, however, was comforting: all definitions of the Midwest covered at least some geographical area, a region of the interior of the United States. If you consult all the authorities—government agencies, commercial organizations, geographers, historians, meteorologists, agriculturalists, and sociologists—you will find that their geographical definitions of the Midwest vary according to their purposes.[1] Yet they vary within definable limits. If no one can say what or where the Midwest is, all can agree what or where it is not! So if you take the highest common factor of many definitions and exclude all debatable territory,

[1] The classic work of reference which comprises most definitions for all the regions of the United States is Odum and Moore's *American Regionalism* (New York: Henry Holt & Co., 1938). They admit (p. 84) and describe marginal belts around their regions but, for the purposes of their book, stick to state lines as boundaries.

you get a Midwest core which virtually all authorities agree is undeniably the Midwest. And extending beyond this core you get a marginal belt which is Midwest territory for some pundits and their purposes but not for others.

It is this way of definition which I have followed. I agree in the main with Odum and Moore that the Midwest region comprises the states of Ohio, Michigan, Indiana, Illinois, Wisconsin, Minnesota, Iowa, and Missouri;[2] but I know that the territory inhabited by people with Midwest background, attitudes, psychology, and institutions goes in many places way outside the political border of these eight states, and in a few places it falls back within it. In other words, the real Midwest, the Midwest of the midwesterners, is the core composed of most of the area of these eight states; but beyond that core you will still find a Midwest, thinning out into something else the farther you go from the center.

Of course, the more your criteria of the Midwest, the more numerous become your "Midwests." For example, if you take areas of farming alone, you get a corn-hog region of the Midwest which sprawls beyond the western borders of Minnesota, Iowa, and Missouri; but in the southern portions of Missouri, Illinois, Indiana, and Ohio that corn-belt line would leave great tracts outside the Midwest region altogether; and the Midwest has a dairy belt in the north. The same would be true of geological or soil boundaries. Again, if you define the industrial Midwest by reference to transport centers, routes to market, routes from sources of raw materials and "belts" of industry, you will find yourself in a quandary on the eastern border of the region; for the Pittsburgh-Wheeling-Akron-Cleveland-Youngstown area of heavy industry covers large tracts of western Pennsylvania and northern West Virginia which are generally placed in the "industrial East" of the United States.[3] Yet these tracts contain cities and people which display as strong midwestern as they do eastern characteristics; and if you look back to their settlement and industrialization, or at their present dependence on the internal routes of industry, you find them as much a part of the Midwest industrial region as of, say, the eastern industrial region which lies away over the mountains toward the sea.

The natural demarcation of the Midwest by its soil and vegetation

[2] *Ibid.*

[3] Odum and Moore (*ibid.*) place them together in the Northeast region for purposes of convenience; though (p. 84) they note that if they used marginal belts around their six regions of the United States, West Virginia would qualify for admission into any of three separate regions.

4

is both important and instructive. It automatically decided and localized the types of farming and, thus, the nature and distribution of the first and succeeding settlements, highways, and trade routes. But an equally important, and allied, demarcation of the region was provided from the outset by water; water, water everywhere; the Great Lakes, the rivers that empty into them, and, just over the little ridges forming the western and southern rims of the Lakes, the great tributaries of the Mississippi. These little ridges, forming the rim of a saucer, were the Indians' portages. They were great watersheds, yet only a few score feet in height and within walking distance of the shore of the Lakes. To this day you can stand on any Chicago skyscraper and, looking northwest, make out a ridge beyond the factories. It is scarcely more than a hundred feet high. On the eastern side of it, little rivers drain into Lake Michigan and so to the Atlantic Ocean. But to the west, many tributaries flow into the Fox, the Illinois, and the Mississippi. The Indians had only to carry their canoes a few miles from the Lakes, and they could go from Canada and the East to New Orleans and the Gulf. One place where they did so is now in the Chicago area. In Indiana and not far from Cleveland in Ohio or from Erie in Pennsylvania are others leading to the Ohio River and the Mississippi. There are many in Wisconsin.

These lakes and great rivers of the Midwest were its first entries and exits, its first highways. They later formed many of the water-level routes of the railroads. They were then an unmixed blessing. But as men massacred the forests and prairie grass and tilled not wisely but too well, the savage onslaughts of Midwest summer rain and winter blizzard washed much of the finest soil on earth down the great rivers. They carried it away to silt up the sandbars, which a young engineer of the United States Army, Robert E. Lee, first successfully removed and thus saved St. Louis, or to build up the Mississippi delta and clog the floor of the Gulf of Mexico. The Midwest lands fared better than the Great Plains to the west—the high, treeless, and sandy topsoil of which, once the scrub and grass had been removed and the plows had bitten beneath, was simply blown or washed away.

The life of the Midwest is more than just the life of the lowland prairies and corn belt. It is not by any means a flat region. There are the northern forests or dairy pastures, amid rolling and sometimes, as in Wisconsin or Minnesota, almost mountainous country—country to which Swiss and Scandinavian settlers understandably gave Swiss, Norwegian, and Swedish names. These settlers, however, on this soil, followed fundamentally the same pastoral pursuits as did settlers from

5

New England. Far, far different, however, was the type of agriculture and pasture followed by the first frontiersmen, hunters, and settlers who, coming into the interior from the hill country of the Old South, pushed beyond Old Virginia into what are now Tennessee, Kentucky, West Virginia, the southernmost portions of Ohio, Indiana, and Illinois, and southern Missouri. They settled on poorer land than the rich core of the Midwest but better land than was left in the East. Coming from the hills and hill valleys, they settled amid new hills and valleys, but they did not greatly alter their way of life. There was no need. The hill country of Kentucky, the Ozark plateau in southern Missouri, and the rolling lands of southern and eastern Ohio, southern Indiana, and southern Illinois were more fertile than the hills of the Old Dominion; they demanded no change of methods, or, indeed, of domestic architecture, for the climate was milder than it was farther north in the lowland prairie and forest lands of the Midwest proper. Many of these southern settlers and their descendants stayed put. They are still to be met in the southernmost fringes of Ohio, Indiana, and Illinois, throughout the Ozark hills, and, of course, across the Ohio in Kentucky and West Virginia. This is still today an unmistakable line forming the northern frontier of southern life and influence. That is why today as soon as you leave the core of the Midwest and cross this line of southern influence, which forms the inner boundary of the Midwest's marginal belt, you are stepping into debatable territory.

I would, therefore, include within the Midwest marginal belt the south of Ohio, Indiana, and Illinois, because influences from the core of the Midwest have definitely affected and modified those areas. But from the Midwest I completely exclude the Ozarks, for the same reason that I exclude all of Kentucky. Their life is in no way that of the Midwest, nor do they look to the Midwest for anything except local trade, tourists, and, perhaps, entertainment. They are not even parts of the marginal belt around its economy and way of existence. For all the foregoing reasons, too, I exclude what the American census includes in the larger Middle West: namely, the two Dakotas, Nebraska, and Kansas—though part of all of these four states comes well into the marginal belt.

A singular no-man's land runs from the Canadian border down to the Missouri-Kansas line. This is the "dry-weather belt" of the Midwest. Here our marginal belt is fairly wide, though, unlike the margin in the Ohio and Indiana territory, it is thinly populated and is almost wholly agricultural. This northwestern marginal belt takes in the eastern portions of North and South Dakota, Nebraska, and Kansas as well as

6

the western portions of the Midwest states of Minnesota, Iowa, and Missouri. The reason for this northwestern marginal belt of the Midwest is compounded of soil, vegetation, geology, and climate. Roughly between longitude 95° and 100° west, and above latitude 37°, the Midwest prairie and hay belts peter out on the rising ground of the Great Plains; the tall grass gives way to the short; and a fairly clear-cut agricultural "watershed" (due to lack of rain) occurs. In the north, dairy pastures disappear and are replaced by wheatlands, small-grain lands, or range country. Farther south the last traces of the corn belt vanish, and the prairie gives way almost exclusively to high, flat wheatlands. This marginal belt shifts from year to year and from decade to decade with the wide variations of rainfall. Only up the river bottoms, all tributary to the Missouri from the high Rockies farther west, can you trace the last vestiges of Midwest prairie or dairy farming; and even there the modern irrigation, which is bringing a new kind of agriculture into the Great Plains, is spreading its influence.

In all these margins, and most definitely inside their ambit, lies the authentic Midwest.

NATURE'S TERRORS

Forced by a savage climate to manufacture his own defenses against it, and to surround himself with the greatest material aids and comforts yet devised by humanity, the midwesterner today scarcely gives a thought to the natural obstacles around him which had to be endured and overcome by the pioneers of his grandfather's day. Of these obstacles, none was worse than the climate and the weather of the region. It is no wonder that so many of the domestic mechanical contrivances and defenses against this climate were invented or manufactured in the Midwest.

Of all the regions of the United States, the Midwest has what seems both to Americans and to other visitors the most unkind climate and the most inclement weather. That probably explains one of the general practices of the better-off, and one of the general aims of those hoping to get rich enough, which is to leave the Midwest at least twice every year on vacation. Many of them ultimately retire altogether from it. In every case the aspirants make for the sun in winter, for dryness at all times, and for a temperate zone in retirement. Lest I be thought grimly facetious, or just an Englishman preoccupied with that English weather which has been one of the stock American vaudeville jokes for three generations, let me develop this point.

There are colder American regions in winter, and regions which are

7

hotter in summer, than the Midwest; and the Midwest apologist, with the Americans' consuming passion only for the averages in statistics (and in almost everything else), points to the average or mean winter and summer temperatures in the Midwest. But, as usual, averages signify little. What is significant is the variation of extremes about an average; and, as I said earlier, the Midwest lies in the latitude and longitude of American extremes and within parallels of paradox. Nowhere else in America do you have to suffer during the year such wild combinations, rapid changes, and wide extremes of weather varying around climatic averages. Thus in the South, Southwest, Rockies, or Great Plains, one season will be either hotter or colder than it is anywhere else in America; but in those regions Nature's compensation is the long mildness of the other seasons. This is even true of Maine, Vermont, and New Hampshire in the Northeast. But not so in the Midwest. There, and even in the most extreme portions of the region, the mercury in winter seldom falls below an average of 10° below zero, and in summer seldom rises above a mean of 90°. That seems extreme enough to any European except perhaps someone from the heart of Russia; but it is as nothing compared to the extreme variations between these summer and winter averages.

The Midwest is, of course, vast and is bound to show within its ambit great variations. On its confines—in Missouri and in the south of Illinois, Indiana, and Ohio—winter is always milder than at the core of the region. These were the territories settled by the first pioneers. The summer of these southern territories of the region is, however, correspondingly fiercer; temperatures often reach 105°. Yet both their summers and their winters are relatively drier. There is not so much humidity. So in the north and extreme west of the region, in Minnesota, upper Wisconsin, and North Michigan, the summers are milder but the winters fiercer; the mercury often falls to 35° below zero. Yet both summers and winters are drier. Humidity is not such a nuisance.

It is the core of the Midwest which has the worst weather: the area east of the Mississippi including the northern halves of Illinois, Indiana, and Ohio, the Michigan peninsula, and southern Wisconsin. This is the coastal area of the Great Lakes, which here exercise an attraction on the transcontinental lines of temperature and pressure and form a kind of water pocket around which the great winds sweep snow, rain, and cold spells.

Dwellers in the belt that runs from Milwaukee to Chicago, the big cities along the Indiana-Michigan coastal rim, Detroit, Toledo, Cleveland, Erie, and Buffalo and a long way inland, during the ferocious

8

winters are weighed down by a cold humidity and blasted by icy winds reaching gale dimensions. They are snowed-in frequently by blizzards that blacken noonday and paralyze all forms of traffic. They are exposed to the packing of snow into miniature but almost as deadly Himalayas of solid black ice on every path from the home driveway to the sidewalks of the metropolis. Blizzards snow-in the suburbanites to this day; and the normal snows are heavy enough to make shoveling and cleaning, overshoes and snow boots, an indispensable part of every midwesterner's winter. Rare, indeed, in any winter in this wide core of the Midwest is an ideal winter-sports day: clear, dry air, bright-blue skies, hard, strong sun, no wind, and zero or subzero temperature. When such a day dawns, everyone talks about it: commuters and housewives and storekeepers and school children.

In defense against the bitter winds and cold the Midwest has developed artificial heating in its houses, offices, and vehicles to a point at which its people are alternately baked and frozen a dozen times a day. It is not fantastic to suppose that this contributes to that extraordinarily widespread Midwest affliction known as "sinus trouble," and it certainly contributes to the pallor of the people in winter, just as the equally savage summer sun, the wind, and the extreme variations of natural and artificial temperatures contribute to the more numerous lines and wrinkles of Midwest faces.

In this core of the Midwest there is no spring—a significant natural phenomenon which may account for at least one big gap in the romantic literature and poetry of the Midwest.[4] Winter lasts, solid and remorseless, from Thanksgiving to March. Then it often begins to relent for a tempting few days which fool plants and people alike. Next, the fierce solidity of winter gives way to chill, howling winds, torrents of rain which seem as if they should be falling at another season in the tropics, a long period of ground frosts, and day temperatures in the forties and fifties. At this time the thaw and the rains swell the big Midwest rivers into floods which devastate the countryside far down the rivers and outside the region and drown or render homeless hundreds and sometimes thousands of people.

This inclement spell generally lasts well into May or even the beginning of June—making both the fierce and the milder portions of winter into one season of six or seven months' duration. Then, the trees and plants and birds and animals having crept gradually and imperceptibly

---

[4] A delightful French writer of my acquaintance said that no one could call the Midwest "the latitude of love": it was either too hot or too cold! There is, alas, no spring; no "small rain."

into a chill, bedraggled version of spring, suddenly the gales abate overnight. Meanwhile the sun has long been fooling everyone by clambering stoically up to the summit of the heavens for almost half the year, but with benefit of light alone. Equally suddenly he now explodes in heat ranging between 80° and 100°. (Republicans will not quickly forget their Chicago convention of 1944!) Frosts in May, 100° in June, are more regular than irregular. Flowers, shrubs, birds, and mankind drink in the sun for an ecstatic week or two; the grass and the leaves are spring-green for only two or three weeks in the year; and then "summer has set in with its usual severity."

"Severity" is the word. When the summer heavens are not as brass, which they are for periods of a few days and often for weeks at a time, they pile up with majestic and terrifying cumulations of rain and thundercloud. The summer storms provide, with the star-spangled moonless nights of winter and fall,[5] the most majestic display of the Midwest heavens in the entire year. Then the Midwest becomes tropical. Nowhere in the so-called temperate zone—from which I think the Midwest should be forever excluded—do you encounter such thunder and lightning, such torrential rains, such an opening of the fountains of the great deep. The temperature often does not fall. Instead a steamy, clammy heat pervades everything. The storms are over as quickly as they begin, but meanwhile much of the topsoil in garden and field alike has gone down to the rivers and oceans—unless the owner has level land, or has drained, terraced, or plowed by contour, or repaired the gullies on his land. Out comes the sun again and with methodical cynicism proceeds to bake the remaining topsoil to terra cotta. This then cracks into new fissures, eagerly expecting the next waterspout to widen them.

The dust, too, comes from the topsoil, whipped up in the remoter areas of the Midwest by the little embryonic "twisters" or whirlwinds which, drunkenly, waltz across the fields like pillars of cloud by day, or blown off by the sudden blasts which precede and follow the savage summer storms.

In the country the summer means dust: dust which permitted, and in many parts still permits, the poorer children to walk safely and comfortably barefoot into the pages of the Midwest's folklore, thus establishing an almost necessary qualification for the childhood of midwestern presidential candidates. The sidewalks of the towns in summer

[5] I have not seen in over twenty countries starlit heavens to compare with those of the Midwest when there is no moon; not even in the blackout in wartime Britain. They fully justify James Joyce's apt phrase, "the heaventree of stars hung with humid nightblue fruit."

10

are as uncomfortable to rapidly tiring feet in all-too-light footgear as they are in winter to ankles, when the surface is knobbed and craggy with black ice.

In high summer come the insects: flies, mosquitoes, winged bugs of every shape and color—all of them "bigger and better" than in Europe—which necessitate the ubiquitous wire-screen doors and windows. This also necessitates the semi-annual chore of paterfamilias, who has to put the screens up and take them down—unless he is one of the five per cent who live in town apartments offering janitor service or are rich enough to employ gardeners or hired men. It is impossible to sit in a Midwest garden in summer because of the insects, except for two weeks in May or June.

Summer, too, conditions the household appliances: iceboxes; that figure of smoking-room folklore, and favorite of all children, the ice-man; automatic refrigerators, which betray their origin by still being called iceboxes; and the new deep-freeze repository either at home or at a central store of private lockers. Suburban and country folk take to that most civilized institution of the Midwest summer, the sleeping porch, wire-screened on three sides. But even then the nights are treacherous for parent and child alike. Frequently the tropical storms break in the wee, sma' hours; the rain is blown in; the lightning and thunder wake the sleeper; and what begins as a welcome drop in temperature for man and beast quickly degenerates into a deathtrap by way of pleurisy or pneumonia. The temperature first yields, then falls, then drops, then plummets downward. Again paterfamilias or mater-familias plods around, this time closing windows and covering the awakened children. In the morning, heavy-lidded and loath to part from sleep, they find the sun beating down with refreshed zeal upon a porch well on the way to becoming a Black Hole of Calcutta.

When storms do not vary the monotony of heat and humidity, night succeeds night in a remorselessly growing tedium of rising temperature, and sleep comes ever more and more slowly to a humanity already exhausted, worn, and dehydrated by the rigors of successive brazen days. What winds or breezes then blow come from the Great Plains to the west, sweeping across half-parched prairies, more suggestive of a prairie fire than of the frolic wind that breathes the spring or summer's gentle zephyr.

Another trick of the Midwest summer and early fall is to bring out the grasses and weeds whose pollenation causes thousands of sufferers from hay fever and other allergies to spend agonizing days and weeks. The newspapers print the day's pollen count on the front page—sure

11

sign of its general importance! The worst sufferers can be seen wearing a kind of gas mask that makes them look like Martians. Those prone to the ubiquitous sinus trouble are also among the sufferers. Thus is the prairie revenged on the children of its destroyers!

Nor is there in the Midwest summer the purifying influence and refreshing ozone of the sea. No one born in England is more than sixty miles from sea water; so on this point I am, though trying not to be, a prejudiced witness. But the great and smaller lakes and rivers of the Midwest certainly do not perform what Keats called the "task of pure ablution" about their shores. Quite the contrary. The cities often empty their sewage, fully or not so fully treated, into these lakes and rivers, with results, down-current, that make the visitor wonder not so much at the widespread outbreaks of disease, which often become epidemics, as at the authorities' ability to keep them within any bounds at all. Nature is kind; the Midwest and its waterways are vast; man is puny; and all animals naturally become conditioned and self-inoculated in a given environment. Happily, the well-to-do all build swimming pools; there are innumerable clubs; and cities build and operate pools which only occasionally have to be closed because of one epidemic or another.

As with the natural water, so with the air of the region: coming into the Midwest from the seaboard in summer, one has the impression that one is living under "that inverted bowl they call the sky" the air of which has all been breathed before. There is iodine and many another property in seaside air, and, at least if we are to go by the results of inquiries by European experts, the folk and their cities by the sea are on the whole healthier than those deep in continental interiors.

Yet the Midwest has one season which, though only of two months' duration, goes some of the way to redress the overweighted balance of wicked winters and savage summers. It is the fall. From mid-September to mid-November, with short interruptions of chilly, rainy days, the Midwest gets its only temperate period of the year. It is much finer, much more beautiful, than what is conventionally called "Indian summer." The days are warm and the nights cool, with occasional light frosts gradually becoming more intense. The foliage slowly takes on those remarkable shades and colors which make the fall in America and Canada unique in the whole world. "Great clouds along pacific skies" rarely explode into the wrathful and regular thunderstorms of summer. The last tiring insects become fewer and lazier. The skies become more brightly blue than at any other time of the year.

Paterfamilias takes down his screens, puts up storm windows, and

12

rakes leaves. The air is mildly imbued with the thin and acrid smell of wood smoke. The winds are tamed; the dust dies out of the atmosphere; and the only real breezes of the year gently rustle the long, crackling, dried-out leaves of corn on the stalks. Berries of all kinds and colors deck the hedges and shrubberies. The very heart of the cities becomes finally comfortable. Over all, a different suffused light from the sloping sun strikes street and building, forest and field, in a strange way, throwing shadows into unexpected places and illuminating what for most of the year lay in shadow. The sunsets, always imposing in the Midwest, now reach their majestic climax. Homeward-bound commuters see the red sun making the west look like that "dark and bloody ground" whence the Midwest itself sprang. The fruit is picked, bottling goes on in kitchens or basements, and late root vegetables alone are left in the fields or gardens. And so imperceptibly, but with the logic of seasons and Nature and the pioneers' history, the Midwest draws toward that peculiarly American family festival of Thanksgiving, to the accompaniment of the first flurries of new snow.

Thus the Midwest ends its year mildly and with promise, as if Nature were relenting after so much savagery during the other ten months. Being a region of such violent natural extremes, it is small wonder that its people have come to reflect wide extremes in their individual and collective characteristics. They have had to adapt themselves to sudden and violent changes of weather. All they could do was to perfect mechanical defenses, to live as much indoors as possible during the most extreme three quarters of the year, and "worry through." There is a saying in Chicago: "If you don't like our weather, wait ten minutes; it'll change."

Such rapid and violent changes take it out of the people more than the midwesterners, looking at their long-limbed, corn-fed husky youngsters, are prepared to admit. But a stranger sees the youngster and the grown man. There is a perceptible and, I should say, premature tiring in the Midwest. It is generally masked by the rapid, restless tempo of social and business life, and by what passes for entertainment and is properly called in the vernacular a "whirl." This tiring is naturally more noticeable in the cities and towns than in the country; but even there, after forty, life manifestly does not *begin*. It is beginning to run down. Less can be physically tackled. Though I shall have more to say later on the social causes of this tempo and its fatiguing effects, I must say here that I do not think the Midwest climate is kind to human beings. I would not go as far as an Italian friend of mine who, after his first visit to the Midwest, said that he now knew why the Indians of the interior had never been numerous. But a climate and weather with wider and more violent extremes, and more rapid shifts between them, than in any other region on the face of the globe—except parts of the interior of Russia—must either take toll of its inhabitants or compel them to adapt by recruiting their energies in repose. Yet repose and recruitment of energy are two things which midwesterners, to a man, and especially to a woman, now flatly reject.

It was not so among their forebears, the pioneers. That is why they stuck it out and lasted. But the pioneers had time on their hands—a season at a time. Time on their hands is now the greatest fear, almost a phobia, of the overwhelming bulk of midwesterners. That may also be an all-American characteristic. But, to me, the significant feature is that, in the other regions of America, Nature does not impose such savagely alternating and wearing trials upon the people; or, if she imposes trials, as in the deep South or extreme North, the people conform, live out a pattern of life, and save themselves. What the outcome will be I cannot say. Midwesterners can ponder it and, no doubt, refute me.

The Midwest has been made and populated by European peoples; yet no people in Europe—except again the Russians of the Russian interior—has to live in a climate and weather as extreme as those of the Midwest. It is therefore natural that the descendants of these people as time went on, and as it goes on, should show marked physical and other deviations from their European fellows of the same stock.

But what utterly defies one's imagination today is how the original pioneers ever stuck it out. There were no metals, no nails, no window glass, often no windows, and only homemade wooden utensils and implements. When one thinks of those three-sided open-face camps, or the four-sided log cabins through the crannies of which the blasts and blizzards penetrated—like that in which Lincoln was born or that in which his father lived in Illinois forty years later—one does not wonder at the original surplus of men and the original rarity and preciousness of women and children in the Midwest. That preciousness is only four generations old and goes far to account for the singularly high indulgence accorded to women and children throughout the Midwest—and, of course, in varying degrees, in the rest of America—today.

It accounts for more than this, too. The only form of portable central heating among the pioneers was whiskey and other forms of hard liquor. It was drunk neat, sometimes with a "chaser" of tea or water or even milk, for breakfast, dinner, and supper. Women drank it as toddy. It was given to children a few months old. Its universal use throughout the early Midwest has conditioned drinking habits in the

14

region to this day, despite the excesses and personal tragedies to which it gave, and gives, rise, and despite the periodic and perfectly understandable waves of agitation for temperance which have always begun in the Midwest from the earliest times. There is little physical reason for the drinking of hard liquor today in the Midwest; but once upon a time there was. It is as well to remember that today. Habits are quick to form and hard to kill.

The climate continues to influence other habits, however. Dress poses a difficulty. In winter and summer you are often too hot or too cold, and it is impossible in summer, except as to footwear, to be always prepared for drenching rains. Americans laugh at the Englishman's umbrella and pity him the constant need of it; but more midwesterners of both sexes carry umbrellas than do other Americans, or else they ruin their clothes and sit in damp apparel—which many have to do, ruing the consequence with colds, "sinus trouble," and kindred ailments. The difficulty of being adequately clothed for a day's emergencies, summer and winter, is frequently resolved by wearing enough "in case."

As often as not, this results in the wearer becoming overheated, with further consequences which can be gauged from the omnipresence of printed and spoken admonitions to guard against body odor, preserve "personal freshness," "daintiness," and what-all. This is by no means a promotional stunt by wise guys who manufacture such aids to the making (or keeping) of friends and to the influencing of people in a pleasant way. There is a real demand; the need had to be met; and it is. Cleanliness is now ranked above Godliness in the Midwest, for virtually all people really practice the cult. Laundries, washing machines, and other aids for washing testify to the personal cleanliness of nearly all midwesterners: frequent changes of linen, more frequent than perhaps anywhere else, are a conventional necessity. Much of this, too, dates from a century ago when it was possible for women to wash the family's clothes only four times a year and not at all in winter.

What difficulties Nature provides anyway, Man has added to in the shape of air-conditioning in summer and artificial heat in winter. Try as they can, midwesterners of both sexes cannot now go out in the morning—or at any other time of day for that matter—and be even reasonably sure of being suitably clothed for all the natural and artificial temperatures and weathers of a typical Midwest day. Nowhere, I think, do people hang so much on the weather forecasts over the radio. Who would blame them?

All these terrors quickly tempered the initial optimism and resilience of the pioneers into a justly famous and indomitable will to master them; but that is not the tale of all the pioneers. It is only the tale of the fittest for survival. Thousands fell by the wayside, victims of agues, "the shakes," the plagues like the fearful "milk-sick" which prematurely carried off Abraham Lincoln's exhausted mother, and epidemics which still occasionally convulse the Midwest under newer and un-English names. These thousands are not numbered in the book of life of the region. But they were of a Great Company. Over their worn-out bodies the rest passed safely forward. The survivors had to develop a toughness different from that other toughness of discontent and unease which had impelled them forth from the more settled and stable order of the colonial East. It was a toughness to match, withstand, and overcome the naked elements in a savage region. Because their own loved ones went to the wall young, because the violence of Nature and of Nature's son, the red man, was ever at their elbow, because of their own hair-breadth escapes, the pioneers who survived held human life cheap. They had every reason to.

But their sons and their sons' sons made life safer and made one of the leading regions of the earth where there was only a wilderness two or three generations before. Even so, in that region of America's greatest extremes, life is still held cheaper than in almost any other part of America. Habits of mind are even harder to alter than physical habits. Fire and flood; impenetrable forests; savage beasts; thunder, lightning, and rain; snow and ice; damp cold and moist heat; cloudburst and whirlwind; famine and pestilence—from all of these and among them all, year in and year out, came the cornfields and great cities, the highways and railroads, the homes and farms and factories of close on forty millions of mankind today.

More than that: among these violent natural extremes and among the artificial extremes which they impelled men to add, came extreme ideas, ideals, and attitudes, and extremes in that human society which both made the Midwest and was in turn made by it. Thereby, too, hangs another tale.

In the American East and even more so in more stable and settled, stratified West European nations, the progress of industrialism took much of the old adventurousness out of masculine living and gradually wore away the primeval and primitive masculine pride in strength, cunning, assertiveness, and "fight." But the natural elements and human environment of the Midwest remained—and still to some extent remain—as an arena in which these virile qualities could still play a satisfying and profitable part. These masculine values are among the few masculine values still honored there. In commerce and politics, as we shall see, they make one of the notable Midwest paradoxes: namely, an unbending conservatism in a region which was made, and made great, by innovators, progressives, radicals, and pioneers.

These values fulfilled, and still fulfil, an even more important role. In the more stable and stratified regions or nations of Western civilization, the mass of mankind has long been chafing against the drudgery and automatism of industrial technique, against the disappearance and disrepute of personal skills and prowess, and even against the humdrum tedium to which the individual seems condemned in modern democracy. There is no element of "fight-play" or "battle-games" for these masses; so, to use Ortega y Gasset's title, we see a revolt of the masses. Instead of the games and civilian skills with which to flex their male muscles, they took willingly to real warfare. It is, significantly, a revolt by males against their emasculation and devitalization, against their mechanical degradation into robots or serfs of a soulless social machine. They are even ready to follow false gods—Demos led by demons. As a result, all the world has been plunged backward into a barbarous arena where masculine virtues have once more been accorded due recognition —but at a cataclysmic cost to humanity and to a laboriously acquired Western civilization.

The Midwest, the region of extremes and violent challenges, has from the outset afforded, and still to some extent affords, a natural and social arena in which the struggle to survive, fitness, combat, aggressiveness, and cunning always were and still are at a premium. The male virtues, and vices, can be used to their utmost there without any effort to find ways of doing it. True, they are now less exercised than ever before in the Midwest, but more so than anywhere else in Western civilization today; and more so than anywhere else in America.

Is it fanciful, I wonder, to link this element in Midwest life with the Midwest's admitted aversion from war, with its high concentration of pacifism, and with the simple, uninhibited, often naïve psychology of most of its inhabitants? That psychology is so often derided by other regions of America as "unsophisticated." May it not be that, because of the natural combativeness, assertiveness, struggle, and competitive prowess needed in the everyday life of most midwestern males, the people are in the main less inhibited and that in consequence there is less need in that region for a revolt of the masses? May it not be that all their combative faculties were flexed and exercised to the full already, simply by the violent challenges of their natural environment and of the man-made milieu which it called forth? May it not be

17

that what was called "isolationism" in the Midwest is really due to the full satisfaction of aggressive impulses in "civil" life and in time of so-called peace? May it not be that the Midwest was relaxed, satisfied, exercised enough, somewhat tired, and, in any case, self-sufficient?

I cannot answer these questions, and we shall have to consider their implications later. But it seems right to pose them; and I think they should first be asked while we notice Nature's own extremisms in the region.

II. "FRONTIER INFLUENCE"

THE MIDWEST HAS GIVEN SO MUCH FOLKLORE AND MYTHOLOGY TO America—and to the youth of the whole Western world—that in the first century of life, from about 1790 to 1890, no one really studied all aspects of its miraculous development from a primitive frontier territory to a leading industrial and agricultural region of the globe. No one could, for the region was still making seven-league strides forward and the American internal frontier of "free land" did not officially close until about 1890. For too long, therefore, Americans, and still more foreign observers, were content with glib generalizations about "frontier" characteristics, Indians, lawlessness, and the mythology that goes therewith. This attitude to the Midwest, except among a handful of American historians, persisted—and to a remarkably unjustified extent still persists—down to our own day.

The early acquisition of this vast, vague interior by the young United States was perhaps the greatest single factor compelling the original thirteen states to stick together and form "a more perfect Union" between 1784 and 1800. Especially was this so in the very critical three decades of divisions and differences between 1790 and 1820. The stake of each and all of the original thirteen states in the development of so vast a territory over the mountains was even then obvious. Not quite so obvious was the fact that this new West would, as it developed, make it harder for the Union ever to break up. Indeed, it was the

19

Midwest that was really to toll the death knell of the ill-starred southern Confederacy's attempt to break that Union more than two generations afterward.

French explorers, trappers, traders, and Roman Catholic missionaries from Canada were the first white men to penetrate the American Midwest, under the guidance of Indians and by canoe. They came by the easiest of all primitive routes, the waterways, along that fantastic chain of lakes and rivers which thrusts right through the North American continent in the tracks of old glaciers. With their canoes, following the aboriginal Indians, they crossed the surprisingly short portages along the southern or western edges of the Great Lakes. Thus they hit the tributaries of the great rivers and proceeded down them. French and Roman Catholic influences are still stronger than most people think in the Midwest; they came from a long-established and well-administered colonial life in the north: French Canada. The weak influence of Spain and the Spanish Catholic missions, on the other hand, coming upstream from the Gulf, is scarcely even traceable in the region today.

Two features are to be noted at this early date. First, the New England and Middle Seaboard colonies were not too interested in the great American interior beyond the frontier. They had already established their trade and their financial and shipping connections with countries which could be reached for commerce only by ship—Canada, the other coastwise British American colonies themselves, the West Indies, and Great Britain. It was the middle and southern American colonies which first looked inland.

The second feature arose between 1748, when the Ohio Company was formed by a London "Forsyte" of that day together with some of the First Families of Virginia, and 1763, when the so-called "French and Indian War" was officially ended by the Treaty of Paris. "The American frontier" began its first real move from a narrow colonial seaboard, east of the mountains, into the interior. It was in 1753 that Governor Dinwiddie of Virginia precipitated the war by deciding to send an official emissary, the twenty-one-year-old brother of the first local manager of the Ohio Company, to Venango, a French fort near the origin of the Ohio River in western Pennsylvania, to warn off the French. The young surveyor was George Washington. His mission was a failure for everyone except himself, for he returned empty-handed, yet imbued with realization of the possibilities of the interior. There, later, he bought more land than he ever had in his native Virginia.

The victories in the war of 1754–63 really decided that the British

20

and not the French would control the interior. But they did not allay the British colonists' discontents with their government in London, and, as the colonists' frontier slowly moved into the interior, these discontents grew. The frontier in 1750 was reached virtually in a day's hard ride on horseback from tidal water almost anywhere along the Atlantic coast line of the British colonies. By 1776 it had marched many leagues inland, but mainly from the middle and southern colonies, not so much from New York and New England. It remained for the Revolutionary War to thrust it—from Virginia and Maryland and Pennsylvania—over the great spine of the Appalachians into the real basin of the Midwest.

Very quickly, between 1763 and 1776, the interest in the settlement and development of this region became inextricably intertwined with the seaboard colonists' interest in independence. This was natural, since royal proclamations and orders after 1763 had tried to keep the colonists out of the Midwest and preserve it for the French, the Indians, the British, and the Indian fur trade. The Quebec Act of 1774 annexed to the British province of Quebec all the lands north of the Ohio and voided the pre-existing claims on western lands by the seaboard colonies and land companies alike. When the Revolutionary War had broken out, the two interests, expansion and independence, became one. All the leading independent states then joined in a scramble to resuscitate their earlier claims to the newly won "western lands."

In 1778 George Rogers Clark, intent upon clearing the British out of the territory forbidden to colonial would-be-settlers by the royal orders and the Quebec Act, marched into what had been French Illinois to capture, for his independent Virginia which claimed the territory, the remaining forts on the French trade route from Canada to St. Louis. But the British, who had inherited the forts, had already decided to evacuate the region. Clark arrived at Kaskaskia, Illinois, with his Kentucky Virginians—not many more than two hundred—to find only a French caretaker. "There were no birds to fly!" It was almost the same story at Vincennes (Indiana) and as far as Detroit. With a few hundred men and hardly a scuffle, Clark acquired most of what is now Michigan, Ohio, Indiana, Illinois, Wisconsin, and Minnesota. Clark would not have recognized his territory seventy-five years later.

The background to this story is also illuminating. Clark had differed with General George Washington, also a Virginian, and so had Governor Patrick Henry of Virginia, because the hard-pressed Washington badly needed Clark's handful of Virginians back in the East. Accordingly, Clark took possession of the vast territory in the name of Virginia and of its governor, Patrick Henry. To this day, hanging in the state capital buildings at Springfield in Illinois, the portrait of "the first governor" of this territory is that of Patrick Henry of Virginia.

Virginia claimed what is now Kentucky and the bulk of Ohio, Indiana, and Illinois, together with part of Michigan, Wisconsin, and Minnesota. The northern colonies, which had hitherto showed comparatively little interest in the western lands, now rushed in. Massachusetts claimed much of what is now Illinois and Michigan. Some states jointly claimed the same territories. Connecticut claimed a narrow but immensely long tract running from the western border of Pennsylvania clear through to the Mississippi. North Carolina claimed what is now Tennessee. South Carolina and Georgia extended themselves straight back to the Mississippi. The squabble between the eastern "have" and "have-not" states—the latter led by Maryland—became so bitter that the states could not even secure unanimity for the adoption in 1777 of the Articles of the American Confederation. The squabble dragged on until, one by the one, the various "have" states agreed on the sensible course, demanded by Maryland, of ceding their western claims in favor of, first, the Continental Congress and, secondly, the United States. Even then, significantly, New York readily gave up her western territory. Connecticut, annoyed with both the Union and Pennsylvania, was the last to cede her strip—the Western Reserve along the southern shore of Lake Erie in what is now Ohio—in the year 1800. This was the same year that Spain ceded her great Louisiana territory to Napoleon.

This transfer of the entire Northwest Territory was a decision second only in momentousness to the Revolution itself. It gave the Confederation its first real federal assets. It strengthened the civil as against the military elements in the Revolution. It rendered necessary federal funds and finances and the first federal civil service. It prevented, in time, the domination of the future Union by the Old South, or New England, or the entire East alone. It meant that the new entity called the United States had to acquire not only these vast western territories but, therewith, the power to administer and regulate and control them, and to decide when and how new states should be carved out of them and admitted to the Union. The big land companies could not face tasks of this magnitude. The question first came to a head in 1784. Thomas Jefferson, who a decade earlier had attacked the British government's proclamation and orders and the Quebec Act as unprincipled restraints upon the seaboard colonies' rights to their own hinterlands, drafted a plan for the transitional organization of the vast terri-

22

tory until it could be settled, populated, and split into sixteen new states. This was the first Northwest Ordinance, adopted but never carried out by Congress.

It was a good thing that it was not executed, for in 1785 came the more influential Land Ordinance, which resulted in the rectangular survey of the western lands; the six-mile-square "township" composed of thirty-six "sections," each of one square mile; the reservation of four out of each thirty-six to be the property of the United States for disposal and of one section in each township as a source of revenue for public schools. This land survey represented a defeat for southerners, who wanted to see their older land pattern carried westward. So this, too, was important to the development of Midwest life and institutions. Land offices were set up, and the regulations deliberately and very politically and profitably arranged that the United States, the states, and the big private land companies were the only agencies through which any ordinary settler could obtain a quarter-section—or more, or less. This greatly helped the Union finances and the land companies but not the settlers, who were often exploited. To this day as you cross the Appalachian herringbone by air, flying westward, you see at once the wide rectangular pattern of the land which forms this frontier between colonial and new America. The Midwest began as "public domain."

In 1787 came the new and effective Northwest Ordinance, providing for full freedom of religion, and the famous ban on slavery in the new region which, despite Jefferson's insistence upon it, had failed of inclusion in the first ordinance of 1784. This exciting series of Jefferson's political triumphs reached its climax—one long studied and foreseen by Jefferson—when, as President in 1803 and contrary to the Constitution, he bought by private treaty the Louisiana territory from Napoleon for twelve million dollars. Thus were the internal barriers to American development into a continental nation pulled down.

This inadequate story of momentous beginnings is worth retelling because right at the outset were planted seeds which grew to great events during the next hundred years. These events were on the grandest scale imaginable; they were epic in their grandeur and in their tragedy alike. Today we tend to forget that the Revolutionaries' and Jefferson's victorious struggles for control of the Northwest Territory and Louisiana raised the specter of the greatest American tragedy, the Civil War; for here the first issue over the extension of slavery to new states was raised; here, too, began the decline of the erstwhile dominant South and New England; here, also, began the struggle between South and North along the seaboard for the allegiance of the Midwest.

23

Within less than a decade the influence of the Northwest Territory on Congress had become so great that, despite the strong opposition of the New York and New England sea-traders, the War of 1812 with Britain was forced on the administration by popular pressure. This war was largely fought in the Midwest and resulted in the first real wave of Midwest self-awareness and self-assertiveness in domestic American politics, at the expense of the East and South.

It is idle to speculate in historical futures—what the world might have been if Cleopatra had been homely, if Charlemagne had married the Empress Irene, or if Napoleon had not fired a "whiff of grapeshot" at a mob—but nothing is more interesting today than to speculate on what America and the world might have been had Jefferson not lived. It is he who deliberately fostered Midwest settlement to offset the dominance of commercial New England. It is he who sacrificed New England's seaborne commerce and merchant marine in this attempt to give the new Union a perpetually agricultural and equalitarian basis, which the commerce and cities and wealth of New York and New England threatened to undermine. It is he who saw in the new Midwest the basis of a free peasant-farmers' society which would never (he thought) be run by city mobs and a city proletariat. It is he, rather than any other, rather even than Washington who supported Jefferson's views of the future of the interior, who should be hailed as "the father of the Midwest"; yet, like Moses, he saw the Promised Land but was never to enter it.

Between 1790 and 1820 the thin pre-Revolutionary trickle of mainly southern pioneers into the south of the Midwest (as opposed to the more settled Kentucky and Tennessee) gave way to a more general migration into the region from the South and the East. These people were bent on pioneer agricultural settlement. This became a rush after the War of 1812. The moving frontier of practically settled (though not continuously settled) land jumped from western Pennsylvania and little more than the shores of the Ohio River in 1800 to an uneven line running from beyond Detroit in the north to the banks of the Missouri River in the southwest in 1820. Within these two decades, Ohio, Indiana, and Illinois were admitted to the Union as states; and in 1820, by that compromise which, "like a fire-bell in the night," awakened the aging Jefferson and filled him with terror at "the knell of the Union," Missouri was admitted as a slave state, offset by Maine in the North. Thus by 1821 the core of the Midwest was clearly visible as it has remained to this day: Ohio, Indiana, Illinois, and Missouri. In 1837 Michigan was admitted: in 1846, Iowa; in 1848, Wisconsin; and, last, in 1858, Minnesota. Beginning with the Northwest Ordinance of 1787 and the Louisiana Purchase sixteen years later, and ending in 1858, the political bounds and states of the Midwest were established. Thus the formative period which made the Old Midwest was the century from 1763 to the Civil War.

Within that period of less than two lifetimes, the frontier of free land was moved away from the edges of the eastern seaboard states to form a great arc around northern Michigan, central Wisconsin, central Minnesota, and Iowa until it crossed the Missouri River into Nebraska and Kansas. The Old Midwest was made before the Civil War. It was made by human hands, the horny hands of pioneers. It was hewn from the timbers of a forest primeval that practically covered the ground. Its agriculture was first implanted in the clearings of that forest. Its beginnings were dark and bloody, in declared and more often in undeclared wars against white men and red men alike. It certainly was a frontier region in every respect until the close of that worst kind of war—war between men of the same kin—in 1865. But what kind of men were they who made this region? What did they bring with them?

Southerners were the first colonial settlers in the Midwest. The influences from the South were real; but they most certainly were not influences which a well-to-do southern planter or the First Families of Virginia, then or now, would either have applauded or recognized as peculiarly southern. For the first southern pioneers and settlers, like Clark's soldiers, were largely "roughnecks," malcontents, dissidents, misfits in a stable or stratified colonial society; they wore chips on both shoulders. They were rough and tough and plucky; they were notably honest; they were mighty hunters of man and beast; they were excellent if undisciplined soldiers; and many were also shifty, improvident, and, like Lincoln's father, bone lazy except when they had to work or were going hunting. The first civilian entrants into the Midwest were quickly swollen by land-hungry veterans of three wars: the French and Indian (Seven Years') War of 1754–63, the Revolutionary War, and the War of 1812. Of the first groups of settlers in the Midwest, the southerners and the war veterans are the most striking. It is still worth recalling that the United States began the process of government-sponsored land grants on favorable terms to war veterans right from its own national beginnings until almost a century later.

These two elements among the first pioneers—poor southerners and war veterans from all over the thirteen states—shared a peculiar psychology. To begin with, they were very anti-British, also anti-French, because of the three wars; and all of those wars, to them, meant the winning of the West and the right to settle in it. But they were more "anti-" than just anti-foreigners. They were anti-imperialism, because they were against empires like those of France or Britain and because they were against any kind of domination of man over man. Was not slavery prohibited from the outset in the Northwest Territory?

The civilians from the South and East were largely disillusioned with the more settled and rigid society of the seaboard colonies before they decided to pull out. Indeed, it was to find opportunities for a freer and wider life denied to them in the East that they went over the mountains. But the veterans, too, were of almost the same psychological makeup. They were quickly disillusioned after their victories—as armies always have been. They hated war. They quickly discovered that they were not going to get the "new deal" or "new order" in the victorious thirteen eastern states for which they thought they had been fighting. Independence in these seaboard states merely changed the men at the top but not the system of society—at least not for a generation or two. The men at the bottom, many of whom did not even get the vote, found that the two-hundred-year-old colonial pattern of society went on, to the personal profit of a new set of men and new "classes."

Discontented, poor, and anchorless people point to, and aim at, a new order of society. The older British gentlemen whose little group had directed and won the Revolution—Washington, Jefferson, Jay, Adams, Monroe, Hamilton, Madison—were more closely akin to the English gentlemen of London or Bristol in their social and economic thinking than they were to their own veterans, their own poor, and their own artisans. If anyone doubts that, let him remember what an American today would call the shockingly undemocratic and un-American views of the greatest liberal of them all, Jefferson, who did not want to see the artisans of the eastern cities given the vote lest it break the rural and agricultural basis of the American peasant farmers and squirearchy! There were soon great disillusion and frustration among the poor and the unsettled veterans, who were jobless and futureless, displaced from or misplaced in society; and the new eastern American society had not yet become sufficiently elastic and progressive to promise economic opportunity. Indeed, much of the development of the Midwest from 1789 to 1860 was due to the lack of opportunity in the settled East, just as much of the development of the Great Plains and beyond after 1865 was due to discontent with the more settled conditions of the Midwest.

These dissenters from eastern society quickly became anti-colonial-society, anti-class-society, and anti-eastern. Beyond the mountains, promised and made available to them by a Congress which seemed quite ready to be rid of them, lay a vast region where, except for Indians—a hazard that did not seem unnatural after wars with white men —there were no human beings at all; and the Indians did not really settle.

This was part of the psychological prompting behind that westward moving of the American frontier which was to go on for more than a hundred years, until the American tide filled the continent and began to eddy around and even ebb. It was not, of course, *all* that psychological prompting. There were many other elements to it. There was a real hunger for good land in the original thirteen states under their old colonial systems of land tenure and their wasteful systems of agriculture. Land could still be had, cheaply; but it was cheap because it was poor; and it was often poor not only because its soil was poor to begin with but also because eastern farmers and planters took everything out of good soil and put nothing back, until they just sold out to newcomers and moved farther off where the soil was good. Thus, a hundred and fifty and two hundred years after the Pilgrim Fathers had landed, new waves of "pilgrims," dissatisfied with a rigid society, struck out westward. They were mainly men without a status in the existing order of the older community in the thirteen states. They were looking at a region in which almost anyone could make his mark, a virgin territory in which—if for no other reason—their pale faces and rarity would stamp them as Somebodies, even if only to each other. There would be a new and real equality, an equality of social significance.

It was such men who went into the wilderness; who established a social, political, and judicial order for themselves, modeled largely *in form* after the one they left behind in the East but operated *in fact* from the bottom up, not from the top down. Their order, and their method of establishing and executing it, arose from their own primitive needs and at the level of those needs. (There was nothing quite like it in the world; and it is doubtful if there ever has been any adventure quite like it.) And this new Midwest order of life naturally took on, from the outset, the color of its makers' psychology. That psychology pervaded everything in the Midwest until this century: dissent, contrariness, differences in religion and politics, dislike of other nations, dislike of eastern American society, hatred of war, an intense desire and striving for material comforts and possessions, and a deep feeling for the equality and brotherhood of man.

It would be neither accurate nor fair to give the idea that the pioneers and first settlers were all men with chips on their shoulders. The mere

27

existence of the Midwest had a lot to do with prompting easterners and southerners to migrate. Where else could they go? The wild life of the vast forests, the virgin richness of the soil once the clearings were made, the fact of virtually free land to be had for the taking, the adventurousness of wild and open-air living, the important opportunity for the male to *build* something of his own (which our civilization well-nigh denies him), the absence of practically all restraints except those inside a man—all these attractions worked. The Midwest had a lot to offer as well as a lot which appalled.

It is also a big mistake to think that the pioneers went into the Midwest—the Northwest, or just "the West," as it was called for one hundred years—to found a Utopia, a new order of human society, a land of heart's desire, a new system of human government. They did quite a lot to achieve all of these, but it was accidental and incidental to their main reason for going: which was just to go from where they already were, to quit, to pull out, to move where they thought land was more plentiful or easier to get or to work, to shift where a living could be had with greater ease and freedom from social constraint, to migrate from crowds and crowdedness and all that goes therewith.

Anyone who thinks the first settlers were Pilgrim Fathers or Crusaders or Mormons should look at the first legal, political, religious, and governmental institutions which they set up for themselves. These were almost indistinguishable in form from those of one or more of the thirteen original states which they had left. One of the most cogent promptings which made them quit the East was their realization that the East would develop and crowd upon the available land and cities and jobs and opportunities there and that this "jelling" of eastern and southern society would mean a class society again, a hardening of the social arteries, a government by the privileged. Where they intended to go, they would be the only class; they would be the only privileged (at the Indians' cost); and, whatever they made or built, their children could inherit and make or build into something better, and again for themselves alone. There, if at all, would be real equality of opportunity —if not of hand and brain.

There were a few pioneers and first settlers who, from the outset, did want something like a new order of society. Some of them had what we think are "queer" religions which did not go well with the rigid Protestant and Roman Catholic churches of the East or of Canada and France. Others just preferred the free life of the wilderness. They liked neither the settled and stable life of the town nor that of farming country. All these men moved constantly onward, always the first wave

28

of the tide. The Thomas Lincoln family's migrations are an example of this type. As the territory around them became washed by later and more numerous waves, became more settled, involving formalities and lawsuits and federal or state officers and civic duties, this first wave of men—the real pioneers—moved on.

In time, as the Midwest filled up, men of this stamp finally quit the Midwest itself and followed the moving American frontier and the "free land" out to the Great Plains and the Rockies and the Pacific Coast and the unchanging hill country. That is where "the Bible belt" and the "queer" notions, ideas, schemes, and religions are mainly to be found today. Whether they were original pioneers of the Midwest, or whether they were later settlers who became (like the original pioneers when they were in the East) discontented or restless in the life of the Midwest as it filled up and became stabilized, they moved on and left the Midwest to a majority who quickly showed that they wanted stability, order, and social institutions like those back in the East. This was the beginning of one great Midwest paradox: a region made by radicals and progressives which soon became most conservative and traditional.

This majority of stay-put settlers was an amazing mixture of people. It multiplied enormously between 1815 and 1865. Britain's "pioneers" and frontiersmen—the British call them empire-builders—generally went out from Britain all over the world with a fairly wide background of culture and civilization, an education that was reckoned good anywhere at that day, a keen European historical perspective, and an overwhelming equipment of British ideas which often amounted to an exasperating "presentment of Englishry" wherever they went. The American pioneers and frontiersmen, on the other hand, scarcely knew what being an American yet implied. Down to 1835, most pioneers still at work had been born as colonial Englishmen. True, the colonial "folk type" was defined long before 1776; but so it was in the West Indies or Canada, and so it quickly came to be in Australia, New Zealand, and elsewhere. What was not defined was the American. Much less was the midwesterner defined.

The pioneers and first settlers were dependent on two sets of people for everything from the outset: themselves first, and then their neighbors. For defense, house, food, fuel, clothing, aid, comfort, consolation, counsel, healing—even for childbirth and burial—they had to depend on only the paradoxical qualities of self-reliance and neighborliness, aggressiveness and kindness, individualism and altrusim, egocentricity and gregariousness. It could not be otherwise.

29

The federal government was a remote myth. Only the state governments seemed real. This self-reliance, tempered with communal effort between self-assured people, showed itself to the outside world as much more than mere rugged individualism on the farm or in business. To it was added the sense of triumph over the wilderness, of realization of the dreams which had driven them forth from the settled haunts of settled men, of that bragging and boasting which was seen at its most violent and pathological in the "ring-tailed roarers" and other "roarers" of the big rivers and the frontier. There was much of the Irish slogan *Sinn Fein* about it: "Ourselves Alone!" (No wonder the Irish felt so much at home in the Midwest and why they made, and still make, such a disproportionately big mark in its politics.) Self-reliance, pride of achievements, pride of possession, and a sticking-togetherness in a new American way of life made the Old Midwest distrustful of the federal government, of eastern financiers, of even its own senators and representatives, to say nothing of those of the nation as a whole in Washington assembled. The Midwest belonged only to the people who made it and to their sons. The new Midwest states ought to own their free land and administer it; not the United States or Congress. Even the successive waves of new immigrants were viewed askance and had to "qualify"; and professional men, mainly lawyers like young Stephen Douglas, coming out from the East, were almost universally viewed at first as "city slickers."

The Midwest and its folk quickly became, in their own eyes, the élite of America, the salt of the American earth, the people who chose themselves, their Canaan, and their priests and judges. (Some of them even chose their own gods.) They were, in their own eyes, set apart, distinctive, different. They were "bearing the white man's burden" against the Indians. And the East and South in their turn helped to intensify these feelings in the Midwest by looking down on it, treating it as a region of boors, and at the same time exploiting its producers and their products.

If the South to this day still thinks of "damn Yankee" as one word, the Midwest still thinks of "damn foreigner"—if not "damn easterner" —in the same way, and understandably. This characteristic midwestern dislike of foreigners was the reaction of the first Anglo-Saxon settlers to the non-Anglo-Saxon settlers, too. The midwestern élite did not like later newcomers. Many midwesterners still think "damn Britisher" is one word; and that has an explanation not too remote in time. The Midwest has a short history, but midwesterners have a long and unconscious memory of their history. Men who fought for their inde-

30

pendence against the British in the war of the Revolution, and then settled in the Midwest, died there only one hundred years ago. Men who fought for the Midwest in the War of 1812 against the British died after the Civil War. Men who, like young Captain Abraham Lincoln, went out in their Midwest state militia to fight the war against the pro-British Black Hawk[1] in the 1830's called the Indian warriors "the British band"; and most of them died in the 1880's and 1890's. Battles with Indians went on until the 1870's in the Midwest; and each time popular memory, handed down at the Midwest hearth, coupled "damn Britishers," which leading American historians today agree is scant justice, with the Indians who treacherously attacked and burned and scalped. Experiences like these set the midwesterners apart from the American East and the other stable societies of the world. And from what one has consciously set one's self apart, one ends by disliking—to justify one's self, if for no other reason.

Very largely it was this same sense of being a virile and equalitarian "elect" which naturally drew or threw the Old Midwest first into the political camp of Andrew Jackson and his "Western boys"—which, incidentally, must have made Jefferson turn in his grave, since he had planned for a Midwest of solid, sober, and conservative farmers to offset the mobs of artisans in the big cities of commercial New England and New York.

In this first adoption of "frontier democracy," the Midwest showed all its distrust of the eastern commercial and financial monopolies or near-monopolies. It was against the Bank of the United States. Land booms had collapsed; poorer land could not be sold; and many another Midwest bubble had burst. Up to the thirties and early forties the Midwest was too primitively poor to produce any surplus—over and above what it had to see going back to the East as payments or interest or dividends—from which the Midwest might pay for education, communications, or its own local industries. Nor did the federal government until this time do anything significant in these respects for the midwesterners. The pioneers' old discontent and frustration, therefore, lay behind this Democrat movement. But in the late 1830's and 1840's, when midwesterners themselves were a more settled and crowded society longing for freer land, improved communications, and their own industries, and when yet another depression had afflicted them, they turned away from the old Democrat party to Henry Clay, Daniel Web-

[1] Black Hawk was old. He had fought for the British in the eighteenth century and in 1812–14, and, perhaps remembering British justice to the Indians in the Quebec Act of 1763, he admired them. He could scarcely be expected to admire the American settlers who had taken his lands.

31

ster, tariff protection, the financial and manufacturing class of the East, and the rich planters of the South as organized in the Whig party. The Whig party was the first in the East to adopt the policy of using federal powers to win the Midwest. In 1840 the Whig candidate, General "Old Tippecanoe" Harrison, was elected President in what was known as the "log-cabin" campaign. It was the most ballyhooed, buffoonish campaign in American history. This candidacy was the eastern Whigs' deliberate sop to the new Midwest, which could not forget that it was "saved" by the man who in 1811 beat Tecumseh and his braves at the river Tippecanoe and, as the Midwest thought (indeed, still thinks), beat the British, who were alleged to be behind him.[2] The change is symbolized in young Lincoln's break with his pioneer family's Democrat politics. He went over to Clay's "American system." His family never voted for him later.

This swing-over to what Clay himself significantly called "the American system" was a watershed in Midwest thinking and in the development of the region, for it put political as well as economic responsibility for the opening-up of communications and the industrialization of the Midwest on the shoulders of eastern Whigs. It began that process of turning midwestern eyes from fields to towns, from agriculture to new industry behind tariff protection, from rivers to railroads, which was to alter not only the face but also the foundation, form, and fashion of Midwest life. It linked the Midwest with the industrial and financial East against the Old South in politics, in trade, and in those great moral issues soon tragically to arise: the right of secession from the Union—and slavery. Jefferson's idea of the future Midwest was finally to be justified but not in the way he thought. The Old Midwest was not to offset, but rather to complement, eastern industry and finance. It was certainly to preserve the stability of the Union; but only after a civil war which the Midwest itself did as much to render inevitable as to win.

The people of this Old Midwest up until the end of the Civil War, its pioneers and first settlers, were overwhelmingly Celtic and Anglo-Saxon. You need look only at the names on every official document, newspaper, or church list to see that. The first "West"—western Pennsylvania in and over the mountains, the Ohio Valley, Kentucky, Tennessee, and the south of Indiana and Illinois—was pioneered and settled mainly by these men. Only from Pennsylvania was there any marked

---

[2] "Tecumseh's league would have been formed and Tippecanoe have been fought if there had not been a single Englishman in Canada" (Morison and Commager, *The Growth of the American Republic* [3d ed.; Oxford, 1942], pp. 413–14).

admixture of those old German eighteenth-century settlers in the seaboard colonies, known as "Pennsylvania Dutch."

From the South came the main body of migrants who made the Midwest up to about 1830; they were English, Scotch-Irish, and pure Scottish. They were a remarkable people; good colonists, honest, imbued with European folklore if not with its culture or civilization, but extremely superstitious and in religion very emotional. Even in religion they were paradoxical: they were overwhelmingly Protestant and "nonconformist"—Calvinists, Baptists, Methodists, Presbyterians, but few Roman Catholics or Episcopalians—yet given to such exhibitions of extreme emotionalism in their rituals and observances as shocked European travelers more familiar with the names of these sects than with their American manifestations. The sprinkling of old-line Germans were Lutherans: more sober and dogmatic, as they still remain.

After 1825, when the Cumberland Turnpike, the "national road" to St. Louis, and the Hudson-Erie Canal became increasingly usable, the tide of American emigrants swelled. For the first time the majority came from the Middle and Northeastern Atlantic States. These settlers went north of the limits of southern influence in the Midwest. They came from Pennsylvania, New Jersey, New York, Connecticut, Massachusetts, and even from the smaller states. They followed the old routes from New York, New England, and Pennsylvania. They were still Anglo-Saxons: "Yankees" and New Englanders; and they brought into this middle lateral belt of the Midwest many of those characteristics and characteristic institutions which still signalize New England. They were frugal, farsighted, commercially enterprising, capitalistic, modest, and reserved, whereas the southern immigrants were more improvident, blatant, happy-go-lucky, ostentatious, and gregarious. Their religion was also mainly Protestant, but they were neither so emotional nor so superstitious; and their religion had for over two centuries issued in everyday life into a far stricter personal morality— especially in observation of the Sabbath, sexual matters, and indulgence in liquor—than that of the southern immigrants. They were more used to settled village or small-town ways. They did not like forests and hunting. They settled in the older parts, too; but also, in time, in the newer Midwest along the northern waterways, the Great Lakes, and the great inland ocean of prairie. Indeed, they did not come in any numbers until they could reach the prairie easily by the new turnpike or the water route. They were every whit as self-reliant, though not as aggressively self-assertive, as the southern immigrants; they laid much greater stress on the need for education and "improvements"; and they were,

33

naturally, a strong force in making the Old Midwest swing over to the Whig party's platform in 1840.

Thus the Midwest by 1850 was a melting-pot within which southerners, easterners, and New Englanders of many differing backgrounds strove, with success, to make new American metal.

After 1830, and up to 1865, a third wave of immigrants into the Midwest began. It was the first to be composed mainly of foreigners, and it powerfully affected the pre-existing amalgam in the melting-pot. The newcomers came, first, from the sad and unhappy Ireland of the "hungry forties"—hundreds of thousands of them, "working on the railroad" or on canals, roads, and new construction projects in the big towns which were beginning to shoot up throughout the region.

They were sad, hungry, poor, discontented, frustrated, and they were Roman Catholics—no Scotch-Irish Presbyterians or Ulstermen, these. They were God's answer to the despairing Roman Catholic priests of the interior surrounded by an ever rising tide of Protestants; and they were a headache to the city fathers, especially on successive St. Patrick's Days and "days of the Faith." Finally, the city fathers abandoned their defenses; and the Irish, far from their native land, won powers and liberties of which Mr. De Valera never dreamed and which he certainly never realized or made one-tenth as profitable for himself or anyone else in Eire. They were also, alas, by their mere presence the cause of acute religious strife in the Midwest for the first time, and not only there; but we shall have more to say on that later. These new town settlers from overseas also led to the first big outbreaks of "native Americanism" in America and in the Midwest, where the original Anglo-Saxons resented their presence, ideas, and Roman Catholicism. It was then that the Know-Nothings and Native Americans made their great and alarming surge forward.

Next came the German immigrants. They, too, were resented. They were not all as liberal as their descendants made out; many of them were imbued with the radicalism of German cities. They came overwhelmingly from these larger German cities and not, as did the "Pennsylvania Dutch," from the rural towns or the land. These Germans were displaced by the upsets due to the political and industrial revolutions in the German kingdoms: unemployment, old restraints, and despotisms or reaction like that of the young Bismarck. To some extent they were in mentality not unlike the original pioneers, though among them were many fine and outstanding liberal intellects. Among them, too, again unlike their "Pennsylvania Dutch" cousins, were hundreds of thousands of Roman Catholics. These Germans, however, shared another significant characteristic with their Irish companions. It was one almost new to the Midwest, and it was to grow and grow until it largely changed and dominated the life of the region. In fact, it rang the death knell of the Old Midwest.

They each made for the towns and cities; they each settled in those places in "national groups," as close together as they could; and they did not, in the main, settle on the land. For by this time there were cities and rising towns in the region, towns to which the artisans or traders of Europe could emigrate. The Germans after 1840 went to the towns for trade and handwork; and the Irish, after they had done with railroads or such big projects, went to the towns to help raise bigger and better cities, but incidentally raised bigger and better political funds and bigger and better churches, convents, seminaries, and schools. St. Louis, Chicago, Indianapolis, Milwaukee, Cincinnati, Fort Wayne, South Bend, Dubuque, Cleveland, Columbus, Pittsburgh, Buffalo, New York and Brooklyn, Jersey City, Philadelphia, Boston—these are the big American cities which at this time bounded ahead, swollen and assisted by great crowds of German and Irish immigrants.

In this same period the first significant flow of emigrants to the Midwest from Britain and from Canada arrived: English and Welsh and Scotch and Cornish. Except for the miners, most of whom were Welsh and Cornish, they settled mainly on the land. They were overwhelmingly Protestant and nonconformist; they were quiet and retiring, except when in liquor; and they did not go into politics, probably because they did not dare. Their sons and their grandsons did. Many of their names are household political words in the Midwest today; but it is worth noting here that, despite a constant stream of British and Canadian immigration into the United States during the last hundred years, there has never been in that century a British "minority" or "racial" or "national" group in the life of the cities or the states or the Union. No one was ever troubled by a "British lobby" or had to watch his "British" group of voters. This may have made them different from other American groups, but it made them good Americans.

After 1850 the region began its unimaginably rapid transfiguration. Development fed upon development. Owing to improved methods, implements, and communications and to a fantastically swelling *adult* population—immigrants provided the Midwest with hands and mouths, whereas babies provided it only with mouths for ten years— the Midwest not only fed itself and covered its payments to the East but for the first time also netted a surplus. With this surplus it could afford education, new public services and amenities, new state and other governmental functions and functionaries, new local enterprises; and it could afford to begin to risk its own capital in new opportunities.

Just when this period might have settled down into the steady progress of a Victorian "Forsyteism," the thunderclouds of sectionalism piled up on the horizon, and the storm of the Civil War broke out. When the surviving Germans, Irish, Scotch, southerners, Yankees, and British of the Midwest returned in peace to their region, it was to find that the war had been a powerful stimulus to the economic development of the Midwest. This soon resulted, inevitably, in a further stimulus to immigration.

While it is true that before the Revolution there had been quite a sizable immigration of non-British peoples into the seaboard colonies —of which the "Pennsylvania Dutch" were the most numerous—and some of this spilled over the mountains together with the original Anglo-Saxon pioneers, the great waves of non-Anglo-Saxon immigration into the region came between 1870 and 1914—indeed, right up to the middle 1920's, when legislation shut it down. Whereas from 1840 to 1860 many non-Anglo-Saxon immigrants arrived and went straight to the Midwest, either to work in towns or on the railroads or to settle on the lands given by Congress to the railroads to get them built, after 1870 the waves of such immigrants were more mixed. They were of widely differing national, racial, and religious origins. They went to all parts of the developing and now continental United States. Some of them—mainly Finns, Swedes, Norwegians, Danes, British, Canadians, Bohemians, and Ukrainians—deliberately emigrated to become Midwest farmers. Others, and this included by far the majority of all immigrants—Germans, Italians, Greeks, Russians, Poles, Swedes, Bohemians, Austrians, Hungarians, Slovaks, Croats, Serbs, Bulgarians, Rumanians, Belgians, Armenians, Syrians, Albanians—deliberately emigrated from the lower-income groups in European and Asian towns and cities to settle in the new towns and cities of America. Among them were very many Jews.

These waves of urban dwellers from Europe settled all over America. The first waves spent themselves on the eastern seaboard cities, which, after 1860, show big increases in population; but they were increases in figures which had already proclaimed these eastern cities the largest in the New World. The greatest *percentual* increases, and the highest *rate* of growth, were shown in the towns and cities of the Midwest from 1870 onward. At first hundreds of thousands, and then millions, of European townsmen and citizens flocked direct from the American seaboard to the big cities of Cleveland, Detroit, Chicago, Milwaukee,

St. Louis, and Cincinnati and to the rising industrial towns of Ohio, northern Indiana, southern Michigan, southern Wisconsin, northern Illinois, and northern Missouri. At the same time a new wave of internal migration set in. Many earlier European immigrants to Boston, New York, Philadelphia, and other eastern cities came out to the Midwest to better themselves.

The London *Daily Telegraph* printed Lincoln's obituary on April 27, 1865, and could say of him that he "contrived by shrewd mother-wit and robust integrity of character to win the esteem of the stout men of the West,—a nobler type of Americanism than the motley tribes of New York." But after 1870 it became increasingly more difficult, and soon impossible, to contrast the Anglo-Saxondom of the great West with the "motley tribes of New York."

Whereas between 1830 and 1860 only four and a half million immigrants came in from abroad, from 1860 to 1900 immigration into America from Europe alone accounted for nearly fourteen millions; and from 1900 to 1929 it reached another fifteen millions. This meant that in 1860 only 18 per cent of Americans had been immigrants since about 1820; but in 1900 over 18 per cent had been immigrants since 1860; and even in 1930 over 12 per cent had been immigrants since as recent a year as 1900—that is assuming that they lived throughout these periods. But if they did not live, their children did. Immigrants from overseas between 1860 and 1930 were equivalent to *one-quarter of the entire population in 1930* and, what is more striking, were almost exactly equal to *the entire population of the United States in 1860*. So if the 1860 population had merely reproduced itself and no more, the American population would still have been doubled in one lifetime by European immigrants alone.

Between the census of 1840, when the Midwest was overwhelmingly agricultural and peopled by Anglo-Saxons, and that of 1880, America as a whole did not quite triple its population, while that of the Midwest almost quadrupled. Roughly a quarter of the increase of America's population in those forty years was due to immigration. But nearly a half of the proportionately larger increase in the population of the Midwest was due to immigrants. Between the censuses of 1880 and 1930, when mass immigration was halted, the American people grew two and a half times larger yet, while the population of the Midwest increased in roughly the same proportion. In that later half-century after 1880, roughly two-fifths of the American people's growth was due to immigration; *but immigration accounted for more than a half of the parallel growth in the population of the Midwest.*

37

Even with a higher infant death rate, most of the European immigrants and Negroes had, and have, more surviving children than the older Anglo-Saxon, Pennsylvania Dutch, and colonial stock of the Midwest. Since 1840 this slower differential influence has been steadily going on. But parallel with it there was a quick and enormous increase every year in the *net* number of new adult European immigrants and European children arriving in the region, reaching its peak between 1900 and 1920. All the immigrants in turn, growing more rapidly as a group of adults, reproduced their kind at the higher rate. The effect has been cumulative on the stock of the region, especially on the people of the cities and towns. Many farmers of the Old Midwest left the region for the Far West or the near Southwest or the Great Plains. They took much of the Old Midwest and its characteristics with them. But the bulk of the immigrants between 1870 and 1930 were urban dwellers, and they stuck to city and town life. They moved a great deal but, in the main, only to other towns and cities in the region.

The later non-English-speaking European immigrants reproduced their kind faster than the pre-1860 native Anglo-Saxon, German, or Scandinavian stocks of the United States—and their *survival* rate was even higher than that of the Negro—so the melting-pot after 1870 really had an increasing flow of raw material, in vast quantities, on which to work. What is most important to bear in mind is that about one-third of these immigrants went into the Midwest and that the bulk of these went to, settled, and stayed in the Midwest cities and towns. As time went on, more of those who had originally settled in the eastern cities moved out to the Midwest.

With growing frequency, as the industrialization of the Midwest made it vulnerable to the swings of trade booms and depressions, the resentment of the older midwesterners flared out against the newcomers. After 1865, Roman Catholics and Jews together outnumbered other single groups among immigrants into the Middle West. The partisans of other persuasions among the older residents were not slow to resent this, to organize against it, and to give concrete evidence of their organization. Thus began the group intolerances of the Midwest which are still one of its characteristic features. It is worthy of note that the Ku Klux Klan began in the Old South after the Civil War as a secret organization championing "white supremacy" but that a revived Ku Klux Klan invaded the Midwest during the war of 1914-18 and achieved its highest political power in Indiana in the 1920's as a violently anti-Catholic movement. So also with anti-Semitism and dislike of foreigners in general. The New Midwest, which began after the

Civil War, had to endure the sorrows as well as the successes of being America's melting-pot.

The sorrows, like the successes, leaped to the eye; for they occurred mainly in cities where "news" is made. What takes place among farmers is generally kept in their own little local circle and "isn't news." But the Midwest population made its gigantic forward strides mainly in cities and towns. In these, the masses of new immigrants settled, just like their Irish and German predecessors of the 1840–60 period, in sharply defined localities. There were many reasons for this localization of national groups in the cities: among them, the need for neighbors of one's own tongue and customs and religion; the strangeness of the long-time residents, and often their ill-concealed resentment or disdain of the newcomers, a disdain which quickly passed into common speech in the shape of opprobrious nicknames—"squarehead," "bohunk," "wop," "kike"—and innumerable tales about them; the lack of housing and the resultant real estate booms, which tended to make the newcomers flock either to old vacated areas or to new sites developed by speculative builders; and the clearly seen ability to "get things done" for themselves in politics by forming blocs whose votes could later be used as a bargaining weapon. It was in this way that the Polish districts of the Pittsburgh area, Detroit, Chicago, and Milwaukee developed; the Hungarian centers of Cleveland, the northern Indiana lake shore, and Chicago; the Bohemian areas of Pittsburgh, Cleveland, and Chicago; the German centers of Milwaukee, St. Paul, St. Louis, Cleveland, Indianapolis, and Chicago; the Italian populations of Chicago and almost every other big city; the Scandinavian centers of Illinois, Iowa, Wisconsin, and Minnesota; and the southern Slav populations of Pittsburgh, Detroit, Cleveland, northern Indiana, and Chicago.

THE HUB OF AMERICA

Movement made the Midwest, and the Midwest made movement. Perhaps no political revolution ever made as much difference to a country as the revolution in transport made to America. Because of its vast interior this was only natural. As the war of the Revolution and its aftermath sent the pioneers into the Midwest, so the age of steam, with its railroads and steamships, developed it. The result was a miracle.

The natural trend of trade, communications, and ideas, for over two centuries until the early decades of the American Union, was along a north-south line, in either direction. This held colonial society in one mold, one pattern, whether of the New England kind or of the South. But within one generation after the Midwest was safely acquired,

39

roads were built to aid the pioneers and settlers, and canals were dug to link the rivers or lakes on the east and the west of the Appalachian ranges. At the same time the steamship and railroad were first introduced. The Midwest was bound to become linked with the seaboard, but with which section: North or South? At this beginning of east-west development few midwesterners and few easterners saw as far ahead as the leading southerners, who were quick to sense not only a danger to their profits but also to their dominating political position in House and Senate. The development of the Midwest meant new states, which in turn meant more senators and representatives. How, and with whom, would they vote? And for what?

The first means of locomotion by land into, and inside, the Midwest between 1785 and 1825 were as primitive as any in human history: shanks' mare, oxcart, horses, solid wooden wheels or rollers, and the sled. The latter was not, as its name implies for Europeans, a winter vehicle. It was the equivalent on land of the flatboat on the rivers of the Midwest, and it was necessary because in the dense and matted undergrowth and close-packed forests of the region it was often impracticable for the pioneers to use even rudimentary wheels: wheels are no good until there are fairly clear tracks, and they sink or cut into the ground. The sled was used in summer more than in winter, for in the winters of the Midwest none moved if he could help it; and the phrases "tough sledding" and "hard sledding," which are still used many times daily in Midwest conversation, stem from the pioneers and do not refer to easy sliding over snow.

The primitive trackways, unimaginably befouled in winter and in the thaw or rains, radiated from the great riverways of the region. These waterways were the first roads, and along them the first settlements were made. The sites of great Midwest cities today were first located at fords, portages, and narrows, or where the shortest overland trackway hit the river: Detroit, Green Bay, Portage, Prairie du Chien, La Crosse, Chicago, Peoria, Joliet, Vincennes, St. Louis, Kansas City, Cincinnati, Dubuque, Rock Island, and many another. The rivers flow down to the Mississippi, draining from what used to be the northern ice cap. They form one great drainage basin. They run inward from the foothills of the Rockies on the west, and from the slight spurs of high land surrounding the Great Lakes, and a little way inland from their southern and western shores, on the east. Terre Haute, Highland, Akron, and many place-names including "falls" or "bluffs" mark these spurs. The pioneers had only to strike these lesser or greater tributaries of the Great River and they had an easy, if tedious and meandering, means of locomotion from north and east toward the west and south and eventually right down to New Orleans and the Gulf. These rivers are mighty. The Illinois at Peoria is far wider than the Danube at Budapest.

These routes were all, in the final analysis, north-south. They made the Old Midwest look mainly southward. They strengthened the influence of the southern pioneers who first came into the Midwest. They made it natural that the first Midwest should align itself with Andrew Jackson, himself a pioneer in Tennessee.

The life, traffic, and traffickers on these rivers fill volumes of Midwest folklore, history, fact, fiction, and travelers' tales. Incidentally, someone should explain why fresh-water sailors and watermen have always been so quarrelsome, loud-mouthed, and foul-mouthed. The bargee in Britain enjoys the same reputation or position in folklore as the Midwest watermen and Mike Fink. Yet it is hard to find such legendary salt-water sailors. Many of the self-assertive, pompous, braggart, quarrelsome, argumentative, and extremely exaggerating characteristics of midwesterners, as testified in American and other visitors' books and as still observable in modified forms today, derive from this river epoch. It was a rough, tough, chip-on-the-shoulder, coat-trailing period.

But it was short lived. The steamboats which only began to ply regularly on the rivers in the 1830's—and incidentally for the first time to chug *upstream* with bulky return cargoes from the South—were themselves to become extinct within four decades as their land cousin, the railroad, carried all before him. The steamboats, however, did begin a revolution in moods and influences in the Midwest. The Hudson-Erie Canal was opened in 1825, carrying freight to and from New York by the navigable Hudson and then through the Mohawk River Valley to Buffalo and so into Lake Erie. The steamboats linked the Great Lakes with this new east-west route—the first east-west route for goods and persons in any bulk—and immeasurably cut down both the time which was required before the 1830's to reach the heart of the Midwest and the cost of getting to or from it. Much more important, however, the canal and the steamboats were the first elements in a long chain of causes, finished by the first railroads, which also followed the water-level routes. These causes very quickly—amazingly quickly—forced an east-west pattern of trade and thought upon the Midwest and weaned it from its former north-south outlook. In the 1840's the British traveler in the interior, Mackay, not only prophesied the abolition of slavery or the end of the Union. He also said that the mere existence of the Mississippi Basin, the Midwest, would prevent any permanent separation of North and South, for the Midwest could not permit the mouth of the

41

Mississippi and its long, level, inland valley to fall under the control of a foreign government.

New Englanders flocked as emigrants by the new route into the Midwest and largely took over the task of breaking the prairies or building up the first midwestern factories and industries and financial institutions. Eastern cities and their capitalists also vied with each other, and even with British capitalists, over the building of Midwest railroads; and, as the first modern communications and factory industries were taken into a Midwest that was eager for them, the products and trade of that Midwest necessarily became directed and "keyed" to the commerce of the East—which in turn was intimately and long connected with the trading needs of Europe, especially Britain. This was the influence which led the Midwest to farm not only for America but for countries overseas; and it led to the rapid settlement and development of the prairies. By the same token, it laid the farmers open to the movements of world prices; whereas the tariffs of Clay's "American system" and of the new Republican party insulated the manufacturers, at the Midwest farmers' expense, from the world prices of manufactures.

When Midwest communications were dependent on waterways, settlements could not be located too far from them. The vast spaces or forests between rivers were slow in being cleared and settled. That is why, to this day, the Old Midwest is still more discernible along the rivers, and within a day's walk or ride of their banks, than it is on the prairie, where water is more scarce and the rivers farther away. This Old Midwest was settled, therefore, by reference not to the best soil but to the best land available within these distances of the rivers or lakes. So the coming of the railroads caused a revolution in agriculture, too, as well as in the mere settlement, peopling, and industrialization of the region. The railroads could run anywhere provided, as was true of the prairies, the contours were not too steep and the forests, tall grasses, and undergrowth could be cleared and swamps drained. The most populated settlements then in existence were, of course, those located at the junctions or crossings of waterways; and, wherever these could be easily reached over gently rolling forested or flat prairie country, the first railroads either spring from them or toward them, whereas the building of highways across such country would have been unnecessary and impossible. Accordingly, the first locomotive bells rang the knell of the great primeval Midwest forests as well as that of the six-foot grasses of the prairie; they were a voice in the wilderness preparing a path for the automobile and highway.

42

But the railroads embittered that struggle between South and East for the allegiance of the Midwest which was to end in war and even to survive the war. From 1840 down to 1880 this struggle—magnified and extended to transcontinental proportions—went on. The railroads slowly strangled the southern river traffic and pulled trade eastward, which was one reason why the North won the war. Therewith they killed many small but flourishing midwestern and southern river towns, whose skeletons can still be visited, just as the small rural town had killed the pioneer frontiersmen and sent them off to follow the frontier as it was pushed westward. All this, too, worried the South, whose senators and representatives saw the Midwest taking on the shape and habit of the North and East. The Civil War was not the only, though it was the most violent, expression of this southern anxiety. It was not just a war over slavery. Nor was it just a war between South and North. It was not only the question whether slavery could be taken into new western territories. By 1860 it was obvious that the Midwest was bound to become the chief entry to the Far West, the link between the industrialism of the Northeast and the continental development of America. At the same time the Midwest trade down the north-south line of the Mississippi was bound to decline, leaving the South, as it was, internally "blockaded" from the main bulk of a new, developing, industrial, and commercial America. Thus, the northern victory in the Civil War, despite its effects below the southern line of cleavage inside the Midwest, had a great influence on the industrialization of the region and the development of its communications with the East.

The unconscious, unplanned revenge of the South on the Old Midwest for enabling the East to win the Civil War came very quickly. Since 1900 it has been increasingly obvious. The North won, but the Old Midwest disappeared as a result of the ensuing spread of big business and little business, of cities and towns. One northern economic unity, one industrial and financial pattern emerged, obliterating much of the Old Midwest. This northern economic unity in its swift onrush peopled East and Midwest alike with strangers who had to be assimilated but who, in the process, to a great extent assimilated the assimilators. A "revolt of the masses" in cities and towns imposed pressure on parties and politicians. Before long, by 1900 and with increasing frequency thereafter until 1933, began that great extension of power of the federal government which virtually all businessmen of America, including those of the South, oppose and detest. But it was especially opposed and detested by those of the North, by the industrial and com-

43

mercial two-thirds of America's cities, towns, business, and trade which lie in the East and Midwest.

As early as 1844 Emerson could contrast "the nervous and rocky West" with the East, which had "imbibed easily a European culture," and could hope for an emergent "American genius" from the influence of that West. "To men legislating for the area between the two oceans," he said, "betwixt the snows and the tropics, somewhat of the gravity of nature will infuse itself into the code." This is the germ of F. J. Turner's theory of "frontier influence." But, as Bryce said, Emerson would have been disappointed.[3] He would have been more startled than disappointed today, a century after he spoke. For the "new and continental element," which he expected, has not intruded "into the national mind," making a new "American genius." Instead, new and utterly unforeseen elements have intruded into the national mind, the continent has become a nation, and an American genius has certainly emerged; yet they have done so mainly from the east, from Europe, and from the fusion of both in the crucible of the Midwest. The resultant mixture has been applied to the whole nation. As the nation has become more standardized, so it has become more centralized.

Thus, after almost a hundred and fifty years, came that consolidation and that concentration of power at the center which all the states feared in 1788 and have feared ever since. Calhoun of the South told the Senate on December 27, 1837, that the conflict at that time was between the notions of a truly "Federal Republic . . . . and a national consolidated republic in which the constituent parts were the aggregate mass of the American people." He could not possibly have foreseen how prophetic were those words: "a national consolidated republic *in which the constituent parts were the aggregate mass of the American people.*" Daniel Webster in his last and greatest speech in the great debate of the Senate on March 7, 1850, could truly say: "Ere long the strength of America will be in the valley of the Mississippi." Ere long, indeed. That strength was already there in the Civil War, and it grew mightily thereafter. But, as it grew, it grew into the strength of the entire North. The Midwest had dovetailed more and more with the East; and the "national consolidated republic" based on "the aggregate mass of the American people" had emerged. Not even the South was immune. Its Bourbonism, diverted into the all-American pattern of business after 1900, kept to the name and party of Democrats. But after 1933 even the "solid South" began to liquefy; and the Bourbons, once the haters of

[3] *The American Commonwealth* (London and New York: Macmillan, 1888), II, 713–14.

"damyankees," began to cleave to the all-American businessmen's philosophy of the new North.

But if midwesterners were molded and affected by all this, so were Americans throughout the country. Nation-wide influences which affected all regions were released. It spread eastern industrialism and enterprise beyond the Midwest to the Northwest and Far West. Inevitably, in so doing, it made of the Midwest a vast clearing-house, entrepôt, emporium, manufacturing center, and transport or transfer hub. It made it a region of crossroads; a central area for the exchange of moods, ideas, and attitudes; a melting-pot of more than men or nationalities; a focus of all-American influences.

Two developments, directly due to geography and transport, had a particular influence on the nature of the Midwest. The first was the discovery and working of the iron-ore deposits in North Michigan and northern Minnesota on the rim of the Great Lakes shortly after the Civil War. Feeder railroads quickly took this ore to the ships, and the new Soo (Sault Ste Marie) Locks—which now carry more traffic in eight months than the Suez and Panama canals combined carry in a full year—passed the ships along the Lakes to lakeside iron and steel works which otherwise would not exist: Hammond, Gary, and Indiana Harbor in Chicagoland; the Detroit district; Toledo, Cleveland, and many other parts on the Ohio shore of Lake Erie. It then went by rail or water to the Pittsburgh-Youngstown steel area between Ohio and Pennsylvania; and to Buffalo in New York State. Railroads bring the coking coal from the Appalachian or West Virginian coal fields up to the Lakes for transshipment as a return cargo or direct to the iron and steel mills by rail. This peculiar interaction of natural resources and transport routes along the Great Lakes and their hinterland—of iron ore, coal, stone, lumber, and wheat—was of crucial importance in the extension and location of American cities and heavy industries along that narrow hinterland, from Buffalo in the Empire State to Duluth in Minnesota. It contracted an industrial marriage with the new railroads and steamships. Of this natural union of steel and water, coal and steam, was born the industrial revolution of the Midwest after 1860.

The second factor was the differential freight rates of the railroads, which favored the Midwest. Almost but not altogether by chance, the Midwest region became the national hub of the railroad network. Anyone in Chicago can go by train to New York, Washington, New Orleans, Houston, or Denver in the Rocky Mountains overnight—that is, from 750 to over 1,000 miles between about four in the afternoon and nine the next morning. Similarly, within the Midwest region—

north of the Ohio River, west of the Appalachians, and east of the Great Plains—the great cities grew great by virtue of their rail connections with the lesser areas around them, which they served as a metropolis, and over which a minor rail network was spread. Coupling these networks with the transcontinental routes and the shipping on the Lakes, the Midwest could scarcely help becoming the region in which the shortest average rail-hauls led either to the biggest retail markets or to the sources of the necessary materials of industry; and most frequently the freight trains bringing the raw materials for one industry were able to return taking finished products to market. Few were the "return empties." This resulted in that simultaneous, mutual, and complementary development of midwestern agriculture and industry, and of midwestern and eastern industry with southern borderland coal and northern ores. Today, and for a long time past, it has made Ohio, Indiana, or Illinois the best center for a factory making consumers' goods and has made the bulk of America's retail market lie east of the Mississippi and north of the Ohio. Most graphically can this be seen in the steady march, decade by decade, of the center of the United States population from east of the Appalachians to Illinois.

One final influence of transport in the development of the region must be mentioned. It is the automobile, which killed the old horse and buggy and necessitated those paved highways which, from the air, make the interior of America look like the unending aftermath of a ticker-tape celebration. Before 1918 the highways were, at their rarest and best, macadam and, at their most frequent and worst, just plain dirt roads— mud in the rains and dust in summer, comfortable for horses and bare-foot boys and for nobody else. The cheap automobile after 1912, the truck and trailer, were a boon to the Midwest. To the farmers they meant, first, cheap tractors, pumps, and light engines to save labor and time on the farm. They meant transport which could effectively compete with the disliked and distrusted railroads on the shorter hauls. They meant bringing the regional town or city into what would have been termed mere riding distance before. They meant an evening-up of land values, since land near rail heads up until this time commanded a higher price. They meant a welcome diminution of dependence on weather, bad roads, and horses and wagons. They meant frequent and larger meetings of farmers over a wider area. And they meant the possibility of more mixed farming for the nearest city or large town.

To the urban dwellers they meant nothing less than a social revolution which powerfully affected manners, vacations, sports, health, crime, sexual morality, the solidarity of the family, the natural Midwest

46

insularity of outlook, and the keeping of the Sabbath. They sent unwanted farm labor and farmers' sons to the cities and towns. They gave a powerful impetus to the industrialists' desire to quit the highly taxed centers of cities, since now each worker could afford to go to and fro in his own car on cheap gasoline. Therewith they aggravated the problems of the cities.

The internal combustion engines and the highways they necessitated set the seal on that final *internal* development of the Midwest which the railroads had really begun. Automobiles virtually obliterated its remaining unsettled, uncleared, but cultivable spaces. They gave the well-to-do Midwest city dwellers their first practical possibility of acquiring farms. Hundreds of thousands, having begun life on them, had nostalgically but vainly ached to own or retire to them. These farms could now lie as far as a hundred or two hundred miles from the owner's, or part-owner's, urban workplace and yet be visited and superintended each week end. From each Midwest city, too, the big distributing, wholesale, retail, and mail-order firms could now extend their radius of activity—delivering by truck and trailer, knocking out the characteristic village stores and sometimes the village itself, increasing their own size and turnover and influence on the manufacturer, spreading the gospel of standardized products to the rural population, reducing costs of production and increasing profits and dividends—though not always reducing the cost to consumers, who regretted the passing of the crossroads store and its social focus. But the internal combustion engine also brought better roads, the delivery truck, the doctor, the ambulance, and the school bus.

In this way the Midwest in the automobile age became even more of a melting-pot than ever. The city went to the country for pleasure. The country children went to the town, and so to the city, for careers. More cross-fertilization occurred, more crisscrossing of attitudes, ideas, and ideals. The Old Midwest, hitherto insulated in the farmlands, began at last to lose its compactness and its uniformity. The New Midwest of the cities began to have its first serious doubts.

THE MELTING-POT

Thus there quickly came about a great transfiguration of the Midwest. In 1860, except for the Irish and many of the Germans, the population of city and town and farmland was almost uniform: it was Anglo-Saxon, Protestant, equalitarian, and, except for Negroes, free of any sign of economic "status" to which a group or class or nationality were, tacitly or avowedly, ascribed. But an economic and social

47

élite quickly developed, and established its social claims, in the cities of the Midwest. (It had always existed in the East.) It was overwhelmingly Protestant, Anglo-Saxon, or early American.

It could not, except in very few cases, notably from the Old South and New England, claim pride of parentage; but it could rightly claim distinctions of achievement, as proved by great wealth. The wealth was made from the rapidly rising real estate values or from producing or purveying the produce or requirements of the region; or from furnishing its utilities and transport: meat, grains, liquor, groceries, hotels, department stores, and railroads. Later came fortunes from steel and machinery and oil. Beneath this apex of the social pyramid in the Midwest came the attendant professions and services; and beneath them came layer after layer of economic functions, many of which were accounted respectable and many not, ending with those the performers of which had to live "on the wrong side of the tracks." These infinite gradations in the pyramid of Midwest society were largely caused by the immigration, which in turn was caused by the increasing complexity due to industrialization. These complications and social gradations multiplied after 1900, and, as industry itself became more delicately complex, they became more rigid.

They differed, however, in two notable particulars from the social pyramids of the East and of industrialized or industrializing countries in Europe. First, and always excepting the Negro, if it was relatively hard for the father to emancipate himself from a lower economic grade and move to a higher, it was still relatively easier for him than anywhere else on earth, and quite easy for his sons and daughters if they were healthy and capable. Secondly, great wealth, however come by, could break the charmed limits of these grades in Midwest urban society—which it could not always do in Boston or New York or the South and could not do in Europe.

To this second exception there were, in turn, two exceptions: the Negro and the Jew. They could never "break into" society; and the Negro, unlike the Jew, could not even get rich. With exceptions in the Midwest today that could almost be named and counted on the fingers of two hands, the Jewish families—at least, those known to be Jews—settled in defined districts and were "restricted" from refined ones. They are still kept out of the select residential districts and clubs and have therefore established their own. And the Negroes, flocking more into the Midwest than into any other region after each of the three big wars since 1860, have been kept to the lowest social and economic strata of the social pyramid, thereby making the "Negro problem" as acute in Midwest cities as anywhere in America.

What happened to Negro and Jew in the Midwest, however, is only an extreme example of a social process observable all over the Western world, even where there were no Jews or Negroes. It was not due solely to ill-will on the part of the older residents of the Midwest. It can be seen in all the rapidly growing cities of Western countries, in which economic undertakings and functions have tended to become frozen. It is the problem of our civilization: the urban proletariat. It has been the universal accompaniment of rapid industrialization, modern mass-production methods, and the decline of handicrafts and skill. Accordingly, in the Midwest, as elsewhere, it has happened to all the lower-income groups or lesser economic functions in cities, irrespective of race or nationality. No region of the world has been more rapidly transformed, from a primarily agricultural economy with a racially simple and uniform society, to a leading industrial region with a racially complex and highly differentiated society. This transformation has taken place entirely in its cities, leaving the old, pre-1860 Midwest, with its simpler and more uniform patterns of life, religion, and thought, still perceptible on the farmlands.

So the visitor to the Midwest today finds not one people, not a uniform type of midwesterner. He finds, instead—if he is careful, observant, and slow to judgment—many Midwests with many midwesterners inhabiting them. Some of these Midwests, defined only by the characteristics of their people or their economic status and functions, are as much a part of the East, South, or Far West and their cities as they are of the Midwest proper. In the Midwest proper the visitor finds the wealthiest midwesterners now in its big metropolitan cities. They are mainly Anglo-Saxons, Germans, and Jews by origin, owning big businesses and exercising professions, living a life of material privilege and luxury which is as extreme as, if not more so than, that of Manhattan or Los Angeles. He finds the Italian, Greek, Lithuanian, Polish, Hungarian, Czech, and Negro factory worker or service worker at the base of the social and economic pyramid, but still in towns and cities. Between these extremes he finds, still in towns and cities, a vaguer and less rigidly defined middle class of white-collar workers, run-of-the-mill professional workers, artisans, and workers in the distributive trades, transport, and public service, who are of all European national origins.

All these people are the children of the New Midwest which came into being after 1865. The visitor finds this New Midwest revolving in

49

its cities at a dizzy and wearing tempo: vigorous, excited and excitable, mercurial, intemperate, immoderate, blatant, dirty, but with all the blatancy of its vulgar vigor, and all the dirt of its fantastic work and output; irreligious, yet sheltering all conceivable religions; of one nation, yet of all skins and accents and statures; of differences, extremes, contrasts, and paradoxes, yet of a rude equality and a growing uniformity; of great economic and other social distinctions, yet of a growing standardization of reaction, response, and pattern of thought; cynical yet kind; irresponsible yet affectionate; of violent and rash prejudgments, yet avid for new ideas and for learning.

But if our visitor leaves the cities and goes out to the farming lands, beyond the limits of the cities' truck-farming areas, he finds farms and little farm towns which provide the most striking conceivable contrast with what he has just left. Here is the Old Midwest which came into being between 1800 and 1860 and still remains: virile, still mainly Anglo-Saxon and Protestant, speaking mainly with the same accents, quiet, unexcitable, scrupulously honest, devout, clean, sober, hardworking, living at a steady tempo of natural routine, full of an old culture and of much unconscious memory or history, unsophisticated, philosophical, slow to judgment, inflexible when convinced, and far less volatile or mercurial than its counterpart in the cities.

Thus the Midwest reflects in its popular composition today the two great periods of its own making: the era of primary pioneering and agricultural settlement up to 1860 and the era of urban industrialism thereafter. These two Midwest epochs go on living side by side today. The New Midwest of the towns and cities constantly recruits itself, at the lower levels, from the children of the farms and from immigrants and, at the upper levels, from leading professional and businessmen who come to make a better material living in it from other American regions.

In the still existent Old Midwest of the farms, however, there is little new recruitment. There is little social or economic mobility in it. Accordingly, the psychology and way of life of this older, more settled, more solid, rural Midwest bulks smaller every year in the life of the region as a whole. It remains—if observed at all—as a reminder to the city dwellers of the human qualities of the pioneer and settler who prepared a way in the wilderness for the railroads and factories and cities which, to a cynic, seem bent on making it into another kind of wilderness: grime and mean streets, slums and saloons, graft and rackets, mob politics and lawlessness, group tensions and intolerance, social divisions and conflicts of economic interest.

The people, their widely different origins and outlooks, their conflicting religions and pursuits, made the Midwest as we see it today. They also made themselves, the midwesterners, since, however different they were in their origins and whatever they brought in with them, they all had to adapt themselves to the new and growing life of a new and growing region. It was always, and still is, "becoming." It has not yet completely "jelled" into something immutable and irrevocable. Within a setting fixed only by natural boundaries, soil, and climate, everything else was highly mobile and fluid; institutions, governmental systems, ideas, and Midwest society itself were constantly, and are still, in flux—as you would expect of so vast a melting-pot and such vast quantities of different alloys. The easterner, like the European who came still farther from the east, quickly became altered in this fluid society and took on many of its peculiar characteristics. True to its own origin in great natural extremes, and in the hands of men of great extremes, the Midwest in its miraculous development produced extremes far greater than those of any other region.

Nothing perhaps exemplifies the midwesterners today better than a short inquiry into their genealogy. One typical Chicago family of my acquaintance in 1945 carries its family tree directly back through Prairie du Chien, Wisconsin, to French chevaliers in Canada who were in the fur trade under Louis XV; to Czechs from Brünn, under a Hapsburg emperor, who went to farm in Iowa eighty years ago; to Englishmen who came up from Virginia to farm near Peoria in Illinois over a century ago; to Norwegian dairy farmers who settled in Wisconsin seventy years ago; to a Connecticut Yankee merchant who came to Chicago one hundred years ago; and to Scottish Presbyterian industrialists who came down from Canada about seventy years ago. The family today is "on La Salle Street"—bankers and investment brokers. That is the story of the Midwest in the making. It is a story of the hopes, fears, and triumphs of many nations and peoples. It is a story which is still unfolding, still to unfold. It is the story of "an awfully big adventure."

III. "UNCONSIDERED EARTH"

Most americans think fifty years ago is old, a century antique, and a century and a half ancient. No people in the world so ignores its own newness, its own youth, the recentness of everything, and the effects of all this. In nothing is this more striking to the visitor than in the parallel, simultaneous, and current contrast between life in the Midwest cities and life on the farms.

One hundred years ago for the first time the proportion of the population of the United States which lived in towns rose above the figure of 10 per cent. Until 1840 nine-tenths of the people of the Union, and those were mainly easterners, were engaged in rural pursuits. Today that seems surprising. But infinitely more surprising and more rapid has been the transformation of the Old Midwest—the Midwest of the "frontier," pioneer, forest, and farmland—into a region in which urban population now exceeds rural and the prairie farms exceed the older farms of the first clearings. When Bryce was writing in the early 1880's, less than 30 per cent of the population lived in towns. He pointed out that "the West" (as it was then called) was more populous than the East or South and that it was still overwhelmingly agricultural. Yet, in 1940, only Minnesota and Iowa in the northwest of that region had a majority of rural population; and in Wisconsin, Illinois, Missouri, Indiana, Michigan, and Ohio the urban population—living in incorporated towns of 2,500 inhabitants or more—was in the great and overwhelming majority. That is the measure of the Midwest's newness.

Towns, especially those with populations between 2,500 and 5,000, do not, however, always mean factories and industry. They also mean services, transport, trade, professional advice, and administrative agencies for large areas surrounding them, in which live farmers. Such towns, and some of the towns with as many as 20,000 inhabitants, lead a way of life quite different from that of a manufacturing town. Their life is keyed to the farmer's life, which they serve. They are agricultural county seats or the center of "townships." Their life is fundamentally not very different from that of a corresponding town in the agricultural provinces of England, France, Germany, Sweden, Czechoslovakia, or Hungary.

In 1940 the "truly rural" population of the United States lived on isolated farms and in small unincorporated places. This really rural American population was less than 50 millions, or 37.8 per cent of America's 132 millions. Over and above these isolated pockets of people were 6,715 rural incorporated places, each with a population between 500 and 2,500 souls and amounting to a little over a further 7 million people, or 5.7 per cent of the country's inhabitants. Altogether, the rural American population amounted, therefore, to just over 57 millions, or 43.5 per cent of the whole. In this figure are included the "poor whites" and Negro settlers of the South, "hired men," lumbermen in forests, and many miners and other isolated workers who are not farmers.

The Midwest region, as defined in this book, has only a very few "poor whites" and Negro settlers in the extreme south, but it still has some lumbermen, miners, quarriers, and trappers in the extreme north. So its rural population is overwhelmingly engaged in farming: fruit, corn, cotton, small grains, cattle, hogs, poultry, and some tobacco and cotton in the extreme southern belt of "general farming" which we have described; corn and hogs, dairy cattle, and wheat in the great central corn belt; and dairy cattle, hogs, poultry, some corn, fruit, wheat and small grains, and some tobacco in the hay and dairy belt which runs across the north of the region.[1]

This Midwest today contains 30 per cent of the people of America. But it produces well over half the entire American production of corn and hogs and over one-quarter of the beef cattle. That is the national significance of the prairie and the corn-and-hog belt. It is for this that the farmers of that belt endure the swings of the "corn and hog cycle."

[1] See above, pp. 4–7.

It is also to a large extent the basis of the meat-packing industry of Chicago, Milwaukee, Omaha, and Kansas City. But the region is also responsible for more than half the national output of butter, almost a half of the production of milk, and two-fifths of the output of eggs and poultry. That is the significance of both the corn and the dairy belts. Of the national output of household vegetables, potatoes, and melons, the region accounts for one-quarter. Of fruit, largely owing to its severe climate, it produces only about one-tenth; but that is an important crop in Michigan, Iowa, and the southern belt of Illinois, Indiana, and Ohio. In the extreme west, northwest, and southwest of the region, over one-fifth of the country's vast wheat crop is harvested; and in the same areas large quantities of small grains—oats, barley, rye—are raised. Recently the soybean has become an important crop on the prairie farms, too. In the south of the region a very little cotton is still grown, and both there and in the north a little less than one-tenth of the nation's tobacco is produced.

Thus within a century the Midwest has grown to be the most general agricultural region of the country. Other regions raise much more of particular products, but none is so richly endowed that it can raise almost all forms of agricultural produce. The Midwest is therefore still largely an agricultural region; and two-fifths of its population are engaged in farming or rural pursuits. Yet the personal incomes of the townsmen and city dwellers, per head, are well over three times those of the farmers. The farmer's average personal income is about one-third of the average personal income of the entire Midwest population, *including the farmers.*

This is the measure of the revolutions in industry and transport which transformed the region and its people in less than a lifetime from a region of agrarian pioneers and settlers to that of nationally vital cities, towns, industries, trades, and communications. These revolutions have gone on around the Midwest farmer, often ignored and deplored by him. He has largely continued the way of life, mentality, and make-up of the original settlers of one hundred years ago or less. If he or his forebears were immigrants, they adopted, and adapted themselves to, that life. Virtually throughout the Midwest climate and weather are cruel hazards to him.[2] We of the cities know full well that there must be farmers. What makes any man a farmer, anywhere in the world, may tax our imaginations. What makes them enjoy it—those who do— is a source of wonder as great as that which coal-mining and other such

[2] See above, pp. 7 ff.

occupations cause the thinking townsman. There is probably very little deliberate decision about entering such vocations.

But what makes the commercial farmer of the Midwest today is indeed a conundrum. To settle, as did the original settlers, for self-sufficiency and a way of life is one thing. To do it for a living amid, and for, an industrial society and for remote or foreign markets is quite another. True, the soil was virgin and good—better than that which the original settlers left behind them in the East. When the brazen sun of a short, fierce summer finally came out to bake waterlogged soil, things shot up so fast you could almost see and hear them growing. (This was an amazing experience to me, as a European, when I cultivated a little Victory garden in Illinois, broken from the grass roots.) But to the uncertainties of prices, fixed by townsmen or foreign traders, are added all the hazards of violent Nature; unseasonable frosts or blizzards; unpredictable tropical rains; voracious prairie grasses, flowers, weeds, and vines; more insect plagues and pests than ever vexed Pharaoh; cattle diseases; droughts; floods; dry rot; fires.

The first farmers who made of the forest and prairie the larder of America naturally developed at the same time singular, profound, and enduring qualities: the faith of Abraham, the patience of Job, the vision of both Saints John, the constitution of Elijah, the zeal of St. Paul—together with some less laudable qualities of Lot, David, Ahab, and the Pharisees, which all men share. No wonder the first settlers had a vehemently emotional religious sense: that they fostered and released it in frenzied camp meetings. No wonder it became the "Bible belt." No wonder William Jennings Bryan, out of Illinois by way of Nebraska, leading the Populists and Grangers of plain and prairie against the men of the cities, thundered biblical imagery: "You shall not press down upon the brow of Labor this crown of thorns; you shall not crucify mankind upon a cross of gold." No wonder Midwest farmers, and many other farmers, still expect to end on a cross between two city slickers, an American on one side and a foreigner on the other.

Farmers and their characteristic qualities are proverbially slow to change. Yet Midwest farmers have changed their ways of farming in the past few decades; but their characteristic qualities penetrated deeply into Midwest life and society, including those of the big cities, from its beginnings. They still permeate it, and these qualities are still more clearly perceptible among the farmers. The rural, farming Midwest today is the clearest survival of the Old Midwest, though it is now much diluted and modified. It is worth bearing in mind that Midwest farming today, and the rural life based upon it, are almost as new as Midwest industry and city life. In other words, in settling the land of the region and farming it during the past century or century and a half, there have been almost as many revolutions in the rural Midwest as the revolutions which made towns and cities.

A large proportion of the original pioneers and settlers had never been farmers at all. That is a fact fraught with significance in the formation of the Old Midwest and of the rural psychology of the region to this day. Pioneers and settlers who had been farmers elsewhere naturally came with a more settled, stable rural outlook; with more determination to "see it through" and to remain farmers, whate'er betide. To such men and their families the new and often heartbreaking problems raised by the strange soils, climate, and other conditions of the new region seemed part of inevitable Nature and could be endured. But as the tide of agrarian immigration cleared and settled on most of the land of the region up to 1890, the proportion of settlers who had never been farmers, especially those who had never been owner-farmers, increased.

These men were different from the pioneers and first settlers. They were more changeable, more ready to quit under prolonged adversity. As the towns and cities grew simultaneously, there was also somewhere to go and much to do there if their spirits broke. Thus from about 1850 onward—that is, after the first fifty years of pioneering and settlement—the rural life of the Midwest became marked, though naturally to a smaller degree, by that same mobility and the characteristics that went with it which distinguished the urban population and the immigrants to the cities. This resulted in a Midwest farming population which, contrasted with that of New England or the South or any European country, was less stable, more mobile, more likely to make radical changes; a farm population which had a higher rate of turnover than any other in a settled region or country; whose sons began to quit the farms and enter the life of the towns and cities; a rural life which was less traditional, less conservative, more progressive, and more closely aware of, and identified with, industrial and urban developments alongside it than any other.

THE PATTERNS OF FARM LIFE

The original pattern of Midwest rural life can best be seen from the air as you fly westward over the mountains from the eastern states. The Northwest Ordinance of 1785 and the rectangular land survey finally settled by Congress in 1796 set that pattern, beginning with all Midwest lands on the west side of the Appalachian ranges. (The results of the earlier unplanned, indiscriminate settlements and claims are still clearly visible as soon as you fly over Kentucky or Tennessee.) The six-mile-square township containing thirty-six mile-square sections, each in its turn (and in time) capable of having its 640 acres further subdivided into smaller holdings, made that characteristically uniform, enormous, unending, and rigidly rectangular face of the rural Midwest which so impresses the visitor today.

This survey, coupled with the newness and vastness of the region, had an important and unforeseen result. The first communities of the overwhelmingly agrarian Old Midwest were small and infrequent: for land was cheap, there was plenty of it, and the rule was "each man for himself." Consequently, the rural life of the Midwest from the outset did not, as in Europe, begin from the village or manor outward to the "common fields," which later became "enclosed" into private property. *It began with private property in land. The settler owned a piece of America.* There was no feudal regime. There was no ancient folk-memory of fields owned and tilled in common. There were no degrees of freedom or property or honor or work liability or rights. There were practically no differences of land tenure. Midwest life began from the private property of a man's own fields and worked inward to a few necessary central points—river landings, ferries, crossroads, and later rail depots—which ten or twenty cabins and, later, a few wood-frame houses made into what was called a "town," with a church or two, lawyers, stores, a post office (the only evidence of the federal government), and a few state or local representatives or officials. Vandalia, capital of Illinois in the 1830's, had less than a thousand inhabitants and no sidewalks. There were only tracks leading to it. Thus, while the Old Midwest certainly developed settlements which it called towns, these were what a European would scarcely call a hamlet; they were for the convenience of a population which was virtually 100 per cent agrarian, rural, and isolated in small farms or larger homesteads. These little original towns could not grow very much before 1850 unless—as was the case with the largest and best known—they were on those waterways which were the Midwest's only reliable means of internal transport. And by the time the railroads came, preceding ordinary highways, the lines, furrows, and creases in the face of the Midwest had already been set.

It was mainly a region whose people lived in their own farmhouses, homesteads scattered around the landscape and separated by rigidly rectangular big fields, from forty to many hundreds of acres in extent. Village, town, or "community" life was mainly confined to one day a week. The other six-sevenths of the time only very near neighbors saw each other; so the rare but regular community life was the occasion for much boisterous merrymaking, drinking, fighting, and devout, emotional religion, by all of which emotions and tensions were relaxed. Neighborliness, that most striking quality of the Midwest, had its roots in the first settlement of the region.

When the railroads and towns simultaneously developed in the Midwest between 1840 and 1860, the towns had to spring up along the railroads, for the same reason as, earlier, they had had to stick to the rivers. But the railroads were quicker and covered great distances. Accordingly, as the big towns rapidly grew and extended their influence, the little Midwest river communities lagged, as they still do. But, what is far more important, *after* 1860 the rural village, as it is known in Europe, where it plays the central role of rural community life, never struck root at all. The few which existed in the Old Midwest, and mainly in the south of it, were killed by the railroads, cities, and industries of the New Midwest. From about 1870 onward the original villages of the Old Midwest disappeared in favor of the county town or, as a European would say, the market town: the town which served either the county or its subdivision, the township. As the Midwest land filled up and the smallest practical administrative centers were townships— they are vast by European standards—the European village and its life, imported only half-consciously and in rudimentary guise from the colonial East by the settlers of the Old Midwest, finished playing its part. This took place sometime between 1860 and the 1890's, nearer the latter date according as one goes farther from the big cities. The *coup de grâce* to the Midwest village, properly so called, was delivered by the automobile and the highways built for it. That blow also removed two characteristic Midwest rural institutions: the little red village schoolhouse and the social focus of the village store. The villages lost; the cities and towns won. But the farmers on their separated homesteads remained a society of individuals set apart from the towns.

The rural society of the Old Midwest was the most uniform of any in America. Its first characteristics were those of pioneers and settlers who owned the land they had cleared and worked and were to all intents and purposes equal in their own eyes. Their institutions sprang from their own soil, from themselves. They did not trust the shadowy federal government which they never saw. They did not trust any banks but the local bank, and they distrusted branch banking, which would have located the control far away from the home community. They were self-reliant, and they did not trust even their own representatives. In strength, abilities, and personality they were, of course, like all men at birth, unequal; and their first games, sports, and diversions, significantly enough, were highly competitive, as if to obtain public recognition of personal distinction among so much general equality. They were extraordinarily boastful, vehement, exaggerating, and quarrelsome. They would fight "at the drop of a hat," and even without that excuse, for fun, and with no holds barred. They were fond of violence and were less upset by murder than by many other crimes. They were also extremely obstinate, always being involved in lawsuits in which they bankrupted themselves and lost their farms rather than give up the suit. Often the suits were over a matter of a few dollars or cents, yet batteries of grass-roots lawyers were retained on each side. All these characteristics spelled individualism, aggressiveness, and a desire for local publicity or distinction. This characteristic striving for personal and publicly recognized distinction is one of the few which have come down direct to the Midwest society of today, where it is now seen at its highest among city folk.

There were many other characteristics of the old rural Midwest which passed, in varying degrees, into the life of the new cities and are still visible there. We have mentioned the abnormally high mobility and turnover, right from the outset, which meant quick change and a demand for the strange or new: a characteristic not to be wondered at when one thinks of the isolation and monotony in a settler's surroundings during most of the year. This mobility was intensified in a society in which all were virtually equal in opportunity.

Then there is that inordinate love of gambling which still earmarks in particular the midwesterner, and most Americans besides. A passion for gambling arises from boredom, monotony, drudgery, jadedness, and an inability or unwillingness to read, contemplate, or think. It has always been an escape mechanism, throughout the ages. So some of the midwesterner's gambling propensity goes back to isolation and boredom, just as some soldiers will gamble with one live cartridge in a revolver, spinning the chamber at random—"Russian roulette"—when they are literally "bored to death." The Midwest was conceived, born, and nourished by gamblers in land, transport, supplies, and (if we think of the Indians) human life. Land companies, federal and state governments, banks, railroads, wealthier settlers, and farmers: all were gamblers.

Land values varied enormously between 1800 and 1850. A vast new country was in the making. Men, by no means "adventurers" as we use that word today, came to the first small towns or villages, as Chicago was in 1830; actually started penniless; and made millions of dollars within a year or two, all in land speculation. As frequently, they lost it. The booms and depressions decreed by Nature for all wholly agricultural peoples were heightened and deepened by speculation in land, which spread like a prairie fire throughout early Midwest society, among farmers and townsmen alike. In that fluid, mobile, creative society, everything interacted instantaneously. A boom in land or a bumper harvest spelled prosperity, which gamblers' syndicates and even politicians tried to exploit by "forestalling" and "cornering" in all walks of life—a characteristic still strong in the Midwest cities—just as a crop failure and a bursting of such bubbles spelled general ruin and disaster. The disasters of the 1830's were terrible throughout the Midwest, but they were accepted as inevitable.

Thus, within this society that began as equals, great differences of wealth and political as well as economic power developed almost overnight, providing a basis for the midwestern city dweller's deep belief—equated with his religious belief—in self-help, individualism, and private property. Here, too, emerged another pair of those extremes which always marked, and still mark, the Midwest: the rapid and violent alternations between prosperity and poverty—"shirtsleeves to shirtsleeves," whether by gambling for the fun of it, or extreme risk-taking, or speculation, or natural disasters. The farmer's son who began as a barefoot country boy and came to the town was as much inured to, and adept at, gambling as any boy of the streets. There was a reason, an end, for gambling. All led hard lives up to 1870 and many until much later. All wanted material comforts, wealth, money, and all needed them quickly. There was no graded society; no European sense of fixed status or "calling"; no thought of slow progress; no familiar tradition or sense of historical continuity in the Midwest, for it had no history then. It was a caldron seething and bubbling with animal vigor, appetites, ambition, and zeal; and this was almost as evident among farmers as it was in the towns.

Other characteristics were impressed by the farmers on the life of the Midwest as a result of hardship, disappointment, and disillusion there. Such qualities naturally reinforced those characteristics, already described, which the "dissident" pioneers and settlers brought with them into the region.

The first farming in the Midwest, like the southerners who brought it with them, followed the patterns of the South. It was not that of the big plantations but that of the poorer, upcountry Piedmont owner-farmers. It was confined to forest clearings, owing to the settler's utter dependence on timber. The prairie lay a waste until the 1840's. The southern pioneers working up from the Ohio, clearing forests and planting only enough corn or vegetables for themselves, brought southern methods, southern razorback hogs which had to "root or die," southern horses for riding and not for draft purposes, and southern cattle which foraged on what they could find. This type of husbandry was carried up river banks as far north as Chicago before 1840; yet the settlers had stuck to the forests and wooded land for their fuel, fences, and homes.

No one knew how to handle the prairie, with its grasses taller than a man and their twelve- or eighteen-inch-deep roots that defied iron plowshares. It was first viewed as "commons," open range country, good for steers which could forage for themselves before being sent on the hoof to Cincinnati or eastern cities in vast and damaging "drives" by tough cattlemen. It was practically appropriated by the cattle interests who, in the Illinois legislature and elsewhere, were powerful enough to get the legal responsibility for damage by cattle to settlers' crops and property placed on the settlers themselves, who were legally compelled to fence their own property. But on the prairies there were few or no trees; and what there were had been cornered for town buildings by wily townsmen who thus secured the monopoly of timber for houses and rails and fencing.

Thus at this early date (yet it is only a century ago) there was great hardship on the prairies; prairie settlement was apparently indefinitely held up; and intense resentments and animosities against the towns accompanied the misery and crudity of early Midwest farming. Much of the animosity was already being vented by farmers against towns, state legislators, political parties, bankers, railroads, and, ominously enough, "vested interests."

Though the best black earth in the world could be had under federal provisions at $1.25 per acre, it could not be properly worked, for no one had yet broken it. No one knew how it could be plowed; that it needed hedges, trees, fencing, steel plowshares, and cultivating tools; that the wretched prairie cabins would need to be rebuilt as wood-frame houses; that animals, to give good yields, needed barns in winter; that wells were needed for the abundant water that lay underground, and trees for shade and protection from the winds and weather for man and beast alike; that some degree of mixed farming was necessary if this vast inland ocean of primeval grassland were ever to become the prairie Midwest of a few decades later. Here, indeed, was the promise of an agrarian revolution matching in scale and effect the industrial and transport revolutions that made the cities of the region during those same decades.[3]

By the irony of history it was the northerner, the New England Yankee, who found out how to break and settle and develop the prairie. If the southerners were first in the region, the Yankees made it. Yankee immigrants into the center and north of the Midwest improved the strains of cattle and hogs; applied the first "horsepower" to the prairie farms; invented and developed better plows and implements; organized to break the lumber monopoly, and broke it by the railroads; discovered trees and shrubs for hedges and fences and plantations; eventually developed wire fencing and reapers and binders; and—with all this—agitated and organized, full of the religious and economical zeal of New England, for rural education, better roads, railroads, measures of public health and, above all, improvement in the lot of the scandalously neglected wives and children of the settlers and farmers.

Social conditions were not good among the settlers in the wooded regions; but on the prairie they were simply nonexistent. No Americans had ever been called upon to lead such a benighted existence as the first settlers on the prairies, for the Pilgrims at least had educational standards and religious instruction. On the prairie there was nothing. In thaw and rain the prairie was swamp-ridden; and in summer it was plagued with mosquitoes. Women and children died off like flies. Typhoid fever, agues, and dysentery carried off thousands before their time. Typhoid killed Lincoln's first love, Ann Rutledge, and her father within three months of each other in 1835. A man often had two or three wives in succession and children by each. The children who survived naturally were tough. Children grew up there, if they survived, with only a fraction of their parents' inadequate literacy or education. Here, again, came a revolution which reinforced the settlers' naturally high valuation of their women and children and their belief in education. It is to the everlasting credit mainly of New Englanders in the Old Midwest that, within one generation of the original tragic errors, a change was begun which led not only to the settlement of the prairies but also to a settlement which brought out the best, and not the worst, in human life. Thus New England characteristics went very deep into the life of the Midwest, on the prairie as in the new industries of the cities. The Midwest was being forged out of South and North into that region of 100 per cent Americanism which it is today.

[3] See Lloyd Lewis, *John S. Wright, Prophet of the Prairies* (Chicago: Prairie Farmer Publishing Co., 1941), for a fascinating account of these problems and the men who tackled and overcame them.

Resentments, however, arose on all sides. Much of the midwesterner's acute dislike of the easterner today is not altogether due to a sense of inferiority—though there is clearly some of that defense mechanism in it. It is largely due to the agrarian Midwest's early and long-lasting resentment at the financial and commercial monopolies in Chicago and other Midwest market cities, where New Englanders were the most go-ahead, and in the East. The banks and markets of the big Midwest cities and the East formed "rings," long before Sherman's and Clayton's antitrust legislation was imaginable, and shamelessly exploited the farmers whose produce could ultimately go only to those centers for a market. The main consuming markets were in the East or in Europe, which meant letting the Midwest cities and the East handle the produce. The Midwest railroads scarcely behaved any better.

Farmers everywhere are slow to combine; those in the Midwest were no exceptions. But their individual hatreds go very deep. I wonder how many Americans in a smoking-car today know that an Ohio farmer led a movement in the 1840's to break the New England woolen mills' stranglehold on Midwest sheep prices; that he was named John Brown; that he was the same who, a decade later, led antislavery forces into "bleeding Kansas," whose body was hanged in Virginia for what he did at Harper's Ferry, and whose soul is marching on? The intense feelings of such men have taken long to die out among Midwest farmers, who are still not very enamored of the big cities of the Midwest, the eastern states, or foreigners. Again, all this is not a hundred years old.

REVOLT ON THE PRAIRIE

The main prairies were really settled after the Civil War at about ninety persons to the square mile; and the tide of settlement, bearing the bitter but fruitful experience of the first prairie experiments with it, went on westward. The big railroads, too, lured many to quit the Midwest and go to the Great Plains. It was chiefly then that immigrant farmers from overseas came to take up farms all over the Midwest and beyond; and it was mainly at this time that the different national groups settled all over the region and formed distinctive localities which still remain.

The southerners and their descendants on the whole remained south of the "line of influence," though many of their descendants, especially the younger sons, profited by the New Englanders' experiments and moved up into the prairies. New England farmers and their descendants to this day can be found in the corn-and-hog belt, from eastern and northern Ohio along through the northern halves of Indiana and

Illinois, into Iowa and northern Missouri, and so out to the Great Plains. Michigan's agricultural land was largely occupied by German, Dutch, Polish, and British-Canadian farmers; there were few New Englanders there, and fewer southerners, though a goodly contingent of New York farmers settled there and along the rim of the Great Lakes. To Wisconsin and Minnesota in the main went the immigrant Scandinavian farmers, Germans, Canadians, and the "Russians" (Ukrainians) who finally went on to the Dakotas. In northern Ohio, Indiana, Illinois, and all over Iowa are still to be found many descendants of original Bohemian farmers. Scattered round the prairies and throughout the corn-and-hog belt are Finns, other Scandinavians, and Bohemian, Lithuanian, Estonian, Serb, Croat, and a few Italian farmers. The Scotch are scattered, but the Welsh mainly kept together and are in pockets in Iowa, Illinois, Indiana, and Ohio. Yet the most striking feature to the visitor today is the speed at which all these farmers of different national origins have taken on the same patterns of work and thought as those which the original Anglo-Saxon settlers and farmers first brought with them and then modified in the Midwest.

The mixing in the Midwest melting-pot has been far more effective among farmers than in the cities. That is partly due to agriculture itself, the natural conditions of which do not permit much variation within one climatic area. But it is not solely due to that, for there are wide enough differences in soils and climate within the Midwest to have allowed much wider differences between farmers and their outlooks or attitudes. In fact, it is only when you cross the line of southern influence in the region that you sense any great difference of outlook today. There are, I think, two main reasons for this quickly acquired uniformity. First, since the prairie was settled, farmers, new or old, have had to meet the same natural conditions—climate, soil, crop experience, methods—and, in addition, new farmers were interspersed with old all over the region owing to the uneven rate of taking up public land and the relatively high mobility among Midwest farmers.

Secondly, and far more influential, all Midwest farmers had to face the same man-made problems arising from the growth of the cities and the development of the region and the whole country—vested interests and "lobbies" of industry and transport, especially railroads and processing firms; the working of the "price scissors" in remote markets; local improvements; social conditions; and so on. In European countries farmers of equal efficiency and character, working under exactly the same natural conditions on either side of a frontier, might have quite different fortunes according as their governments differed in protecting

64

or subsidizing or improving the lot of their farmers. True, there are a few agricultural frontiers between American states—applying particularly to fruits, dairy products, livestock, competition from oleomargarine, and so on—but, on the whole, the absence of internal tariffs insures the quickest spread of influences, common conditions for all farmers in a locality, and a common experience.

In its very beginnings, the Midwest was farming. The first state legislative assemblies were composed of farmers' representatives who were often farmers. But the lawyers, bankers, and industrialists rapidly ousted farmers from these bodies, and the farmer has had a chip on his shoulder ever since. It is really surprising how quickly the Midwest's legislative assemblies fell completely into the hands of lawyers and bankers and others, representing syndicates for canals, railroads, and some franchise or other, but not representing farmers once they were elected. The process was complete by 1840, which is also the date at which the Midwest first departed from the Jacksonian Democrat fold and linked its fortunes to the "American system" of internal improvements and high tariffs. One obvious explanation was that these professional men were abler than the farmers and that the states wanted to develop industries and other large-scale activities which, in the long run, might well be thought to advantage all farmers as well. The groups of rich men behind the growth of Midwest cities and transport; the men behind the governors, mayors, congressmen, and senators; easterners allied with midwesterners; all rich from forehanded and foresighted speculation which they dignified with the name of risk-bearing—these men placated the farmers only at election times. Meanwhile they largely ignored agriculture and its problems, especially the personal problems of the farmer. The triumphs of industry, finance, and the cities of the Midwest were so much more exciting—and profitable. They succeeded each other so continuously that few of the directors of this industrialization could think of farmers.

The virgin strangeness of Midwest soils at the outset, a century and more ago, meant ignorance. Ignorance meant waste; waste of soil, of other natural resources like timber, of labor and time. Anything would grow, and there was enough land for everybody. As long as there was free land anywhere in the Midwest or to the west of it, a farmer could easily use his own hands or utilize the laborsaving methods and machinery of the Deeres and McCormicks and others; crop the prairie or the cleared fields; and, when the curve of prices turned downward for a spell, sell out or default and be sold up, move to the towns, or "go West" and begin again. Midwest literature is full of such family experiences. Few foresaw that the day was fast approaching when there would be no more free land anywhere in America, when the internal "frontier" would close, when the cup would be brimful. When that day arrived, new methods would be needed; agriculture would become more intensive and require more capital; agriculture and the farmer would become a *national* problem.

That day arrived between 1880 and 1890. The date is significant. It was at that psychological moment that the Midwest and Great Plains farmers exploded in Grangism, Populism, and Progressivism. But it was also at that same moment when, the "expanding frontier" having closed, the first big tussles in the cities between embryonic trade-unionism and industrialists also broke out. The aftermath of the prairie revolt, which shook both the old political parties of the nation like the convulsions of an earthquake, was still being heard around the Midwest in 1914. While the war of 1914–18 stilled it for a season, it broke out again when the wartime agricultural bubble of prosperity burst in the 1920's. Only the New Deal—which incidentally weaned the despairing Midwest farmers in large numbers away from their old-line Republicanism back to the Democrat fold, as farmers everywhere tend to be weaned away from traditional allegiances during a revolution in agrarian conditions—brought back the Midwest and other farmers to the old-line two-party political system and killed the hopes of a third, or farmers', party in the region.

The farmer had tried to copy the industrialists, the bankers, the power companies, the trusts, and the utilities and build his own "lobby." But, though he had the votes, he had not the financial resources, and he could not speak with a nation-wide, uniform voice, as could an industry. Moreover, no "lobby" could cope with differences of climate, or with Nature, seasons, and a run of seasons. The farmers' problems were long run, not short run like those of the industrialists. The farmer did not want to quit farming. He wanted to remain solvent and to get "a fair return"; a certain regularity and reliability about prices; a reasonable assurance that he could safely continue in his way of life and see his wife and children enjoying benefits comparable with, if not as great as, those of city dwellers. But all that seemed dangerous radicalism to those congressmen and senators, and the bankers or industrialists behind them, who spoke out loudly and clearly for the virtues that had made America great: rugged individualism, self-reliance, and to the wall with the inefficient, i.e., the unsuccessful. Here, again, we meet with that extraordinary paradox of the midwestern man of property: he prides himself on being more go-ahead and more full of initiative

66

and progress than anyone else, yet after about 1880 he became more traditional, hidebound, and even reactionary in social outlook than any British Tory. In this case, and at this time, he was as violently opposed to the industrial workers of his own cities as he was to the farmers. It was certainly an omen when Populism exploded alongside trade-unionism: the one from the prairies, the other from mean city streets.

There was another typical midwestern paradox in this. The bankers and industrialists and manufacturers were owners, men of money, men of property; and up until 1890 the Midwest farmers were also men of property. They owned their own farms. They might therefore have been expected to make common cause with the businessmen who owned their own businesses and to oppose the trade-unions of the city workers. They did no such thing. Trade-unions and farmers alike, from different angles and with little if any collusion, demanded a better return for their labor and better security. To the businessmen and bankers who dominated the Republican party, security meant—and still means—rendering the costs of industry rigid, thereby hamstringing competitive enterprise and imperiling the foundations of American economic life. Thus from the close of last century the farmers of the Midwest began to play an important political role; often a "marginal" role, according as they threw their votes this way or that. And this in turn involved both the traditional political parties in competition for the farmers' vote, at a time when the new trade-unionism was growing as an organized or organizable vote of great dimensions, and turning to the more liberal of the parties. The story is familiar to Europeans.

Meanwhile, the great change swept on across the face of Midwest agriculture, altering its long-run prospects and affecting the outlook of the farmers. At the turn of the century it was clear that the qualities of the Midwest soil were not permanent; that waste could no longer be afforded; that as big a revolution in methods as the revolution which first brought the prairie into cultivation was now necessary to save it; and that the older farms, off the prairie, might be in even worse plight before long. The casual plowing, recurrent tropical rains and hot suns, tearing-up of the grass-mat of the prairie, destruction of forests, constant cropping, lack of cattle and horses by which to feed manure back to the soil—all these had either washed much of the Midwest farms' topsoil down the unrepaired gullies into the big rivers or else tired the land. New agricultural settlements in the Northwest and Southwest, and older, well-tried methods in the East, began to show the wasteful and thoughtless among Midwest farmers that Nature could rebel, too. It was harder to meet competition; in other words, it cost more; and some

67

farmers could not cover the extra costs, or alter to meet new conditions. The great awakening came when the farm boom burst after the war of 1914–18.

It is significant that tenancy in the Midwest, as distinct from ownership, made such strides between 1890 and today. The tenant-farmer and the cropper, so antithetical to the nature of the pioneer and settler, now cultivate farms practically all over the Midwest; and in the farmlands of northern Illinois, Iowa, Minnesota, northern Indiana, and Ohio there are large areas where they predominate over other types of farming. In other words, tenancy in all its forms, sharecropping, métayage as it would be called in France and old European countries, has not come into the Midwest on its poorer southern lands which were first settled by southerners. Nor is it strongly in evidence in the northern dairy belt. It has come, or broken out, in the prairie farms, in the best land of the corn-and-hog belt. In fact, where tenancy and sharecropping of all kinds mark the majority of farms in the Midwest today, it is in the corn belt. This trend to tenancy reflects not only the dangers looming over Midwest farming: the need for capital from townsmen to cover the cost of improvements to the land and new methods and new implements. That is a problem in European farming, too. It also reflects the ability of many a son or grandson of a Midwest farmer, who went to the cities and made good there, to return to the land in the guise of an absentee landlord or farm capitalist. It spells a little more mobility between farm and city; but at what cost, if it continues to extend? What does it mean to the temper and mentality of Midwest farmers? It has, meanwhile, intensified the farmers' resentment toward the city. On the other hand, during the second World War, big farmers themselves have tended to take in more land, either on lease or by purchase, and then they have allowed it to be cultivated on a sharecropping basis or on some other kind of tenancy. In any case, there is a new group of Midwest tenant-farmers; it has been expanding steadily since 1890, its mentality and outlook very different from those of the owner-farmers.

THE MIDWEST FARM

The life of the Midwest farming community is often derided or looked down on by most Midwest city dwellers. The more thinking minority in the cities, however, prize it, are inclined to overidealize it, and want to buy a farm or retire to one. Few, indeed, know how the farmer and his family really live.

Much of the social instability, uncertainty, doubt, tension, and conflict of interest in the cities of the world during the last two decades is bound up with the vanishing of that reasonable Victorian ability to *count on things happening roughly as one expected them to happen.* In those days the curve was ever upward. You could be sure of things and of yourself. But when standards collapsed, dependability, foresight, rationality, and a lot of other virtues collapsed too. Now no one can plan as an individual for his and his family's future in the way that our grandfathers planned. (That is why, in our age of anarchy and chaos, private enterprise and the individual planning on which it is based give way to demands for group planning.) In the Midwest farmers' life the ability reasonably to foresee and to forecast has always been smaller than it was elsewhere; yet, living separately and individually on scattered farms, they have managed, more than the cities, partly to solve the problem of individual versus community effort. True, the outlook before them today is as somber as at any time since the days of the settlers, and their future is clouded. Yet this has not affected their individual and community life half as much as it has affected those of city dwellers during the last half-century.

Life on Midwest farms varies, of course, with the size of farm, the soil, the agricultural region, the amount or quality of machinery, buildings, and equipment. It cannot be uniform, and yet it has more uniformity than that of the city dwellers. But, before you accompany me to a few typical Midwest farms, there are certain facts which we must bear in mind.

First, life on the best farms is hard. It is harder than life in the city, where labor is limited to so many hours a day and where amenities are greater. Despite all laborsaving machinery on the farm, it is still a hard life. It is no life for amateurs or "gentlemen farmers"—which may explain why the well-to-do city men, going "back to the land," seek tenants or croppers to work their acres. Secondly, while the best farms and their farmers can afford the most modern machinery and buildings, the overwhelming majority of Midwest farms now seem undersized and undercapitalized by reference to what modern machinery and adequate capital could tackle. This would not be surprising on European farms but may seem strange in America—above all, in the New Midwest, where instalment selling and the world-famous equipment-makers of Chicago and other big cities stand behind the farmer. Yet so it is.

Except for the poorer southeastern region of the United States, the region of Negroes and "poor whites" and sharecroppers par excellence, the Midwest has the greatest number of individual farms as well as the greatest proportion of farms under a hundred acres each. Only about one-third of all its farms have water piped into the house. Its farm buildings alone, however, are surpassed only by those of the Middle Atlantic States, and this jumps to the eye when you visit Midwest farms. The Midwest farmers do not hire as much labor as those in most other regions; for one thing, the reserve of casual labor does not exist. Nor, strangely enough, do they employ as much machinery and capital equipment; though in both respects they make a better showing than the South or Southwest. The automobile comes into its own among Midwest farmers, who, together with those of the Great Plains, own proportionately more cars than other American farmers. In no Midwest state today are more than one-fifth of the farms without an automobile. Both new and used automobiles are cheaper in the Midwest than elsewhere, being nearer the factories.

The farmhouses and farm buildings of the Midwest are, to a stranger, uniform, somewhat severe but clean, solid, and handsome. All the houses are white, wood-frame, and either rectangular or L-shaped, with the front porch and entrance in the crook of the L. The simple porches are fairly deep and generally screened in summer. They are the rest places of a summer evening and on the Sabbath and have passed into the literature, songs, and folklore of America. Most houses have four or five rooms, excluding the ample kitchens, basements, or outhouses where the preserving and laundering are done. The houses of the better-off farmers often have seven or eight rooms. The wooden farm buildings are almost universally kept in good repair, regularly painted brick-red, and often picked-out in white. The severity of the climate on man and beast alike makes every good farmer think of his buildings before his house; and recently the wealthier farmers have begun to lay out the buildings so that you can pass from the house through the buildings with the minimum of exposure to the elements. The barns, mainly Dutch, seem to European eyes, with their huge interiors and massive doors, enormous; but they serve a greater number of purposes than a barn or grange in Europe: cow barn, stable, granary, hayloft, workshop, garage, machine shed, and storehouse. One or two lesser buildings house poultry, pumps, any odd vehicles (relics of horse-and-buggy days), dairy, and so on. There is generally a windmill for water, at least on the prairie. Virtually all farms have a silo, like a round medieval watchtower, for silage as winter feed. Adjoining the buildings are the wired hog pen and its hog houses, the topsoil rooted away, pocked by hogs' snouts and thick with corncobs, both winter and summer. In the beginning the prairie settler tried to leave cattle out all winter, with disastrous results. Now they are brought in, which is another reason for the disproportionately large size of the farm buildings compared with

70

the house. Again, owing to the severity of the climate, the farm is nearly always surrounded and overhung by trees which, growing quickly in the Midwest, shade and shelter the buildings in summer and winter alike. This is especially remarkable on the prairie, where they have all been planted within the last hundred years.

Then come the fields, stretching away along the concrete highways, macadam or dirt roads toward the neighbor's farmland, and generally devoid of hedges. Practically none is wood fenced except in the south of the region; most are wired in, with metal posts (metal on the prairie is still cheaper than lumber). "Good fences make good neighbors," says Robert Frost of the New England farmers; but the contrary is true in the Midwest—"something there is that doesn't love a wall." The need for larger fields, to utilize machinery to the full, is doing away with fences all the time. Near the farm is usually a small meadow, but there are comparatively few ponds, since most water is distributed from the wind or motor pumps; if there were more ponds, the rolling land might be better drained, gullies stopped, and soil erosion prevented. Few prairie farms are on or near streams; though farms away from the prairie, being older, are generally located by them, to the intense delight, and sometimes the peril, of farm children.

The majority of farms in the Midwest have electric light and power, radios, refrigerators, and vacuum cleaners. The better-off farmers' wives have electric washing-machines and other devices. Instalment-buying has made this possible, too, and revolutionized the life of the farmer's wife. The farmer, too, has innumerable electric appliances in his buildings, obtained in the same way. The overwhelming majority of farms have telephones.

Not all Midwest farms, however, are like this. A minority of about one-quarter of the farmers still live at very low standards of housing, buildings, sanitation, household and farm equipment, and cash income. Many have a cash income of only a few hundred dollars a year for a wife and generally many children; and sometimes not that. Here the picture is far from idyllic, though not as dark as in one or two other regions of the country. It is estimated that in the Midwest alone one farm family out of every five has a thoroughly bad and unbalanced diet. The children in these families do not even get enough milk, eggs, and green vegetables; and sanitary, physical health, and intelligence standards among them are deplorably low—as the recruiting agencies discovered in the second World War. I mention these things here, as I mention other such facts, only to show that attitudes and characteristics can scarcely be of a uniform pattern, even in the more uniform life of

71

the Midwest farming community. There are still many "dissident," discontented Midwest farmers; and some of them cannot blame anyone or anything else but themselves. Happily these are a tiny minority, though they form a social problem.

I visited many farms throughout the region, but a few stand out in my memory, not because they were outstandingly kept, or belonged to the minority of well-to-do farmers, but because they were typically well run by hardworking, thrifty, conscientious farmers who loved their land, their state, their country, and their calling.

I recall in particular two farms near Mason City in Cerro Gordo County, northern Iowa. It is not a century since that county was established, taking its name from the Mexican War. It is only seventy-six years since the first railroad came into Mason City; and many old farmers can remember Indian wars and the breaking of the first sods for farm land. The land was prairie and very swampy; there are big lakes quite near. But luckily there were vast brick-clay deposits which were later turned into tiles and bricks to enhance the value of drained land and double the county's population. The first farm on which I called in a cold January was about ten miles away. Let us call the owner Mr. Jones.

I was unannounced, and the young lady with a babushka round her head, whom I took to be the daughter, turned out to be the farmer's wife. I guess she was about twenty-eight. It was only when I saw her full-face that I noted the natural fresh complexion and the weather-marks at the corners of her eyes. Her husband, a man of about thirty-six, was working on his farm buildings, re-roofing with composition material and enlarging one end of an outhouse. He had 180 acres, which he described as "middling." His father had been a farmer in central Iowa, and his grandfather had come from Ohio. Mrs. Jones was collecting eggs from some hundred hens. There were about twenty milch cows and some thirty hogs. Jones had a tractor which pulled his numerous and clean field implements and machinery. There was a milking-machine in a clean barn; electricity was in use everywhere; an electric pump delivered water not only to house and cistern but through wrapped pipes to troughs in the nearest corners of the fields. He had a mobile, power-driven hopper which he connected with his field trucks to deliver corn to the loft, whence it was fed by gravity through a chute to ground level. All these, he explained, were bought "on terms." In the yard was a trailer full of corn, and Mrs. Jones went about the business of taking corn to the hogs while we talked. The fields were rotated to corn, clover, grasses, a little oats, and fallow. Jones kept two horses—

"just in case, and anyway I like to see horses on a farm; don't seem a farm without 'em; not that I use 'em much; but the kids like 'em."

The Joneses had three children, two girls and a boy; two of them went to school about six miles away by bus and had their lunch there. The six-room house was white clapboard and L-shaped, as most are in Iowa. They had telephone, refrigerator, radio, vacuum cleaner, and washing-machine. They had had this farm for eight years, since they married. Jones did not want to change, but he wanted " 'bout 'nother 100 acres, I reckon, if I could be sure of help." (He farmed the 180 acres alone with a little seasonal casual help.) When I asked him how he had made out during eight critical years, he said, "Not so bad; wouldn't change; lot better'n most, I reckon." But he did not want his son, aged about seven, to be a farmer.

"Why not?"

"He's smart. He could do better'n I've done, in town. Besides, by the time he'll be fit to farm, folks'll need bigger farms anyway; a lot bigger farms; I don't see how he's going to buy and I wouldn't want him to be a tenant." I left the Joneses with something like homesickness.

In the same county I went in late fall to Mr. Robinson's. Robinson was sixty, perhaps older: gray-blond, leathery, thin, spare, tall, wrinkled, blue-eyed, quick, and almost nervous in his movements; most unfarmer-like, I thought. I wasn't surprised to hear that he had started life in North Carolina. He had worked on the railroad. "Came out here about forty years ago; saw this country; liked it [pause]; never went back." He told me that his family records showed their origin in East Anglia in the seventeenth century. His speech was quick and clipped, unlike the drawl of the native Iowan. His wife, whom he met and married in Iowa, was tall and dark; she was Holland Dutch, born in Iowa. She, too, was busy with about six hundred head of poultry when I arrived. I think she was about five years younger than he. They farmed 160 acres of their own, leased (for cash) another 160 acres and farmed it, and two miles away they had also leased (during the war) a further 100 acres. Robinson said he was getting old and could not tackle as much as he used to; he maintained the buildings. He and his wife tended the cattle, hogs, and poultry and went to the town with the truck or trailers; but their two sons (a third was in the Pacific on an aircraft carrier), aged about twenty-eight and twenty-four, were both fully engaged in running most of the 420 acres which was cultivated. They had no other help. The entire quartet worked on the farm. Mrs. Robinson had no help in the house, but she had every conceivable type of domestic labor-saving device.

73

Robinson told me he had tiled and drained his own 160 acres with "cuts" four and a half feet deep every 60 yards, all running into a main drain, at his own cost and with his own labor. It had cost $1,700 ten years ago. He thought that in a few more years all of Iowa and most of the Midwest would need a great amount of capital for draining and fertilizing—especially on the prairie farms.

"Maybe they'll put by enough of what they're takin' in these days; but I doubt they will. Folks seem unlike to remember bad times or what's in store. It's always crazed good times, and then crazed depressions. Folks been takin' everythin' from our soil 'n putt'n noth'n back f'years, 'specially in this war. See this land here," he continued, pointing to a barely perceptible declivity in the middle distance. "Rains come heavy here early on in year, 'n *thet* land gits waterlogged; gummed up, it is. All we c'n do to git tractor 'n plows 'n discs threw't. Same in the thaw. An' I drained mine. I don't care t'remember what *thet* piece were like 'fore I drained it. But there's thousan's won't drain; 'least, they don't. Yew sh'd see what we git threw in fertilizer, too."

Out to the big fields we went in a big Buick with a trailer behind. Round and round the elder boy was guiding one of their tractors pulling a combine and a trailer behind the combine. He was harvesting soybean which was periodically dumped through a canvas hopper into the substantial homemade trailer-truck behind our Buick. This trailer, which the boy had made, was on an old model-T Ford chassis. (Nearly every Midwest farm boy is a natural mechanic, which stood the United States armed forces in good stead in the war.) It needed to be substantial, for, when we went back, the Buick was pulling over a ton of soybean in that trailer. The rotation on this 160-acre of "home farm" was corn, oats, clover—clover for more than a year—and then soybean. Robinson had about forty-five head of cattle, Herefords and black Angus, and his own bull. There were the usual fifty or sixty hogs.

I, the townsman, stood a long time watching the elder boy running that combine with the other homemade trailer astern. Round it went gathering, stripping, shelling, and delivering the beans to the trailer. Regularly he brought the seemingly unwieldy equipage exactly alongside the other trailer behind the Buick, to transfer his load; and I could not help imagining that under the vast, blue Iowa sky and the warm sun we were out on a far more tropical ocean and this boy was bringing a small warship alongside. I do not think that more boys join the United States Navy from inland states just because the inland states are more numerous. A certain aptitude is gained on the vast inland

74

ocean of the open spaces—and a desire for the sea. Don't ask me to particularize. The United States Navy knows that it is so.

We moved on in the car to the farther 160 acres. Here the younger boy was disking a 100-acre field with a 16-foot-wide harrow behind the second of Robinson's tractors. Like his elder brother and unlike his father, this boy, too, was tall, gangling, very dark, with intensely bright black eyes—perhaps there had been Spanish blood in Mrs. Robinson's ancestry in the Netherlands. Young Robinson said he also had a 21-foot-wide disk-harrow, and that in spring, from sunup to sundown, he regularly disked 75 acres, or 50 acres in winter. I remarked how this put West European agriculture, with its smaller fields and hedges, at a disadvantage. He showed me that he was making a straight run of half a mile without a hedge in sight; the furrows were dead straight. I could not see a tree for a landmark. That boy, too, would have made a good navigator! He had only to go through the wire or over roads (also without hedges, or trees), and he could go on for weeks until, literally, he had disked or plowed the county. Young Robinson could not understand why West European farms used and depended on so much "old-fashioned human labor and horses" per acre. I asked what the tractor and harrow had cost. He told me: $1,150 for the tractor, brand-new, and $60 for the 16-foot disk-harrow, slightly used. They had taken two years to buy the tractor on instalments. Back in the farm they had a less costly third tractor as a stand-by, together with mechanical corn-strippers, corn-huskers, mobile hoppers, milking-machines, milk-separators, manure-spreaders, drills, and so on.

I made a mental note that what was true of the industries of Western civilization was beginning to be true of the farms. We make them capitalistic. We make production more laborsaving. Yet fewer people tend to work more, and more people tend to work less. I also made a mental note that here was, basically, a 400-acre farm, owned by the farmer, and wholly run by his family. Yet, apart from the value of house, buildings, and stock there must have been $10,000 of capital equipment on it in the shape of laborsaving farm machinery. In any West European country that equipment for a smaller farm would have cost the equivalent of $12,500 or $15,000, owing to tariffs, less efficiency, and less capital per industrial worker employed. Here was not only a comparison and a contrast with farmers of the Old World but also a tribute to what the industrialization and urbanization of the Midwest had been able to do for the farming Midwest.

Back at the farm Robinson showed me where the entire family, including his wife, were building a new machine shop, implement shed,

75

and storehouse. They had surveyed it, drawn up the plans, and ordered the supplies, acting as architects, quantity surveyors, bricklayers, carpenters, and plasterers. The building was about 100 feet long, 25 feet wide, 40 feet high, with a steeply arched roof and big eaves to distribute the weight of snow or quickly get rid of it. The base was of local cement, and up to a height of 9 feet the walls were of local brick tiles, mortared, two such tiles in thickness. On these was raised that systematic and symmetrical network of timbers which makes the inside of the roof of a Dutch barn look like a medieval village hall in Europe. Many of the timbers were old and weathered, having been taken from former buildings which they had pulled down. They expected, when finished, it would have taken them six months of "spare time" to construct.

As this farm land was of deep black earth, I asked Robinson about crops, weather, seasonal variations, and farm fortune. He had only one complaint: yields varied greatly with the highly variable weather. Corn, for example, needed a good steady dose of sun after good rain. But that year, 1944, corn was still on the stalk on October 27. He had turned more and more to mixed farming during the last fifteen years because he resented the slings and arrows of outrageous weather. Soybean and dairy cattle were an offset to the average Midwest prairie farmer's dependence on the corn-hog cycle. In 1943-44 hemp had been grown very successfully for the first time in northern Iowa. Within a 100-mile radius of Mason City there were eleven plants processing it; it grew well on the best corn land; and it averaged a net profit of perhaps $75 per acre. There were, he said, 4,000 acres of hemp in Cerro Gordo County alone, and might be more in 1944-45. Robinson and his family were game to try anything, and they were going to try hemp.

Quite different from the Jones or Robinson farms in Iowa was the farm of Mr. Brown in the southern quarter of Illinois. Brown and his wife had four children, the eldest aged nine. They farmed only 85 acres of that rougher land which lies south of the prairies and was originally settled a hundred and twenty-five years ago. There were old trees along the bottom of a stream and about 15 acres of uncultivable land. An orchard—apples, peaches, plums—covered about 20 acres. Corn and hogs and a little poultry took up the remainder. Brown had no tractor; he had two indifferent Belgian horses and old, rusty implements. The house was in poor shape. It was "old"; that is, it was built over sixty years ago. The few buildings were in no better condition. Brown owned the farm, but he wanted to move. The land, he said, was worked out and had never been good to start with. He "aimed to sell during the war" and then go as a tenant on a prairie farm. There was no electricity, though there was a telephone. Mrs. Brown cooked with oil, and there were oil-gas lamps. Water came from a hand well. The winters were milder but the summers were fiercer. Indeed, the summer suns had tanned and lined the Browns' faces far more than the winds and snows had those of the Iowans. The nearest town and railroad were eight miles away, and the town numbered two thousand inhabitants. It, too, was dusty, neglected, and poor-looking, though I was there in February. You can find many such farms scattered through the Midwest. Generally they are situated in the southern part of the region, on the lands first broken and settled. But poor farmers do not "localize" in any country. You get good farmers on poor soil, and poor farmers on good soil.

Round the prairie and in Wisconsin, Michigan, and southern or eastern Minnesota, generally near big cities, are all sizes of dairy farms with big pastures and fine herds of dairy cattle. These are the more modern farms, more recent in origin; but the life of the farmers is almost exactly the same as that of the Iowa, Illinois, or Indiana corn and hog raisers. The farms and farmers in central, northern, and eastern Ohio partake more of the characteristics, and even of the appearance, of those in western Pennsylvania. But in southern Ohio, as in southern Indiana, the farming is more difficult, the country more rolling and uneven (though more beautiful), and the visitor gets the impression that there are more run-down farms in those areas.

During the hundred years since the breaking of the great Midwest prairie, agriculture has steadily become more and more influenced by the cities, their needs, their industries, and the capital equipment they produce for the farmers. As a result, Midwest agriculture has steadily tended to become more and more of an industry, more and more "capitalistic" in its nature. Its demand for human labor has fallen and is still falling. The capitalism and the industrial outlook went with the increasing amount of capital equipment needed on the farm. This may account for the parallel decline, among the better-to-do third of all Midwest farmers, of that radicalism which first characterized the Midwest farmer and broke out again and again when times were bad. No new agriculture sprang up in Europe alongside new inventions like those of a McCormick, a Deere, a Case, or a Ford. But, almost from the outset, Midwest corn-and-hog farms or cattle ranges were linked with meat-packers in cities, as they still are; or with the more recent meat-, fruit-, and vegetable-canning industry, which has even left the cities and invaded the countryside; or with the patent cereals and breakfast foods and dairies, the factories of which can be seen in the

77

heart of the farm lands of Michigan, Wisconsin, Indiana, Iowa, and Minnesota. As the cities, their industries, and their consumer populations bulked ever larger in the political life of the states, industry and agriculture tended to dovetail—causing the conflicts described earlier—but by the same token the farmers modified their output and methods.

The versatile soybean is but one recent example of this. Cattle feed from the bean serves an agricultural use as a waste by-product, but the main products are oil and food for human beings and material for industrial plastics. Midwest farmers have had to modify and change and adapt more quickly than almost any farmers anywhere, for their soil is now getting tired, needs fertilizer, and needs conserving. In this recent process, success is largely due to the great, efficient, and beneficent role played by the state agricultural colleges and the agricultural experts who range from officials at the capital to that Good Samaritan, the county agricultural agent. Nowhere are these institutions and individuals more strikingly effective than in the Midwest states. Perhaps one reason why farmers' co-operatives have never developed in the Midwest to the degree they have reached in other regions of the country, which is itself only a fraction of the degree reached in European countries like Denmark, is the great public provision of agricultural expertness which serves the cause of private, individual farm ownership and farm operation throughout the heart of America. Another reason is the high degree of organization and technical knowledge available through the Farm Bureau, the Grange, or the Union—the farmers' own professional associations and "lobbies." Indeed, individualistic as Midwest farmers are, they have also the American, and particularly the midwestern, genius for organization and association to further their common interests.

THE FARMING COMMUNITY

The rural towns to which farmers repair are an enormous influence in, and a particular feature of, the Midwest. They have generally from one to five thousand inhabitants. They follow a distinctive over-all pattern from Ohio to Minnesota or Missouri with but slight, though important, local differences. They have grown, in the main, from a corner store at the crossing of crude trackways, among a few log cabins, or from a river landing or railroad depot. The pattern of that crossroads is still there at the heart of the town today, often a green square with singular memorials to those who fell in the Civil War and all wars since.

Along the sides of the square, if the town is a county seat, are the

78

county buildings and courthouse, the bank or banks, a battery of lawyers' offices—farmers must still be as litigious as the original settlers, or else land titles are inexplicably confused for so young a country— two or three drug stores, some taverns, barber shops and at least one beauty parlor, doctors', dentists', and veterinaries' offices, the news- paper, and the usual array of hardware, clothing, and other stores. Among the stores are a surprising number of jewelers, for farmers ap- parently buy much gold when times are good. They were most certainly doing so during the second World War, and jewelry stores have multiplied. Here is perhaps a lingering trace of the farmer-settler's long- pent-up demand for luxuries and distrust of "paper" and banks. During the last fifty years the taverns which used to be, and are often still, called "saloons" have dwindled as the drugstores have increased; a commentary on trends among farmers and their families. The first church—Methodist or Presbyterian or Lutheran or Baptist or (more rarely) Episcopalian—is "on the square." The other churches, like the movie and the grade and high schools, are usually a block or two from it, as the town grew.

The store fronts look modern, if rather cheap and standardized, with neon signs; but, if you cast your eyes upward, you will see good, well- laid Flemish bond or other traditional bricklaying, and windows of the 1860's or earlier. There are no hills, except in Wisconsin or along the Ohio or in Minnesota; so you see no skyline from the center of the town. It is as if the welkin were a big sun umbrella balanced on the central market place. The streets, paved only in the center of town, run straight into a middle distance of overhanging trees beyond which lies open country. Along them brick alternates with clapboard until, still surprisingly near the central crossroads, every building becomes a home and all are clapboard. Before them are little lawns and no hedges or borders, but vines over the porches and flowers by the house. Within a stone's throw of the crossroads are many gas stations, warehouses full of farmers' implements and supplies, and seedsmen's stores. If there is a railroad depot, it is usually a few blocks from the center; it will have one combined waiting-room and ticket office on one side of the tracks. Round it are warehouses; along the tracks are generally loading-pens for cattle and hogs; and there is certainly a sizable truck depot near by. The nearness of the real countryside to the center of all rural Midwest towns is a great and an ever present influence.

Outside the chief public and commercial buildings in summer, and inside them in winter, farmers and local worthies always find time to talk; and good talk it generally is. Everyone uses "first names." They talk slowly as if they savored it rarely, which is probably the case; and it is simpler Anglo-Saxon, with less city slang in it. During the hours of daylight, as if by common consent, the talk is mainly of personalities and trade and purely local affairs. In the evening, whether in town or at a neighbor's in the country, talk turns to state and national politics and issues of greater pith and moment. The farmer still comes into town with wife and family (except those at school), for his wife has as much to do in the town as he himself, and young children have to be brought with the mother. Where buggies used to line the square and the whinnying of horses was heard on all sides, there are now mute, serried ranks of automobiles of all ages and descriptions, with and without trailers. The farmer's standing can still be roughly gauged by the make and age of his automobile.

There is always one leading hotel in or near the central crossroads, and the lobby chairs are nearly always occupied. Here meet for lunch, on their respective days, if the town is large enough, the Rotarians, Lions, Elks, Kiwanis, Buffaloes, or other service clubs; banquets are given; and local functions take place. It is one of the very few common meeting-places. On the mezzanine or the second floor is usually the local Chamber of Commerce, if the town boasts one. Few rural towns do, but most towns of 5,000 inhabitants and more have one, if only to "boost the town." The Farm Bureau, Grange, or Union has an office or chapter in the town. There are often in the larger towns a Y.M.C.A. and, less generally, a Y.W.C.A. If the rural town is the county seat, there will probably be a public library, but otherwise it is a rarity.

Much of the shape, layout, compactness, communal solidarity, and social familarity of Lincoln's Springfield still fills these rural towns of the Midwest. In town and county politics almost every voter knows the candidates and they him; or, if they do not, they know someone in town—tradesman, banker, editor—who does. It is much the same in social affairs. Life is intensely personal. Business and politics and social matters are arranged or "fixed" by a few informal talks. A group of worthies runs the community. They trade, talk, and visit with one another. They were nearly all born there or near by. They stay put. They become the arbiters of community life. Each knows, likes, and is liked by a group of surrounding farmers; and in this way the rural town is the social focus of an area often as big as one or two hundred square miles and with an agricultural population of some 10,000–25,000.

If the district is overwhelmingly agricultural—as it will be in central and southern Ohio, Indiana, and Illinois, or most of Wisconsin and Iowa and Minnesota, or the center of northern Missouri—the county seat may be a rural town of between 5,000 and 20,000 inhabitants, and there may well be no other social center of that size within a radius of twenty to thirty miles. This partly reflects the insulation of farm life and small-town life in the Midwest; but it also explains the compact solidarity of these smaller communities and the immense influence they have wielded on the lives of their tradesmen's or professional men's or farmers' children during the last century.

Many a successful midwestern businessman or professional man between his fifties and seventies in the big cities came from these smaller towns or from the farms which serve, and are served by, them. A certain amount of his present outlook, caution, susceptibility to public opinion, toleration, and forbearance will remain from his youth. His successful colleagues and competitors, city-born, do not have these qualities to the same extent. There is much more to be said for life in the public eye of a small community than most people seem willing to confess today. (Perhaps it is just because they fear the public eye.) But in the formation of the Midwest character, the farms and the small country town have done most and best—at least among midwesterners aged fifty and more today. The monotonous life may have driven its sons and daughters forth, but it has left its indelible mark upon them. Much of their success in the cities is due to it.

One of the chief social problems of the farming community and the rural town is the scarcity of diversions; and, as leisure time increases, the problem grows with it. At home there is now the radio, which, however, is almost 100 per cent weighted with "big-city talk" and the characteristics of cities. It has therefore been a disturbing influence on the family life of the farms, while being at the same time a great boon. In summer and fall there is all the sport of the open air; hunting and fishing and boating—there are lakes or rivers within driving distance throughout the region—and motoring to this or that center of amusement or interest. (Water sports are surprisingly popular throughout the Midwest, which may help explain the popularity of the Navy in the inland states.) There are the forests, too. But winter and the so-called spring take up half the farm year. Then rural towns provide the only diversions, and they are limited: taverns, bowling, nickel-in-the-slot machines, one movie house open once or twice a week, and little else. Dances are still arranged by families and societies, as they were a century ago; but there is more attraction for the young, initiated by radio, in the newer kinds of dancing and dance halls, which they have heard of or seen in the cities and of which the religions of the farm belt do not approve. Consequently, social and family life on the farms and in the rural towns is undergoing great and growing tension. I have been in scores of rural towns in which there was no public library, no community center, no social focus of any kind. (The middle-sized towns and the cities are far ahead in this respect.) The young have no secular meeting-place save the drugstore or the tavern, though the churches or the Y.M.C.A. and Y.W.C.A., where the latter exist, provide some kind of social or religious focus on some week nights. The service clubs and the city fathers are anxiously trying to find a solution to what, after all, also vexes parents in the largest cities of America and the whole Western world. But meanwhile the thousands of farm communities and rural towns of the Midwest—which has more of them than almost any other region in the world—feel the impact of modernity upon youth much more keenly.

The social life of the parents is simpler and far less pretentious. To that extent we may be on the eve of a great social and familial convulsion in the Midwest, brought on by the automobile and radio. It could easily result in the disappearance of certain original, fundamental, and currently strong midwestern characteristics within a score of years from now. The farmer and his wife today, if they are aged forty-five or over, were not nurtured on radio and gasoline.

I recall many winter evenings with Midwest farmers—in Illinois, Wisconsin, Iowa, Ohio, Minnesota—when, neighbors having been advised (or, perhaps I ought to say, warned), about twenty would foregather in one farmhouse just to talk. The visiting wives would get someone to look after their children and come over to the host's farm to help the hostess with the baking and preparations. They would bring jars of this or that, or a pie, or a cake. The men would bring bottles of this or that, too. The icicles would hang by the barn door, swordlike. The snow would crackle underfoot in the temperature of zero to 30° below. Through the double storm windows far away the little lights of nearest neighbors would twinkle like grounded stars. At six we would see the headlights of cars steadily eating up the straight, white, snow-deep roads and finally snaking along the driveway up to the farm. Muffled, their occupants would come in, greeting each other only by first names: "Ned," "Matt," "Charlie," "Mis' Clarke." There would be an intense, hushed, and entirely propitious bustling in the kitchen in the rear. The summons would come, and we would sit down, nine or ten aside, host and hostess at either end, the other ladies "in waiting," to a dinner which fairly sang of Midwest hospitality: fresh mushroom soup; two kinds of chicken or pork; lima and string beans, baked potatoes, corn biscuits, preserve of baby strawberries and butter with the biscuits; salad of lettuce with fresh cranberry and pomegranate jello thereon; ice cream and maple syrup or three kinds of pie; and coffee. (I know they did not eat like that ordinarily. But I also know they could do it regularly for the enjoyment of their friends and for an evening in their own home.) In the offing, over the banisters, curious and wide-eyed youngsters, regularly shooed off to bed and as regularly returning, would give the false impression of Christmas eve. Afterward the ladies washed dishes—none would dream of leaving that pile for the hostess next morning—and then we would talk, and the ladies would join us.

Of all the talk and discussion I had in the Midwest, I think I relished that in the farmhouses most; and not only because of the preliminaries. It was direct, elemental, simple, often oversimplified, but extremely rational and open-minded. There was an evident readiness to change opinions upon fair, logical conviction. Those fundamental and re-markably searching political discussions in the stores, taverns, farms, and courthouses of Ohio and Indiana and Illinois before the Civil War do not seem so long ago when you go among Midwest farmers to-day. This may seem very near to romantic idealism; but it goes on. It simply is not heard of by the three-fifths of the population who are city dwellers in the Midwest. And that seems to me a pity for both of the great divisions of the Midwest people. "There is a great gulf fixed. . . . ."

One reason for this division is the greater speed with which the Mid-west farming community has assimilated foreign or other-American immigrants to an over-all pattern of rural life. This assimilation is al-most complete and utterly unlike the state of affairs in the cities and middle-sized towns. Almost anywhere in the region today, if you take one of the county seats and look at the land titles or records, or comb the area around, you will find American farmers of Anglo-Saxon, Celtic, German, Scandinavian, Bohemian, Ukrainian, and other Slav origins. You will find Methodists, Baptists, Presbyterians, Congregationalists, Unitarians, Episcopalians, Lutherans, Roman Catholics, Greek Ortho-dox, Jews (only in the town), Quakers, Christian Scientists, Seventh-Day Adventists, Jehovah's Witnesses, and many you may never have heard of before. But if you leave an area with a majority of German or Scandinavian Lutheran farmers and go to one with a majority of Anglo-Saxon Methodists, or to one with a majority of Russian Ortho-dox (and I have been to some), or to one with a majority of Bohemian Hussites, you will note only slight and superficial differences among those communities, no different pattern of life, and only differences in politics or outlook on national or international affairs.

83

In one county seat of 14,000 souls in Ohio, for instance, I found Americans of fifteen national origins with twenty-three different churches, excluding different branches of one and the same church. Mason City in Iowa, with 27,000 inhabitants, when I was last there had Episcopalian, Roman Catholic, Presbyterian, Baptist, Congregational, and Greek Orthodox churches and a synagogue; but it had two Methodist churches, five Lutheran—two German, a Norwegian, a Swedish, and another Eastern United Lutheran church—two Negro churches, and one remarkable evangelical, undenominational "radio church" with a big unseen congregation of listeners. The people of the city came from forty different national origins in Europe, including Iceland, and some years ago they were from fifty-five such national origins. Mason City, apart from being the seat of an agricultural county, is partly a manufacturing town and is, in any case, not "truly rural"; it is a middle-sized town. I mention it again in this context because I have described its near-by farmers. But these cases could be paralleled, with variations, throughout the agricultural areas of the region. Yet the social uniformity and single pattern of farm life covers them all.

The morality of the farmers in the Midwest is strict. In both their private and their community life their religions, no matter how great their differences of dogma or theology, have budded forth into an ethic of fair dealing. The sins of the rural families and communities in the region are naturally as human as those of any city dweller, but they are less varied and more elemental: mainly crimes of sex and personal violence, often ascribable to liquor. There is more looseness in sex morality than appears on the surface—or in court! The "shotgun wedding" is still common, even if a shotgun is no longer necessary; and the two parties resume a respected position in society. There is much less theft and almost no housebreaking, robbery with violence, holdups, racketeering, blackmail, and so on. In the farming and rural community, the greater social uniformity is reflected in a greater uniformity of morality. Indeed, there is a more commonly recognized and observed code of behavior there than in the middle-sized manufacturing towns and cities.

I have already noted the unparalleled neighborliness and mutual help of the rural community in the Midwest; but it is worth noting that there are severe and recognized limits to this. Kindness in "trouble" and mutual aid—"trouble" is a capacious portmanteau word in the region—are general and dependable. But the same farmer who will help out on a sick neighbor's farm will not give him an ounce of seed, or yield an inch while bargaining, if he feels that the context is one of

84

trade or business and not of human need. They are as tender, sympathetic, kind, and hospitable as their womenfolk toward the visiting stranger or the needy; but with the non-needy they drive the hardest and closest bargain possible. And townsmen are an object of initial distrust—with good reason, if you are to go by the history of prairie settlement or the ubiquity of smoking-room stories about the behavior of "drummers."

The severe self-reliance in the farmer's struggle with soil and elements, his geographical insulation from others most of the time, individual responsibility for his acts and decisions, the dependence of his kith and kin and way of life on those acts and decisions, the headship of his little family-community in its isolated acres—all these things make him tend to bring up his children with a sense of the hardness and unpredictability of life. Wherever the children go in the rural community they get the same philosophy, except at school. It is part of the social uniformity. Accordingly, the rural background of the Midwest has been a forcing-bed to so many promising youngsters. The better they were at school, the more, by contrary tugging and opposition and rebellion, did they strive to leave the rural life. Thus the farms and the rural community have engendered much ambition and energy —especially the energy of contrariness and "anti" feelings—and have tended to say what the Scotch say of Scotland or the Irish of Ireland: "A fine country to get away from!" And look what the Scotch and Irish have done in the world—or in England, for that matter—and where they now are in it! The farm boys of the Midwest have been, and still are, its "Scotch and Irish." Again, perhaps it is the contrariness and desire for change which drives so many farm boys away to sea, or into the air, or into the cities. Moreover, there is no room in the Midwest for every son of every farmer to become a farmer, and the room is shrinking.

Few city dwellers realize how pervasive in the Midwest is this influence from farms or rural towns. Some states in the region—Wisconsin, Minnesota, and Iowa—are more dependent on farms and farm products than on anything else. With few large cities, these states form the newest, northwest section of the region. It is predominantly agrarian in its pattern of life and therefore different in atmosphere, political outlook, and attitude from the other five Midwest states. This has significant results. For example, of the roughly two and a half million souls in Iowa, about half form the male and female electorate; and, after less than a century of settlement in the state, a surprisingly large proportion of them actually know, or know of, nearly all political candidates personally and have relatives or connections by marriage throughout the state. Such social compactness in an overwhelmingly agricultural region is rare. It is not found in Europe or in the East of America, where families have been settled far longer but have forgotten or ignore their relatives. I should like to add here, as a pointer to the impact of war on the farms, that, of Iowa's one and a half million souls of both sexes and all ages over eighteen, more than 300,000 went into the armed forces of the United States in the second World War.

This vast reserve of farming communities throughout the Midwest, always going on with their steady life behind the cities and towns, is of enormous importance to the region as a whole—and to the people of the towns and cities, even if they only think of the farmers when they go motoring or cannot get something for their table. For, vastly different as the life of the cities is, many of the city dwellers' characteristics came, and are still being renewed, from the farming communities.

THE MENTAL CLIMATE OF THE FARMER

All these influences have combined to create a mental climate of the Midwest farmer—a climate different from that in which the city dweller grows up. This mental climate naturally declares itself in the farmer's characteristics. Perhaps only the visitor to the Midwest clearly sees that region's most striking paradox and extremes: what Karl Mannheim called in his portentous phrase the "contemporaneity of the noncontemporaneous." In this case it means the existence of a farming people, whose folk-memories are longer, alongside one of the most highly industrialized city-dwelling people of the world whose memories, if any, scarcely go back two decades. The farming community is a more uniform society, both in national origins and in social structure. The cities and towns are melting-pots, always bubbling. Here is the real division of the Midwest; the real tension; the real cleavage in attitudes. Two-fifths of the midwesterners are still bound up with the soil, leading an agrarian way of life, serving the cities and to a less extent served by their manufactures, yet not of these cities. They were once a majority. The region once belonged to them and to their way of life. There is much influence and counterinfluence between the two divisions of the people; yet the cleavage remains, and in many ways it is greater now than it ever was.

Farmers, unlike city dwellers, have "time on their hands"—or perhaps it would be more accurate to say they have "time on their minds," for their hands are always busy. As soon as the foreign visitor leaves a Midwest city or middle-sized town and spends a few days on the farms, wholly with farmers, he feels that he is on more familiar ground. More

86

especially does he feel that he is in a familiar mental climate, even if he knows nothing of agriculture. The Midwest farmer has long and arduous tasks, but, while his limbs are coping with them, he can ruminate or contemplate or just not think at all. He cannot cart the radio about on his tractor or on his horses or cattle, though I know of one who does! The farmer cannot dash for the newspaper. The movie is a long way off. Unlike the first settlers, with their "groceries" among every little group of cabins, the farmer today is sober. He drinks, but very little and hardly ever to excess—if he does, he fails as a farmer and very definitely loses caste among his fellows. (Here is a change in a century!)

The farmer is at the mercy of Nature and knows it. He is more profoundly religious than city dwellers; and he seems to be more philosophical, more profound, and to think more deeply about current affairs, domestic and foreign. He may not think as often or as frequently on these matters as most city dwellers think *they* are thinking on them. But he does think, and, like all real thought, it is painful. His mental climate is both more elemental and more fundamental than that of the city dweller. It is often confused and contradictory—whose isn't in our day and age?—but he gives the visitor the impression that he is not regurgitating predigested conclusions or snap judgments, that he speaks thoughts which are his own, that he has thought them out for himself, and that he has "looked before and after." He sees things over a longer run, and on a more general canvas, than do his contemporaries in the city. He is what midwestern city dwellers call more unsophisticated than they. But he is also more direct, more sober in judgment and habits, more obstinate when his mind is made up, and less volatile.

For this there are many explanations. First, the competitive tempo of Midwest city life is lacking; the farmers do not so obviously have to compete with each other in trade, nor do their wives in social events. "The Joneses" live in towns; they are not so frequent, they are not ubiquitous, in the country.

Secondly, life on the farm has a prescribed annual, seasonal, weekly, and daily routine which dare not be flouted; and routine, contrary to popular belief among city people, does not kill; it economizes life. You can try to run your business or profession in the city on a hectic nine-hour day, then meet your wife (whose day now dawns) for cocktail parties, do a theater or party of some kind, crawl into bed in the wee sma' hours, and get up again for the new day's business when the hours are only a little bigger. You can even try to do this regularly, breaking into city "society," and learning to pay for it, as so many businessmen and professional men do. But if you are a farmer, want to remain a farmer, and cannot be anything else but a farmer, you cannot do that even if the opportunities are at hand—which, happily, they are not. The overwhelming majority of Midwest farmers today conform to a routine and pattern of life which is partly prescribed by Nature, partly by tradition, partly by the compelling force of local uniformity. All other farmers are in the same boat. They save their bodies—the Midwest rural areas produce long lives, as long as those of the two other best regions of longevity, upper New England and the West Coast, to which so many Americans retire to die—and it can be argued that they save more of their souls, too.

Thirdly, they are, in fact, more interested in their souls than are the city dwellers. As you would expect, their religions—overwhelmingly Protestant and evangelical "nonconformist," with scattered pockets of Roman Catholicism and Episcopalianism—contain stronger doses of determinism than the same sects show in cities: doses of Calvinism, fundamentalism, verbal inspiration, and Seventh-Day Adventism. Religion is also still more directly emotional in the farm communities, as it was in the beginning of the Midwest. There is more dogma and theology in the sermon and in the minds of the congregation. But, in addition, there is an evident admixture of natural philosophy. In many places—Ohio, downstate Illinois, Iowa, Missouri—there is at times almost a pantheistic tinge to discussions in the narrow circle formed by the pastor and a few others. Wordsworth would have been quite at home on the prairie. The "genius of the place" would have affected him as it affects all who stay in it; who see its remorseless growth and movement, its tough obduracy, its vast skies, its vigorous and luxuriant life. Outside the prairie in the North and West of the region, Lutheranism is strong. Here there is no trace of pantheism, little emotionalism, and much more dogma.

It is strange that in a region which is so new, so recently settled, superstitions and remnants of paganism from the Old World are still alive among its people. Perhaps this is part of the unsophistication. Certainly much of this superstition came in from the South; but it was strange to me to find, among farmers of Anglo-Saxon and Bohemian and German and other national origins, superstitions which have their counterparts today in Wessex and Hungary and Scandinavia. Midwest farming may be the newest and most modern in the world, but the way of life is very old, and the farmers are no younger than those of Europe, whence came their forebears. For the same reason, I suppose, there are still strong traces of that consuming bigotry which marked the pioneers—as it did the Pilgrims before them—the bigotry which runs like a vivid streak throughout the life of the Midwest; the bigotry of small-town morals, of Lovejoy and the Abolitionists, of slaveowners, of New England and the South combined in the Midwest. This bigotry still has something to do with narrowing the life of the farm and driving the youth to the cities.

Fourthly, despite railroad and automobile and radio, the Midwest farmers are far more isolated—or, rather, insulated—than the city dwellers. The farms are separated; the towns are miles away; the routine has to go on, and, except in winter, there is not much spare time. Thus the Midwest farmers from the outset felt they were cut off: an "elect" people, subduing a wilderness. Later, they felt they were being exploited. Many farmers today cannot know their congressman, senator, or representative in the state legislatures unless they go miles to see him, and on very rare occasions. They do not often go to the big cities. Their contacts with the world of trade and finance, which rules their individual destiny, are local, through agencies at the nearest railroad depot or their "lobbies." Their life has the great blessings of intimacy and privacy, but it has little else. It is natural that they should have developed so quickly, and retained, "anti" characteristics, phobias, and resentments at big soulless and even person-less bodies or corporations, governments, government agencies, banks, railroads, packers, grain dealers, and suppliers and shippers, by whose remote control, they feel, their lives are involuntarily directed.

Their attitude has always been that of the debtor to his creditor. This colors their attitude to monetary problems, to industrialism and industrial capitalism, and, if they are tenants, to landlords or cash partners. It is perfectly natural, therefore, that they should tend to view great national and international economic issues only in the light of transactions affecting the farmer: for instance, the nonpayment of the debts after the war of 1914–18, the Bretton Woods proposals, the gold standard, devaluation of the dollar, and so on. What is surprising is the degree to which the farmers can and do take a detached view of current national and international problems. This is certainly borne out by the various polls of public opinion which specifically contrast farmers' views with those of others in cities. Doubtless the "time on their minds" enables farmers to "think through" so many problems, to see them steadily and see them whole. It would be dangerous, however, to judge by the polls taken since 1940, for in that period the financial prosperity of the farmers has resulted in the repayment of mortgages at an unparalleled rate. The total of mortgages on farms has been reduced in five years by 25 per cent; and in no region has the total of such repayments been as great as in the Midwest. So there is, temporarily, less evidence of this debtor's mentality.

Among themselves, few people in the world are as neighborly, as hospitable, as friendly in time of need. This is not, of course, a characteristic unique to the Midwest farmers. It is general among American—but not among all European—farmers. Owing to their insulation and isolation on separate farms, to their settlers' habits and traditions, and, above all, to their sense of community, it is carried to a marked degree in the Midwest. The family plays a part in this. The farmer's family life today is the closest knit of all in the Midwest. It is breaking down as the influences, attractions, and communications of the cities draw the girls and boys—and sometimes even the whole family—into town life and occupations. (This only intensifies the Midwest farmers' dislike of townsmen and their way of life: "How're ya gonna keep 'em down on the farm?") But it is still obvious to the visitor that the stability and solidarity of Midwest farm life—contrasting in this respect very greatly with that of the city—repose, first and foremost, on the family. In these farm families there is still a familial division of labor between husband, wife, elder children, and, of course, the hired man—if there is one. The hired man is still reckoned part of the family, together with his own family if he has one. In this characteristic kindliness lurks some trace of the pioneers, when all inhabitants of a single-room log cabin lived as a unit—parents, boarders, relatives, children—and dressed and undressed without shame before each other.

The farmer sees more of his wife and family than the city dweller. If he does not think more of them—and I am not sure that he does not—at least they fill more of his mental horizon. The housewives, real heroines of the forest and prairie that claimed so many of them in untimely death, led and still lead an arduous existence. Tempered as that existence now is in many of the better farmhouses by electricity and laborsaving equipment, the majority of Midwest farms still have no bathroom and no inside toilet. There is little "help" for the farmer's wife, who copes not only with all the household chores and the share of the farm work which devolves on her but also with the care of children. And the farm children of the Midwest are generally sturdy, well tended, well fed, and never spoiled. The farmer therefore thinks not so much in terms of government enterprise, or legislative activity, to provide his family with a minimum standard of life more comparable with that of city dwellers. He thinks of his calling, his way of life, as a necessity to the nation; and he firmly believes that it should get its reward, that it should not be knocked hither and thither and kept down by the vagaries of city or international life. He remains very largely an individualist, but he is very tired of being the one American individualist who is always forgotten.

Many travelers through the Midwest have testified to the casual, genial, kind, but blunt, matter-of-fact, and "don't give a damn" manner with which the city dwellers, the public servants, waiters and waitresses, and others treat the stranger. They are most helpful. They treat you well. And they let you know who they are and how they are treating you. But the Midwest farmer knows he is your equal. He does not shout it in your ear and blazon it upon his forehead. He takes it for granted but quietly. There is far more unstudied, unconscious courtesy —the real courtesy of real equals, like that between eighteenth-century aristocrats—among "Nature's gentlemen" in the Midwest than in the cities. Indeed, the farmers in all income brackets have an effortless, natural poise. They are more open-minded and—strange as this may seem—I think they have more imaginative qualities than the city dwellers: at least, on all subjects save perhaps sex and religion. They are interested and more patient to learn another person's views. They are more sympathetic, which means they can imagine better. It is noteworthy that so much of the imaginative literature, humor and fiction, and so many of the great literary figures of the Midwest during the last hundred years have sprung from its farmers' sons and daughters. This is as true today at it was when the Midwest was all or mainly farms. What the constant permeation of city life by characters and characteristics from the Midwest farm has meant to the life of the Midwest will perhaps never be adequately appreciated. It has not been without cost and heartache on the farms, where it is a great and growing problem. But it is still going on. It is a great and good influence.

THE BEAUTY OF THE LAND

The observant European who walks in the procession of the seasons through the Midwest countryside cannot fail to be struck by majestic beauty on all sides. Indeed, I am surprised by the general American belief that the Midwest is "weary, stale, flat, and unprofitable." There is a bewildering and impressive variety of beauty, at all seasons; but those midwesterners who travel abroad and enthuse over European beauty—which is admittedly striking—come always from cities. They are the same midwesterners whose first impulse, when deliberating about a vacation, is to go to California, Florida, Canada, Maine, Arizona, or the Old South. As we saw, there is a climatic reason for wanting

91

—nay, needing—to get away from the region. But there is no compelling aesthetic reason for leaving the Midwest countryside, except a desire to see another kind of beauty.

The country is vast and still largly primeval. You can really see Mother Nature in the Midwest countryside. The clearing and destruction of the forests and the breaking of the prairie have not really taken from the country its virgin aspect. The monotonously rectangular fields, farms, and road patterns are more obvious when you are at speed in car or train or airplane than when you are at rest among them. Take that region of the Midwest which comes in for so much disdain: the prairie. When you walk across it or stay still in it, as few do, there is extraordinary beauty of bird and beast, grass and flower, around and above those vast fields. There are skies to which only the Dutch and Flemish or the East Anglian school of English painters could do justice. (They worked in flat country, where alone one can really see the heavens by day or by night.) The size of the heavens above the prairie; the blend of horizon with the sky; the clouds, both pacific and like "black battalions of the gods"; dawns and sunsets; the wind and rainstorms and the mantling of the blizzards; the rare trees; the verdure of the stream beds and river bottoms; the infinite ways in which sunlight and moonlight strike the great masses of land and the scattered habitations; above all, the constantly shifting colors and light and shade— these make the prairie itself as restless and changeable as the sea. It is to midwestern farmers what the sea is to sailors.

In winter the deep snow smooths away the rectangular lines of buildings and wire fences and reveals a hugeness which has to be seen to be felt; something like the hugeness of that sea of tall grass which rippled through the Midwest until less than a hundred years ago. Here is the naked bosom of Mother Earth, reduced by snow to bare form and nothing else. Tiny and more solitary than ever seem the farms, perfectly and naturally camouflaged. The land is out in the elements, alone. Man and beast are in-a-door. This is the only time of the year in which the prairie reverts to some semblance of what it was; and it then has an ageless grandeur. But when the sun climbs and the snows melt, the rivers and streams overflow, and the black earth is turned inside out again, the prairie pulses with that primeval life-urge which astounds and transfigures a few days or weeks later. In a day, the heat will strike from forty degrees to over eighty, and then on to ninety and more, and the prairie heaves and labors and gives birth. Round the farmhouse and farmyard and along the headlands of the fields and roads, the descendants of the Old Prairie push forth in every shade of green at an unnatural pace and in almost frightening profusion. The orchards put on their unseasonal snow. To fly over the Midwest at this time is like flying over Hungary, Slovakia, Bulgaria, or Rumania in the spring. Summer comes in with a thunderclap. The fierce sun which takes toll of man and beast brings life to the fields, and the brilliant green corn parades in militarily symmetrical files across the wide landscape, rank upon rank. Even the droughts bring a savage sense of beauty. As so frequently, what is human tragedy is no less natural grandeur. The grass is scorched brown, and withered to the ground, by August; but the skies are still there, and the shimmering heat waves make vague horizons tremble.

But it rarely lasts long, even if long enough to spell the farmer's ruin. The wild storms bring tropical rain, and the growth of weeds and plants is redoubled. The oncoming fall turns leaves and brings new flowering weeds and shrubs. All the country goes amber, then gold, then russet, then red, like the sumacs round the house. The heavens become clear of dust, Mediterranean or Mexican blue by day and velvet blue and brilliant by night. And so to the frosty crackle of winter again.

The impressiveness, the majesty is, of course, that of size. The bigness of things which so impresses and inspires the midwesterner of the cities lies all around him. It is the Midwest; and the Midwest is size. Yet the country has the beauty of little things, too. Either on or off the prairie, in the forests or the river bottoms or along the banks of the little streams, there are brilliant birds and shy beasts. Round the houses and in the near-by fields or woods are chipmunks, field mice, squirrels, groundhogs, gophers, possums, raccoons, rabbits and jack rabbits, and scores of other fur-bearing "critters" no longer trapped—to say nothing of the skunk, that creature whose defense mechanism so startlingly, and unfortunately so enduringly, belies its beauty. They are all handsomely attired and attractive to watch. Through the trees and shrubbery near the houses or about the streams or woods go a bewildering variety of gaily dressed warblers, woodpeckers, sapsuckers, nuthatches, and tree-creepers with their acrobatic finesse: the handsome flicker with his staccato hiccuping; the red cardinal and his russet lady; bright orioles and tanagers; raucous but garish blue jays and the somber, humorous catbird; smart thrushes with their liquid song and their cousins, the delicate ovenbirds; the little booming, backing-and-filling humming-birds in the orchard; tame and cheeky chickadees with their delicate legs, and juncoes who, like the cardinals and woodpeckers, stay all winter; whippoorwills and bobolinks, unseen but only too frequently heard; a surprising selection of pert wrens, finches, and sparrows (far handsomer and with more real song than the house sparrow); the vulgar robin, crow, and grackle; owls of all kinds lamenting in the night; heron and duck and waterfowl by the lakes and streams; pheasant and partridge everywhere in the fields; and, above, hawks and buzzards on lazy pinions, gliding and scrutinizing. Audubon's pages unfold before your eyes if you sit quietly in any wood or river bottom in the Midwest. Then there are the insects and frogs in late summer days and nights, humming, drumming, booming, whistling, and croaking: toads, frogs, katydids, tree frogs, grasshoppers, locusts; fireflies and the bright bees; multitudinous butterflies; and gigantic moths in the evening, stupidly clogging the screens; and the huge, regal dragonflies over the streams and round the shrubbery. For three months there is prodigal life and color about the Midwest.

To walk slowly along some little brook or "lick" or river bottom in a Midwest May, or through those woods which are the remnants of the great Midwest forests, is an experience. The willows and alders, and many reeds, put forth their new greenery. The woods are full of young trees and shrubs growing in haphazard profusion, the survival of the fittest among so many fallen seeds and fruit. The crab blossom startles the woods with its coral spray and reminds you of Johnny Appleseed's journeyings. Oak, maple, cottonwood, sycamore, elm, all come out at different times and with varying tones of green and yellow. The white candles of the catalpa take the place of the European flowering horse chestnut. The European misses the cuckoo, the nightingale, the primrose, the bluebells, and other birds and flowers which form so much of the literature of spring in the Old World since its early dawn. But here in the Midwest is great beauty, too; wild but luxuriant, strange but vital and prolific; the struggle of vine with tree trunk, the battle of green shoots through the leaves of centuries. I always think of the morning-glories as emblems of the Midwest before I think of the old familiar faces—violets, trillium, iris, tiger lilies, anemones, celandine, Aaron's-rod, wild geranium, and, near the habitations of men, forsythia and bridal wreath, magnolia and lilac and japonica, jasmine, and almost every flower in the herbaceous borders of Europe. Only the lawns, the greensward of northern Europe, are missing. The summer sun sees to that; and if you want them, you must sow again each spring and roll and water incessantly—as they do, at great expense, on suburban golf courses.

The land is as beautiful in its bigness as it is in its manifold little haunts of beauty. That is perhaps Nature's penance for the savagery which she makes evident in so much. It is a mixture of Holland and

Slovakia, Scandinavia and Hungary, Russia and Spain. It is not yet a region for diversions and relaxation, in the popular sense of those terrible words. It is no recreational region for the rest of America. (That is its good fortune; it has remained itself.) But for its own people, in farm and city alike, it has beauty and health and repose to offer— abundantly; on its innumerable lakes; in the beautiful north woods; by sand dunes and among pines; on horseback through forest trails; in remarkably good hunting and fishing almost everywhere; in cabins and log camps, or canoeing and trail-blazing. Its restless city dwellers—aided by the automobile and airplane and railroads, their own curiosity, and the deliberate "boosting" of other parts of America—have mainly employed their spare time in going away from their own region. They do not seem to know it very well. They have missed a lot.

This, then, is the *country* of the Midwest, the rural region distinct from the towns and cities where three-fifths of its people live. This is the Midwest of farmer and lumberjack which contains the only living legacy of the first pioneers and settlers. Here some of their qualities and characteristics are still most clearly perceptible. And here the Old Midwest is carried onward by an economic and social momentum which has lasted longer in the fields than on the city streets. But it is changing, too, though at a slower pace; and the life of the cities is changing it.

IV. "THE CITIES RISE"

ALL OVER THE WORLD, CITIES AND CITY LIFE AROSE IN THE WAKE OF communications, trade, and industry; but nowhere and at no time did they arise as quickly as in the Midwest. One of the most striking Midwest extremes or paradoxes today is between its cities and its country. There are two distinct Midwests: one, the older agricultural Midwest with separate, scattered farms and small village towns, each with anything from a few hundred to twenty-five hundred inhabitants; the other, the larger, newer Midwest with a network of towns and cities above that limit, forming wide industrial areas. The Old Midwest was broadly settled, in its present familiar outlines and way of life, by the end of the Civil War. The industrial, urban Midwest dates from after the Civil War. Both Midwests have interacted and changed, but the change has been vastly more striking in the New Midwest.

In the Civil War, survivors of which are still alive, the center of population and of industry of the United States was inside Pennsylvania, though it was over the mountains and in the west of that state. The center of industry and population by 1890 had passed westward into Ohio. Today it is in eastern Illinois. This westward movement of industrialism was naturally linked with the transcontinental development of America and the spread of cities and towns, for, since the industrial revolution, manufacture has been an urban process. Consequently, the way Americans live, "the American way of life," has rapidly changed from an overwhelmingly rural to an overwhelmingly urban way. You can tell a people by its songs. Today the majority of mid-westerners are city dwellers or townsmen. But at the Rotary or other service clubs their songs are of Dobbin and the shay, of the old mill stream, or of working on the first railroads, or the songs of Stephen Foster and of other regions of America. Since those songs were written, the only new and popular songs are the radio ditties of all-American cities. There is Midwest history in a nutshell: from cornfields to neon signs without a pause.

In this rapid change within half a century—roughly from 1840 to 1890—the older East of the country underwent almost as striking a change as the newer Midwest and West. The only outstanding difference was that in the East the older commercial towns were magnified into industrial cities as the country towns were drained of their population, while in the Midwest entirely new towns sprang up and soon became big industrial cities. In both regions the rural country towns were drastically reduced in their total number and in their size. They have never regained their former importance, either in the East or in the newer Midwest. While the total population of America between 1790 and 1890 was multiplied only 16 times—and that is a fantastic growth compared with any other people's—the population living in towns was multiplied 139 times.[1] Rural towns, townships, villages, and even counties lost population after 1880, while towns and cities picked it up and added waves of immigrants to it. This was the beginning of the great cleavage between town and country which so strikingly divides the Midwest, its people, and their ways of life to this day.

In 1860 there were only three cities in the Midwest with 100,000 inhabitants or more—St. Louis, Chicago, and Cincinnati. They were engaged in handling the agricultural products of the region and serving its farmers and settlers. In the most thickly populated Midwest states not more than one-seventh of the people then lived in towns of 2,500 inhabitants or more. Yet by the end of the century, within only half a lifetime, the region had fourteen cities each with more than 100,000 souls; in the entire region one-half of the people lived in towns of 2,500 inhabitants or more; and more than half the people of some Midwest states had become urban dwellers. Chicago had a population of more than 1,500,000 in 1900, whereas half a century earlier it had well below 100,000.

If you can bear with some statistics in this section, you will find it

---

[1] Arthur M. Schlesinger, *Political and Social Growth of the United States* (New York: Macmillan Co., 1933), pp. 61 ff., gives a graphic picture of this process.

worth while. (You may not gain knowledge from them, but, as Carlyle said, they may save you from having ignorance thrust upon you!) They will help to put in perspective the recent suddenness of the industrialization of the Midwest, the division between town and country to which it gave rise, the significance of the European immigration into the region between 1870 and 1929, and the problems thus created in city and farming communities alike.

Ignore for the moment my "marginal belt" around the Midwest. Think of the region as containing just the states of Ohio, Michigan, Indiana, Illinois, Wisconsin, Minnesota, Iowa, and Missouri. Now compare this Midwest with the older East, into which we will put Maine, Vermont, New Hampshire, Massachusetts, Rhode Island, Connecticut, New York, New Jersey, Pennsylvania, Delaware, and Maryland. Thus we contrast our eight Midwest states with all eleven eastern states —including as eastern both Maryland and Delaware. As far back as 1880, this Midwest actually exceeded in population the eleven eastern states: 15,800,000 to 15,400,000. In 1910 the eleven eastern states had a total population almost exactly equal to that of the Midwest eight (East, a little over 27 millions; Midwest, a little over 26 millions). Now jump to 1940. These same two groups, East and Midwest, were then in almost the same relationship: East, 38 millions; Midwest, just under 36 millions.

The difference in the numbers of towns and cities—or, as the census puts it, the difference in urbanization—between the two regions is not nearly as great as many Americans imagine. In 1940 the eight states of the Midwest had nearly 60 per cent of their people living in towns of 2,500 or more; yet the eleven states of the "industrial" East (including Maryland and Delaware) had only 65 per cent. No Midwest state was as rural and agricultural as Maine and Vermont; but no Midwest state, either, was as urban as Massachusetts, Rhode Island, New York, and New Jersey, each of which had more than four-fifths of its people living in towns.

Table 1, which also puts the national capital into the eastern region, will quickly show how the two most important and most populous regions of America compare. Remember, as you look at the table, that two-thirds of the entire American retail market lies east of the Mississippi River, north of the Ohio River, and north of Washington, D.C. Remember that the national capital is here included in the East. See how evenly the two regions are matched; the one old, the other young; the one thriving a century ago, the other barely even settled. See how heavily they bulk, combined, as a proportion of all America.

You will note that even when we put the recently swollen national capital into the East—where it is doubtful if it rightly belongs, since it is unique in its way of life—the eight Midwest states make a remarkable showing alongside the older eleven states of the East *plus* the capital. If, in addition, you note the disproportionate bulk of the state of New York, which houses the nation's metropolis and has more than

TABLE 1

THE EAST AND MIDWEST COMPARED: 1940 CENSUS

State	Population	Per Cent of U.S. Population	Per Cent Urban	No. of Cities over 50,000
Ohio	6,907,612	5.25	66.8	12
Michigan	5,256,106	3.99	65.7	9
Indiana	3,427,796	2.60	55.1	8
Illinois	7,897,241	6.00	73.6	9
Wisconsin	3,137,587	2.38	53.5	3
Minnesota	2,792,300	2.12	49.8	5
Iowa	2,538,268	1.93	42.0	5
Missouri	3,784,664	2.87	51.8	4
MIDWEST	35,741,574	27.14	57.3*	55
Maine	847,226	0.64	40.5	1
Vermont	359,231	0.27	34.3	. . . .
New Hampshire	491,524	0.37	57.6	1
Massachusetts	4,316,721	3.28	89.4	16
Rhode Island	713,346	0.54	91.6	2
Connecticut	1,709,242	1.30	67.8	5
New York	13,479,142	10.24	82.8	13
New Jersey	4,160,165	3.16	81.6	13
Pennsylvania	9,900,180	7.52	66.5	16
Maryland	1,821,244	1.38	59.3	1
Delaware	266,505	0.20	52.3	1
Washington, D.C.	663,091	0.50	. . . .	1
EAST	38,727,617	29.40	65.8*	70

* Arithmetical averages by states.

one-tenth of the American nation living in it, the comparison becomes even more striking.

But so far we have compared regions which are defined by state boundaries alone. This is misleading if we are more concerned with the characteristics of their people or their particular ways of life. For instance, the most populated state of the Union, New York, is also one which has some of the largest unpopulated or underpopulated areas. The bulk of New York State's population now lives in a "great wen" down at the mouth of the Hudson, and then straggles back in manufacturing towns up that river through Albany to Schenectady and

99

across the valley of the river Mohawk to Lake Erie and Buffalo, passing places like Utica, Syracuse, Rochester, and others on the way. Yet many of upper New York State's towns, and certainly those of western Pennsylvania and northern West Virginia, are as recent in industrial development, and in their populating by immigrants, as the manufacturing cities of the Midwest proper. The movement of industrialism away from New England or the Middle Atlantic States and across the Appalachians is a fairly recent development. It is hardly more than a century old. Consequently, the characteristics of the newer manufacturing towns and their people in the western portions of the East—their people being either foreign immigrants or migrant Americans from the East—are similar to those of the Midwest, whether the new towns were only just over the mountains in Pennsylvania or upper New York or northern West Virginia, whether they were in adjoining Ohio, or whether they were in Michigan, Indiana, Illinois, Wisconsin, and Missouri. Thus our "marginal belt," which runs round the Midwest roughly from Buffalo to Kansas, Nebraska, and the two Dakotas, contains a surprisingly large number of manufacturing cities, the populations of which increase or decrease the total Midwest population according as we include them in, or exclude them from, our definition of the Midwest.

Now the table above makes no allowance for this "marginal belt." It is based simply on state boundaries. It gives all of Pennsylvania to the East, despite the development of the Pittsburgh steel region together with that of eastern Ohio. Similarly the table does not include in the Midwest that narrow eastern strip of Kansas, Nebraska, and the two Dakotas which is inside the line of Midwest agricultural methods and contains towns and cities industrially and financially linked with the Midwest—and not with the Great Plains or Rockies or Far West beyond. So let us, as an experiment, leave Buffalo with the East, but include in the Midwest and its "marginal belt" the boundary cities or industrial regions of Erie, Greenville, Sharon, New Castle, Pittsburgh (Pennsylvania); Wheeling (West Virginia); Kansas City, Topeka, Atchison, and Leavenworth (Kansas); Lincoln and Nebraska City and Omaha (Nebraska); Sioux Falls (South Dakota); and Fargo (North Dakota). To be accurate about the Midwest, let us also omit from it the Ozark region of southern Missouri. As soon as we do this, we have to knock 1,000,000 souls off the East and add about 1,500,000 to the Midwest. The Midwest—eight states and a marginal belt—then has roughly 37,250,000 inhabitants. And the East, including Buffalo and Washington, D.C., and all of Maryland and Delaware, has 37,750,000.

Of course, all this juggling with figures is arbitrary, for you cannot be sure you are right in including Maryland-minus-Baltimore in the "East," or in excluding the Pittsburgh steel region from it. Nor can you be sure you are right in leaving Buffalo with the East. But, however you juggle, two facts always emerge. First, the Midwest and East are surprisingly near equality in size. Secondly, there is a marginal belt of debatable territory around the Midwest, and it contains many big manufacturing cities, the profile and way of life of which are very largely midwestern.

Now let us look more closely into this "urbanization"—the numbers and sizes of towns and cities in the two chief regions of the United States. For this purpose we will leave the Pittsburgh region to the East again; we will also leave to it the national capital and all eleven states; and we will stick to state boundaries in the East. But in the West, as we fairly can, we will take in the few "Midwest" towns and cities on the eastern edges of Kansas, Nebraska, and the Dakotas. Here again some remarkable features emerge. The figures are from the 1940 Census of the United States. The best way I can set them out is in paragraphs, like this:

1. AMERICA HAS 14 CITIES EACH WITH OVER 500,000 SOULS: *17 per cent of all the people live in these 14 cities. The 14 cities' total population is 22,400,000.*

   THE EAST *has 7 of the 14 cities, with a total population of 13,100,000. Of these, New York City alone accounts for 7,500,000; the others are Boston, Philadelphia, Pittsburgh, Baltimore, Washington, D.C., and Buffalo.*

   THE MIDWEST *has 5 of the 14, with a total population of 7,300,000. Of these, Chicago (city only) accounts for 3,400,000; the others are Detroit, Cleveland, St. Louis, and Milwaukee. Thus in the class of the biggest cities, the East—mainly because of New York City—is overwhelmingly predominant, not only over the Midwest but also over all the other big-city regions of the country put together.*

2. AMERICA HAS 23 CITIES EACH WITH 250,000 TO 500,000 SOULS: *a further 5.9 per cent of all the people live in these 23 cities, the total population of which is a further 7,800,000. So 30,200,000 people, say one-quarter of all Americans, live in 37 cities each of which has more than 250,000 souls.*

   THE EAST *has only 4 of these further 23 cities, and the 4 have a total population of 1,300,000.*

   THE MIDWEST, *however, has 7 of the 23, and these 7 have a total* population of 2,600,000. They are, in order of size, Minneapolis, Cincinnati, Kansas City (Missouri), Indianapolis, Columbus (Ohio), St. Paul, and Toledo. Thus the Midwest has twice as many persons as the East living in cities each of which has between one-quarter and one-half million souls.

3. AMERICA HAS 55 CITIES EACH WITH 100,000 TO 250,000 SOULS: a further 5.9 per cent of all the people live in these 55 cities, the total population of which is, again, 7,800,000. So 28.9 per cent of all Americans live in 92 cities, each with more than 100,000 people.

   THE EAST has 22 of these further 55 cities, and the 22 have a total population of 2,900,000. They are mainly the industrial cities of New England, New York, New Jersey, and Pennsylvania.

   THE MIDWEST, however, has only 14 of these 55 cities, and those 14 have a total population of 2,100,000. Thus the Midwest cannot compare with the East in the number of medium-sized cities each having between 100,000 and 250,000 inhabitants.

4. AMERICA HAS 107 CITIES EACH WITH 50,000 TO 100,000 SOULS: a further 5.6 per cent of all the people live in these 107 cities, the total population of which is 7,300,000. So 34.4 per cent of all Americans—over one-third—live in 199 cities, each with more than 50,000 people.

   THE EAST has 37 of these 107 cities, and the 37 have a total population of 2,600,000. These 37 cities, too, are concentrated in New England, New York, New Jersey, and Pennsylvania.

   THE MIDWEST again has fewer than the East. It has 30 of the 107 cities, and these 30 have a total population of 2,000,000.

5. AMERICA HAS 213 CITIES EACH WITH 25,000 TO 50,000 SOULS: a further 5.6 per cent of all the people live in these 213 cities, the total population of which is 7,400,000. So 40.1 per cent—over two-fifths—of all Americans live in 412 cities each with more than 25,000 people.

   THE EAST has 75 of these 213 cities.

   THE MIDWEST, however, has 71 of them. The Midwest almost equals the East in the number of cities each with 25,000 to 50,000 persons; and, more important, the 71 in the Midwest have a total population slightly greater than the 75 in the East. In other words, the average size of these cities is larger in the Midwest.

6. AMERICA HAS 665 CITIES EACH WITH 10,000 TO 25,000 SOULS: A further 7.6 per cent of all the people live in these 665 cities, the total population of which is 10,000,000. So 47.6 per cent of all Americans—nearly one-half—live in 1,077 cities each with more than 10,000 people.

THE EAST has 246 of these 665 cities.

THE MIDWEST has only 166 of them. So it is not nearly so "small town" in this group of cities as many people think.

7. AMERICA HAS 965 TOWNS OR CITIES EACH WITH 5,000 TO 10,000 SOULS: a further 5.1 per cent of all the people live in these 965 cities, and 52.7 per cent of all Americans—the majority—therefore live in 2,042 towns or cities, each with more than 5,000 people.

THE EAST has 279 of these 965 towns or cities.

THE MIDWEST, however, has 286 of them.

8. AMERICA HAS 1,422 TOWNS EACH WITH 2,500 TO 5,000 SOULS: a further 3.8 per cent of all the people live in these 1,422 towns, and 56.5 per cent of all Americans therefore live in 3,464 urban places each with more than 2,500 people.

Of these 1,422 towns each with 2,500 to 5,000 souls, the Midwest again has more than the East; but for the first time, in any of the foregoing groups of towns and cities, the rest of the country has slightly more than the East and Midwest combined.

It is true, therefore, to say that the Midwest is more of a "small-town region" than the East, if you confine "small town" to urban places with less than 10,000 people. But, surprisingly enough, the Midwest outranks the East in the number of cities each with more than 250,000 people; and the East heavily outranks the Midwest in the number of cities each with 10,000–250,000 people. In the group of cities which you could still legitimately call "small town"—that is, each with 10,000–50,000 people—the East outranks the Midwest in the ratio of 321 to 237. That is a surprisingly heavy predominance for the East.

There is at least one catch in all this. In the large group of cities each with 10,000–100,000 souls, the East has a greater number because the eastern cities have many more suburban communities which, under local government provisions in the East, have split off from the parent-stem and become incorporated as separate cities. They are listed as separate cities, but they adjoin, and their life is still that of, Boston, New York City, Philadelphia, Jersey City, and so on. In the Midwest, on the other hand, except for the very few suburban communities of Detroit and Chicago and the separation of Kansas City, Kansas, from Kansas City, Missouri, there is nothing like the same extent of what you can call the "self-seeding" of cities. Consequently, the figures given above underestimate the number of Midwest cities each with 10,000–100,000 people and overestimate the number of those in the East. Even with that correction, however, it remains true that the East has an

103

overwhelming predominance in the group of cities each with 10,000–100,000 people.

Another interesting feature is that the predominance of the Midwest over the East in the really small towns only begins clearly to emerge when you get to towns with about 6,000 people and less. It is not apparent in towns each with 6,000–10,000 people. It becomes increasingly apparent, and eventually heavily predominant, as you go below the figure of 5,000 for a town; then below 4,000; and so on, down to 2,500. In other words, the Midwest is only peculiarly "small town" in nature when you get down to the very small towns; and, of course, the overwhelming bulk of these in the Midwest are rural towns serving the farms and farmers.

Anyone looking at the map of the country will be struck by two further points. First, the older East, with its eleven states and the national capital, is a region of a few straggling big states, with huge industrial and financial resources, and a great proportion—more than half—of small, mainly rural states with a very big city or two in them. Its internal differences are enormous: compare Maine, Vermont, and New Hampshire with New York, New Jersey, or Pennsylvania; compare Rhode Island and Delaware with Massachusetts. The eight Midwest states, on the other hand, being flatter and bigger and owing their existence to an over-all federal plan of settlement and land survey, have more social, agricultural, and industrial uniformity as states. Each of them is more like the others than any eastern state is like the other eastern states.

This is even true despite the great cleavage in the Midwest between town and country, between industry and farming. The industry or farming of any Midwest state is in fundamentals more like that of another Midwest state than is the industry or farming of one eastern state like that of the others. The East includes the farming and fishing of upper New England; the international finance and commerce of New York, Boston, and Philadelphia; and the domestic industries of the region from Massachusetts and Rhode Island down to Wilmington and Baltimore and back through the mountains to Pittsburgh or Buffalo. The farmers of Maryland, Pennsylvania, upper New York State, and upper New England are vastly different people engaged in very different farming with very different methods. Many of them are subsistence farmers or serve only the nearest individual city of the East. They are not big, cash-crop farmers, working for export as well as for home market. You do not find that degree of internal difference and contrast in the eight Midwest states. Life follows a much more uniform pattern, whether in cities, in towns, or on farms—whatever be the industry or the farming.

The second point bears on politics and sectional jealousies. The eight Midwest states, as we saw in the foregoing statistics, are remarkably near equality in their population to the eleven eastern states *plus* the national capital. But they only get sixteen members in the more powerful United States Senate, in contrast to the twenty-two senators from the East. (As the citizens of the national capital are disfranchised, we can for this political purpose deduct them from the East, in which case the two regions become much more nearly equal in population.) True, this contrast between eastern and midwestern representation in the Senate pales into insignificance when we remember that, combined, the nineteen states of both the East and the Midwest contain 56 per cent of America's population but get less than 40 per cent representation in the Senate. Their recompense, if it be one, is their overwhelmingly proportionate predominance in the House. Nevertheless, this does not prevent the regular recurrence of political tensions between Midwest and East which are directly bound up with their respective sizes and populations.

The most astonishing of all astonishing events in the building of America has been the swift making of the Midwest and its equally swift change-over from an agricultural community of settlers to a region nearly identical in size, numbers, and industrialization with the older East. Between 1840 and 1890 that change was practically accomplished. Since 1890 the Midwest has been steadily more industrialized and its people have more and more become city or town dwellers. Therewith, a great change has come over their way of life. Inevitably they have become more like easterners; for cities are cities everywhere; and everywhere their social and municipal problems are largely the same. Modern industry, too, has methods and problems which vary very little, in essentials, from one region, or even one country, to another. New communications and their increasing speed have more and more closely dovetailed the industrial, urban Midwest and East; and in nothing is this more obvious than in the way of life of city dwellers and their problems.

Since we are still talking of comparisons, let us carry the story of population to its logical conclusion and see how "civilized" and "urban" (if not urbane) the Midwest has become in so short a time.

Still taking the eleven states and the national capital as the East, and only the eight states as the Midwest, look at the comparisons in Table 2. Again, if you subtract the Ozarks from Missouri and the national capital from the East and, more legitimately, if you add the "marginal belt" in Kansas, Nebraska, and the Dakotas to the Midwest, the comparisons become even more striking. The approach to equality is closer.

As far as the big difference in the last entry goes, we should do well to remember that many federal income-tax returns filed in New York City and Washington, D.C., are not really those of easterners at all but of Americans from all other parts of the country who have retired there or gone there to settle. But, by the same token, it does show that "the money is in the East," as many midwesterners still say. They forget that, in the country as a whole, nearly three-quarters of "the money" is in the East *and* the Midwest!

TABLE 2

The East and Midwest Compared: Material Standards

	Per Cent of All in U.S. in 1940	
Item and Standard of Comparison	Midwest (8 States)	East (11 States plus D.C.)
Occupied dwellings............................	28.0	29.2
Residence telephones...........................	34.3	33.2
Homes wired to electricity......................	30.7	36.4
Passenger automobile registrations................	31.0	27.9
Family ownership of radios (est.).................	29.3	31.8
Total of federal income-tax returns of individuals *...	28.0*	42.8*

* For 1938.

One other set of figures, and we can push statistics out of sight. This happens to be a very important set, however, and if you can bear it in mind as you read farther, so much the better. In 1939, the last year of so-called peace, the eight Midwest states and their western "marginal belt" accounted for 31 per cent of the retail trade (in dollars) of the nation, while the eleven eastern states *plus* Washington, D.C., accounted for 35 per cent. Again, that is pretty close; but, more important, it means that these two chief American regions *together* account for two-thirds of the retail trade in the whole country. And that, too, reflects a growing similarity between the ways of life of the easterners and midwesterners who live in towns and cities.

"A BUSINESS PEOPLE"

There is much of chance and accident in the spread of modern industry, much of human calculation and foresight. In the 1830's the bankers

106

of Shawneetown in Illinois, on the Ohio River, were asked for a loan to help develop a little village of cabins in the swamps beside Lake Michigan. They sent directors and others on a visit of inspection. Their decision was that none but fools would locate a human settlement there, so they would not lend any money. But the "fools" built there; the cabins in the swamp became Chicago, a city of 100,000 souls within less than twenty-five years; and Shawneetown lapsed into obscurity.

Beau Brummel in Regency England set the fashion in beaver hats. Under the French, the trading-post of St. Louis had become a great fur-trading center; and in time it became the second largest fur-trading center in the world. So it took to making beaver hats and, thereafter, almost any kind of hat. It drew thousands of people to it, many from Germany, and became a great city. Beau Brummel therefore deserves to have a statue erected in St. Louis more than does John Jacob Astor, who went out of the fur trade before the beaver hat! Henry Ford, tinkering with gas pipes and an engine in a shed at Detroit, realized an idea and made it work. He founded the automotive industry of Detroit, Dearborn, Pontiac, Flint, Toledo, and other cities in Michigan and near-by Ohio. He made cities, and his industry made the society of those cities.

The Pittsburgh steel industry began before there were railroads; and even today it is poorly served by rail—its most severe bottleneck—owing to the mountainous country and approaches. The industry spread over to Ohio and northern West Virginia. But all its ore has to come across the Great Lakes from Minnesota and North Michigan and be transshipped on to the rail; its coal comes up from the South by rail; and its products go out in all directions, but only by severely limited canal or railroad connections. As America developed and the center of population moved westward, steel men looked for a new western manufacturing center from which distribution would be easier. They found it among the sand dunes at the foot of Lake Michigan, south of Chicago, in both Illinois and Indiana. The ore ships had a much shorter distance to come, and they did not need to transship to the rail. They could unload alongside. Thus sprang up Gary, East Chicago, Indiana Harbor, Hammond, and the South Chicago steel works. They now cover many square miles of flat land with innumerable rail connections for distribution to any part of the country from this greatest railway hub of the world. The workers were there, available beforehand, for only management and foremen are technical and really skilled in steelmaking.

Now Texas wants its own steel industry; but has Texas the steel-using

107

industries to act as market? Not yet, say the Texans, but give us the steelworks and they will bring the market. That is not how industry spread through the Midwest. The market was there first. The immigrants had arrived, and were still arriving, in droves. The towns were growing by an unparalleled process of new babies *plus* brand-new adults simultaneously. The consumers of manufactured goods outpaced suppliers almost every year. The Midwest farmers, having broken the prairie, changed from pioneer subsistence farming to commercial farming, raising and selling, and even exporting, virtually all their produce for cash; and cash meant more consumers' demand.

In this way the Midwest, unlike the East of yesterday and the Far West of today, became a vast converter of farm products and maker of farm implements; then a vast network of communications, north-south and east-west, in the new interior of America—a vast conveyer belt between consumers and producers; and, finally, a vast internal market, made up both of farmers and of urban workers. Though the farmers fell behind as a percentage of this market after about 1890, when America's internal frontier of "free land" disappeared, the industrial process was not halted. Iron and steel, metal works, railroad equipment and maintenance, automobiles, auto accessories, domestic laborsaving machinery and devices, machine tools, instruments, farm implements, chemicals, patent foods, canning, oil and oil-refining, printing, wearing apparel and clothing trades—the making of machines for capital equipment vied with manufacture for the needs of consumers on farms or in the bulging cities. One egged on the other.

Between 1840 and 1890, in the railroad age, there came an unparalleled era of chance, opportunity, accident, haphazardness, gambling, speculation, and good solid construction in the Midwest. Rural agricultural towns declined in numbers and size, and manufacturing or distributing towns and cities grew phenomenally. The steamboats, the river trade, and the cities of the Mississippi depended on a line from north to south. They therefore tried to stop development of the country along the east-west line and to prevent the consequent predominance of newer cities—Chicago, Detroit, Cleveland, Des Moines, Indianapolis, Kansas City, Omaha—based on railroad connections. One of Abraham Lincoln's last law cases, before he was elected President in 1860, took place in Chicago when leading citizens of St. Louis subscribed an enormous sum to make the Rock Island Railroad and its subsidiary, the Rock Island Bridge Company, liable for interference with north-south traffic on the Mississippi. A St. Louis river steamer had smashed against the piles of the bridge across that river near Rock Island, the stoves had been overset, and the steamer had burned. The Chicago jury was "hung"; the case was therefore never decided; so the east-west railroads went on building bridges over north-south rivers; the nation "went West"; and the burghers of St. Louis, Cincinnati, Memphis, Cairo, Louisville, and many another river city were mortified and resentful.

Gambling and risk-taking, vision and accident, thrift and speculation, "lobbying" and "rigging" of state legislatures or Congress or municipal corporations on a truly cosmic scale, bribery and graft of gigantic proportions, the organization of city and state political "machines" recruited from poor and ignorant alien immigrants, personal and bipartisan "deals," ruthless commercial and interurban cutthroat competition, even gerrymandering of state constitutions or electoral districts or "apportionment"—all these were the commonly accepted methods by which the Midwest and its "internal improvements" were developed between 1840 and 1890. The wonder is, not that many of these characteristics continue in the cities and towns of the region, but that they are not stronger and more apparent. For it is all so recent, and the typical midwesterner does not think of that. He is not interested in the past, not even in his own. So he does not see what that past still does in the present—and must, inevitably to some extent, still do. The social pattern into which he was born was laid down beforehand. This rough-and-tumble process of building and making an industrial nation affected the whole of American life, its city life in particular. But nowhere was the process rougher and cruder than in the far more rapid making and building of the Midwest.

Nowhere was it as quick or as new, to begin with. The East had something to build cities on. The Midwest built them from scratch, thrust them up the rivers, scattered them along the railroads, dumped them in the prairie or the forest, and then blew them up, like balloons, with immigrants. Young men who came as settlers to build their own cabins among earlier cabins, and bought little lots on which to build them, found themselves rich men, running big industrial cities before they were seventy, living from the colossal rents of their little original lots—now huge office buildings in the heart of the commercial section of a brand-new city—and forming a social élite of wealthy persons who could buy privileges. Such a new élite never emerged in the East because settlement and civic development had gone on for centuries there, and the élite was already old. The Midwest minority of civic arbiters by 1890 faced thousands or hundreds of thousands of poor immigrant factory workers, speaking alien tongues, confined to the oldest or worst or cheapest housing areas. Of strange habits and customs, the bulk of them were utterly foreign to notions of personal freedom or self-government or, indeed, to any notions of government whatever.

National, state, and city political "machines" were well known and well established by 1860; but the development of American cities after that year most powerfully clamped the "machine" upon the country. Nowhere can that process, either, be more clearly observed than in the Midwest. Lincoln Steffens, son of a well-to-do pioneer family in California, one of the most cultivated and "educated" Americans of his day, first opened the floodgates of "muckraking" (as it was called by those responsible for the "muck") in his articles and book, *The Shame of the Cities*; and his studies of eastern and midwestern cities in the 1890's came as a shock to the whole of America—and the world.[2] But what he described in such circumstantial detail was not new. It had "just growed" like that; and it had "growed" most quickly in the cities of the brand-new, lusty, tough Midwest.

Midwest industry and business began by being strictly localized. Railroads were few and far between until after 1850. It was an early era of many small, independently owned factories, employing few men. Two words passed into the American commercial vocabulary during this period: "distribution" and "merchandising." Both of them arose from the great difficulties, and distances, of travel from the centers of production. As recently as 1890 there were at least sixty separate areas of trading or distribution in the Midwest. By 1930 this had been reduced to about twenty, mainly by the advent of the truck and good highways. In 1945 it was estimated that it could be further reduced, in peacetime, to five! Consolidation and concentration of industry grew up with the region. Production of any given item tended to concentrate in fewer places, and these places were chosen far more deliberately by reference to the areas of distribution—the markets. Therewith, big cities grew bigger; so did the medium-sized cities serving wide areas. The small rural cities and towns lost population or "stayed put" at the best. But therewith, also, between 1890 and 1930, many industries in the Midwest tended more and more to be run by "big business." The "little fellows," the small and independent manufacturers, began to feel a draft which, after 1930, became a hurricane.

Because of the rapidity of America's industrial and urban transforma-

[2] Lincoln Steffens' *Autobiography* is one of the great books, anyway; but the sections on the American cities are, to my mind, the best, most informative, and most exciting. Steffens was a king of journalists in his prime. He did not then know what his political views would be a generation later; but those views do not invalidate his earlier journalism.

tion, the businessman of the city or town became the most effective type or symbol of "the American way." Gone was the gentleman-planter of the South. He vanished after 1865, except as a myth revered in the South. Gone was the rich southern and New England landowner-lawyer as a type of American leader: Washington, Jefferson, Calhoun, Clay, Webster, Adams. Gone were the settlers and Midwest lawyers: Lincoln and Douglas. Gone, within thirty years, were the Union generals and officers in politics.

Industry and the city brought forward the businessman, the railroad magnate, the big manufacturer, and he rapidly becomes the real hero, the folk type of the American leader: Rockefeller, Vanderbilt, Carnegie, Pullman, Hill, Gould, Ogden, Morgan—the list comes down to our own day with living and almost venerated figures, Henry Ford and Henry Kaiser. There could only be one Washington or Lincoln; but, as industry never dies, so the businessman never dies. *Le roi est mort; vive le roi!* Each new American generation of businessmen, like Tibetan priests, went out to find a new incarnation of the industrial Dalai Lama. And there, sure enough, he always was, which was both a comfort and a justification for it all. The heroes of business are living, abiding heroes. Like old soldiers, they never die; so they do not need to be relegated to history—which is only studied in America while you are at school. Each new big businessman gets part of the sanctity of earlier big businessmen grafted on to him. He cannot help it. He grows, and is made to seem, like them; just as early Christian saints had the best qualities of the older pagan heroes grafted on to them by popular acclaim. The demand arose that presidents and governments and Congress should be more business-like, should have more of business and businessmen in them.

This rise of business and businessmen to a position of the highest eminence was naturally both a cause and a result of the overwhelming importance of cities, town life, trade, manufacturing, utilities, and communications. The East and South, with their older and more established pattern of society, held out against it—and still do in Boston, Manhattan, Philadelphia, the national capital, and the South; but even there it is a hopeless, if gallant, rear-guard action. American society is the most fluid in the world. The younger generation of the eastern élite marries into Hollywood or Chicago or Omaha or Detroit; it even does it two or three times running; and the bounds of eastern society are already blurred. In the Midwest there was no such eastern society or élite to begin with. Thomas Wolfe, if he had been a midwesterner, could not have written about his gracious old relatives as he did. There were no First Families of Virginia in the Midwest; no Bostonian or

111

Manhattan Dutch gentry. There were descendants of them, but in the rough equality of the new Midwest they had to "go midwestern" to survive.

Industry and cities and big business burst upon a Midwest society of small-town grocers, hardware merchants, meat-packers, real estate lawyers, shippers, and storekeepers. Porkopolis could be the name of many a Midwest city, even now; and "pork-barrel" politics became natural in the region. The businessmen seized their opportunity. Easterners and eastern capital joined with them to develop the Midwest; and, presto, the cult of the businessman completely routed and ousted that of the farmer and even of the necessary professional men, the doctor and lawyer, in the great heart of America. The businesssmen, becoming rich, became richer yet, acquiring real estate and railroads and utilities and political power and so on. They were both Midwest society and its gods, at one and the same time and in one and the same lifetime. They became heroes of a new mythology while they were yet living. Midwest business and businessmen made the region more typically American in this respect than any other region—for business was all the Midwest had with which to impress or express itself. And it did it nobly.

The leading Midwest businessmen after 1850—the makers of industry and railroads and cities and machines (both mechanical and political)—became a model, an ideal, for smaller traders and businessmen. It was perfectly natural. The "giants in the land" had made the region. The highest levels of urban society and material well-being were achieved by these giants within their own lifetime. The region had been transformed by business and businessmen. The Midwest cities and towns were their children. Businessmen had made it a region of miracles, America's fairyland, what the Rhine and Rhineland are to the Nibelungenlieder and to Germany. The age of pioneers, of gun and ax and rail-splitters, vanished into songs and storybooks. It "went West!"

The second and third generations of Midwest businessmen, big and little—the third is with us today—grew up in this creed. They were suckled in it. Its ritual, slogans, catchwords, and vocabulary of advertising surrounded them from their salad days. "Don't knock; boost!" became the slogan of every Midwest businessman, city, town, and tradesman. Midwest society was always and in every way growing bigger and better. Slumps were due to easterners or Wall Street or foreigners or money-changers. There was nothing wrong with the Midwest itself. The Midwest businessman's attitude today therefore pervades Midwest towns and cities. His attitude to contemporary big businessmen of

America, in and of whatever region they may be, is what that of some citizen of an ancient Greek city-state would have been if Jason or Ulysses or Hercules had suddenly come walking down Main Street.

But a change has come. It came between the third and fourth generations of Midwest businessmen; between those who are now over sixty and those now under forty; it came in the critical years of our century and reached its climax after 1929. Today the myth of the big Midwest businessman is under a cloud. The high priests, over sixty, still beat the drums and blow the conch horns and call on the faithful to bow down and worship that competition, laissez faire, individual enterprise, and risk-taking which made the Midwest. But, as in some other religions, the high priests are not today the most fervent believers. They are more than a little dubious. They are realists. They are honest with themselves. They know they cannot act and acquire and control and climb as the Goulds and Hills and Rockefellers and Ogdens and thousands of others did. There are limits today; and the big businessmen of the Midwest recognize limits, which their fathers or grandfathers never did. Of course, they do not admit this for the record, or in politics, or in their "lobbies" or public relations. But they sadly admit it in private, and they give to Mr. Sewell Avery the loud and well-earned applause which is always accorded to the Grand Old Man, the champion emeritus, of any time-honored game of skill or prowess as he stages a comeback.

Most of their sons, who are generally too old to have been caught up in war, do not altogether take part in this applause. They are too worried, too busy, too harassed by the extremely technical problems of modern industry. They are the younger owners and executives, now in their prime. They know that you cannot bull and lobby and thrust your way to riches and power through the maze of modern problems. These now arise from government, industrial technique, and labor— and not, as they arose fifty years ago, from finance, competitors, obstinate politicians, franchises, freight rates, or communications.

In the Midwest today it is the substantial army of "little business" and its businessmen, those employing up to a hundred or two hundred men, which bears in the van the banner of the crusade against cartels and trade-unions and for laissez faire and untrammeled competition. They chiefly believe that "there is always room at the top" and that all of them can be really big businessmen and run the Midwest on the lines of "the American system" of Henry Clay. The contemporary big businessmen in the Midwest rather pity them—again, privately; for the big businessmen know what it is, and what it takes, really to run big

113

business. They are under no delusions. It is the little businessmen who are under delusions. They are riding the waves of a wake. They are living in the time lag, way behind the big businessmen. That is why they do not like big business, though they admire big businessmen. They have suffered from big business, but they want to be big businessmen.

All this has had far more effect on the people of the big midwestern cities and larger towns than on those of the East. The big eastern cities have roots in history and in eastern society, in the old America. They have a greater social stability—though far less than that of cities in the Old World and though eastern city dwellers are still mobile, volatile, mercurial, and socially fluid, as are all Americans. But the big cities and larger towns of the Midwest are so new, have altered and grown so rapidly and so recently, that they and their people alike have never struck roots. As a matter of fact, those that did strike roots mainly withered! Here and there you find exceptions where easterners, southerners, or the older peoples of Europe first sent down roots: in St. Louis, Cincinnati, and some of the old French cities or towns of Wisconsin, for example. (And the typical Midwest city dweller thinks these cities rather "stuffy" in consequence!) The overwhelming majority of Midwest cities and large towns have been in a whirl since their first beginnings. They and their people had not really settled down when the acute social, political, and economic problems of our day broke over them, to find them largely unprepared. And, of course, to add to the confusion in the Midwest picture, while all this was disturbing the life of cities and towns and their people, the life of the farmer went on along quite different lines, toward quite different problems. This is yet another example of the cleavages and tensions, the extremes and paradoxes, the breakneck tempo and confused restlessness of the region as a whole.

The Midwest farmers and businessmen for three generations—between 1850 and 1929—were taught that in the sweat of their brows should they eat their bread. (There, again, was the Bible belt.) Everything else was largely parasitical. Of course, lawyers and doctors and ministers were necessary. But Wall Street, the federal government and its agencies, railroads, big utilities, trade-unions, and any public measures for social security—all these, to the Midwest farmer and manufacturer alike, were unwestern, dangerous, and parasitical, even if they held stock in some of them, and even if they had recourse to, and benefited from, all of them. So great was the Midwest feeling of "ourselves alone" that foreign trade was thought to be rather immoral; indeed, to a surprisingly large extent in the Midwest, it still is. Lending abroad, shipping across oceans unknown to the insulated interior of America, handling of midwestern products by seaboard Americans, debts and interest reminiscent only of eastern bankers and eastern "city slickers"—all these seemed, and still largely seem, un-American.

"The American way," Clay's phrase "*the* American system," meant developing the Midwest and exploiting its own resources first. It was not "America first"; it was "Midwest first." It meant tariffs which, however, *did* mean federal action. It also meant the free import of human beings; but not, of course, the free import of goods for them. Those goods should be made by the protected Midwest manufacturers who made and often controlled the new and growing cities, and who could thus exploit a growing market of consumers without any of the still-hated foreign competition, generally and still currently termed "sweated labor." On the other hand, the Midwest should sell and sell and sell, on equal terms with any other producer, American or foreign. Selling, salesmen, distribution, sales policy, "selling the idea," "sold on something"—all this was the hallmark of a region which produced big surpluses for sale; which could not feel dependent on anyone or anything but itself and its own resources. There should be no labor legislation or trade-unions to render rigid a Midwest manufacturer's costs. Contradictory and paradoxical, illogical and inconsistent, maybe; but that was the commercial mentality of the Midwest until within the last decade or two. And that, very largely if not overwhelmingly, it still is. Climates of opinion change slowly and very little within the space of one lifetime.

Even more paradoxical was the close link between Midwest trade and industry, on the one hand, and national, state, and municipal politics, on the other. Politicians and government might be thought by Midwest farmers and manufacturers to be largely parasites; but you could get only the laws you wanted if they were passed by politicians, and you could get only rail and public utility and other franchises from them. No wonder the politicians took a leaf out of the businessmen's books and "charged what the traffic would bear." From the very beginnings of the Midwest, the morality, ethics, practices, attitudes, and mentality of trade and of politics were like Tweedledum and Tweedledee—except that there was never a "monstrous crow" to scare them. The farmers were frozen completely out; hence their periodic fury. How could you develop a virgin territory as big as Western Europe in one lifetime, shove railroads and canals through it, settle its land, build roads, set up public utilities, build cities and service their people—unless the financiers, traders, manufacturers, and contractors were either in the closest relationship with the local authorities or else were those authorities? (Remember, the remote federal government could not, under the Constitution, do it directly.) The Midwest and its cities—apart only from the national domain—belonged to itself, to its own states, and they gave franchises and incorporated cities, which in turn had power to give valuable franchises and launch or facilitate great enterprises. Both "buying" of politicians and lobbying were inevitable.

It is because public opinion in the Midwest recognized this inevitability that so many midwesterners are worried about the relation of business to politics today and in the future. What on earth is the use of blaming politicians or constitutions or mayors or parties or city fathers or what-not, when right from the very outset, from their birth in the Midwest, trade and commerce and manufacture and communications and public services—nay, the entire economic development of the region—were due to a close relationship between business and political life? Remember, again, what we saw earlier; by the 1840's the farmers were out of the state legislatures; professional men were in; and when industry and cities were growing up together, nothing was more natural or more inevitable than that business should control politics. After all, who and what made the cities that brought the population, that had the votes, that put the city fathers and politicians into power—and that could put them out, too, if they did not do what was required of them?

The businessmen kept their part of the bargain. They paid the taxes (and more besides) to politicians. They certainly did what the consumers required of them. They made and delivered the goods—goods of high quality and very soon so cheap that most of them did not need the protection of tariffs. The businessmen of the new Midwest cities and towns were in the main thrifty. They were not generally ostentatious in their wealth. They plowed back a big proportion of their huge and ever increasing profits. Capital accumulated until the Midwest today does not even need eastern capital. (Then the dislike of dependence on Wall Street changed to the dislike of Wall Street as a competitor!) Laborsaving machines and methods were the shapes that this capital took; and new industries sprang up to make the machines. The output per man in the leading Midwest industries, with their new methods of mass production, rose to more than double what it was, or is, anywhere else in the world. But the specter of unemployment rose, too. The great populations of manufacturing cities and towns began to show their brand of restlessness. They felt jealous. Extremes of welfare and ill-fare emerged only in the cities. The saga of heroes in business,

116

still adored by most Americans, began to sound a little off-tone and off-beat to the industrial workers. True, they got the consumers' goods all right, but the conditions in which they consumed them formed too striking a contrast to those in which the businessmen enjoyed theirs.

It happened in the 1880's, again in the 1890's, and again very badly indeed in 1907. Then it seemed to become endemic—except for a mad heyday, altogether exceptional, between 1922 and 1929. The industrial Midwest was no longer insulated. The industrial East and Midwest had become like Siamese twins. Worse, industrial America had somehow become entangled with the economic influences and economic tides of the world. That was a revolting and revolutionary thought to the typical Midwest businessman and especially to the manufacturer, distributor, and trader. It meant that the insulated prosperity of the region, based on its resources, economic development, and population by immigrants, had passed. As if to make the shock worse in the 1880's and 1890's, trade-unions began to form in the Midwest; and they began overwhelmingly, like a kind of nemesis to the manufacturers, among the poorer European immigrants who settled directly in Midwest cities. The bombs of the "anarchists" in Chicago in the 1880's and the great teamsters' strike a little later took place simultaneously with the Grangism and Populism of the prairie and Great Plains farmers. It was the writing on the wall for Midwest businessmen. It was the "revolt of the masses" who had not risen in the social or economic scale.

The big businessmen did not give in. They fought back with every weapon in an extensive armory: state governors, state politics, city police, privately hired vigilantes, lobbies, newspapers, representatives, and senators. Violence occurred on both sides to a degree seldom reached in civil contentions in any other country of the Western world. That, too, was natural; for freedom in business and freedom of opportunity had become articles of religion. So what elsewhere might seem an economic or political clash of interests became in the Midwest a "holy war" on the businessmen's part and a rebellion for independence on the part of the city workers. What Lincoln warned against, the "mobocracy of the artisans," what Jefferson before him had feared and striven to prevent by opening up the Midwest, seemed now to be breaking out in Midwest—and other—cities which neither Jefferson nor Lincoln could possibly have imagined. But the Midwest was more violent, quarrelsome, litigious, individualistic, property-minded, and extremist than any other region of the country, in 1840 as in 1890— more so than the Old South had ever been on any subject, except slavery.

What had happened in the meantime was that businessmen and men of property in their own lifetime had become a privileged and powerful social layer. They had risen by taking every opportunity, by thrift, and by very hard work. They had climbed above city populations which had been brought in by millions from abroad and had been taught that America was the land of equal opportunity. It was no longer the Old Midwest. The businessmen themselves had been the greatest and most successful revolutionaries. The boyhood friends of Lincoln and the first settlers on the land, dying in the 1880's and 1890's, could not recognize the cities or their people. They died bewildered and rather pathetic figures.

One must not underestimate the importance of the time lag in our own day from this recent era. One must not underestimate the role of the Midwest businessman, either for what he does or for what he is as a symbol. His views must be understood. Many American liberals seem to a foreign observer both unscientific and wrong when they merely criticize or attack the attitudes of Midwest businessmen (who form the backbone of the National Association of Manufacturers), or poke fun at them, or think them benighted. (You don't get far in life or war or politics—which are all a struggle—unless you try to understand your opponent.) It is not these men alone who made, or make, the problems of the Midwest—or, for that matter, of cities all over the world. The Midwest of today, its very towns and cities, were made by the revolution, and revolutionaries, of trade and industry and business. The people wanted it that way: that was the demand which business supplied. True, New Englanders and English capitalists helped—for a handsome profit. But it was the Midwest's own great resources which were being developed. They were there, in the Midwest, and belonged to it. Out of swamp and prairie and forest came vast cities and factories and the bulk of forty million souls, all achieved by trade and industry and communications within one lifetime.

The older settlers and their sons saw it happening and gave honor where honor was due; for they could remember log camps and cabins without windows and leaf-stuffed mattresses. But the immigrants who came to the Midwest towns and cities, whether from Europe or from the older American cities of the East, had not passed through the pioneering or settling stage. They were the first in the cities to explode into political and industrial action. It was a shock to the Midwest businessman, as indeed it also was to his colleague in New York, Philadelphia, or Baltimore. It was much the same shock which the good southern planter experienced when a slave ran away, or a bunch of

118

slaves rebelled. Were not slaves better off than they had been in Africa? Were not the workers of Midwest cities better off than if they had stayed in Europe? The answer was "Yes" to both questions.

By 1900 the cities and larger towns of the Midwest were filled with overwhelming majorities without a drop of old American blood in their veins; who were ill assorted to live cheek by jowl with each other; who had failed for centuries to do so in Europe; who, in the main, stuck together in great blocks in cities or social groups in towns; and who were treated more handsomely than any working people in the world at that time. They got American citizenship and the vote very easily. They were a great reservoir of raw material for lobbies or political machines. The political system and its politicians soon taught them their power. They were far better fed and clothed, and their children better educated, than they would have been if they had not come to the Midwest, or than any other city workers were at comparable levels of skill anywhere in the world. Housing, admittedly, was bad. It never kept pace with population. But it was slowly improving. Social reforms and social action were being slowly pushed forward by farsighted businessmen—often against the opposition of politicians. But the average "old American" employer, businessman, or professional man in Cleveland, Cincinnati, Chicago, St. Louis, and hundreds of smaller but rapidly growing towns heard the first mutterings of the revolt of the masses in the 1880's and 1890's with amazement—amazement at what seemed to him black ingratitude. Thus rapidly did the conservative and radical elements develop, also within one lifetime, in the region. Some of those businessmen or their sons are alive today, running Midwest business. And immigrants or their sons are running the trade-unions.

Another point must be remembered. The businessmen who made the Midwest had to work in with politics and politicians, as we saw. They had no alternative. Midwest society and politics gave them none. But they really disliked having to do it. They disliked it much more after 1900, when the "new masses" became so important to both political parties and to all city machines. It is from 1900 onward that the trend of the cities' workers toward the Democrat party is clearly seen; and from the same critical date can be traced the hardening of tempers, the emergence of class conflict and tugs-of-war in the cities. The businessmen never really dominated politics and politicians after 1900; at least, not as continuously and as reliably as they did between 1850 and 1900. Consequently, today, if a Midwest businessman's son at the age of eighteen said that he thought of going into politics as a career, the businessman would ask him "not to tell Mom"; he would almost as lief set him up running a disorderly house. The Midwest businessman knows modern politics and politicians perhaps better than most other American businessmen. He has had to grow up with them, because politics in the Midwest city or town or state was from the outset closer to the roots—such as those roots were—of the new Midwest society. When Midwest businessmen saw their own employees beginning to turn votes away from the Republican party, the party of "the American system," born in the Midwest, as they began to do after 1890, it meant far more of a shock and a challenge to them than it did in, let us say, Democrat Boston and New York or Republican Philadelphia. City machines were old in the East. They were new and still being built or altered in the cities of the Midwest.

Politics to the Midwest businessman meant paying politicians either to get something for his business or to leave that business, and its employees, alone. The thought that politics, especially national politics from the East by federal action, might condition or affect Midwest business was heresy. Anyone, midwesterner or not, who harbored that thought was a traitor to the Midwest and to the spirit and principles that made it. Hence the anathemas hurled by Midwest businessmen against Bryan and the La Follettes, or against trade-unionists and Teddy Roosevelt and trust-busters, with equal zeal and impartiality. They were, said businessmen and many city dwellers, monkeying with the buzz saw. They might lose their fingers. That didn't matter. But suppose they jammed the saw. Where would the Midwest get another as good?

Great as were the achievements of the traders and industrialists of the Midwest for the consumers after 1860, they could have been even greater—at a cost. Few Americans, either in the Midwest or outside it, seem to realize that the breakneck making of the Midwest was partly because of bad social and economic conditions—and not the reverse—just as the Russians lived very badly for nearly two decades after 1919 while they were forcing capital, the "forced savings" of doing without things, from the mass of their people to build railroads and factories and make modern Russia. Part of the capital which was constantly plowed back into the industrialization of the Midwest could have been spent on improving social conditions and standards of health and living in these centers. But then the process would have been slower. There would have been less room for immigrants. America's advance would have been more gradual. That economic advance was as natural—humanly natural—as it was unplanned.

It might have been more humane if it had been slower and more planned—or, shall we say, more "deliberate," if you do not like the word "planned." But as it was, it was haphazard, violent, vigorous, amazingly effective, and dizzily swift. And that has left its mark in many ways on the region and its people. Swiftness, newness, recentness, cheap temporization, provisional solutions, shoddy extemporizing, making do, "getting by," slums, wood-frame firetraps in all its cities, uneven street-paving, waste, extremes—all these were inevitable if the Midwest, and its politics and government and cities, were to be made at such a rate. They are visible to a smaller extent or less striking degree throughout industrial Europe's cities, where the process was slower. The standards of the mass of the people in Midwest cities were uneven. They had so much of most kinds of food, right from the outset, that until the second World War they wasted lots of it, as the Argentines, Australians, and New Zealanders wasted meat. It was their social life, the life and institutions and equipment of their cities and towns, their life in the factory, which had to lag until very recently. And in some things in Midwest cities and towns that lag—the price of the town and its size today and the speed at which it grew—is still clearly visible.

On the other hand, look round the industrial and commercial sections of the city or town. Compare what is now there with what was there fifty years ago, and you see where the capital and the foregone consumption have been put. Then, indeed, you marvel. What would the life of the Midwest, of America, have been if they had consumed more as they went along? It might have been better. But it might have been far worse—far more of an orgy. It was the businessman who stopped a greater and worse orgy. (Yes, I know; he was living better than most; but he was working harder, too.) I repeat, he was the real revolutionary of the Midwest. He made the region what it is today. He made its cities, their masses of people, their problems. He did all this because he was more successful, more energetic, a faster worker than any businessmen have ever been anywhere, and because he took bigger opportunities in a bigger way. His sons and grandsons may not realize all this today because they face his legacy and many do not recognize it as his—or theirs! Their problem, the problem of all America, is to keep it all going. That is what worries them.

What the closing of the frontier of "free land" was to the farming population of America after 1890, the war of 1914–18 and the immigration acts of 1917 to 1929 were to the cities. There was a lag of a generation between the filling of the agricultural cup and the filling of the industrial cup. Farmers organize more slowly than the workers

121

of the cities. After 1929 the two problems of America's future—on the farms and in the towns and cities—simultaneously merged into one problem, dominating the social, intellectual, and political life of the whole country, cutting across the lines of city and county, class and party. Again, in no other region of America today can you see this process and its implications more clearly than in the Midwest. It is only natural that most Midwest businessmen and men of property should continue, uncritically, to believe in an article of faith which produced such works all over their towns and cities and landscape. It is equally natural that, in the age of self-examination and of the swiftest spread of ideas, a minority of Midwest businessmen and men of property (especially those in big business) should, like their fellows elsewhere in America and abroad, anxiously scan political and economic horizons. Thus here, too, divisions, tensions, and extremes have arisen among businessmen themselves, and between different generations of businessmen. Add these to the divisions, tensions, and extremes produced, on their side, by a still disunited American labor movement, and you get plenty of elements of new restlessness to add to the traditional and original restlessness of midwesterners.

A word is due on trade-unions. The Midwest is peculiarly affected by American labor movements. It is a coal-mining region, so it partakes of Mr. John L. Lewis' United Mine Workers and of other coal-miners' unions, which are at odds among themselves while they are all at odds with the other American labor organizations. Being the railroad hub of the nation, the Midwest has the strongest regional stake in the independent railroad brotherhoods, which have not joined with the Congress of Industrial Organizations or its great rival, the American Federation of Labor. The Midwest cities and towns, especially the medium-sized ones with their manifold industries, trades, and processes, provide a big proportion of the A.F. of L. Unions' membership. And, finally, the big Midwest cities and their industries—those of southern Michigan, Ohio, northern Indiana, northern Illinois, and southern Wisconsin —are the national stronghold of the new C.I.O. You could not, if you tried, make a bigger or better boiling-pot of labor movements and labor opinion out of any other region of the country. The labor mixture seethes and bubbles in almost every Midwest town or city—and sometimes out in the countryside, too. This, also, does not make for unity, uniformity, and a calm, dispassionate atmosphere.

This region, which offered the biggest material opportunities in the world for the space of a lifetime, became responsible in the second World War for forty per cent of America's output of war material and food. It was arsenal, mine, refinery, granary, dairy, butcher's shop, and distributor combined. It built submarines and corvettes on Lake Michigan and tank landing ships on inland rivers, and sent them by water round Chicago and down the Illinois and Mississippi to the Gulf—the way of the Indians and first white men who explored the region. At Seneca, Illinois, in what was a cornfield, the Chicago Bridge and Iron Company built 157 "landing ships, tanks" on a $200,000,000 contract and employed nearly 11,000 workers from all over America, within the space of three years. Down the Illinois and the Mississippi and out to Europe and the far Pacific went those ships. Electronic devices, tanks, ordnance, ammunition, and ships were made in factories which had made toys, cars, railroad equipment, radios, washing-machines, and refrigerators. Meat, eggs, cheese, milk, soybeans, corn, wheat, sugar, fruit—all these and more flowed out of the region to meet national and international needs. Its railroads and waterways worked overtime. Old cars were rushed back into service. The biggest network of transport in the world bore unimaginable strains and stresses, and did it with little apparent fuss and little real inconvenience to the people of the region.

It seems only right and fitting to mention this now because, as I write, survivors of the Civil War are leading a Memorial Day parade in Chicago and in other Midwest cities. How could such things be imagined by them when they were young men of eighteen or twenty? They went to that war from an overwhelmingly rural, agricultural, and Anglo-Saxon Midwest. In their old age they live in an overwhelmingly industrial region, peopled by the children of fifty nationalities, who live mainly in big cities and towns and work in factories, transport, trade, and city offices. Such a rapid change may not have affected the little minority of survivors of the Grand Army of the Republic; but it has profoundly affected the majority whose memories cannot travel so far back. And yet how near it really is. The moral becomes tedious with repetition: how could such violent, unbridled growth and transformation take place without convulsions and growing pains? How could there fail to be divisions, diversity, and differences and the tensions and extremes which accompany them? The real cause for wonder is the degree of unity and uniformity in the life of the Midwest.

THE CITIES AND THEIR PROBLEMS

The pioneers and settlers easily ran their primitive social life. They were scattered, and the few hamlets were far between. Even in the 1840's it took almost a week to get from Ohio into Illinois, or from Michigan down to the Ohio River. In the Great West of America, law, government, and the social institutions with which the citizens of every Western country are unquestionably familiar today sprang from the grass roots, from below, from among rough-and-ready equals. But the real social problems, the cleavages, tensions, conflicts of interest and strains and stresses imposed on government and law, came with the towns and cities of the Midwest and with the American migrants or foreign immigrants who flocked to make them. These places offered the greatest material opportunities in the world to any resourceful or hardworking man at that time, and limitations, social questions, restrictions, or conventions did not fence him in.

The frontier society of the pioneers and first settlers had been rough but moral; crude but fervently religious; individualistic but imbued with a deep sense of liberty and equality and fraternity; solitary but uniform and tempered by dependence on neighbors and the little, almost nonexistent community. The swiftness of the growth of towns and cities from 1850 to 1900, their newness, bigness, obvious extremes and differences of people, and jostling mixture of races and nationalities and characteristics, changed all that. As soon as there were great economic opportunities in urban communities, and ease of travel and speed of communications, the new city dwellers did not feel so strongly about equality, community, fraternity. They did not even feel so deeply about morality, religion, and scruples. How could they? Man's own wits and strength and not Nature were producing consumable goods. They were the first midwesterners to be packed together with strangers, compelled to "root or die" in city surroundings, forced to look after themselves, by themselves, or go to the wall.

The life of the average citizen in these new towns was strange, chaotic, fluid, highly mobile, intensely individualistic and competitive, immoderate, intemperate, and, above all, materialistic. If it had not been so materialistic, the towns and houses and railroads and factories would not have been created with such furious zeal. The waves of people did not wash into these towns and cities because of some deep inner spiritual compulsion or some feeling for liberty and equality and fraternity. A very few did. Most did not. They were far more practical and realistic. They came to get away from something materially worse to something materially better. They were material-minded. The majority of the workers were not interested very much in forms of government. They merely asked that it should leave them alone so that they could get as much material welfare as quickly as possible. Never having had much, if any, material welfare, they ranked that, quite naturally, first. Of course, after a time, some social-minded citizens would pay

124

for churches and go to them once a week; and (after a long time) for schools and send their children to them; and (after a longer time) for some rudimentary public services and use them. But they were not out for a quiet, steady, sober, and settled life. In fact, few of them seem to have thought very much of their own lives entire, their "long home," and the "whole duty of man." Of all men in the world at any time, the makers of the new Midwest towns and cities seem to have been the most temporal and materialistic, and so were the workers who labored for them.

We use the word "materialistic" as if we were ashamed of it today, so let me explain what I mean. These men were young, vigorous, and filled with visions of what they could make of any town or city or business in their own lifetime. No one had had such an opportunity in modern history—to build a city from the wilderness and die, rich, in it. They did not, except spiritually, look beyond their lifetime; and as we with our hindsight see and marvel at what they accomplished, we ought to understand why they did not. They were so busy. They were, I think, busier, more hectically and frenziedly busy and hardworking, than any men have been anywhere: hewing, hacking, building, struggling, organizing, traveling, competing, convincing, arguing, persuading, lobbying, directing, and transforming. Preoccupied with natural resources, money, materials, machinery, and men, these businessmen were shouldering enormous risks. They had seen the region in the raw; seen it yield to human effort and enterprise; and seen in one, two, three, four, and even five decades the wilderness, prairie, and log cabins give way to railroads, wood-frame and brick towns and cities, and completely settled farm lands.

Many who had lived in cabins hewn from the trees of the great forest lived to see the electric trolley cars, the "elevated" in strange new cities, and the first automobiles. How could these builders of cities made with their own hands also dream and plan for the lives of their children and grandchildren, for the arts or graces of life, for the highest principles and practices of individual conduct and government? A surprisingly large minority of Midwest businessmen did bring colleges and institutions of learning, grace and arts and sciences, to their cities. The majority did not. How could they, looking back on their own lives, believe that any human life would be so settled that you could plan for your grandchildren's city or for a center of art and beauty? They saw the crudest in men, and the crudest of men, around them every day. They had to handle men from fifty nations of whose languages, morality, religions, and customs they knew nothing, and cared little if at all. They were

125

making more than a town, a city, a business, or an industry. They were making a nation and passing it on to their children, and to the even vaster numbers of foreigners' children, to safeguard, administer, and run.

The future, in which they could not share, was not their problem. The present was. It was enough in all conscience. Omelettes do not get made so quickly and on such a scale without breaking eggs, wasting some, and making a bit of a mess on the floor. The point is: everyone knew it was an omelette. Everyone wanted omelettes—and quickly. Everyone wanted a share. Everyone got it. It was all as simple, and as materialistic, as that.

But it was all as different from the old frontier Midwest as chalk from cheese. Only a few of the pioneer characteristics passed into the life of the new towns and cities: constructiveness, resourcefulness, individualism, toughness, an immoderate love of liquor, display of self or of one's prowess, familiarity and informality, boasting and tall tales. The energy and zeal which showed itself so strikingly in the making of the towns was only partly "frontier" in origin. It certainly came into the towns with the most energetic, restless, and frustrated of the settlers or their sons. But it also came in large measure from the New England Yankee or from the eastern cities and from some of the immigrants— the Scotch, the northern Germans, even the English, and (if they stuck to one business or vocation) the Irish, especially the northern Irish and the Scotch-Irish.

The old pioneer sense of community and mutual aid did not emerge in the new towns until after more than a generation had passed. It came when the social problems of the towns shook the citizens' consciences, and when the community sense had begun to grow again, as it first did among the pioneers, in rather sad and lonely communities: the groups of non-English-speaking immigrants who stuck together in urban localities for their mutual comfort and support. Churches came into the towns in much the same way, by groups of each cult or sect as they could afford it; and they became as numerous and bewildering as were the different social groups or immigrants who wanted them. The uniformity of pioneer and farm life gave way in the growing towns to an intensely concentrated diversity of peoples, tongues, customs, habits, religions, sects, and moralities.

The farmers hated it all. They still do. It is surprising, and yet not so surprising when you stop to think of all this, how the farmers of the Midwest hated and still hate Chicago and St. Louis and one or two other big cities of the region.

126

Liberty and equality and fraternity became split up and diversified in the new cities; for running such growing cities could not be a uniform business. It was, and still is, a terrible problem—greater than that of running any non-American city. The Midwest has no uniform pattern. It was born and grew without any foundation in uniformity. Liberty was greater for some than for others. It came to mean not liberty to do anything you liked but liberty from purely *governmental* interference with your life. The businessman, the local political boss, even the police might interfere with your liberty in these towns. They might control or wreck your life. But the state and the federal governments would not and could not.

So with equality: the old uniform equality of the settlers stopped at the towns. Levels and gradations of society formed in them, as they have done throughout history. But in the new towns of the Midwest there were Negroes, many different nationalities, and a rapidly growing group of leading citizens from the old Anglo-Saxon families who owned much real estate and belonged to the old-time religion or the original Methodism or Presbyterianism. A right side and a wrong side to the new railroad tracks developed.

But equality also got split up. It changed to mean equality of opportunity. "Anyone" could go and start meat-packing or railroad construction or a steelworks or a newspaper. To many an immigrant it became the equality which Bernard Shaw epitomized when he said, "The law is free and open to all, like the Ritz Hotel."

As for fraternity: a midwesterner, born in the 1840's, might just be fraternal with a Yankee; but it was hard to be fraternal with the Negro and the strange new Slavs and Italians and many others who were flocking into the cities as they grew. You could know almost everyone worth knowing in Chicago, Springfield, and Illinois in 1840; but in 1890 it was a physical impossibility. The people were so different one from another. They were like the grasses, flowers, and plants of their prairie: bewildering in their diversity, energy, and vigor. As they learned English in the schools, the words "law," "liberty," "equality," "opportunity," "freedom," "community," "union," and "morality" did not mean what they meant to an old Anglo-Saxon or Pennsylvania Dutch American in the Midwest. (Make the experiment of translating those words into Italian, German, Polish, or Russian, and you will sense the difference even today.) Worse, as the cities grew, the children of the "foreign groups," as they were called, had to grow up in areas of one and the same nationality where the speech, customs, culture, and morality of the "old country" prevailed with disconcerting obstinacy. So even

127

the second generation born of immigrant parents grew up with accents, spoke the old tongue at home, stuck together, and pulled (or were pulled) together in trade-unions or in municipal, state, and national politics.

All this took place between 1870 and 1914. But these influences, modified and weakened, are still felt today. It would be a miracle if they were not. The makers of Midwest cities could build and people a whole urban civilization in a wilderness; but it has proved mighty hard for their sons and grandsons to alter, transform, and reform those cities and their people, once they were there. Cities and towns acquire a life and an obstinate momentum of their own.

It still seems strange to the casual visitor that, in this young, new, and intensely democratic interior of America, its cities so quickly reproduced the evils of European cities which are centuries older. The obvious answer is that the *industrial* cities of Europe are scarcely, in fact, any older than those of America; that industrialism and "metropolitanism" are of about the same age all over the world. What the big cities of the Midwest showed most quickly, because they were so new and grew so swiftly, were far greater differences among citizens and far greater extremes of welfare and ill-fare than in other American cities or in most of those in Europe. For this there were many reasons. Government and politics, state or municipal, did not interfere with business. That was part of the bargain, as it was also part of the Midwest's faith. The full and uncushioned impact of the new industrialism thus struck Midwest cities while they were still in the process of being built and peopled from all over Europe and America. Much of the building was therefore haphazard, provisional, and unplanned; and as new waves of immigrants or (after 1865 and 1916 and 1941) of Negroes hit these cities, sections of the older housing areas became overcrowded or dilapidated. The better-off moved to the newer homes and suburbs as fast as they were put up and as fast as the rapid transit lines were extended.

Secondly, the grouping of many immigrants and the Negroes into urban localities formed a new problem. It meant the segregation of groups of citizens who were engaged in well-defined jobs—the rougher work in factories, construction, utilities, public services, and so on. Though London, Paris, Berlin, Vienna, Budapest, and many other big European cities contained areas in which performers of the rougher jobs were compactly settled and localized—for instance, London's East End, the Paris *banlieu*, or Berlin's Neukoelln—these workers were all

128

of uniform English, French, or German nationality, language, customs, or morality and with fewer religious differences.

In Chicago, St. Louis, Milwaukee, Detroit, or Cleveland, on the other hand, really big sections of the city by 1900 became almost solidly settled by groups of Irish, Germans, Italians, Poles, Bohemians, Hungarians, Lithuanians, Greeks, and many others; and, of course, there were compact Negro districts everywhere, even in towns with as few as a thousand inhabitants. This resulted in an involuntary and non-deliberate "grading" of Midwest city life, not by deprivation of any constitutional liberties or civic rights, but by the social attitudes of one group to another. There was no ill-will about its origin, though its almost inevitable development caused, and still causes, much ill-will, resentment, tension, and division. Just as the mulatto or octaroon in the days of slavery looked down on the pure-blooded Negro socially, so the poorer white immigrants in Midwest cities looked down on the Negro (and felt better about their own lot). And above that "level" one group felt itself better than another. It also resulted in a kind of economic grading, which in turn aggravated social feelings; for one nationality or race was deemed to be more skilled at this, less apt for that. The Negro could be employed for this but not that; and so with Lithuanians and Greeks and Italians, up through various Slavs to Germans and Scandinavians and Anglo-Saxons. Accents played a large part in all this, leading to much heartache on the part of immigrant parents as they grew older and found their children becoming strange and "American."

Thus in the cities of a region which had been hewn from the forest and prairie by men of a rough-and-ready equality came a fair equality of political or individual rights but great inequalities of economic or social status and, once again, all within one lifetime. The life of Midwest cities did not, could not, and has not yet become that of a uniform society, despite the brilliant achievements of American standardization in education, in the press, and in all the material things of life. Here is the effect of another time lag, which only a historical sense can explain and enable one to understand. But it is also one of the Midwest's greatest extremes and paradoxes. This democratic standardization in so many things on the surface goes parallel with bewildering diversity and with abysses formed by economic and social distinctions and extremes.

Many Midwest city dwellers think the English are the biggest snobs in the world, have the greatest extremes of welfare and ill-fare, and live under a benighted system of castes and social classes, from any of which it is impossible to move into any other. But the Englishman living in a

Midwest city becomes as bewildered as the midwesterner who, on living in an English manufacturing city, discovers that the local lord is an automobile manufacturer who began as a bicycle renter, the local Member of Parliament is a trade-unionist boiler-maker, and the local society is made up of factory managers, lawyers, doctors, the bank manager, and brewers. The Englishman living in the Midwest finds that he is cordially and emphatically treated as an equal by the electrician, plumber, milkman, waiter, train conductor, and the boy at the gas station but that he does not meet these people at the home of plant managers, newspaper editors, and so on. If he wants to meet a Negro, he has to go to the Negro's home or choose a restaurant carefully. He will even have to be careful where he is going to live, and about whom he asks to meet whom; for he cannot, as in England, ask any Jewish friend to meet anyone or everyone.

Well, says the midwesterner, why shouldn't people live in separate groups as long as they are, in fact, equal? You can't meet up with the whole city. Anyone can be anything, if he wants to, in the great Midwest. And the Englishman then wonders about the Poles of South Milwaukee, and the Greeks of Chicago's West Side, and the Sicilians of every Midwest city, and the Lithuanians, Hungarians, Serbs, and so on, to say nothing about the Negroes. These people, strangely enough, do not seem to mix socially in the Midwest cities, except if they are at the same economic level, or in the movies, at the game, in their taverns, or at work. Often they are not all mixed at their work, because they do better in teams or groups of roughly the same kind. They will meet in a real equality at service clubs and separate to a social inequality again. There is really a surprising amount of social gradation in all Midwest cities. It is correlated with income brackets, kinds of job, and groupings of national origin: Anglo-Saxons, Germans, Scandinavians, and Celts (but not the poorer Irish) at the top; then Bohemians and Poles; then the other Slavs and the Magyars; then Italians; then Greeks; and so on.

Negroes and Jews are two groups apart. The Negro is socially segregated by all whites except those who do the roughest work. The Jews get varying social treatment according to their economic, intellectual, or artistic status.

To the visitor it often seems that the result of the Civil War was not as happy for the Negroes who settled in, or came to, the North as the press and mythology of the North have made out. Society in the South of the United States was, and to a great extent still is, somewhat like a Bach fugue. It takes place within a universally accepted framework of harmony and counterpoint. It moves in an ordered pattern, conventionally and traditionally, easily and logically, toward an inevitable conclusion which is always in the same key as its beginning. The Negro can be on the land or in the city. His position has to be respected, provided he respects the position of the white. There is a rough but practical harmony of duties and obligations. All know the rules to be observed. All, white and Negro, know the penalties. In that southern life, the Negro had, and still has, a humble yet difficult part in the score—just as the coachmen and gardeners of some German margrave in the eighteenth century, fetched in to perform for their master, had to play short but very difficult passages in Bach's *concerti*. All mankind, rich and poor, are happier in a stable and ordered society which performs like a good orchestra. All the players get a measure of happiness out of their little or big contributions to the great harmony of the whole. If you doubt that, pause and think of our society in the leading nations of the world today and try to answer the greatest riddle of all: are we happier for owning more?

But the society of the new Midwest was unordered, unstable, hard, and confused. That of the growing Midwest cities, especially after 1860, was more like a scratch orchestra of gifted amateurs trying to play for the first time a composition by Stravinsky or Shostakovich; but the Negroes, sharing in much of the delight at this new and bewildering composition, were restricted to very few instruments. They did not know how to handle the more complicated and interesting ones, anyway; and they never got a chance. They were given important but limited parts: servants of the public, laborers, and menials of the cities. They could not go on the land. They were and still are largely bewildered by this city life, to such a narrow sector of which they are restricted. And they are equally restricted in the small towns.

The magnitude of the problem as it arose, and the seriousness with which it is now being tackled in almost every Midwest city and town, must not be underestimated. In Chicago alone it is estimated that there were about 360,000 Negroes in 1945, densely settled in a very few localities. They poured into the new midwestern towns and cities after 1865, then as the cities grew, then in 1917 to 1929, and then again after 1940. The movement is still, on balance, from South to North because there is more money to be earned in good times in the northern cities and towns. But it has magnified the social problems of these cities; and, though the Negroes find more money, more possessions, more variety, and more diversions, they do not, it seems, find more happiness. Why should they be any different in that respect from their white fellow-citizens who have had much the same experience, coming from the farms to the towns or "from quiet homes and small beginnings"? One big difference remains: the white is not "restricted"; the Negro is. His children are born into a fixed status and have to stay in it. Thereby comes yet another form of social tension in the cities.

The case of the Jew was different. Many cultivated Jews and large numbers of eastern and southern European Jews who were less cultivated flocked to the new Midwest. To be "restricted" was not strange to the mass of them. But, unlike the Negro, they were white, they were traders, and they or their children could enter virtually every profession or business. It is very hard for the visitor to find out the cause of the widespread anti-Semitism and social discrimination against Jews in Midwest towns and cities. The feeling seems more vigorous than in the cities of any European country except Germany or Hungary. It is a peculiar kind of anti-Semitism. Individual Jews are well liked. They are and have been outstanding in business, the professions, academic life, and in the making of the Midwest. The most successful of them have been great collectors, donors of art collections and museums, large subscribers to that charity which for so long took the place of social security in Midwest city life, and endowers of schools and colleges and institutions of learning. But the Gentile midwesterner did not, and often does not, like the "lesser breed" of Jews in the towns and cities (Jews do not settle on the land). He calls them by opprobrious names. If it be because they seemed thrusting, blatant, vulgar, and ostentatious—well, so was most midwestern city and town life in its beginnings, and so were most of the Gentiles in it.

The small minority of Jews and Gentiles "at the top" in Midwest cities seem now to understand, respect, and get on well with each other. But below this thin upper stratum, Gentiles still dislike Jews more than the midwesterners of German origin dislike the Greeks, or the Greeks the Italians, and so on. Perhaps it was part of the waves of intolerance, of "anti"-ism, which billowed through America last century and spent themselves in this. It is, of course, quite illogical, because vast numbers of authentic, though unorthodox, Jews transliterated their names into good American, while older and prouder Jewish families preserved honored names but therefore remain unmistakably Jewish. Again, a Bloom or a Blum was recognized as Jewish; but a Virag (Hungarian for "bloom") was not; and so with millions of Magyarized, Russified, Rumanized, Italianate, and Greek names of Jews. The apartment houses, residential districts, clubs, hotels, and vacation resorts which were "restricted" to Gentiles got more Jewish blood in them than they fondly imagined; but they kept the bulk of the more obviously Jewish, among them many citizens which any country would be proud to own, out of social intercourse with Gentiles. The Jews responded to this kind of challenge by erecting their own clubs, apartments, and so on; and they had the funds. So the gulf was made and perpetuated. Happily it is slowly being bridged, but from the top down, not from the bottom up.

There is an exception to this social gradation. It works only in favor of the Midwest citizen of any grouping below those of Anglo-Saxon, German, Celtic, or Scandinavian origin (except the Negro) who has made a success of life, in trade, finance, industry, arts and letters, academic life, or anything famous or well publicized. It is significant that he does not need to have made merely a *material* success; though that, of course, helps. If he has made that success, he has proved the point of equality of opportunity, the career open to the talents; and for all practical purposes—though not by any means for *all* social purposes or occasions—he has "arrived." His wife and children can practically be viewed as Anglo-Saxon or German or Celtic or Scandinavian. For practically all purposes he and they can move socially among those favored nationalities that form the apex of the social pyramid in Midwest cities. But he must first make the success. He must be a "successful" man. He must be "up and coming," which phrase suggests social gradations, as well as ambition, energy, and ability.

This accent on success is, of course, part of the Midwest's commercial history which is still current. It reflects a real, popular, and general emphasis on material achievements. The successful man is accepted, whatever his national origin—unless he be a Negro or, to a less extent, an "obvious" Jew—because he has paid his dues to Midwest urban society. He has made his contribution to the development of the region. In nothing is this more striking, right from the outset, than in the real estate of the Midwest cities and towns. This feature deserves closer examination because it is so typical.

The speed with which towns and cities grew resulted in fantastic rises in the value of urban real estate. Farsighted men, or men who were lucky enough to buy and hold on to city lots in the early days, made such big fortunes that Henry George's *Progress and Poverty* and the single-tax movement were natural expressions of concern in America, and gambling in real estate became almost a national obsession until the 1920's. Many leading families in Midwest towns and cities today owe their wealth and social position quite as much to the rise in the real estate which their fathers or grandfathers acquired as to their businesses.

Families which were and still are the arbiters of elegance, "the glass of fashion and the mold of form," were made rich without needing to do much about it except hold on to pieces of land situated in or around growing cities. To this extent, too, Midwest city life runs true to European patterns. There are many such cases in the cities of Europe. Some aristocrats of land or commerce did well out of the cities. But in Europe the speculator in land, the real estate dealer, the *Bodenspekulant*, was socially frowned on; and, in any case, real estate values rose by comparison so slowly in Europe that, to reap the profit, you had to stay in the business, which made you a commercial fellow. In Midwest cities the real estate dealer was, and still is, a kind of civic patriot, boosting and maintaining the values of local property. He and his chief clients are responsible for the "restricted" areas and for keeping them "restricted." He, also, now scans the future with anxiety.

There were more Victorian "Forsytes" in the Midwest than ever flourished in England, and they made bigger fortunes. More important, the phenomenal rise in real estate values inevitably became linked with municipal politics from the very outset; for here was an apparently unlimited source of public revenue from which to pay for the services demanded by the citizens. The "frontier" characteristics of bragging and boosting were brought in to help; and, as they do to this day, every little town or big city began to beat the drum and print the Chamber of Commerce pamphlets which proclaimed it the best or biggest or most rapidly growing community in the region—all for the ears of intending manufacturers, distributors, transport firms, parents, and institutions who "looked to the future." Big deals were made between cities, railroads, and state politicians to insure and secure bigger and better rises in real estate values, to the profit of all concerned. The quicker business and population came to the towns and cities, the quicker real estate values rose, the better were the city treasurers and the assessors pleased, and the happier were those who got a share of the estate. "Bragging saves advertising." When you hear a citizen of a Midwest city or town bragging of his home town today, he is unconsciously passing on part of a mythology which, like most mythologies, is founded on hard fact. The only difference is that this particular Midwest mythology of real estate "paid off" handsomely to all concerned while it lasted.

It did not last, mainly because of the stopping of immigration, the filling-up of the American cup, and the coming of rapid transit and the automobile. As the Midwest cities and towns expanded, dormitory suburbs and satellite communities grew up with a life of their own,

134

peopled by "commuters" who were better-off and by automobile owners who drove to work. This was an enormously important development, the effects of which are still being felt. It created terrible problems for the cities—slums, poor and declining central residential areas, the exodus of the well-to-do, a constant fall in taxable property within city limits, and, finally, the exodus of the factories themselves—which are among the most acute problems facing the Midwest cities today, and still unsolved. It meant that Midwest cities from 1900 onward were increasingly left with a proletariat of Negroes and lower-paid white workers, all concentrated in the inner bounds of the cities. Inevitably they became a species of Roman plebeians for whose votes politicians and parties contended—the vision of Jefferson and Lincoln again!

The city fathers could tax only commerce, industry, utilities, the professions, the very rich few who still could afford to keep a town residence, and the commercial centers of their cities. The masses of poorer residents were not very taxable, and, if they were taxed too heavily indirectly, they would make a political change. The city dared not drive taxes too high for fear that the businesses might quit their city and go to a more favorable and better publicized competitor. The problem was, and still is, to find new sources of public revenue to meet the growing demands on city treasuries. The railroads and trolley cars began it: almost all of them run by commercial undertakings which, for a time, paid handsomely. Then came the automobile and the bus, and they greatly increased the building of sprawling suburbs and the drift of the people toward them. And, finally, the new big factories sprang up outside the cities, and the older factories in the center were abandoned. The firms moved outside and utilized the truck and trailer. And when this process was fully developed, the suburban railroads and trolley cars began to run into financial difficulties, together with the city treasuries. Only then did citizens begin to talk of public transport and public undertakings.

The suburbanites had newer homes, air and space and light, community houses, and lower taxes. The Midwest city was healthy and sound on the outside and for some way in; but something went rotten at the core. And the strange thing is that this pattern has been followed, in varying degrees, in virtually every Midwest city and town, down to towns with as few as 25,000 inhabitants today. All are arranged in roughly concentric circles, broadly conforming to the historical growth of the community and to the levels of the citizens' economic or social status. The better-to-do "lie a little farther off." The less well-to-do and the Negroes are very near the tracks. There is nothing strange in

135

finding that pattern in any European town or city. But it is surprising, to the European, to find it so faithfully reproduced, within a lifetime, in the Midwest. It may account for the widespread resentment among Midwest businessmen at what seems to them an invasion of the Midwest by "European" social and political problems.

Today as you walk through the centers of many midwestern cities, you may be surprised at the number of vacant lots turned into parking spaces, or the number of grand old homes going sadly derelict in poor surroundings, or the number of buildings condemned as "tax delinquents." You will notice that in winter no one clears the snow and ice from the adjoining sidewalk. In summer no one sows grass seed along the little border of earth. And in all seasons paper, orts, and shards lie around. These are the no-man's-land of the cities. They are a pathetic reminder of the transfiguration which these young, sprawling cities of the Midwest have undergone in so short a time. So are the slums, the older "white" districts which have had to be invaded by the growing number of Negroes, the rows of little wood-frame houses badly needing repair, the localities where fires or epidemics strike most heavily, where overcrowding began and still grows, where a baby can be severely mauled by rats while its mother's back is turned.

It is easy to talk of rehousing and slum clearance; but the makers of state constitutions in the Midwest, distrusting public officials and even their own descendants, generally wrote valuation laws into the constitutions. You can get the right of "eminent domain" to clear slums by passing a new state law. But where do you get the cash? Changing a state constitution now, in order to change the tax laws, to establish new systems of valuation or to raise revenue, is about as quick and easy as poling a flatboat up the Mississippi. Thus, the very success of the real estate boom in the Midwest cities, during their growth, made real estate the main source of taxes; the cities and states grew and raised assessments; a flight to the suburbs took place; the automobile worked against the cities which manufactured and sold it; slums developed at the center; and real estate in the cities had to take the rap. Again, this was a kind of nemesis after a short, a very short, time lag.

Here, too, emerged another big problem of the Midwest—a problem both political and economic. The growth of the cities brought great wealth and revenue to the states, but it put a constant strain on state politics because the population, the voters, became more and more concentrated in the big cities or industrial areas. State constitutions provided for regular reapportionment of electoral districts to meet this change: for example, every ten years. But in reapportionment rural, small-town, and less populated areas were bound to lose representation in state legislatures, and their representatives often held up the re-apportionment. Very few politicians rush to commit political suicide, anywhere, even for the public weal. So the thickly populated and growing metropolitan areas in each state have always tended to be underrepresented, and the rural or declining urban areas to be over-represented. Thus, when the big-city areas demanded reapportionment or new state laws to solve their problems, the representatives of the rural and less populous areas enjoyed strong bargaining power. They would give a bit on this, if the cities' "machine-made" representatives would also give a bit on that. Party politics did not generally decide this issue. It was not a party question. It was, like so many in the Midwest, a question of the city and its machine against the farmer, the countryside, or the small town; of local interest against local interest. In the political dickering, chaffering, and lobbying little could be done quickly. There were long delays while the problems grew. They were greatly aggravated by the usual and traditional American provision that puts state capitals and legislatures in small cities or towns.

Of the eight Midwest states, only Indiana and Iowa have their capitals and legislatures in the state metropolis; St. Paul, the capital of Minnesota, lies alongside its bigger offspring, Minneapolis. So the metropolis, the dense areas of industry and other big cities in most Midwest states were generally in a tug-of-war either with, or in, the state capital and legislature; which means that they were tugging against the rest of the state. As state legislatures and constitutions had great powers which they could exert over the big cities, while the contrary was not true, the citizens of the Midwest during their short history of hectic growth were generally more interested in these local divisions and tugs-of-war than in matters of greater American or world-wide moment outside the Midwest. Naturally they were. It lay closer to their homes and their everyday lives. And these home-town or home-state problems are as acute today as ever they were. It is as well to bear this in mind, for, though struggle and competition and contrariness were features of Midwest society from the outset, the local struggles seemed more vital and more absorbing, and in many cases still do.

THE FACE OF THE CITIES

The cities and towns of the Midwest are different from those of the East, South, and Far West, but it is hard to say exactly why. In appearance they are like most of America's new industrial cities and towns. They always have good and big hotels, for midwesterners are always

137

traveling in the region, and the smaller towns are as important, in their sum, as the big cities. The salesmen and businessmen demand comfort, and it is supplied; and good hotels mean satisfied clients and visitors. There are fine new skyscrapers and apartment blocks. There are older declining or slum areas. There are good, solid bourgeois and often splendid stores, and at night almost every store or cafe on the streets is ablaze with neon signs. The store fronts are always being changed and modernized, while the façade and upper stories of most buildings remain as they were, like a woman who has put on smart shoes and a new dress but wears an old hat and has forgotten to attend to her face. The wrought-iron fire escapes cling to the fronts, sides, and backs of buildings like prairie vines. The old trolley cars rattle and clang along the middle of the chief thoroughfares, except in St. Louis and a few other cities, where new sound-deadening wheels have been fitted; but the cars and lines remain. In this respect the smaller cities and towns have been luckier; they were never big enough to have trolley cars, and now they can go straight to busses and private automobiles without tying up capital and disrupting the life and traffic of the streets.

The railroad casts perhaps more of its spell over Midwest towns and cities than over those elsewhere, as you might expect; and it also casts prodigious quantities of soft-coal dust, smoke, and grime over them. Locomotive bells, grade crossings, and noises of shunting are never very far from the center of town—least of all in Chicago—and in smaller towns "the depot" is still a focus of business and social life, the contact with a pipe line to the world.

There is a definite if undefinable flavor to a Midwest city or town. While the cities may all look alike, it is the people who make the life and atmosphere of them; and the people are different. You sense this different atmosphere as you step down from the train on arrival. You hear louder voices and greater noise of crowds. To begin with, there is far more equality, individualism, elbow-thrusting, casualness, square-shoulderedness, slap-happiness, self-assurance, and self-assertion on the part of the people you see in the depot or on the street. They are clearly less inhibited, and, as easterners say, they are also more unsophisticated. (So much the worse for sophistication!) There is more display of sentiment or emotion. There are more contrasts in the types of humanity: tall and short; very dark and very fair. Chic hats mingle with babushkas; bluejeans with English suitings. The waitress reminds you of a Slovakian peasant girl in Nitra, whence her parents probably came. Faces, and the deeper and more numerous lines in them, move more frequently. People seem more natural, but at the same time more rest-

less, hurried, eager, and often grim. That sounds contradictory or paradoxical. Well, that is exactly how the Midwest city and its people first
strike you. Both the cities and the people seem familiar yet strange,
American yet with a difference, natural yet restless, worldly wise yet
unsophisticated, matter-of-fact yet emotional, welcoming and helpful
and polite yet pushing to get somewhere ahead of you. As Muirhead
said half a century ago: "The atmosphere is thick with the emanations
of those who hurry to be rich."[3] Well, why not hurry?

Much of this sounds as if Midwest cities and larger towns were like
all big cities which are not capitals: Bordeaux, Liverpool, Barcelona. It
sounds as if they were what easterners call them: provincial. They are
not. They are too much in movement with other cities for that. Their
traffic in men and materials has been largely with other Midwest cities,
for the region is so vast. They are each like capitals of a big country
round them. Many of the biggest cities in the world are seaports or
near the sea: London, New York, Boston, Philadelphia, Hamburg,
Bremen, Tokyo, Singapore, Marseille, Liverpool, Manchester, New
Orleans, San Francisco, Antwerp, and a host of others. Such cities are
always influenced by trade and personal contacts with other countries
and their people. This is also true of virtually all the big cities in
America except those of the Midwest. The Midwest has only its own
inland seas and its great ocean of prairie, all linked by bonds of steel
rail and concrete highways. The Midwest big cities therefore live to a
very great extent with and among themselves. They trade with the
seaboard and other American cities or regions. But their first "port of
call" is another Midwest city. Even the locomotive engineer who starts
at Chicago drops off while he is still in the Midwest.

Chicago, Rock Island, Des Moines, Omaha; Chicago, St. Louis,
Kansas City; Chicago down to Cairo; Chicago, Milwaukee, St. Paul;
Chicago, Indianapolis, Cincinnati; Chicago, South Bend, Toledo, Cleveland—all these spokes radiating from the hub of the region and the
nation reach a rim which is still midwestern but a very long way from
the hub. The omnipresent trucks and trailers carry names of big
Midwest cities on them. Even the cities other than Chicago are set in
the middle of great agricultural areas and at big distances from the next
city.

The exceptions to all this are those many Midwest cities in the
"marginal belt"—for example, Cleveland, Akron, Youngstown, Canton,
Dayton, Columbus, Cincinnati, Evansville, St. Louis, Kansas City, Lincoln, Omaha, and Sioux Falls. About one-third of the people of the Mid-

[3] J. F. Muirhead, The Land of Contrasts (London and New York: John Lane,
1900), p. 199.

west, both urban and rural, live in that marginal area; and the majority of this one-third live in cities. In this belt the adjoining eastern, southern, or Great Plains regions exert an obvious influence, mixing another flavor and atmosphere with that of the Midwest, making more obvious the issue of the marriage between East and South in the region and the movement farther West.

Chicago is the metropolis of the West. To describe this great city, now the fourth largest in the world, defies one's powers. Abler pens than mine have done it, and yet Chicago changes so fast that their written descriptions are largely out of date or out of truth in a few years. Here is a city of nearly four million souls, with another two millions in satellite communities round it; composed of almost all Caucasian nationalities, Negroes, and Orientals; and dependent on agriculture, mining, oil, electricity, the seaborne traffic of the Great Lakes or the canals and rivers, and the most intricate texture of railroads and highways on earth.

The most impressive first sight of the New World is when you sail into New York harbor—if it is on a clear day. But the most impressive first sight of the Midwest is when you fly into Chicago at night from the East, descending over the blackness of the prairie to the great, ruddy blast furnaces and steel mills, catching the first winkings of the Lindbergh beacon from the Palmolive Building away on the starboard bow, and watching the brilliant rectangles formed by a thousand square miles of straight streets and buildings. Huge, sprawling city of swamp and prairie; one community of many communities, *communitas communitatum*; it is both a Pittsburgh and a Detroit; a financial and commercial center; a warehouse, department store, mail-order house, granary, slaughter-house, and inland seaport; a repository of great wealth and great poverty; a center of learning; metropolis of that million square miles which is the heart of America. It is something of a national metropolis, too, because of its position. It is the national headquarters of the medical, surgical, and hospital associations; of Rotary and other service clubs; of America's library associations; of the mail-order business; of the musical and juke-box industry, which plays so large a part in American life; of the *Encyclopaedia Britannica*; and of the cinematograph equipment trades. It is a part of all American life.

Driving into the city from the airport up Archer Avenue, you could be on the outskirts of Warsaw, Budapest, Prague, Bucharest, or almost any other big central or eastern European city except Berlin or Vienna, which have too many apartment blocks. And in a sense you are, for the names above the stores and on the windows of offices speak all European

140

tongues. Little clapboard houses with unfenced patches of garden remind you of a dozen European nations and their cities. Miles and miles of streets go by, with railyards and warehouses, corner stalls and markets, before you see the strange billowing vastness of the inland sea; the great cluster of skyscrapers and the biggest hotels in the world that sprout inside the central "Loop" of the elevated lines, like precocious overgrown plants in a wired-in forcing-bed; and perhaps the noblest front that any city in the world ever deliberately put on: Michigan Avenue.

This great and imposing front was once washed by the waves of Lake Michigan. Then the Illinois Central tracks came along it on piles and wooden bridges. Then the sandy foreshore was drained and reclaimed for the Columbian Exposition in 1892–93. The work was extended, and today Michigan Avenue is mainly built-up on the western side, facing east across the lake, and looking down on reclaimed and man-made Grant Park, the open-air theater, the Greek buildings of the Chicago Museum of Natural History (the old Field Museum), Soldier Field like a Byzantine hippodrome, the elegant Shedd Aquarium and Adler Planetarium, the richly endowed Art Institute, and the imaginative superhighway of the Outer Drive which takes traffic along the lake front from north to south, away from the Loop, for twenty miles. Driving along that highway by day or night and looking across to Michigan Avenue, the Loop behind it, and the big buildings of the Near North Side, you marvel at this noble city of the prairie on a sea-shore, where the first skyscraper was born.

Just parallel with the northern boundary of the Loop you cross the Chicago River by the bridge which President Franklin D. Roosevelt opened with his famous "quarantine the aggressors" speech in October of 1937. Just here is an example of Chicago's ingenuity, initiative, and enterprise. The sluggish Chicago River, on the swampy banks of which the first white fur-trader settled a hundred and fifty years ago and Fort Dearborn was put up, used to meander through sand bars and reeds into Lake Michigan. Chicago straightened it, put a lock and harbor at its new mouth, and now the river can either flow into the lake and so into the Atlantic by way of the St. Lawrence, or admit vessels and water from the Lakes, channel them round the Loop and down the canal to the Illinois River, and so to the Gulf by way of the Mississippi. One canal, a few locks, and Chicago became a two-way lake port.

Another side to the story is not so impressive. The cities downstream enjoy the trade and traffic, but they do not like the products of the city's effluents which wash downstream when the locks are opened and

141

the higher level of the lake water puts a "head" on the canal and the streams. This is the cause of a long and acrimonious dispute between Chicago, the adjoining states, the cities on the rivers, their various legislatures or authorities, and the national Congress and Supreme Court. All of these authorities are involved in Chicago's struggle for better sanitation and drinking water (it comes from the lake) and in her neighbors' struggles to avoid inheriting Chicago's dirt while Chicago gets clean.

The fourth city of the world, built by "fools" on piles in a marsh at the southern end of a lake, has other problems, too, which grew with its size, impressiveness, and beauty. Life in all American cities is more varied, mobile, and hectic than in any others in the world; but in none is it more so than in Chicago. Chicago has the best human virtues and the worst vices. It is therefore more truly human than any city, and it tells more about humanity. It tells it frankly, honestly, and openly. Nothing is hidden, nothing hush-hushed. The beauty of Michigan Avenue is offset within five or ten minutes' walk westward by the derelict buildings, dirty alleys, and run-down, overcrowded dwellings that any other city would hide or gloss over. Not so Chicago. Look on this picture and now on that, and see what was done and remains to be done. That seems to be the motto of Chicago. It has more extremes and variety than Istanbul, Singapore, or Shanghai, and ten or a hundred times their vigor. The vigor and vitality of the city amaze the visitor. Like an anthill, it is always moving, day and night. Other cities have their quiet times. Not so Chicago. To find a blasé Chicagoan would almost be a relief, so keen, so hungry and thirsty for new experiences, so curious, so divinely discontented and unsatisfied are Chicagoans of all income brackets and national origins. That is why Chicago holds the quintessence of the Midwest.

In Chicago all the extremes and extremisms of the region reach a grand climax. Within a minute or two's walk of the splendid stores and hotels and offices in the Loop you pass the flophouses of West Madison, Canal, and North Clark streets; the hiring offices for casual railroad laborers ("Good Eats Provided" painted white on the windows); the terrible slums and Negro district near the stockyards; the waste lands near the railyards; the hangouts of the bums and especially of the old, wrinkled, slow-moving, pathetic bums. I think "bums" and "bumming around" are still used more frequently in the Midwest than anywhere else because of the size of the region, the importance of its vast railroad network, the building of that network and its maintenance. It is natural, in the region of the greatest mobility in America, that the Germans' *bummeln* should have thus passed into the general slang.

On railroad maintenance, in thousands of factories, in the stockyards, and down south in the steel mills work the sons of fifty nations, all Americans, all midwesterners, all Chicagoans; and if white and colored, Sicilian and Greek, German and Pole occasionally clash, what of it? It is natural: the naturalness of so many different kinds of human nature. A little bloodletting is a small price to pay for such general tranquillity and order. The police are tolerant and extremely tactful, for they are mainly of Irish but also of German, Polish, Czech, and other national origins. Chicago is a League of Nations, a United Nations in itself. But it has been learning for seventy-five years how to live and let live, when to pay out the line and when to reel it in, when to give ground and when to hit hard. It requires a good deal of management and skill to give such a city order and regularity. As with so much in the Midwest, the wonder is that it has so much order, efficiency, and regularity. You cannot achieve that quickly without some show of toughness and force. You cannot let intolerance abolish order. And yet you must preserve liberty.

Who are the Chicagoans? More than New Yorkers, Jersey Citizens, Philadelphians, Pittsburghers, Clevelanders, Detroiters, St. Louisans, New Orleannais, or San Franciscans, they come from almost every race and people. There are Americans from all regions. Germans form solid districts all over, but chiefly in the north and northwest, like the working-class quarters of Hamburg. Poles with their pseudo-baroque Catholic churches with green cupolas make whole areas look like Cracow or Lodz. Czechs and Slovaks keep their homes and little gardens more neatly and reproduce Brünn or Pilsen, Brno or Plzen, in the Midwest. Lithuanians, Latvians, and Estonians have their homes out in the southwest, looking severe and North European in winter. There are Scandinavians of all kinds; Italians of all kinds, too, who keep their feast days and market days as if in the old country and live in solid blocks of the city; Greeks, Yugoslavs, and Syrians mainly on the West Side; Mexicans, Chinese, and Japanese, in their characteristic quarters; Hungarians down in the South and also on the North Side, mixed in with the Czechs and Germans and Yugoslavs, whom in Europe they dislike; British, Dutch, Belgians, Spaniards, Portuguese, Russians, Ukrainians, and Armenians; and, of course, the Negroes.

It was estimated in 1940 that two-fifths—nearly one-half—of adult Chicagoans did not generally speak English (or, as Illinois puts it, American) in their own homes. Nearly all of them can speak it and do, outside, or with their American children. But there are many Chicagoans over the age of fifty who cannot speak it at all; they live in one or other of these compact groupings and do not need to. No wonder there are so many confusing accents in Chicago. New Yorkers and other Americans can make fun at the Brooklyn or Italian accent because in New York these stand out, firm and clear. No one in Chicago makes fun of any particular accent, because there is no single Chicago accent as a standard from which to deviate; there are so many. Chicagoans of German, Italian, Polish, and Czech national origin of the first or second generation, with their children, accounted in 1940 for more than one-third of the people. The others of non-English-speaking origin and the Negroes brought that proportion to more than one-half; a clear majority. Here is a potent source of variety and difference as well as of vigor and restlessness. The same pattern can be traced, with less degree of clarity and intensity, in almost every Midwest city and large town.

Americans from outside the Midwest tend to think of Chicago as Sandburg's "hog-butcher to the world," as being composed of vast stockyards and slaughter houses ("everything used but the squeal"), surrounded by some fairly decent apartment blocks and some necessary hotels and offices in a downtown section called the Loop or the North Side, and peopled by a scared race who go to and from work under a periodic hail of gangsters' lead. Nothing could be more grotesquely inaccurate. The stockyards are vast, surprisingly trim and clean, and localized in a compact area away from the main thoroughfares and traffic (except, of course, the huge railyards which serve them). You can live in Chicago for years and not know that meat-packing goes on there.

Chicago is not the only American city with gangsters; but in Chicago "the Prince of Darkness is a gentleman." They, too, keep to their local haunts, taverns, and night spots. They have a rigid code. The penalty for failure to observe it is quicker and more severe than in normal, so-called "civil" society. The only Chicagoans who see a gangster or hear his shots are those who, out of an inverted sense of snobbery or curiosity, go to the gangsters' haunts to see them or, more rarely, happen to be about in the small hours when the code of gangland is enforced. Even then the gangsters take remarkable care not to shoot up the public. Everything is nicely and neatly arranged so that only the principals—gangsters and police—are directly affected. Crime, racketeering, robbery with violence, other forms of lawlessness—these are more in evidence, as in other big American cities; and on them we shall have more to say later. But the activities and deaths of gangsters are known to Chicagoans in the same way as they are known to all other Americans: namely, in the columns of the newspapers.

The visitor generally sees only the Loop, the Outer Drive, the Near North Side, the offices and hotels, and perhaps one or two institutions on the outskirts: factories, mail-order houses, universities, hospitals. He seldom sees the Chicagoans at home. Their homes are their pride, and rightly so. From over thirty miles north of the Loop to thirty miles west and southwest, or fifteen miles south, and from as near as only three miles, the commuters come into the Loop by steam and electric trains, trolley cars, busses and automobiles. They are very early risers. Chicago starts work at the same hour as New York, where time is an hour later, and often before it. All factories and most Loop offices are working by eight or eight-thirty. From six-thirty in the morning until eight-thirty the commuters go into town; and from four-thirty in the afternoon until six-thirty they go out again. They have little time for lunch; half an hour is quite common. They are a hardworking community.

Their homes are the places where they relax. The variety of suburbs is bewildering. In this respect Chicago is far less standardized than most other American cities. The styles of architecture, layout of the suburb, and density of population per acre vary from the spacious, quiet beauty of Glen Ellyn, Hinsdale, Winnetka, Riverside, Evanston, and Highland Park to the greater uniformity and compactness of Oak Park, Rogers Park, and the South Side, with its more frequent apartment blocks, and then to the still more densely settled communities nearer the Loop. No greater luxury, spaciousness, elegance, and beauty could be found than in the old homes and modern apartments of the wealthy on the near North Side—the "Gold Coast"—or the great homes and estates of Lake Forest, Wheaton, or Barrington. Farther out, too, beyond the thirty-mile limit, are the big estates, summer homes, "farms," or week-end cabins of many of the better-off Chicagoans. But the homes of the great majority of Chicagoans, of the German workers on the nearer Northwest Side and of those of all national origins in separate wood-frame or brick and clapboard houses or in brick, stone, and concrete apartment blocks, are homes indeed. For ten miles around, the terrible grime of the soft coal from the many railyards blackens the windows and the outside, and the drapes or curtains inside; but the interiors are generally kept clean, full of those intimate belongings and that informal atmosphere which make a place a home. Chicago is not mainly an apartment city, like most of New York; nor does it live and eat in public places. It is a city of separate homes to which the visitor or client is immediately made welcome. It is a city of home-proud, city-

145

proud citizens whose fathers and grandfathers came there to "make a home"—and made both a home and a city. And in that it is typically midwestern. It is the product of the South, New England, and central Europe. It is even more of a cosmopolitan city than New York.

This has one interesting by-product. Chicago has little of its own to offer the mere visitor or tourist. It is not a center of entertainment or diversion like New York or Los Angeles, or a national historical center like Boston or Philadelphia, or an old and quaint city of non-American origins like New Orleans or San Francisco. There are beautiful things to see in Chicago; but few tourists want to go to the remarkable Art Institute or the wonderful museums. Children and students flock to them. Few businessmen go, and the life of the Midwest is business. They want relaxation or "fun." The "fun" of the Rush Street or North Clark Street night spots and other such places, many run by questionable persons, is ordinary, vulgar, and raw. For those reasons, these places are well patronized—but not regularly by Chicagoans. The theaters are average; and despite or perhaps because of Mr. Sam Insull's colossal barn of an opera-house, with its indifferent acoustics, Chicago has no permanent opera and for an adequate performance has to depend on New York. The smaller and more congenial Orchestra Hall, hallowed with memories of Thomas and Stock, provides music and a home for a good symphony orchestra. The movie-houses are vast, numerous, comfortable, and always full—day and night. The big hotels put on the best "entertainment" in Chicago; but because there is so much to see and do on the street and because, as in the early days, taverns and night spots are extraordinarily numerous, the visitor for a few days and nights gets the impression that there is much liquor, "fun," relaxation, and diversion in Chicago and that Chicagoans are always indulging in them. Again that is grotesquely inaccurate.

Chicagoans will put themselves to no end of trouble and expense to take a visitor or client round the night spots, the floor shows, to the theater, or on a round of a few of the many taverns. But that is not how the Chicagoan lives when the visitor has departed. The Chicagoan is like the Parisian in this respect: a very devoted home-lover, judged by visitors who hardly ever see him at or inside his home. He is judged by what he provides for alien palates. For this, the Chicagoans are not responsible, though America may be. Much of the less attractive, noisy, blatant, neon-signed, liquor-smelling aspect of Chicago is there for the millions of visitors, businessmen, and passers-by who have to traverse this vast crossroads city between transcontinental or other trains. (The greatest railroad hub in the world still has no central terminal, no

146

through connection for passengers; you have to change stations, to the perpetual profit of the men who own taxis and hotels.) True, many of the 20 per cent of Chicagoans who live in mean streets and poor housing areas and work very hard at the rougher jobs regularly patronize the taverns; as the small minority of unimaginative and unwise business-men, condemned by their fellows as unreliable or unstable, regularly patronize the places on Rush Street and elsewhere. That is because both these groups lack imagination, have poorly stocked minds, and have not acquired, or been able to acquire, any other ideas of relaxation. That occurs with the same groups in every big city. Drowning one's sorrows, or giving them bromide, is not unique to Chicago; nor are the sorrows of humanity. But the vast majority of Chicagoans lead quiet, domestic lives in their own homes and with their neighbors, who are friends.

One feature in which Chicago is very like big British cities is in the size of its suburbs. That is scarcely surprising, since the city has grown by absorbing small outlying villages and converting them to suburbs. These are now the home of the middle class, the clerical workers and the professional men. Being the Midwest capital and metropolis, Chi-cago has a very big middle class—or perhaps, as "classes" are not sup-posed to exist in America, I had better say, as Americans do, "a great concentration in the middle income brackets." But these Chicago sub-urbs of the well-to-do and the "middle income brackets," unlike the suburbs of European cities, are very beautiful; they have also far more variety than those of British cities. They have more of a community sense and community life of their own, centered round their com-munity houses, libraries, forums, clubs, societies, or high schools. Places like Oak Park with 70,000 souls—"biggest village in the world"—Win-netka, Riverside, and Hinsdale set a high standard for suburban com-munity life, and though they are not satisfied, they have already out-distanced most suburbs in overcoming the problems of life in a big city. They have community sense and community achievement to their credit, where the suburbs of cities in the Old World have only apathy and bleak failure. Indeed, the suburbs of most of the big cities in the Midwest are way ahead of others, both in and out of America, in this respect; and that is scarcely surprising, because the sense of community is, and always was, so strong in this new region. But, in making these communities, the community sense has been taken away from the city's center. The problems of Chicago, as of the other big cities and towns in the Midwest and everywhere else, are left at or near the center: the "inner ring" of solid and densely settled residential areas where the

147

manual workers live; the areas of slums, dilapidation, or overcrowding; and these are linked with the level of incomes and the grading of jobs. That leaves the problems with the city fathers while the satisfied suburbanites go free. You cannot take the "El" or the Illinois Central out of the Loop and look out of the windows without wondering when and how Chicago is going to clear its slums, its deathtraps, and its breeding-grounds of crime and social problems.

The tempo of life in Chicago has to be experienced to be believed. It is much faster than that of New York. I am sure midwesterners work harder and more furiously than any people. They relax harder, too. One reason for that is the restless curiosity and experience-hunting of the midwesterner, which is greater than that of the more sophisticated easterner, which in turn is greater than that of the European. Another reason is the extraordinary gregariousness of all midwesterners, which is part of their sense of community. The Chicagoan is a home-lover, and there he really relaxes. But when he is "on the job," whether it is work or "fun," he (or she) never relaxes. Organized and communal relaxation is a business, like American games; "in earnest." The world is the midwesterner's oyster, which has to be opened at sword's point and then quickly swallowed, before he looks round anew for "those of the largest size." In New York, Philadelphia, Boston, there are many different groups in the social or intellectual life of the city. You can join any of them, but not all. Chicago's social and intellectual life is confined to a thinner layer, and whether it is in social affairs, intellectual pursuits, or gay diversions you meet the same people.

In this it is true that Chicago seems still "an overgrown small town"; but that remark is not as unkind as it sounds. The life of the small town rests on more solid social foundations than that of a metropolis. Social and intellectual leaders in such conditions must be prepared to live in the public eye. Thus the great mass of Chicagoans are free to live as anonymously or as publicly as they like, but there is little anonymity for the few hundred social "families" or "big names" of Chicago. They may not want anonymity. Certainly most of them cannot get it; and those who do are thought "snooty." That, in turn, means that life is a very hectic business, somewhat like that of royalty. Like the Red Queen in *Alice through the Looking-Glass*, you have to run as fast as you can to stay in the same relationship to people and events. To a smaller extent this is also true of social life in the other big cities and larger towns of the Midwest. It is not so much a question, as many observers think, of "keeping up with the Joneses"; it is rather a question of just "keeping up"—period. This gives to the surface of things in Chicago an impression of perpetual motion, like the surface of the sea. The analogy is good because in Chicago things happen, and people seem to think, and even move, in waves: waves of thousands or little waves of friends, but always waves. To get an individual alone you have almost to get into an office, bedroom, or bathroom.

Few cities in the world dominate as vast a region as Chicago. London dominates England and, as Cobbett pointed out over a century ago, it has not been altogether for England's good. Moscow dominates a large region of Russia. Paris, Berlin, Vienna, and Madrid do not dominate their countries to that extent. Chicago is still the "big town" to millions of midwesterners; but millions do not like it because of its bigness, vigor, initiative, enterprise, and economic dominance. The other big cities and the larger towns are jealous of it. The farmers distrust it. All of them prefer it to New York; but, for them, that is like preferring the devil you do know to the devil you don't. To many midwesterners Chicago seems, and seemed long ago, like an octopus whose tentacles could not stop growing, extending, reaching out, sucking in. By the same token, Chicagoans have a chip on their shoulder about the entire East, which the East helps to keep there. They also tend to decry the importance, qualities, or achievements of other Midwest cities; somewhat as if they were the New Yorkers, Bostonians, or Philadelphians of the Midwest. Their natural self-assertion and contrariness are thereby heightened.

The oldness of Chicago, the old town, has disappeared with the people who made it. The city is always putting on a new dress—but not always changing its underlinen. It is always on the go, going places, seeking "some new thing." If ever anyone tries to build a bridge out of wedding cake in the shape of the letter S, I am sure it will be a Chicagoan—and I am sure the experiment will succeed.

The city has surprising beauty. The beauty shines through all of its grime, the dirt of hard work. I have stood many a time, of a fall evening or in the depth of terrible winters, on the Michigan Avenue Bridge and looked west to see the girders of the many bridges over the Chicago River and the skyscrapers and the sunset beyond; and I have wondered why a Midwest school of painting did not spring up here. The rich businessmen of the Midwest buy the old and modern masterpieces of Europe; yet the best European artists would have had a field day if they had lived in the Midwest. Grant Wood and other Midwest artists seem more attracted by farm and rural life. Yet the cities have beauty, too; and it is ignored. You have the most beautifully poised masses and patterns of lines, majestic skies, colors, light and shade, depth and distances. Cross the east-west bridges over the southern branch of the

149

river: look at the fortress-like dimensions of Butler Brothers' warehouses; the Byzantine aspect of the Merchandise Mart. How tiny seem the huge locomotives on the Milwaukee Road's tracks beneath, how their smoke billows over the bridges; how the west winds howl under the Randolph Street underpass below the Northwestern Station and rush eastward into the Loop; how the bridges rise and fall so quickly, one after another, to let ships through—at what cost to the city I cannot imagine, for there is a bridge for almost every street leading north and west from the Loop, and they must all be lifted and lowered again. Stand on the top of a skyscraper and look south, along the curving shore beyond Hyde Park and the University of Chicago, seven miles away, to the steel-gray horizon of the steel mills. Go out west to Halsted Street— the longest straight streetcar ride in the world for eight cents, over thirty miles—and see Greek and Syrian, Sicilian and Armenian, at work and play. Or go to Maxwell Street on Sunday morning and see London's Caledonian market, Berwick Street, and Petticoat Lane fused into one, with the color and noise and bargaining of all the world's peoples.

See the city under new snow—be sure it is new—and it is a city transformed. "Windy City" lives up to its name, and to see a modern city being snowed in is an experience. I have seen drifts breast-high against the walls and only a few inches deep at the curbstone, right in the Loop. Go to the remarkable observatory on the top of the Board of Trade Building, above the "wheat pit," and walk all round, looking out for miles across railyards, stockyards, great public buildings, hotels, skyscrapers, each commercial building with its water tank atop, and as far as you can see in all directions but one—eastward where the lake runs straight north and south—there are the evidences of hectic activity: producing, transforming, packing, merchandising, printing, transporting, financing, selling, advertising, bustling, jostling, hurrying—all for the needs of six millions in Chicagoland, forty millions in the Midwest, a hundred and forty million Americans, and millions more in other lands. And then think: where Chicago is now there were about a dozen log cabins five generations ago.

The other big cities of the Midwest have much of Chicago's life and history in them. All of them are more like each other than any of them is like an eastern, southern, or far western city. The biggest difference from life in Chicago is that in all the other big cities the entire "top layer" of the well-to-do lives outside the cities in suburbs. Yet each of these Midwest cities has a perceptible life and atmosphere of its own. That is what many easterners and foreigners do not seem to perceive.

150

Take Detroit, for example. That is a city of factories and factory people. It has more of sheer production in it, less of commerce, finance, transport, and distribution. Accordingly, its downtown commercial area is small. Commerce seems relegated to a back seat. To that extent it differs from Chicago, the Twin Cities, St. Louis, or Kansas City. Detroit is all the world's city of the internal-combustion engine. It has grown faster than Chicago in the last two or three decades and had in 1945 over two million inhabitants. But it has its grades of jobs, its social gradations, its beautiful suburbs—Grosse Pointe can hold its head up with any place anywhere—and its grave social problems at or near the city's center. It is also as flat as Chicago, a city of the plain. It has virtually no public transport because, as the automobile made the city grow, everyone used an automobile, until the gasoline shortage in 1942 showed how utterly dependent on automobiles the city and its citizens were. Here, too, are workers of almost every conceivable nationality, with their different religions and habits of thought; and at Hamtramck, now part of Detroit, there is a completely Polish city within the city. The nearness of Windsor, Canada, and the constant passage of workers of both nationalities across the narrow channel, or through the tunnel beneath, has made Detroiters more understanding of Canadians, and perhaps of foreigners, than the people of any other Midwest city except Des Moines or Minneapolis. Detroit has little imposing about it except the factories, which are more imposing than almost anything else could be. The dirt on all sides is that of incessant production—a production without which it is almost impossible to imagine America being American, or "the American way" continuing. Like Chicago and the other big cities, it serves and is served by a big region extending over most of Michigan and well into Ohio. The cities and larger towns of this region mainly produce either furniture or the General Motors cars (contrasted with Ford, Hudson, and other "independents," which are located in or near Detroit) and the numerous accessories, fittings, and furnishings of automobiles. Detroit is a metropolitan area and, like Chicago, dwarfs its state capital. I have the impression that in Detroit the talk among men is mainly of assembly lines, retooling, programs, models, unions, labor relations, and supplies—in wartime more so, but in peace scarcely less. Yet I recall the concerts of the fine symphony orchestra, the museums, and the paintings of its art collection as yet other examples of what the big Midwest city and its most successful businessmen never fail to provide for their home town. The world which hears more of Ford, factories, Father Coughlin, the Reverend Gerald L. K. Smith, race riots, and labor troubles from Detroit, hears

151

less of the forums, discussions, and meetings of inquiring minds which are a more steady undercurrent in the life of the city, from the city fathers in the council chamber out to the people of the suburbs.

Cleveland is more a city of contrasts than Detroit; more like Chicago in that one respect, unlike it in most others. Like Chicago, it is a metropolis, far bigger than the state capital. From Lake Erie the city rolls back in hills and vales. It is not as new a big city as Detroit and is about only one-half the size. There is still something of a religious quality in the atmosphere of Cleveland, lacking in most other big Midwest cities. Mammon is not quite everything in Cleveland, not even for its richest citizens; and religion seems there to be more than ritual or good form. There is something more of the Quakers and Shakers, something more of New England, something of the Rockefeller family's sense of public service and duty. This is not only because of its New England and Pennsylvanian settlers, founders, and makers, but also because Cleveland still looks eastward and southward as well as westward. The tide of settlement from New England and New York along Lake Erie from Buffalo seems to have made Clevelanders look eastward more than the citizens of any other Midwest city except Cincinnati. Yet, though it is on the fringe of a "marginal belt," Cleveland is undeniably of the Midwest. Its steel, metal, machinery, and other manufacturing plants are bound up with the life of Detroit, Chicago, Toledo, Dayton, Cincinnati, Akron, Canton, Youngstown, and, of course, Pittsburgh—the last of which may also explain its slightly eastern outlook. There is less hurry and bustle in Cleveland than in Detroit or Chicago, but Clevelanders seem to get just as much done. The grand homes on Shaker Heights, its museums and art collections, its huge civic auditorium and public buildings, and its standards of education and learning only partially offset the same social problems at or near the center of the city which mark all the cities of the region. Cleveland has its very poor quarters; its Negroes, its masses of German, Hungarian, Bohemian, Polish, and other Slav origins. Until about ten years ago it was a city in which crime, gangsterism, and racketeering flourished proportionately as much as anywhere in America. But the leading businessmen and professional men of Cleveland seem to have a greater sense of civic responsibility and more determination to run their own city than do their fellows in most other big cities and larger towns of the Midwest. There may be something of the New England village in this respect, too, and something of the earnest young men from Yale (and Harvard, Princeton, and other eastern colleges) who made such a cultural revolution in early Ohio.

152

Cincinnati is as distinctive in the Midwest, and as "marginal," as St. Louis or Kansas City. Like St. Louis, it is one of the oldest cities inside America. Like Cleveland, it rolls back from its waterfront on the Ohio River in hills and vales. Like Cleveland, it still looks partly toward the east, but more toward the national capital, Baltimore, Philadelphia, and the other Ohio River cities. The southern region of Kentucky is on the opposite bank, and you feel something of the South, not the Old South but the newer western South of the pioneers, in Cincinnati. It is a city of just over half a million people. It does not contain the bewildering variety of Americans of as many national origins as Chicago, Detroit, or Cleveland; it is more solidly German. But there are traces in it of the same beginnings in river trade that St. Louis has. It was once the biggest meat-packing city; and superimposed on all that there are now big metal, machinery, and tool works which make it seem like Cleveland and the nearer Ohio cities of Dayton, Akron, and Canton. It is, like Detroit, Indianapolis, and many other Midwest cities, a city of skilled assemblers, precision workers, and fine technicians. Cincinnati is one of the few Midwest cities which seem to keep their citizens close to an average standard of living, with less obvious extremes of wealth and poverty, fewer suburbs of the well-to-do, and fewer slums. It is an extremely well-kept-up city; perhaps its early experiment in the "city-manager" form of administration accounts for that. The suburbs, as always in the Midwest, are handsome and dignified. They are set in rolling woodlands and lack nothing in elegance or amenities. But the small homes of the artisans and even the older residential sections of the city seem not to have fallen upon such evil days as those of other Midwest cities. As in Cleveland but to an even greater extent, there is in Cincinnati an evident interest in the cities and peoples of the regions outside the Midwest, and even in the life and ideas of other countries. In this respect it has changed mightily since the days, over a century ago, when Mrs. Trollope visited it! Its life is more regular, more ordered, less bewildering and hustling than that of other big cities in the region; yet the extent to which its name and products are famous all over the world, despite its smaller size, is evidence of its capacity to get things done, and done well.

Indianapolis, somewhat smaller than Cincinnati, is an industrial city; but it is also a state capital surrounded by rich farm land. It is another flat city without a waterfront, and a city of contrasts. Its suburbs of quiet, beautiful homes contrast with the very poor quarters near the center. As in Cincinnati, the predominant group by national origin is German; but it has more such groupings than Cincinnati; it is more

153

of a melting-pot, and to that extent has many of the characteristics of Chicago or Detroit. Indianapolis is located in the center of a region of big industrial cities and towns and seems to have remained half an industrial city and half a state capital, not knowing whether, and if so how, to grow bigger.

Milwaukee, on the other hand, now approaching three-quarters of a million people, is quite unlike Chicago, Detroit, or Cleveland. It is more like Cincinnati in its earnestness, closeness to average standard of well-being, and predominantly German atmosphere; and it is like Indianapolis only in this last respect. The Germans made it famous for breweries and beer, as they did to a less extent in St. Louis, St. Paul, and Cincinnati. Today it is a most important center of heavy engineering, tool-making, and the metal trades. Milwaukee is older, and was bigger than Chicago in the early days; and today, ninety miles and ninety minutes away from Chicago on the same lake and also facing east, it would be hard to find two cities so near and yet so far from each other. The people of Milwaukee are far more serious-minded, earnest, and quiet. The majority of the citizens are of German or Polish extraction. The city has as many citizens of Polish descent as of German— almost as many as Chicago—and in the outlying districts of the city, as in those of Chicago, you might well be in Poland. There is also, surprisingly, a strong Scottish, Scotch-Irish, and Irish element in the life of the city. The stately old homes on the northern bluffs have an uncanny mixture of North German and Scottish features in their architecture: Bremen combines with Balmoral. The diversity of religions can be imagined: German, Pole, and Celt correspond to Lutheran, Roman Catholic, and Presbyterian or Methodist divisions in the people. The city, like Chicago and unlike Cincinnati, has been sprawling and haphazard in its growth; but, unlike these other cities, it has managed to preserve much of its original self at the core. Like Chicago, it is the metropolis of its state but not the capital. Like Chicago, it has absorbed outlying villages and made them into suburbs; and, like Chicago, though not to the same degree, its system of public transport leaves much to be desired. Milwaukee, like Detroit but not to the same extent, depends on its citizens' automobiles. The city is solid, dependable, *gutbürgerlich*, like the old Pfister Hotel; but, like Chicago and other Midwest cities, it is encountering grave problems of housing and slum clearance as it grows older and bigger.

The Twin Cities on the Upper Mississippi, older and smaller St. Paul, the capital of Minnesota, and newer and bigger Minneapolis, have a combined population of just under one million. Like Rebecca's twins, the younger has supplanted the elder, and the elder is somewhat jealous and resentful. Minneapolis, the more industrialized of the two, has over half a million souls, and they are overwhelmingly Scandinavian and Anglo-Saxon. It has the modern machinery factories, huge flour mills and grain elevators, new skyscrapers, new streets and other buildings, and new suburbs with new homes. St. Paul, less than half-an-hour's car ride across the valley, is as German as Milwaukee or Cincinnati, and more German than St. Louis, though it is also a very Irish city. St. Paul has the beginnings of slums. Minneapolis has not—yet; but it may have before long. Both have their beautiful suburbs. It is interesting to note the predominance of fair heads and taller people on the street in Minneapolis, and of dark heads and shorter people in St. Paul. Yet St. Paul, like Milwaukee and Cincinnati, has something of the steadiness of age and its uniformity of pattern. Minneapolis has nothing like the stately old homes of the first families in St. Paul, the successful makers of railroads, beer, farm machinery—and of farms. It was from St. Paul that the northwest of the region was developed, and it still has the atmosphere not only of a state capital but of a regional capital. In that respect it is what Des Moines is to Iowa and beyond. Minneapolis, however, is more like Dallas, Texas, or Tulsa in Oklahoma: a big city of new buildings which sprang up and grew fast, because in an age of new machines, communications, utilities, and services there was need for a new distributing, merchandising, assembling, and transporting center. St. Paul lost its opportunity; Minneapolis took it. In the Twin Cities you still see pine all round you indoors. You hear of, and see, Indians and birches, and you think of the sources of big rivers and of canoes. The Twin Cities are near the lumberlands, the North Woods, the numberless lakes of Minnesota, northern Wisconsin, and North Michigan. Paper, resin, wood pulp, cellulose, chemicals, balsam, plywood—these are around you; but so, too, are the other old trades of the Midwest, like meat-packing and the making of farm equipment and farm supplies. The people of both cities are more interested in the currents of contemporary ideas and national and international affairs than the remoteness of these cities in the region and country might lead you to expect. Perhaps it is because of that remoteness; but it is also due in large measure to their peoples' commendable concern with educational institutions. Their peoples, too, have an interest in the arts, especially music and letters, which the people of many another city nearer the main current of American culture cannot equal.

St. Louis is a city set apart in the Midwest; in the region, yet not entirely of it; French in origin; German in settlement and development;

155

swaddled at birth in furs and skins brought in by the forerunners of the pioneers, the *coureurs des bois*, the hunters and trappers; owning slaves and still largely southern in outlook; drawn to the North and East by the rail traffic; made into an industrial, financial, and commercial metropolis and a hub of communications; but still more stable, ordered, and settled in its way of life than any other Midwest city. You cannot think of St. Louis without thinking of its great river front and of the Mississippi; of Mark Twain, of the north-south and east-west river traffic of which the city was the junction, and of its relation to New Orleans, Memphis, Cincinnati, Louisville, and Pittsburgh. Today St. Louis has one million inhabitants. The Germans, both Roman Catholics and Lutherans, share leadership of the city's life and business with the descendants of the original French, of New England Yankees, and of pure-blooded southerners from Virginia, the Carolinas, Kentucky, Tennessee, Mississippi, and Louisiana; but in the big industries, German names predominate. St. Louis, like all the Ohio River cities and like Cleveland, runs back from its impressive waterfront up little hills and valleys to wooded suburbs, great campuses of colleges and seminaries and institutions of learning, big estates, and the gently rolling country of Missouri beyond. The city has slums, as do all cities of its size, but it also has beautiful parks, hotels, and public buildings in the center. To this day society in St. Louis has a cultural life older, more vigorous, and spread more generally over its citizens than that of any other Midwest city. It used to be one of the dirtiest cities in the world. St. Louis changed that by demanding, and insuring, smoke abatement. It used to be one of the noisiest cities in the world. St. Louis carried out an effective antinoise campaign, not by words but by deeds. Like most Midwest cities, it has sprawled out haphazardly into the country, and the problem of public transport has grown with the city. Here, again, the automobile has temporarily cushioned the impact of the problem; but the congestion of automobiles at the center has correspondingly grown.

Kansas City, with about 450,000 people, is new. It is another city of the "marginal belt," looking out over the Missouri River to Kansas City, Kansas, and to the wheat lands of the Great Plains beyond. Like Omaha to the north of it in Nebraska, and in the same "marginal belt" looking west to the Plains, Kansas City is like a miniature Rome, though on more than seven hills and the hills are not so little. The bluffs above the Missouri near both cities are high, and behind both cities there is rolling country. Below the bluffs are slums. Trees are more rare and are prized; you are nearing the treeless plains. Kansas City and Omaha have been made within living memory. In a real sense they are the children of contention: of the Kansas-Nebraska Act of 1854 and of the warring factions that were pro- and antislavery in the new states. I have talked with men in Omaha who remember stories about the first trains on the Union Pacific line, and with men and women in Kansas City who remembered the railroads "coming through"—a significant phrase in itself. The mother of President Truman, who flew to visit him in the White House on Memorial Day, 1945, was a little girl when the terrible Missouri-Kansas border wars were going on in the middle and late 1850's. The cities and the larger towns in the "marginal belt" from Kansas City northward to the Canadian border—Omaha, Lincoln, Nebraska City, Sioux Falls, and Fargo—are the newest in the Midwest. Their public buildings and business districts proclaim their newness. They are also more closely bound up with the agricultural life of the surrounding country. Their "big business" is grain, meat-packing, distribution, transport, serving the farmers. They are more like towns which have become cities overnight, and their peoples, accordingly, are newer, less settled—and extremely hospitable and generous, even by Midwest standards. There is old and poor housing in all these cities, but there are no big slum areas: the cities are too young for that. Instead there are tumbledown buildings and blocks here and there. Nor are there great problems of public transport: the suburbs are almost within walking distance—at least, within a European's walking distance—of the center. Though these cities are composed of people of all national origins, there is more sense of community and public spirit among their citizens. There is a great mixture of regional characteristics, too, as you would expect on the margin of the Midwest; but it is not solely due to the nearness of the Great Plains. Southerners, midwesterners, and New Englanders as well as alien immigrants "went West" to make these cities; and to this day, as a result, there is more "all-Americanism" in their atmosphere.

The easterner who makes fun of Kansas City, Omaha, Lincoln, Sioux Falls, or Fargo knows little of what he is talking. Passers-by, or casual reporters from the East sent to "write them up," do not spend the time, or have neither the inclination nor the equipment, to discern the energy, the constructiveness, the great sense of community which have raised up these cities and thereby developed vast agricultural regions around them. They do not see what prompted the leading citizens who made them to pass on to their home towns such beautiful and valuable collections as that of William Rockhill Nelson at Kansas City, and the museums and other public collections at Omaha, Lincoln, and other

157

such cities. Their peoples are far more interested in music, in the other arts, in history, and in the tide of current affairs than New Yorkers, or, for that matter, Chicagoans, imagine. British and continental European conductors of orchestras have been surprised by the keenness of audiences there and by the reception accorded to them by thousands drawn from all economic ranks of their citizenry. (That was certainly the experience of the great orchestra of the Royal Air Force, with its leading British instrumentalists, on its tour of America in 1944.) On these western confines of the Midwest, big cities and large towns are fewer and farther between. Their peoples are in touch with, and surrounded by, the atmosphere of the "great open spaces," like islanders. They have fewer local and social problems; and in consequence their interest in such things seems to be greater than in many bigger, more central, and more closely located cities or towns of the region.

Des Moines, capital and biggest city of Iowa, is also a city set apart in the Midwest. With about a quarter of a million people, it is still a dominant city in a big region, the region of the richest farm land in America. In the main it is also a flat city, but the state capital is perched on a dominating hill, and the expanding suburbs run along bluffs above the river valley. You see more farmers and more evidences of them in Des Moines than in any Midwest city of its size; but you also see great stores, a fine university, and big commercial and public buildings. The open country is nearer. You can see fields and water meadows from the railroad tracks. Country birds fly round the eaves and columns of the Capitol and Polk County Courthouse. Life goes forward easily, regularly, and in order in Des Moines, perhaps because it is more of an agricultural, commercial, and administrative center and has comparatively less of modern industry with its attendant social problems. Like the people of the Twin Cities, Kansas City, and a few others, those of Des Moines seem more keenly interested in the great issues of the day and display tolerance and open-mindedness to a more marked degree. I throw out this suggestion at a venture: it may be because the life of the city has remained more intimately linked to that of the farmers; but, as we shall see later, there are other reasons, too. The people of Des Moines led the American nation in their treatment of the Nisei—the American-born Japanese—displaced from the West Coast after 1941. So also in their many public forums and discussions, the earnestness and fair-mindedness of the people are striking. There is also another point worth emphasis: though Des Moines is both the capital and the metropolis of Iowa, it is relatively small; accordingly, the political, administrative, industrial, agricultural, and commercial life of the state comes closer to the average citizen of Des Moines, whatever his or her calling may be, than it does in states with far bigger metropolitan cities and far smaller state capitals.

All these big cities of the Midwest are new. None of them is older, as a city, than a hundred years, and some have become cities only within the last half-century. The story is not quite the same with the smaller cities. These differ enormously one from another. The capitals of the states are generally smaller cities and often have an air of quiet distinction, beauty, and culture—for example, Madison (Wisconsin), Springfield (Illinois), Lansing (Michigan), and Jefferson City (Missouri). Of all these, Madison is the most beautiful, with an artistic capitol and a famous university poised between two big lakes. Columbus, the capital of Ohio, is really a big industrial city with more than 300,000 inhabitants; yet the city which Mr. James Thurber has immortalized seems still to be more administrative, more dependent on life in its central square, than the many smaller industrial cities of Ohio. It is somewhat like Indianapolis, the center of a region of cities and good agricultural land. Abraham Lincoln would not recognize industrial Springfield, though the old buildings and the center are still there, much as he knew them, and the trees now meet over the wide suburban avenues. The smaller industrial cities of Ohio are legion, and they are more alike than are the big cities of the region. Machinery, metal trades, fittings, devices, gadgets, accessories, household and office and farm equipment—these are the basis of their existence. These made them. You find such cities, nearly all new, throughout the region: the many cities of Michigan; Peoria, Rock Island, and Rockford in Illinois; Iowa has Clinton, Davenport, Cedar Rapids in the bend of a beautiful river among bluffs and woods, Waterloo, Sioux City, and others, all linked with both agriculture and industry; and there are many in Wisconsin— Racine, Beloit, Janesville, Kenosha, Sheboygan, Green Bay, and Manitowoc. Indiana is almost as full of them as Ohio—Gary, South Bend, Fort Wayne, Evansville, Plymouth, and Terre Haute are but a few examples. Each has a life of its own.

Yet among the smaller cities and large towns, quite different, are some of remarkable beauty. They are less industrialized; happily, modern times seem merely to have skirted them: Vincennes, "on the banks of the Wabash" in Indiana, the capital of the Old Northwest and still as handsome as when the Lincolns came through it with young Abraham; Madison (Indiana) with its lovely old homes; Marietta in Ohio with its beautiful colonial and slightly southern buildings, and Athens in the same state. Quite apart from the beauty of age and the elegance

159

of the old-time architecture of the eighteenth century, which is confined to those Midwest towns in the southern part of the "marginal belt," there is an extraordinary profusion of quiet and well-ordered, modern, small towns in the region: towns with between 10,000 and 50,000 inhabitants, dependent on one or more big factories or industries, retaining at their center and in their everyday life much of the ordered regularity of the old rural Midwest. I think particularly of Ottawa, Kewanee, Quincy, Dixon, and Alton in Illinois; of Mexico and Columbia in Missouri; of Winona, Minnesota; of many such towns in Indiana and Ohio, which have more of them than any other state in the Union except Pennsylvania; of Battle Creek and Holland, Michigan; of Eau Claire, La Crosse, Prairie du Chien, and Fond du Lac in Wisconsin; and of Mason City, Ottumwa, and Marshalltown in Iowa. In poking fun at "small-town life" in the Midwest, inhabitants of America's big cities have not often troubled to go and stay in them. The authors of *Middletown* did, with valuable results. The millions who talk glibly do not.

When I think of the smaller cities and towns of the region, I think first of wood-frame or brick and clapboard homes, little gardens, vines, and big trees whose leaves mingle above straight streets; of big but clean and new factories; of the workers who know each other and the inside of their fellow-workers' homes; of the garish and incongruous neon signs of Main Street at night in "Middletown"; but also of goings and comings known to all, the great importance of the wrongly and too often derided service clubs, the birthplaces of men of genius and leaders of business, the centers of down-to-earth religion and faithful ministers of it. I think of places like Salem, Illinois, whence William Jennings Bryan—and his opponent against whom he argued in the famous "monkey trial" at Dayton, Tennessee—both came. I think of county and other public buildings around or near the square; of people who still make time in which to meet and gossip; of old wood-frame houses near the center and new brick and clapboard homes farther out, but still within walking distance of work. I think of housewives who know tradesmen, and vice versa, and whose children know each other. I think of the longer continuity of life among these small-town families and the life of their town or city. All this needs to be remembered whenever anyone talks or writes of the standardization, boring uniformity, and constricting narrowness of small-town life.

Even the smaller cities have not yet lost all their small-town characteristics. Peoria, a city which plays the same part in American as Wigan in English vaudeville, contains three cities: the old one along the level Illinois riverbank; the newer industrial one on rising ground;

and, farther back, tree-lined streets of trim suburbs on the bluffs. There are the buildings and the life of the old Peoria which Lincoln knew; there is that of the huge distilleries and the caterpillar-tractor factories, and the taverns and city life which go with it; and, finally, there is the quiet home life of the suburbs. Yet Peoria has but 100,000 inhabitants. South Bend, Indiana, has Studebaker plants, but also Notre Dame. Fort Wayne has General Electric, but also its art school, museum, civic theater, and parks. Grand Rapids has its furniture factories, but also its art gallery, museums, and libraries. The contrasts of the big cities are there, but there is also more of the small-town sense of community, too, and more of its neighborliness.

It is dangerous, indeed, to talk of the uniformity of the smaller Midwest cities and towns. How can you compare, say, Canton and Akron in Ohio with the industrial "tri-cities" area of Rock Island, Moline, and Davenport, where the Mississippi divides Illinois and Iowa? Or Toledo with Fort Wayne, or even with Columbus? You cannot compare a university town, like Iowa City or Champaign-Urbana (Illinois), with a purely industrial town like Racine (Wisconsin). There are, first, the really big cities of the region, each in varying degree the metropolis of a big region, with Chicago dominating them all. Then there are industrial districts containing many new and purely industrial cities, grouped round one or two big cities. One such area is that which serves Detroit and contains Toledo, Flint, Pontiac, Saginaw, and others. Another such area runs from Milwaukee down to Chicago and out into Illinois and Indiana, embracing such cities as Racine, Kenosha, Elgin, Joliet, Gary, Michigan City, and South Bend. Yet another is formed around St. Louis and, across the Mississippi in Illinois, East St. Louis. The eastern Ohio, western Pennsylvania, and northern West Virginia industrial area is still another. The towns and cities of the Minnesota, North Michigan, and northern Wisconsin iron-ore region, leading to Duluth and Superior, are in another such industrial area and therefore have a distinct similarity, as do the towns near Omaha or Council Bluffs or those near the two Kansas City's. The capital cities and university towns of the region have an obvious cause of similarity between themselves, and of difference from others, despite their wide divergences in degree of industrialization. And the cities or towns, whether big like Des Moines or smaller like Bloomington (Illinois), which work primarily for and with agriculture differ from those like South Bend or Fort Wayne, which work for all of America's industry and the consumers it serves.

The innumerable small county and rural towns do conform more to a pattern, the historical and largely agricultural pattern of their surrounding regions. Both big cities and smaller cities, by railroad, truck, newspaper, and radio, have enlarged their area of influence and altered their own faces, the face of the smaller towns, and even the face of the country in so doing. The variety, restlessness, and mobility which made the Midwest have been changing its life and its appearance. That is more obvious in its cities and larger towns than in its small rural towns and communities. But it is not merely a Midwest process. It is American.

V. FOLK AND WAYS

MIDWESTERNERS ARE COMPARATIVELY AS NEW AND YOUTHFUL IN THE region today as were the old midwesterners of the period from 1790 to 1860. They are different from the people who were there before them, but they are still new and young. It is important to keep remembering that.

Just as the pioneers and settlers had to clear forests and break prairies before they could live in it, so within one lifetime the Midwest businessmen and others had to make the towns and cities of the New Midwest before twenty-five millions of souls could live in them. Much of this making is still going on, much was provisional and shoddy, much was splendid, and little of it has lasted. The hallmarks of the Midwest are change, restlessness, movement, scrapping the old, inventing and installing the new. As the towns and cities were transformed within a decade or two, as their inhabitants were new to them, nothing stayed put—not even the people who inhabited the various residential sections. Constant change seemed to be the stable and settled order of Nature, and "only the provisional endured." The natural extremes of the region were there, as they were in the Old Midwest. Yet rail, automobile, and airplane were lessening distances, knitting life in towns and cities together, and dovetailing the region itself more closely with the East. But while some of the old extremes were lessened, others—notably the psychological extremes of many new races and nationalities and the extremes of welfare and ill-fare—were heightened.

163

The bulk of the adult midwesterners of today cannot go back more than two or three generations in America. Even their Americanism is therefore new, overlaid on the customs, religions, tongues, and patterns of thought of forty or fifty other nationalities. The mixing is still going on inside families in all big cities and towns. The many kinds of European immigrants who settled in eastern towns and cities were more absorbed into the older and more stable American culture there. But in the Midwest they had more than an equal chance to mold and alter the still fluid way of life which they found on arrival. They have left their stamp upon the newer people and way of life of the Midwest. You realize it as soon as you step down from the train in Lima, Elkhart, Decatur, or St. Joseph. You see it in the faces, voices, and statures of the people. You experience it in their restaurants and menus, in their homes, and in their ways of living.

The Midwest is where the most likeable American characteristics are at their most likeable and where the far fewer unlikeable American characteristics are at their most unlikeable. That is what you would expect in a region of extremes. But it is also what you expect of youth. Midwesterners of town and city are youthful, with all the effervescent, illimitable, and often undisciplined vigor of young people who refuse to count the cost, who take great risks, gamble, venture all, and cannot believe in bad luck or bad times. The armed forces of the Old World, friend and foe alike, noted this American willingness to run risks, this élan, this headstrong prodigality, this heroic gambling, in both of the world wars. With this youthful zest and zeal go the crude extremisms and the dogmatic self-assertion of youth; bragging, boasting, and intolerance; the unamenability to discipline, whether of parental, national, or local governmental origins; the individualism and self-centeredness but also the kindliness; and, paradoxically but naturally, youth's temperamental and mercurial sensitiveness.

Youth is not interested in the past, because it has none. So with midwesterners; the overwhelming majority are interested only in making the future into an enjoyable present. In fact, the future is viewed only as something which must be made into a present to themselves or to their children, on whom they therefore build their hopes. "The past is a bucket of ashes." How truly midwestern that is—and how young! The midwesterners of today are young because they have no "folkage," no "folk-memory," behind them. Their history and, indeed, their Americanism are alike assimilated at school, from books and teachers. There is no folklore or family background to it. You do not need to

164

believe in Jung's "collective unconscious" to recognize that the long continuity of families in one country, and one place in it, makes for a stable pattern of society. That is lacking from the Midwest, though it is on the way.

One of the results is that midwesterners do not really feel identified with any history but that of their own region. They do not feel identified with colonial American society, with the East or the South. They tend to say of the attractive grapes in the East and South that they were probably sour, anyway. But it goes farther than that. The Midwest today is the issue of the marriage between a young people and virgin land and resources. The geographical isolation and insulation of midwesterners, their development of the region's fabulous resources, and the speed with which they achieved the highest average standard of living in the world made this young and still unformed people as critical and sensitive toward the federal government or the East and South, as toward all the nations of the Old World from which the bulk of midwesterners came. That youthful sensitiveness is still a marked characteristic. It is almost unique in the world.

You find the nearest equivalent among the Canadian French in their attitudes toward the French of France and toward the British. But the Canadian French today are nearer to the French of France in the eighteenth century, and they are strongly agricultural and opposed to industrialization; in which they are not at all like midwesterners. On the other hand, we may find something like this developing in the great "Midwest" of Russia during the rest of this century, as people flock to it from all over Russia and from the Balkans or eastern Europe. This self-satisfaction and egocentricity is due, I think, to the great material achievements and to isolation and insulation of these regions during their development. But, as we shall see, it is only part of a picture, and the other parts, like everything else in the Midwest, are paradoxical and contrary.

This leads us to the pride of a youthful people: pride in the region, the state, the city, the town, the home, and the achievements of all of them. The Midwest is so much the "home" region of America that the word "home" is linked with this pride in many ways: home town, home state, home folks, stamping grounds. Much of this pride, too, can be traced to the insulation of the region. Just as the man of the Old South was first a citizen of his state and only thereafter an American citizen, so today midwesterners are first Hoosiers, or "from Missouri," or Suckers, or Badgers, and then Americans—but with a difference. Now,

165

the midwesterner thinks of his home region as the real heart of America, always beating true. That heart cannot be false to itself and therefore cannot be false to any man. It is to the midwesterner the real America.

The East seems cosmopolitan and (strange to say) polyglot or Europeanized. The South seems antiquated, "olde worlde," worth visiting. The Far West seems either a playground or remote and strange. The Great Plains seem boring, uncouth, or "flat and unprofitable." The midwesterner looks around him in a region a thousand miles wide and almost a thousand deep, and thanks God that he was born there and nowhere else. He is surrounded, shielded, insulated by the rest of America. He is proud and content with his origin, though he is still too young to be satisfied with his lot. He is still divinely discontented.

His pride is personal to himself, whether he is growing the best corn or turning out the best baby buggies or helping to make the best radios, steel, or laborsaving devices. But it is also in the achievements of any other midwesterners, who thereby become his friends and neighbors—the baseball or football team, the men who manage the home town's real estate values, the local boy who "makes good." Something of this local pride can be traced to the bragging, tall-tale-telling, self-assertive, and aggressive river boatmen; to the delight of pioneers and settlers who became farm owners whereas, in Europe, they would only have been peasants; to the magnitude of the material achievements of millions of hands in their own lifetime; to the "sudden glory which overtaketh a man" when he has done what no one did before.

But it is not just small-town pride, as so many easterners think. There is something in it of the *genius loci*, the genius of the place. Walter Pater's *Marius the Epicurean* would not have found it strange. In it there is something of the restless vitality of the prairie, the vast distances, the great rivers and lakes, the vigorous tempo of city life; the remarkable monuments made with hands; something of the kinship between man and nature, hard work and a hard environment. Rupert Brooke, after his first visit to America before the first World War, thought that instead of the Statue of Liberty welcoming the foreigner there should be the statue of a young, bareheaded, bare-throated American saying enthusiastically, "Gee! this is some country!" That epitomizes the pride of the midwesterner in the Midwest and in his country.

A mature citizen of any country or region will accept any serious and courteous observation, even if critical, in order perhaps to learn something. The pride of the midwesterner, linked with his self-sufficiency and youthful self-confidence, admits criticism only with great difficulty

166

and with no little danger of misunderstandings, even if the critical observer is another American. The proud are always hypersensitive, but not all the proud show it. The midwesterners, being both young and proud, cannot conceal their sensitiveness.

Next comes another paradoxical and contrary characteristic: curiosity, open-mindedness, and readiness to give anyone's idea a "break." Despite the midwesterner's unfailing trust in his own destiny and in his own abilities, he remains youthfully curious. Consequently, he is also probably kinder to young men than any human being anywhere; for young men have new ideas. In England during the last generation, and to a smaller extent in the remaining democracies of the Old World, you were a callow youth in your thirties, a promising young man in your forties, and in your fifties (if any ideas survived) you were barely heard. Americans do not realize how fortunate they are in this respect. Youth in Western Europe was only given a chance to take great responsibilities, or to try out its ideas, in war or under a dictatorship. And in two wars within one generation Europe lost a prodigious amount of its youth and gained instead a series of aging populations—aging doubly rapidly because of the fall in births and the loss of the young. Not so the Midwest, and there lies the secret of its perennial youthfulness, of its vigor, and of their constant recruitment. To be young is to be forgiven almost everything. Where men had less than twenty-five years' expectation of life at birth in the 1850's, they now have sixty; but, despite this, young people are still very precious in the Midwest. The accent is on youth in a youthful region. The only comparable country is Russia, where over three-fifths of the people are under thirty.

Children are generally, and often outrageously, intolerant and unkind to each other when grown-ups are not around; but the surprising thing about midwesterners is that, being young as a people, they are so good to the young. Perhaps it is because the young were once so precious. Perhaps it is because they belong to the future. Perhaps it is because midwesterners believe in them anyway. If so, they are right; and they need not fear for their future.

All midwesterners are full of curiosity: curiosity about the rest of America, the world outside, new notions and gadgets, strangers, new faces, "some new thing." That is also an attractive feature of their youthfulness, their eagerness to know, their hunger and thirst after new experiences. How much of this is due to the solitude of the pioneer and settler, how much to the insulation of the Midwest, how much to the broad standardization of life, and how much to the peopling of the region by strange, non-American folk no one can say for sure. But

167

there it is, and the outcome has been of immense benefit to the Midwest. Despite the dogmatism, prejudice, and self-assurance of youth, the midwesterner is surprisingly open-minded and commendably open to conviction. True, he must be "sold on the idea," and it is indeed hard to convince any midwesterner of an abstract proposition, because it cannot be concretely demonstrated. "Show me," he says; "I'm from Missouri." There the easterner and many foreigners stop, declaring him to be prejudiced, bigoted, or crystal-skulled. That is silly. The Midwest was not made, and is not run, by numbskulls. They occasionally fall for slickers, as all of us do. They fell for them in the past and are wary. But they will give anyone—any crank or crackpot—a fair hearing, in business or on the platform. "Perhaps there's something in it; we'd better see." If the stranger can "show them," can convince them by sound sense and hard facts, no people are quicker to change their opinions or to give a new idea a chance. That is a rare quality in humanity.

It is all a strict matter of business. That is why the word "businesslike" looms so large in the midwestern vocabulary. The person who has the idea must first "sell" it. If he can "sell himself" and his idea, he gets the breaks. Here, the curiosity, experimentalism, practicality, business sense, tolerance, and kindness of the Midwest offset its dogmatism, prejudices, egocentricity, and self-assurance. I know of no place where these contrary characteristics are so evident in everyday life.

Certainly midwesterners are the kindest, most generous, and most hospitable people in a country famed for these great virtues. Here again you cannot be sure from what it derives: the pioneer community and vast distances, or the mutual aid in small communities of strange immigrants, or the curiosity about the stranger, or the long dependence on Christian charity to solve social problems instead of action by governmental authorities. Midwesterners do not use first names quickly or call each other "friend" and "neighbor" without meaning it. A whole people of nearly forty millions do not conform to a general pattern of kindliness, generosity, and neighborliness out of mere ritual, convention, or form. There may by this time be something conventional in the speedy use of first names among strangers. Conventions (in both senses of the word) may have spread this practice. But they did not spread the practical generosity and hospitality. That is proverbial. The only other countries with which it can be compared in this respect are the old Russia and Hungary.

People get an immense "kick" out of giving, entertaining, and putting up a visitor at great inconvenience. ("That's fine. Mom will go in with Sis, Chuck can come in with me, and you'll have Chuck's room!") The visitor offends deeply out of a desire to spare his hosts such inconvenience, except that what would really be inconvenient almost anywhere else is here an obvious pleasure. The sensible visitor, American or not, gives the pleasure and shares in it, and all are happy.

Such generosity shows itself on all sides: at births, marriages, and deaths; on birthdays, Valentine's Day, Easter, and Christmas; and at arrivals and departures. Business-like as ever, the big stores and others, more interested in the practical side of giving, have prevailed on the authorities to institute and proclaim "Mother's Day" and "Father's Day," which are faithfully observed. "Every dog has his day"; but if every dog *needed* to have his day declared beforehand, it would certainly be recognized and he would get a gift. Thanksgiving alone is confined to members of the family, though a passing stranger would not wittingly be allowed to spend it alone.

It is the same in the stores, on the railroads, on the street. Everyone is kind and helpful. People will not say, "Excuse me, could you tell me where So-and-so's is?" They will more probably open with direct fire: "Say, where's So-and-so's?" or, as a genial St. Louisan once blurted out at me in Kansas City: "Brother, am I lost!" (I felt like giving G. K. Chesterton's reply to the office boy: "My friend, we have *all* lost our way!") The kindliness is there; it has a different sound, a different flavor; that's all. It is a conventional necessity in the Midwest to proclaim your equality of status with anyone else. This you do by asking bluntly what you want to know: no frills, no European "aristocratic" fopperies or nonsense, no waste of words (in a region that wastes many in other ways). But, having paid this tribute to Demos, you are then at liberty to be kind, considerate, and polite, either in pleasant smalltalk or in buying a stranger a drink.

Hotels, stores, salesmen, and salesgirls will do more for the customer than anywhere else on earth: take other stores' packages, hold everything until later in the day or for some other member of the family to call for it, deliver messages; "it's all in the service." The customer is never wrong. "Do as the lady wishes," said the first Marshall Field; and it is still the rule. The conductors on the commuters' trains remind people not to forget their parcels, pass on messages, know the various members of each family, and are for the duration of the journey more of a minister than a servant—which is as all service should be. The girl at the cash register tells you that your Mary went by with two other girls half an hour since, with ice-cream cones, and she thinks they were going to So-and-so's. A young couple expect their first baby, and from that moment onward the neighbors offer the loan of this or the gift of that. ("Mary Lou has grown out of it." Or "Don't expect I'll be needing it—least, not for some time!") The community fund, the drives for the Red Cross, the Y.M.C.A., the Y.W.C.A., the tuberculosis and infantile paralysis campaigns, and many another voluntary effort tap the wellsprings of this great generosity. All who can, respond. There are those in the cities and larger towns who cannot. Life is far from being "roses, roses all the way" in the Midwest. But in the main it is a region of hard workers who live in communities and who give and take of this impressive generosity in common.

Youth is gregarious. Midwesterners are extremely so. Like the home, the community counts for much; and from the home as a center the circles of communal feeling spread out to the block, the district, the town, the county, the state, the region, and the nation. This, too, had its origins partly among the pioneers and settlers, partly in the community spirit of New England, partly among groupings of alien immigrants, and partly in the older Protestant religious sects, the circuit riders, the settlements of Quakers, Shakers, and Mormons, and the communities like the Rappites of New Harmony, Indiana. Like most wild animals of the prairie, the people were gregarious from the outset. They had to be; for only in community were security, mutual aid, and succor possible. This sense of community underlies the many service clubs—Rotary, Lions, Kiwanis, Elks, Buffaloes, Optimists, Civitan, and others—the fraternities and sororities of school and college, the chambers of commerce, advertising clubs, and the innumerable voluntary associations for civic service or charity. It is as strongly evident among the women as among the men, and in purely social affairs as in civic matters. It is linked with the home town, with that "genius of the place" already mentioned; and in the big cities it is less evident than in the smaller cities and towns. But it declares itself in the life of the individual to quite a surprising extent.

Individualistic as most midwesterners are, they are also acutely unhappy and often ill at ease if they find themselves alone. One of the most striking differences from the East is in the public vehicles. You notice you are in the Midwest by the easy urgency with which strangers start a conversation on the trains or in restaurants or on the street. The overwhelming majority of midwesterners do not relish being alone. Rather will they risk an argument or an unpleasant encounter with a stranger than be alone and in silence. This may be a part of midwestern curiosity and kindliness. It is also part of the midwesterner's feeling of home: no one should be left to feel himself a stranger; no one should be strange. This has the result that no one should be different

170

from anyone else, and fits in with the new American standardization of life. It does not always seem an unmixed blessing to the foreigner—nor to a small minority of midwesterners.

The person who likes solitude, silence, privacy, or contemplation is thought to be "snooty," queer, or up to no good. This aspect of their communal sense and their gregariousness weighs heavily upon the small minority of midwesterners who like privacy and solitude. They are thought to be putting on airs. They are not one of the community of average persons. They are abnormal, and in the Midwest anyone abnormal and outside the framework of the community is mistrusted and disliked. Such a man clearly has resources of his own which are not, and cannot be, shared. He is not "a good mixer." Worse, he is probably covering up something. He may be immoral. His wife and family are quickly made to feel that. The pressure of Midwest community feeling can be oppressive. It may be partly responsible for the almost general desire of the Midwest's outstanding literary, artistic, and intellectual geniuses—who are many—to quit the region. It also underlies that "cult of the average" in the region, to which we shall turn later. Maybe this community feeling is a protest against *national* standardization; an attempt to find diversion and relaxation outside one's self, among one's fellows, and not within one's self, not in one's own thoughts. In this way the typical midwesterner declares his belief that all relaxation and diversion must be taken in doses, collectively.

But it is wrong to leave it at that. The individual's sense of obligation, duty, and service to his community, to his friends and neighbors, is more developed in the Midwest than anywhere else. Very few successful midwesterners forget their origins. They boast of coming from the farm, or a small town, or a big city, indiscriminately. Fewer rich European aristocrats or successful businessmen donate to their community a fraction of what so many midwesterners have given and still give to beautify or enrich the life of their home towns. The age in which Europeans did so lies centuries behind us—with notable exceptions. True, wealth was and is still made more rapidly in the Midwest, despite the speed with which American taxes and social services have caught up with their European counterparts. But the making of riches within a lifetime or less does not generally result in the voluntary use of part of them for the community's sake. In the Midwest, however, monuments of private munificence and private enterprise lie around you; in fabulously endowed schools, colleges, laboratories, technical research institutes, art collections, libraries, and museums; in symphony orchestras, community centers, clubs, and parks. It took "death duties" to

171

induce most rich Europeans to donate some of their belongings to the nation; but in their own lifetime successful midwesterners, without constraint, have richly endowed their fellow-citizens; and most of it exceeds any limit on gifts imposed by the taxing authorities. Seldom has so much been given so quickly to so many by so few.

The sense of community, gregariousness, and lack of any need of privacy show themselves in the absence of hedges, walls, and fences around the people's homes; in more than a willingness, a desire to live in the public eye; in the frank freedom with which Midwest businessmen will discuss their problems and make available their knowledge to strangers; in the community's feeling of dependence upon the business, skill, and individualistic enterprise of each member. This feeling of identity between the community and its businessmen counts for much in politics, especially for the strength of the Republican party among the well-to-do and those in the middle and upper income brackets in the Midwest: the industrialists, businessmen, professional men, clerical workers, and traders. The Midwest has probably the greatest regional concentration of these people in America. They belong to both political parties and are distributed through hundreds and thousands of small towns, in which they are the acknowledged leaders of the community.

Here the sense of community has been more successfully linked with social and political leadership than in almost any remaining democracy on earth. Yet it is not the leadership of an élite or a class. It is the leadership of many "firsts among equals." In many of the big cities, and in nearly all of the smaller cities and large towns, the movements for greater racial and religious toleration during the second World War began among such leaders, extended next to religious and racial leaders, and then embraced the various service clubs, societies, and associations in a voluntary communal effort to combat America's most enduring and exacting social problems.

Youth is seldom still, hard to restrain, always on the go. It is infinitely adaptable and resourceful. So are midwesterners. Their energy, skill, capacity for work, and devotion to business are well known. Indeed, they are perhaps inclined to carry over their work psychology into their play and make most of life a business. Few easterners, and fewer Europeans, would permit their business, their way of earning a living, so to dominate their life outside nominal working hours. Any hour can be a working hour for the typical midwesterner: at home on the telephone, with friends and neighbors, at a club or restaurant or cafe, or at a show. The Midwest is original and inventive; but in business it is even more adaptable, improving, perfecting, promoting, developing. It

172

takes ideas from anyone, anywhere, and develops them. It is always altering and changing things: new types, new models, bigger and better kinds. It is extremely quick to see the possibilities of any idea and to realize them in practice. That keeps industrialists, technicians, and businessmen constantly on tiptoe.

This absorption in "the everyday business of life" is not just a mark of materialism, of devotion to Mammon, as many superficial observers think. Midwesterners have an extremely free and easy time when they are young. But, once they start to earn their own keep, they are treated as men; and the business of making a living in the Midwest is hard. It is extremely competitive and terribly exacting. Remorselessly it demands eternal vigilance. The Spanish proverb "Sir, there are no curves in Castile" is true of almost all ways of making a living in the Midwest. It is no smooth, rounded existence. It is abrupt, acute, full of unforeseen shocks and surprises, a sea of shoals, a battle of wits morning, noon, and night. There are many stresses and anxieties, many frayed nerves, many stomach ulcers, much worrying over the future of the wife and children. The high standard of living is earned by all of this, too. There are many shipwrecks on the shoals, many personal tragedies in the struggle for existence. The price of giving young men and new ideas a "break" is often the firing of an older man, or the dropping of a whole department.

To an Englishman, living in the business atmosphere of the Midwest is uncanny. It is like living on Mars in the future, but simultaneously it is like being reborn a century ago in early Victorian England. Yet it is real, actual, infinitely more efficient, and infinitely more productive. The tempo, mobility, and fluidity of life are in consequence bewildering. Competitiveness, physical and nervous energy, responsibility, adaptability, resourcefulness, initiative, organizing and reorganizing: these are the qualities necessary to make a fair living in the Midwest, if you are ever to earn more than a clerical worker or an artisan and be able to live accordingly. So there is a constant changing of jobs, homes, and home towns. This mobility and fluidity go from the very top of Midwest society to the very bottom. The farmer or itinerant laborer who is broke will just "up and quit," packing his belongings and family into an old jalopy and lighting out for some other town, or even some other region, where he has heard there is work. But the richest and most successful men are also likely to come home one night and tell the wife to get ready to move to Cincinnati or Cleveland or Chicago or New York for a year or two or more. And very many of the people in the middle income brackets do exactly the same. There is no equivalent to this in the world, except in Russia. It is as if a man who had worked in Liverpool came home and told his wife to get ready to move to Istanbul, and three or five years later to Cadiz. Within a working lifetime, few midwesterners stay in the same small town for long, unless they are of the minority of professional men or tradesmen who like to stay put and grow up with the community.

Frequent movement within this great region is part of the order of Nature. It means constant adaptation. It is as true of teachers, librarians, and doctors as it is of lawyers, ministers, or professors; as true of trade-unionists as it is of foremen, accountants, managers of plants, and directors on the board. True, there is plenty of evidence that this fluidity of society is not what it was; that standardization and stability have permeated the Midwest from the East; and that the new problems of stability are rearing their heads in the region. But it is still true that midwesterners regularly, and up to the age of fifty or more, think nothing of packing up and taking a new opportunity in a new state, city, or town. The opportunity, moreover, is frequently utterly new: the corporation lawyer or banker goes into industry; the artisan into storekeeping; engineers buzz around like bees in honeysuckle; so do accountants, plant managers, and factory workers. Midwestern society is nothing like molasses in January. Even if there is no prior opening, a man will look for one or make one, whenever he wants to move. By the same token, the region gets new men and new ideas from other regions of the country and sends successful midwesterners to them. There is far more cross-fertilization of ideas, and of families, than most Americans outside the Midwest realize. That is also what carries all-American characteristics to extremes in this region.

Something must be said of Midwest manners. Seldom, indeed, have so many kinds of manners been crowded together within so short a time. They have been the manners and customs of many peoples. The energy, restlessness, mobility, and youthfulness of midwesterners might have been expected to result in a lack of manners. Quite the contrary is the case. I doubt if anywhere else in America has Emily Post so faithful and regular a following. Midwesterners are as manners-conscious as they are etiquette-conscious. Their manners differ slightly from those of other Americans, but they have a code, and the proof of that is the general censure of any departure from it. Toward women and elderly people the midwesterner shows a respect which is only partly expressed by considerateness. There is nothing of the ritual of gallantry in it. It springs from the family and the home. The Midwest home and family

174

of Italian, German, Polish, or Bohemian origin are in this respect as important as those of Anglo-Saxon Americans.

Liberty, equality, and fraternity loom larger in the picture of Midwest manners. So does the hurried tempo of life in the towns and cities. For example, there is less considerateness for women in crowds, lines, streetcars, busses, and commuters' trains than there is for those same women in the office or factory, or for women whom you meet at home or at your neighbors' homes. That may be because women have put themselves on an equality with men in the business sphere; and the midwesterner is nothing if not natural. Equality means actual equality to him. First come, first served; waste no time in getting where you need to get. His manners have that ease and naturalness which mark all manners of the people, contrasted with etiquette or mannerisms imposed from above. There is no arbiter of manners in the region, no class or layer from whose habits manners derive. The code is so natural that it must have grown out of long experience of family life and communal living.

There is more politeness in thanking than in asking. That is probably because midwesterners like to be asked to do things or to help and are the most approachable (and approaching) people. One is struck by the extent to which kindliness and considerateness form the basis and justification of Midwest manners. It is as if the mutual aid and comfort of pioneers and alien immigrants had been turned into sympathetic consideration for all men. But it is a realistic sympathy and consideration. For instance, self-help must be exhausted before consideration will be forthcoming. There is more help for someone who has suffered by an act of God than for someone who has only himself to blame or can look after himself. A man will take off his hat before a young stenographer in the office elevator; he will not give up his seat to her in the streetcar; but he will get up for an elderly woman or an obviously expectant mother. When he does get up, there is an awkwardness in his approach because he is doing something good in public: "Here, take this seat," or "You sit right here," he will say. In this there is some evidence of the midwesterners' deep distrust of gallantry and "the gentleman."

This is strange because, between 1870 and 1910, in every big Midwest city there was what is now called the "old school" of courtesy, manners, and elegance: a society which could, on its home ground, compare with its counterparts anywhere in the world. These were "the old men with beautiful manners." Some of them remain. Their world has vanished. Instead, a new school of free-and-easy, familiar, natural *bonhomie* has sprung up. Its members, now in their forties, think the

175

old school "stuffy." They emancipated themselves from the old school of manners during and after the first World War. Meanwhile, however, their children have been in the second World War, and there are evidences of a return to more formal manners in this informally brought-up younger generation. So does the wheel come full circle, and so are parents surprised—and grandparents often delighted.

There are more natural good manners in the homes of midwesterners than in their public life. In public life all are supposed to be free and equal, to show neither superiority nor inferiority, with which most midwesterners confuse European manners. In the homes—until the second world war in one generation began to break up family discipline anew—the manners of the people were reflected in the children's demeanor. Their behavior was extremely good. It was far better than Hollywood, the radio, or the novel have ever led foreigners (or other Americans) to suspect. It was better than in the homes of most other countries.

The freedom, ease, and frankness of Midwest manners have often been misunderstood. Many observers have thought the abruptness, frankness, and directness were crude. In fact, they reflected genuineness, honesty, and candor. Admittedly it is a little hard sometimes to live with "nothing but the truth." (Ibsen made out a very good case for the polished lie in social life.) But anyone who lives for some time among midwesterners learns the formulas of their manners as easily as if he were living in Madrid or Vienna. Much of that abrupt directness is a formula: the tribute payable to liberty, equality, and fraternity. When the overriding human need is there, when the graces of life are urgently required, no one can be more spontaneous, more instant in generous response, than midwesterners; and then, again, there is no mannerism about their manners. There is only a natural, human graciousness.

Finally, youth is incurably and delightfully romantic. So are midwesterners; but, like youth, with a difference. Their romanticism is like that of the Elizabethans in England nearly four hundred years ago. They are youthful, virile, swaggering, intrepid, nationalistic, and resourceful. But, contrary and extreme like all youth, they are shrewd, realistic, and matter-of-fact. With their grass-roots philosophy and down-to-earth realism they are men of sentiment rather than sentimentalists. They are far more emotional than people think. You notice it in their attitudes to animals, children, birth, love, marriage, and death. The occasion or event itself calls forth a great wave of emotion, which is rapidly succeeded by a most realistic lapse into matter-of-factness and everyday resignation. That is surely the hallmark of a youthful people. In sentiments, emotions, and in general sensitiveness while

176

they are undergoing the experience, they oscillate between great extremes. They go from wild optimism to unwarranted black pessimism and back to their prevailing optimism again in the space of a few hours or days. This is all part of the general extremism, youth, and unbridled vigor of the region; but it brings many midwesterners to the verge of a manic-depressive state, and it heightens the general impression of the instability of life.

Tempers, moods, and emotions lie very near the surface, as among adolescents of both sexes. It could scarcely be otherwise in a region which has mixed and molded so many races and nationalities within one lifetime and made them live together and like it. Nothing exemplified this romantic strain better than the effect of Pearl Harbor in 1941 and the death of President Roosevelt in 1945. Both events were unexpected, sudden, dramatic, and cosmic. They evoked a whole people's emotions. Their impacts in the Midwest were stunning, dumbfounding. But in that region the press and radio outdistanced popular reaction by days of synthetic emotionalism. The people had absorbed, reacted, adapted, had taken it all in their stride and had reverted to their everyday realism far more quickly than their organs of so-called public opinion. The greatest crises of individual and folk life give way more speedily to "So what?" in the Midwest than anywhere else in America. Life has to go on. The unknown, the unexpected, has to be assimilated. The present and future belong to the living, the vigorous. This is a feature of the New Midwest. It was not the way in which the old midwesterners received the news of the outbreak of the Civil War, the assassination of Abraham Lincoln, or any comparable crisis.

When all this is said, to what does it all boil down? To this, I think: that midwesterners are a youthful and romantic people with an over-mastering belief in themselves and their children, who are their future; that they are a self-reliant, self-assertive, but extremely kindly folk; that they rate the individual highest, but only if he is part of a community; that they are buoyantly enthusiastic, proud, sensitive, skilful, and hard-working; and that they go by the average in things and people and not by the outstanding. They were once reformists and radicals. They are now more stable and settled and have thereby become more conservative and traditional; in other words, an older people. But, being a folk mixture which has not yet "jelled," they are still paradoxical and extreme, full of the contrariness and confusion of youth. They know they are still "going places" and are not sure whither. In this, they are less sure and certain than their forebears. They are not a deeply spiritual or religious people, in a transcendental sense; they believe more in good

177

works and in life here below—a fact which has led many to think of them, wrongly, as mere materialists. Materialists they certainly are, but not merely so; for their materialism must issue in good works for others, even if the circle of "others" be confined to their own families, which it seldom is.

In short, with all their distinctions and differences, they are very human folk. Nothing human, of virtue or vice, is entirely alien to them. More than any other people I know, they are like the youth of the world. They can hurt as they can comfort. If any people can perform what they promise to be able to do, then midwesterners can. And they do not promise what they do not think they can perform.

MIDWEST MYTHOLOGY

Every people has its myths and mythology. Contrary to popular belief, a myth is founded on something real and true in the people's past; and in their present, myths are very powerful influences. Myths are not unreal or fictional things. They set a framework within which every current issue, every item of popular discussion or conversation, arises and is considered. Midwesterners have a particularly rich mythology. It is the mythology of all America in a Midwest setting and often carried to Midwest extremes. It was not so rich in the old days of pioneer and settler, for at that time very little of the old colonial folk mythology was brought into the region and remained there. There, as decade succeeded decade, the myths and mythology of a new America, and especially of a new Midwest, were built into the life of new peoples as the region itself was being built. Today, as if you were looking at a well-laid brick wall, you can trace these myths and the mythology like string courses, cornices, and quoins at different levels as the eye moves along.

The myths of a people, the common beliefs about their origins and their way of life, are extremely important. To vary the metaphor, they are the mortar which holds the social fabric together. As long as all subscribe to them, the building stands solid. If groups of the people pick at them, or if they weather badly, the solidity of the building and even its endurance become doubtful. It does not matter whether myths are those of heroes or of the way of life of a whole people. The myths of Henry V, Henry VIII, the Elizabethan age, Marlborough, Wellington, and Nelson were even more important and effective in the England of 1940 and 1941 than in that of 1914–18. The myths of the Czars Peter and Catherine, of Kutuzov and Suvorov, were deliberately invoked and broadcast by a new and strange Russia after 1939, with enormous effect. The myths of a Washington, Lafayette, Pulaski, Henry, Decatur, and many another hero are newer and probably even more effective in America.

But America, more perhaps than any other nation except the new Russia, has a rich mythology *of the people* and their way of life. These myths are more effective today in the Midwest than they are anywhere else in the country. The Midwest even has its own heroes of the people: Mike Fink of the Mississippi, Boone, Crockett, Custer, John Brown, Horatio Alger, Huck Finn, Abe Lincoln, and many another from fact and fancy. But it is with folk myths that we are more concerned here. They are general beliefs. They form most of the people's philosophy of life and much of their everyday vocabulary and sphere of discourse. They are more important in the Midwest because they were vitally necessary, as a social cement, after 1870. They were the medium of assimilation for all the peoples who flooded into the New Midwest and helped to make it what it is. Because the folk of the Old Midwest were more uniform in beliefs and social composition, they did not need these new myths. Strangely enough, however, most myths of the Midwest today were taken from the life of the Old Midwest which few midwesterners since 1890 ever saw or knew. To that extent, when midwesterners of today invoke or refer to these myths, they seem like modern Greeks or modern Italians employing the mythology of ancient Greece or Rome. That does not make the myths any less real or less effective; but it should be borne in mind. Moreover, as in almost everything else midwestern, these myths often lead to extreme, contrary, and paradoxical consequences, according as they serve different social purposes.

Midwesterners ardently believe in equality, yet it is equality of a kind and with extreme differences. Men are thought to be born equal. In fact, everyone knows they are not and often wishes they were. All parents know that. But men are supposed to be equal before the law and in opportunity. Again, everyone knows they are not. There are differences of status, different opportunities, different treatments under the law for white and Negro, the children in the schools of one city or township or county and another, the American of non-American descent before a judge of the same descent, the Democrat before a Democratic city machine's judge and the Republican before a Republican, the party member in the machine and the citizen who is not, and so on. Thus the Midwest way of life is closer to that of any other industrial region or country than the midwesterner's myths suggest.

There are highly developed economic strata in the life of the Midwest city and larger town, which we have already described; and these

179

strata are parallel in the main with many of the groupings of different national origin in the towns and cities. True, their able children move out of the parents' strata into other and more highly paid professions or occupations—which occurs in the towns and cities of other countries too; more so than midwesterners, or most Americans, think or will admit. But how do you tell who is able? By instilling the same things into a child or by evoking (educating) different things out of him? We shall have more to say on this when we discuss education, but it is enough to observe here that equality of opportunity is far from perfect and complete in the Midwest. It is, however, greater than in many other regions of America and greater than in most countries of the world.

In whatever occupation or grouping of national origin a midwesterner may be, the practical equality which he enjoys is largely that of his fellows in the same income brackets. The wider life, "the larger hope," expands as levels of income rise in the Midwest, just as it does anywhere else in the world. What the midwesterner really means, and in what he really believes, is the equality of opportunity for the able or gifted to rise in levels of income. If people are poor, if they have menial tasks, it is their level of merit or ability which is responsible. This explains why the passion for equality and for the average in the Midwest is nevertheless utterly and completely opposed to communism. Nowhere in America is communism as anathema as in this region. Equality really means a struggle to rise, a struggle for survival, and the struggle is not and cannot be between equals, despite the myth. It actually operates to produce an élite, as did that of the Victorians: an oligarchy of highly remunerated professional or businessmen who, significantly, are called civic or business "leaders." This is what makes the Midwest seem to European observers the most bourgeois or middle-class region of America—which is what Victorian England seemed to Europe and America.

This leads to the next myth: that of liberty. Liberty in the Midwest is personal. It is individualism begotten by equality out of fraternity. But, again, it is individualism of a kind and with a difference. The citizen must stand or fall on his own and by his merits; but his occupation shows his merits. If he had greater merits, he would have a more highly paid occupation. It is that simple. Individual liberty is exceedingly cherished. Nowhere else in America during the second World War were so many legal cases decided in favor of the defendant, in favor of spies or aiders and comforters of saboteurs, and in favor of men or corporations challenging the powers of the federal government and its

180

agencies. There is much to admire in this, as there was in the great cases on civil liberty laid down between 1840 and 1914 in England. But the myth of liberty as a completely personal and individual possession is not applied consistently and logically to all associations of individuals, and not to all individuals. For example, the liberty of employers, individually and collectively, is accepted far more as an article of faith, as a real folk myth, than the liberty of workers in trade-unions.

The inquiring foreigner is told that this is due to the racketeers and bosses in the unions and to the absence of compulsory accounting to union members, which makes of many unions and their local organizations a "plunderbund." The foreigner recognizes that but also remembers where the word "boss" originated and wonders how the unions, union leaders, and labor relations are ever to improve. Lest it be thought that these liberties are alone in question, he observes that the liberties of Negroes and slum-dwellers of all national origins have availed little in the majority of city courts in the Midwest when they were in conflict with the interests of the owners of the property; and the attitude of the police and other authorities varies according to the prominence or residential locality of the citizens.

Employers, trade associations, and others have the unquestioned liberty of contributing to political funds; but when the C.I.O. established its Political Action Committee in 1944—indeed, ever since—the consuming wrath of the millions in the middle and upper income brackets in the Midwest was greater than anywhere else in America, including Philadelphia and the South. There is the same attitude to socialists as an entire group: even more so to communists, who are illegal as a party in many states. This version of the myth of liberty seems paradoxical alongside the great care with which spies, saboteurs' friends and relatives, and violent criminals are defended and their rights upheld. It would appear that the Midwest, its states, and its courts fear new political and social ideas more than they fear treason or crimes of violence. They may be right, but liberty is thereby particularized. It tends to become what the local police can be told to enforce or not to enforce.

Liberty, in other words, is the individual's freedom within a sharply defined pattern of society laid down in advance and generally interpreted by the local authorities. Changing the application of that great and life-giving principle means changing the life, the pattern, of Midwest society. It is happening, slowly and gradually, but because of influences from outside the Midwest; and many, if not most, midwesterners do not like the change. Thus, in respect of liberty, too, the Midwest which is so youthful, vigorous, and enterprising in so much, is also in many ways traditional and conservative, even by English standards. This paradox, for instance, caused fervently democratic midwesterners between 1942 and 1945 to fear that England was "going socialist." I asked many friends for their opinion when the British Labour party won their crushing victory in 1945. I was often told, "America is not a democracy; it is a republic; it has a written constitution which cannot, thank God, be changed by a simple majority vote in an election." As Li'l Abner and the people of Dogpatch say, it's "confoosin', but amoosin'!" Over a century ago Tocqueville asked why democracies showed "a more ardent and enduring love of equality than of liberty." He could well ask again, today, in the Midwest. The midwesterners' myths, like the people, are new and young. But, as the people are mixed, mobile, and changeable, the myths often get tangled in inconsistency when you seek to apply them.

There are other myths which, upon examination, do not bear out their popular meaning in practice. There is certainly complete freedom of speech, more complete than anywhere else on earth. It is consistently upheld and protected. But the freedom of the press has been tempered by the growth of "chains" of ownership, by the growth in power of the owner and his views, and by the growing power not only to impress but also to suppress. We shall see more of that in a later chapter. Then there is the pioneer myth: the belief that the Midwest today breathes the spirit of "pioneers, O pioneers!" It does in most of its industries, but in the way of life of its people it has steadily become more and more all-American. There is far more questioning of the ability to pioneer today: to start a factory, a newspaper, a radio station, or even a store. Then there is the allied myth that the Midwest is more democratic than other regions of America. This is only true in practice if we define "democratic" by reference to the Midwest conceptions of equality and liberty, already discussed. Midwesterners are more natural, less mannered, more free-and-easy, more prepared to take a man at his own valuation. That may be a sign of being more democratic; it probably is so on the farms; but it is not necessarily so in the towns and cities, as you discover the longer you live there. Then there is the myth of progressiveness, go-aheadedness. Midwesterners believe they are the most progressive Americans. In industry, again, they probably are. But many Midwest myths hold true in practice only of industry or business. As soon as you branch off to social policy, education, local government, civil administration, the arts, or the life of the mind, these myths become more mythical, in the popular sense of that word.

182

There is the myth that government is "we, the people": that it is of the people, by the people, and for the people. That is fairly true in the agricultural districts and small towns, but it is not exactly true of the cities. The minority of the electorate that votes in local elections shows that; and in state or national politics the papers of the party out of power—and often of the party in power—show that the people have little control of their candidates or representatives or of who selects them. And this holds true, on their own public admission, despite "direct primaries," conventions, delegates, and committeemen. Machines of all kinds have their own laws by which they run or are run. We shall see more of this, too, anon. The city machines and the party machines in each state have reached a degree of efficiency which would have staggered Bryce, who thought the American two-party system of the 1880's the most efficiently run piece of political machinery in the world. Caucuses, smoke-filled rooms, "boys in the back room," deals within parties and between them, fusion candidates—the operations and results of these would also have staggered Lincoln, adroit party politician as he was. The important thing, however, is not how a thing works but how the mass of the people *think* it works. There is no doubt that belief in the myth is general; and that, by itself, is a help. It preserves that rule of public opinion which so impressed Bryce, which impresses the observer today, and to which dictators as well as democracies have to pay heed.

There is another Lincolnian myth: the belief that midwesterners more than any other Americans, or non-Americans for that matter, behave "with malice toward none, with charity for all." Like many other human beliefs, it is more of an ideal or a statement of intention than a fact. Alongside this belief you find racial tensions, social tensions, friction between labor and capital, friction between labor and labor, the bigotry of certain religious sects, the narrow-mindedness of the small community, and the overweening political intolerance of extremists in both parties. These tensions, and the violent emotions into which they (perhaps fortunately) often explode and are thus temporarily dissipated, are those of youthfulness and vigor. But they are not less obvious than in other parts of America. With one or two exceptions—the racial issue is one of the exceptions—they are more extreme and more obvious than elsewhere.

Midwest life in the cities and big towns is surprisingly split up into groups of all kinds: of racial or national origin and of the poor at the center; and of the well-to-do in suburbs which govern themselves. The life of the city or town as a whole escapes you. Each citizen thinks it is that of his own locality, and he seldom "visits with" people outside his own income bracket. There is an utterly surprising segregation and insulation of social life. It goes by layers—as, indeed, it does in other countries, but as midwesterners prefer to think it does not in their own region. The life of the Italian, German, Polish, Bohemian, Greek, or Hungarian quarter continues on its way in a partial vacuum. These Midwest city dwellers live cohesively in localities; the Irish, Scotch, British, and Scandinavians do not. Thus you find clearly marked national localities in which "foreign" languages, customs, religions, newspapers, and local politicians are perpetuated and from which only a minority of the young drift away into all-Americanism.

Such Midwest city communities, strange to say, show a time lag in their way of life compared with the way of life of the contemporary Italians, Poles, Germans, Bohemians, and so on in the respective countries of Europe. I have often heard Irish, Germans, Italians, Bohemians, Poles, Greeks, Hungarians, Serbs, Lithuanians, and Croats in many Midwest cities and towns—and more often than not in their native tongues—excitedly arguing and debating "their" peoples' claims or rights, though they were all Americans, most of them were American-born, and most had never set eyes on "the old country." This alone makes for continuing tensions and, if not divided allegiances, at least what psychologists call ambivalence: emotional conflicts. No other country and no other region of America has this problem to the same widespread extent throughout its cities or big towns. It powerfully offsets and modifies the myth of "malice toward none and charity for all," though at the same time it emphasizes and stimulates the need for the translation of that myth into practice. And, for their encouragement and to their honor, midwesterners recognize the gulf between this myth and current practice and the dangers of it more than they do the divergence of any other of their myths from reality. They are right. The attendant dangers are greater, for the less perfectly assimilated midwesterners have long been reproducing themselves at a far faster rate than those who are perfectly assimilated. Political power goes with numbers, as Jefferson foresaw. As numbers increase disproportionately, the omen looms larger.

Finally, there is the myth of "life, liberty, and the pursuit of happiness." I write on this with great doubt and diffidence. Midwesterners are less constrained and less inhibited in their life and their pursuit of happiness than any people I know, American or not. But, as I know of no standards for life or happiness, I cannot say how far the myth corresponds to reality or how it compares with the realities in other regions

184

of America. What is important, however, is that the midwesterners of the cities know that no one knows what these standards are. So with faultless logic and sound common sense they let everyone go his own way and find out for himself. In this respect, life in the smaller towns is utterly different. It is far more restricted to an imposed, average standard. Whenever the midwesterner mentions this myth, as he frequently does, he seems to make "liberty" approximate more closely to "happiness" than to "life." To one observer, at any rate, he seems to mean "the right to do as you damn well please if it makes you happy"; in which case liberty comes perilously near meaning license. I am probably wrong in this; but it is my impression.

The pursuit of happiness, contrary to general belief about the Midwest, is not just the pursuit of money or material things. Money and material well-being help you along the road to happiness, as they also advance you along paths to a good many other goals, including anxiety and outright misery. It depends which kind of way you travel when you begin to acquire money and possessions. In this, the midwesterners of the cities do not differ from other Americans. But they seem to show more sense of "live and let live" in their interpretation of the phrase. In that, they are far more tolerant of foibles, eccentricities, and crankiness than other Americans. If a man wants to walk down the street leading a lobster on a green ribbon, let him. Midwesterners, I think, would show their native curiosity, gaze, linger a little, and pass on. I very much doubt if the police would have to clear the sidewalk or even open with that ominous gambit, "Hey, what goes on here?" It is in this context, rather than in that of civil or political liberty, that "liberty and the pursuit of happiness" become one and the same, complete, perfect. On the other hand, such an event would be as impossible for the resident of a small town as for him to proclaim himself an atheist, a monarchist, or an adulterer. This emphasizes the width of the chasm between city life and small-town life in the region and also of the chasm which this myth tries to bridge.

A man is an individual. He has a right to be himself, whether he is a crank, a crackpot, or just plain crazy. Provided he does not endanger life or limb or hold up traffic, he can go ahead—like the drunk I once passed at noonday on North Clark Street in Chicago offering big bills from a full wad to the passers-by. (Not a soul took one, though I watched his erratic progress for two blocks.) Each to his taste: liquor, crankiness, total abstinence, anti-Semitism, conscientious objection, red-light districts, craps, the numbers, the horses, free silver, any religion or none, Bible belt and Rush Street, dice girls, poker, Moody

Bible Institute, the man who advertises in the Sunday papers that he can guarantee you salvation, and he who also advertises that he can rejuvenate you or "can call spirits from the mighty deep." Who knows where is solace or salvation? What is happiness? Give a fellow a chance. "He knows about it all; he knows; he knows."

CERTAINTIES AND UNCERTAINTIES

In everyday life in this region of extremes nothing strikes the stranger with more force than a nervous restlessness, a lack of repose in the people. It belies all their self-assurance. It is not new, nor is it peculiarly midwestern. Tocqueville over a century ago asked why Americans were "so restless in the midst of their prosperity." But in the Midwest the tempo of life, its constant mobility, and the abundant energy of the people heighten and perpetuate the extremes within which they spend their lives; and these extremes make very many people ride on their nerves. They have such a superfluity of energy and vigor that it spills over. But into what? Their curiosity and thirst for "some new thing" suggest that they cannot be satisfied by the material marvels they have produced. Among the peoples of older countries, in which for this purpose the East and South of the United States can to some extent be included, more developed cultural activities, a more stable social life, more settled religious beliefs, or more privacy and solitude help to contain and assuage modern restlessness. In the Midwest, vitality overflows into a youthful St. Vitus' dance, "gets things done," but also finds its way into extremism, crankiness, and fads. Yet, significantly, these eccentricities are all organized.

This is naturally not true of the farmers or of life in the small towns. But in the larger towns and cities you run into a bewildering array of conflicting and extreme attitudes on the part of many perfectly delightful and kindly people whose lives, judged by material standards, leave nothing to be desired. Widespread feelings of discontent and dislike, passionate expressions, extreme views and utterances, intolerance: these, among so kindly and generous a people, bewilder the stranger. The fact that they are organized and advertised, as if to meet a demand, is even more bewildering. They suggest that there is some maladjustment, some lack of stability or poise, some loss of equilibrium, perhaps even some malaise among these new midwesterners of town and city. Some such evidences we noted among the characteristics of pioneers and settlers, but they were periodic then. This new Midwest is so different from the old; so are the people; and the restlessness, nervousness, and extremism seem continuous. It is a puzzle.

186

Take one example: when most midwesterners "get together," they are less inhibited than other Americans; but their gregariousness seems exaggerated, as if they could only relax or become uninhibited in company. Then come noise, organized entertainment and diversion, and—often—much hard liquor. The interesting question, however, is: Are midwesterners frequently and hurriedly seeking to escape from something in each other's company? If so, from what? Why do they flee solitude and abjure privacy?[1]

Up to the fifties in men, and up to the sixties or even the seventies in women, midwesterners keep moving in huddles: parties, clubs, societies, associations, collective games, meetings, lectures, and so on. They seem always to be visiting or visited; yet, as we also saw, most of it is in their homes. And, as we also saw, they prize the individual and individualism in other walks of life more than other Americans prize them. What lies behind this paradox?

It is one of the most intriguing, and one of the most revealing, of all the paradoxes in Midwest life. It is also one which makes the observer beware of generalizations. When you think these people have displayed a characteristic, you find they have shown only a paradox; and you have immediately to go round and see the other side of it. With these other sides we are now concerned.

The ordinary feeling for the equality of all men in their everyday social lives is probably at its deepest and strongest in the Midwest. Once, up until 1900, there was a "society" in the cities and larger towns which all citizens, when these cities and towns were smaller, respected: not as inferiors respect superiors but as members of a community respect those who run it. That was a period of Victorian certainty about everything. Today, except possibly in St. Louis, Cincinnati, Chicago, and Cleveland, such a "society" has vanished. Even in these big cities, as well as in the smaller cities and towns, fashions, modes, and culture have become more all-American. There is more restlessness; there are more currents and cross-currents. At the same time the community spirit has died out of the centers of cities and grown in their satellites or in the smaller towns. Yet that community

---

[1] "When we examine the moments, acts, and statements of all kinds of people— not only the grief and ecstasy of the greatest poets, but also the huge unhappiness of the average soul, as evidenced by the innumerable strident words of abuse, hatred, contempt, mistrust, and scorn that forever grate upon our ears as the manswarm passes us in the streets—we find, I think, that they are all suffering from the same thing. The final cause of their complaint is loneliness" (Thomas Wolfe, "God's Lonely Man," in The Hills Beyond [New York: Harper & Bros. and Avon Book Co., 1944]).

spirit, greater than almost anywhere else, has in many ways become a more restricting, narrowing, and average-making influence.

Average-conscious neighbors, in a community living wholly in the public eye, can be as repressive, inhibiting, and ruthless as aristocrats: even more so, for aristocrats are few, and an aristocrat is not so concerned how the mass of the people live their lives. They do not impinge on his. In many smaller towns of the Midwest it is impossible for a teacher, professor, civic leader, or politician to drink a glass of beer in public or have a bottle of beer seen in the home. It is impossible for the lady librarian to be in public with a male visitor to the town after six o'clock in the evening. Private and public discussion of any controversial moral issue is highly inadvisable for such people. So you get another paradox: there is more individual freedom to live one's life as one sees fit in the centers of the big and smaller cities than in their satellite communities or the small towns. Yet it is in just these smaller places that communal effort and communal life often achieve the best results. Thus, the midwesterner and his family who form a unit in such a community are in many ways far less free from constraints and conventions than an English, French, Swedish, or Swiss family at the same relative standard of living. Equality and community mean averages. And averages do not make outstanding individuals. This is what Emerson meant when he said "our prevailing equality makes a prairie tameness." If it is equality at the average level, it does.

But it is not an equality of the average. Social classes are not supposed to exist in the Midwest; and almost every midwesterner tells the visiting Englishman that what is wrong with England is its class society. Yet if you ignore labels and look at the people, you find another paradox. In England there are well-defined class *distinctions*, recognized by all classes and marked by accents more than by level of income. But there is also an extraordinary absence of any class *hatreds*, or of anything like a class struggle—much to the disgust of communists after their long, zealous, and arduous labors there. In the Midwest, on the other hand, there are no distinctions of class. Certainly differences of accent do not mark them. There are only levels of income and grades of work or function. But there are plenty of class divisions in society. There are different sides of "the tracks" everywhere. There is a good deal of passionately expressed class hatred, and more recently there has been something of a class struggle—or perhaps I should say a struggle between groups at different levels of income and grades of work. Much of this may be the mere, frothy explosiveness of views and attitudes in the Midwest, but it expresses tensions. The English and

188

other foreigners still have "classes" on their trains; yet many midwesterners seem to think that everyone in America travels Pullman. Again the European servant—domestic, public, or civil—is supposed to be servile. In the Midwest the breezy familiarity of servants, domestic or public, asserts their equality with all men. But in the country and region of service there is more than a trace of defiance in this assertion of equality, as if fellow-Americans were being reminded that the servant is not a servant but an "operative" or a person clothed in some authority —just as clerical workers want to be called "executives" or "assistants" or any other title which suggests a difference from clerks and white-collar workers.

This leads to yet another paradox in the context of equality: the constant striving to give impressions of distinction and inequality. This, too, is American, but greatly in evidence in the Midwest. There is a consuming hunger for recognition as a significant individual by one's community, for "social significance," for distinction either as a person or as a member of a group. Indeed, if distinction from one's fellows and from the average cannot be obtained by individual achievement or prowess, then it is obtained by joining clubs, orders, fraternities, and so on. Nowhere in the world are there so many of these groups per head of population; nowhere is there so much associational life; nowhere in time of peace so many uniforms, badges, conventions, titles, and the use of titles. True, they are all employed in the name of equality or fraternity, and within the setting of the club, society, order, legion, or other association. But they clearly meet a general need. What is it? Friendship, community, service, social solidarity, certainly; relaxation and relief from boredom or monotony, certainly; and to that extent the necessary assimilation of so many different kinds of people, and the cement for the social fabric, are well provided. But something of a problem remains.

It is the same unanswered, if not unanswerable, problem: To what is the restlessness or dissatisfaction due, which drives midwesterners to such a pitch and tempo of associational life? What are he and she seeking? Certainly all the outward evidences of life in the Midwest suggest that they are seeking, hunting, for something. If their discontent is often divine, because it drives them to great achievements, it is certainly purchased at a great price. The incidence of nervous and emotional disorders in the towns and cities of the region is higher than in many European countries, though probably no higher than in the East of America. In the second World War one of the greatest problems in the Midwest, as in the East, was the extraordinarily and sur-

189

prisingly high percentage of mental and emotional handicaps preventing the acceptance of men between eighteen and thirty-eight in the armed forces, and the equally high percentage of those discharged from the forces both before and after combat because of "neuropsychiatric conditions." This has been increasing throughout this century. It is not just because the doctors' activities and definitions have become more comprehensive or more general in application. Nor is it confined to men, or to men under thirty-eight.

The stranger may be wrong but he may be forgiven if he thinks there is a connection between this nervousness and the vigor of the people, the insufficiency of outlets for it, the reduction in hours of work, the speeded-up intensity of work in those reduced hours, and the preponderant (though not, as we saw, exclusive) materialism and the tempo of life. Most midwesterners are in such a hurry to enjoy the present, and turn the future into it, that they seem, like Figaro, to be wondering whether the world will last three months. But after a spell of this, the limits of material and external relaxation, within one city or community, are reached and overtaken. Then what? Either the round begins anew, making first for boredom and monotony and later for a feeling of caged frustration; or else the midwesterner has to seek for resources which are nonmaterial, which are within himself or herself. If those resources do not exist, the same goal of caged frustration is reached by a different path. Nothing and no one is more dangerous than a young person who does not know what to do.

In the rural communities most of the frustrated, bored, and discontented leave. They go to the larger towns or cities, which naturally heightens the hectic tempo of life there. It tempts the observer to think that the problem is solely one of the cities. But that is wrong. What actually happens is that the average folk, the "conformists," stay in the small communities and thereby solve their own problems by conforming to the stricter religious or moral principles of the community. Their ambition and self-expression are limited to, and by, the small community. On the other hand, the "nonconformists," those dissatisfied with the life of the small communities, those whose frustration drives them forth to seek and hunt for some new thing, flock to the cities, where they have greater personal freedom, where they try everything once, but where they also seem quickly to rediscover the frustration after a time lag of some months' or years' experimentation.

This hunt to allay frustration is evidenced on all sides by an astonishing variety of superstitions, palmists, spiritualists, queer religions advertised in the papers, elixirs, cranks' literature and meetings, and

190

advertisements of the secret of eternal bliss or eternal life. They are all profitable at the cost of their patrons, although the effect of the drug wears off. Then the drug and druggist have to be changed. But very often it is the same syndicate working through an employee who is another druggist. I discovered an example of that when I found a Chicago carpenter who had a fat contract to build secret closets behind a medium's wainscoting whence, in adequate gloom, "spirits" could emerge. He was paid by a syndicate which also ran two very modernistic "churches"—one in a well-to-do residential district—and a pool hall: quite a profitable cross-section of life.

But such eccentricities are not only proof of a sense of frustration and a compelling curiosity. They are also evidence of doubts and uncertainties. And here emerges another paradox: self-confident and self-assured as midwesterners are, great as are their capacities and achievements, they show many evidences of an inferiority feeling. They show it toward art, culture, and the life of the mind. They show it toward easterners and foreigners. They have doubts. Their assurance is generally confined to things material. Beyond that, assurance is not so sure; so they shout or whistle louder as they go through dark, strange, or lonely places.

Much of their noise is mistaken for self-certainty, self-importance, and toughness. In fact, midwesterners, as soon as they feel themselves on strange or lonely ground, are engagingly youthful, human, and not a little pathetic. It is this paradox, more than perhaps any other, that causes them to be so grievously misjudged and misunderstood.

The midwesterner of today lives most easily and at his best, like most of us, within a recognizable and commonly accepted framework of conventional society. That is why, as American society has altered and run into crises, particularly since 1929, midwesterners have become more "jumpy" than most Americans. Uncertainties, abstract notions, nonmaterial considerations, trouble them deeply. They feel a sense of inadequacy in face of them, which is a most un-Midwest feeling. It is a strange feeling to people who do not like strangeness, even if they like newness, and even if they are curious.

Midwesterners naturally took to potted culture by the radio or the various printed digests, by the newspaper, the movie, the lecture, and the forum. These are laborsaving. Being very busy and hardworking people, they brought laborsaving devices to perfection. But this had disturbing effects. First, laborsaving devices increased leisure, especially for women; and that led straight back to the old question: leisure for what? In many cases it meant more boredom, more gregariousness, more frustration, more absorption in common of predigested thoughts, and a further quickening of the tempo of life. Secondly, potted knowledge and culture spell standardization. This makes men more and more creatures of habit, more and more conformable to pattern, less and less individualistic. And this again leads to boredom, frustration, and hectic attempts to avert them.

Midwesterners for a long time have put a lower value on the original and creative life of the mind than they have on material things, practical affairs, common sense, and what they term "realism." Accordingly when issues arise, or when they are in contact with ideas, which are critically important but not capable of being measured by business, or even by material, standards, they feel nonplussed. It is on such ideas that midwesterners show ignorance. Like all young people, therefore, they then display the strongest evidences of inferiority feeling or of inadequacy in an unfamiliar setting. An alien world has invaded them. They do not know where they are. And, in that, they are certainly not alone. The Russians today show many of the same characteristics: an outward assurance and dogmatism that may well mask doubts and uncertainties. Even Emerson's self-assured British are no longer so assured and react accordingly.

But midwesterners are different, for their distrust of intellect and the life of the mind is longer and more traditional. In this, there is a straight line of descent from the Old Midwest. Many pioneers thought practical abilities, native wit, and common sense worth more than "book larnin'." The pioneers quickly had to drop the old colonial rationalism in favor of rifle and ax. They became men of action who, later, became the folk type for business. President Lincoln told the soldiers that any one of them could do his job "as well, or better." Behind this there is an engaging modesty. But there is also a belief that all men ought to be equal, ought to be on an average, even if they are not born so. As the Dodo said after the Caucus race: "Everybody has won and all must have prizes." No one must be outstanding—except in business and wealth, for that is the reward to the best individuals. Every soldier must wear marks and badges of distinction. Even if not every soldier is a hero, he can be made to look like one and believe he is one—which is vastly important to a soldier. People must believe that they can all be captains, as in the frontier wars, or, in modern times, in industry. Though this is all-American, it is even more characteristically midwestern.

Culture, mainly brought into the Midwest by the efforts of its heroic women, and to a great extent kept alive today by their grand-

192

daughters and great-granddaughters, was always and is still to some extent thought by most of the men to be effeminate. So are etiquette and any manners which are polished. This has had the unfortunate effect, in turn, of developing in the majority of midwesterners a sense of inferiority in intellectual and cultural matters—a sense which is not always justified. Apologetically they will say they are too busy. Or they will use the defense mechanism of crying down or pooh-poohing the arts, literature, intellectual affairs, "long-haired" professors, and the life of the mind. Naturally, also, they will show a chip on the shoulder about Americans of other regions who accord a higher place to the cultivation of arts, letters, and the intellect; and, by the same token, toward most foreigners. By itself this would not be serious if it did not have widespread social consequences among the mass of the people. If its effects were confined to business, it might be all right—though that is extremely dubious today.

The worst effect is a natural by-product of all this. It is the belief in, and even satisfaction with, popular ignorance. The ignorance of the great mass of the people in the Midwest is assumed to an astonishing and unwarranted extent by the press, radio, advertising agencies, public relations experts, professional charity organizers, and so on. Either they are right or wrong. If they are right, then they present a grave indictment of their society, which is themselves and their fellows. If they are wrong, they insult the public who, however, do not appear to feel insulted. These agencies place astonishingly low estimates on human nature, impulses, motives, reason, logic, ability to think, emotions, and sentiments. No foreigner could ever be as uncomplimentary about midwesterners' level of knowledge, power to discriminate, and general maturity as are the press, radio, films, and advertising media of America. Because such low estimates certainly "pay," in the shape of contributions from the public, it does not follow that the public either merits or likes them. But it is generally assumed that what pays is all right; and "culture and taste don't pay." Accordingly, culture and the intellect are at a discount. Cleverness and smartness are at a premium. Business provides the material things of life. What pays business must be right. It is "what the people want." They do not want ideas or culture. They want washing-machines, movies, soap operas. And if they don't want So-and-so's soap, they can be made to. That is how the argument is put to the stranger.

Again this might be all right if placing the life of the mind far below business were really democratic. That is one of the paradoxes. It is no more democratic in the Midwest of 1945 than when Emerson described

193

it in England a century before. It is no more democratic to make all things and standards bow to business than to make them bow to farmers, aristocrats, kings, professors (as in the old Germany), or red-headed persons. It would also be all right if the undervaluing of cultural and intellectual life, and a sense of inferiority about it, had not spread so widely and led to many completely irrational and intolerant movements among rich and poor alike. The trouble about pooh-poohing or ignoring the life of the mind is that it often leads to a pooh-poohing of human reason, in politics as well as in other walks of life. It is when the stranger thinks of this that the nervously hectic attempts to avert boredom or frustration by midwesterners do not seem so lightly to be dismissed as harmless "fun" or fancy. In this respect the farmers and those who dwell in small towns, despite their cramping of the individual's abilities for self-expression, have sounder foundations beneath their way of life.

Midwesterners are very distrustful of the intellect, of artists, and of culture. Therefore, many of them unhesitatingly accept all sorts of ideas in predigested form. It seems strange, however, that they should so actively distrust anything that savors of propaganda; that they should strain at a gnat which resembles an official statement, yet uncritically swallow a camel of predigested opinion provided for them by private interests. It looks like a complete inability to discriminate. If so, that cannot serve the good of society as a whole, though it may serve some interests. There is one offsetting feature, however, though it is scarcely happy. Midwesterners have recently and very rapidly become skeptical of all print, radio, and other mediums of communication. "It's the bunk," you hear on all sides. This could be a healthy sign if the skepticism were merely blasé; the skepticism of cautious and shrewd men, intellectually well equipped, who kept their feet on sound beliefs. Strangely enough, that *is* the skepticism of businessmen. They have their feet on a set of positive beliefs. But what worries a minority of forward-looking midwesterners is that this latter-day skepticism of the people, in default of trust in human reason and the free life of the mind, may slip easily and quickly over the edge into utter cynicism. Then what would become of the folk myths, the social cement, the structure of Midwest society, the interests of businessman, worker, editor, minister, and teacher alike?

For this, much of the "anti-ism" of the Midwest, from the anti-rationalism of the pioneers downward, is responsible. Today the man of action, the modern pioneer, the rugged individualist par excellence, the man with the gun and the ax, is the business leader. Practically all businessmen identify themselves with him. Like their pioneer proto-

194

types, very many of these men, especially "little businessmen" and small retailers, are fundamentally anti-rationalist, critical of colleges, universities, professors, polite accomplishments, the humanities, and the arts. It is perhaps understandable, as they are the practical romantics of a merchant-adventurers' age. They are dead against permitting any teachers or advocates of these subjects to have any say, or even any activity, in local and national politics or civic and public affairs. Naturally there are many great and, I would even say, noble exceptions. But another astonishing paradox arises: where so many businessmen munificently endow great and small institutions of research, culture, and learning, the majority of businessmen, if not of all Midwest men, want the teachers and their results to have no effect on politics or public affairs. The women and the youth are not nearly so sure about that. In the long run it is, of course, impossible; and happily that is slowly being demonstrated. But "in the long run we are all dead." And in the short run it provokes constant tensions, the frustration of potentially great minds, the quitting of the region by many of its promising people, and many personal tragedies among leaders of the life of the mind and those who want to learn of them.

This extreme Midwest love of the practical and hatred of theory, as they are termed, recalls an apt remark in the German Reichstag last century by Ludwig Bamberger. Twitting Bismarck and the representatives of German big business, he said: "What these gentlemen can't deny, they call theory; and what they can't prove, they call practice." This anti-rationalism and distrust of "the clever" or "the cultured" is by no means a pecularity of the Midwest, or indeed of America; but in that region it seems to be more thrust upon you. In this, as in other things, the Midwest is healthily frank. British and Americans share the unique distinction of using the word "clever" to suggest something questionable or depreciatory about someone. And every traveled Englishman knows how much personal tragedy and frustrated hope lies behind the impressive mask and reserve of Englishry. The very openness and frankness with which this same attitude is displayed and discussed in the Midwest may help midwesterners, as it helps them in so many other ways, to solve, by-pass, or compromise.

Vigorous and youthful, midwesterners marry young, though not as young as southerners. The average age for first marriages among men is a little over twenty-four, and for women about twenty-one and a half. The two-fifths of the people who live on farms and in rural areas marry even younger. This means that many marriages must be contracted very young indeed, to give such lower averages than in Europe. This is good for society because women have their first and other children while they are young, and the social nucleus of family and home also begins young. But it imposes enormous strains on youthful and mainly inexperienced people.

The man is transformed, perhaps too rapidly, from being able to behave as a boy or a youth to being a husband and father. From having virtually no responsibilities and being forgiven for everything by all, he has suddenly to stand on his feet and support one or two more other people on theirs. At the same time in all cities and larger towns he is in the fiercely competitive, thrusting, elbow-jostling business life of the Midwest. "After hours" he shares in the responsibilities and duties of home and, with his young wife, in the gregarious diversions of midwesterners. He is still a young man. Like all young men of Western countries, he is in fact younger in many psychological respects than his forebears were at his age a century or more ago. But he has a longer life, on the average, ahead of him; and if it is less physically strenuous, it is far more nervously exhausting.

True, the region offers great opportunities to able young men; but this ability also means ability to stand the strain. If he makes good, it certainly means more dollars, a nicer home, probably more children, and certainly more for his wife. But it also means that he regularly rises into levels of keener and fiercer competition, on each of which he becomes more and more vulnerable until, in his forties, he becomes established or "solid." The higher, the fewer but keener are the competitors, the greater the responsibilities, the greater the consequences of error. In this respect, the difference between the midwesterner and any other member of industrial society is one of degree only; but it is a real difference.

A century ago and more, the burden of the day weighed more heavily and fatally on the women of the Midwest. They were rare and precious. They died young, often in childbed; and any man could easily be a widower two or three times before he was forty. In Midwest city life today the shoe is on the other foot. Though the majority pull through, at a cost, the strain kills many able men young. The death rate among able executives between their late thirties and late fifties seems to be high. It strikes regularly within the circle of friends and acquaintances. In peacetime it is not uncommon to find women being widowed twice before they are fifty or sixty. There are many widows, and all women have a much longer expectation of life than men. The doctors' testi-

196

mony, the medical columns in nearly all newspapers, the advertisements in the press and on the radio, bear eloquent witness to the frequency of nervous disorders among both sexes. Much of this is due, on medical evidence, to the tempo of business life, to the almost equally rapid tempo of social life, to the kinds of diversion, and to lack of sleep and repose. The pioneer men had to stand only physical strain. A century or more later, midwesterners have invented thousands of devices to drive physical strain away, but many have ended by coming near the verge of nervous collapse. Where the Old Midwest survives, it is different.

The farmers and dwellers in small communities do not show anything like this degree of nervous strain. They are thought stuffy, narrow, or "hicks" by the city dwellers in consequence. That is not because they work less hard but because they relax less hard. The pace of working and leisure life is kinder to them. Home life, privacy, and repose are all greater and more common there. By the same token the masses of manual workers and those in the lowest income brackets in the big cities undergo less strain. Their hours are fixed, work is over when they go home, and they pursue simpler and more natural relaxations.

The man's struggle for a living is hard. No one should cherish the illusion that the higher standards of living of both the rich and the not-so-rich are easily earned and maintained in the Midwest. For most men the intensity of work is either extremely high or work is extremely monotonous. Wages and salaries that seem luxurious in Europe do not, in fact, buy anything like a proportionately higher variety of services, though they buy more goods. Goods can be mass-produced. Services cannot. The cost of any service in which hours of human labor, rather than of machine output, bulk large is three and four times higher than it is in western Europe, to say nothing of the eastern and southern parts of that continent. Accordingly, wages and salaries go farther than in Europe on goods, travel, and popular amusements and not so far on services or on the higher grades of entertainment, housing, and education. Though much money is earned, it is needed and must be regularly increased. The breadwinner, his anxieties, his tiredness, and his efforts to relax at home form the daily features of many national comic strips in the papers. "Poor old Pop" is a national figure with whom all have sympathy, even if the sympathy is not always practical.

All midwesterners, in cities or in small towns, show a commendable, unparalleled, and collective concern for the safety and well-being of women and children. Men are men, pioneers still, individualists. They

197

can, and ought to, fend more for themselves. They seem more tired at forty-five than most Europeans, and more aged. In that, too, they are romantics, adventurers, and Elizabethans. They do not shield themselves; and though their women are most considerate and loyally perform the ministry of marriage in so many ways, they cannot—they do not want to—shield their men. For one thing, the men, being venturesome and eternally sanguine, resent being coddled. They do not believe in disaster or death, just as President Coolidge's preacher was "agin' sin." Mary Baker Eddy founded her church in solid, stable Boston; but its precepts correspond remarkably to the beliefs of Midwest businessmen and townsmen.

The wives naturally demand their relaxation from the arduous rearing of children, upkeep of the home, and commissary's or quartermaster's functions. The women's day begins when that of the men ends. If one partner wants gregarious, organized, and external relaxation, the other may want to stay at home. Thereby differences of nervous stamina and temperament are early and easily heightened. A higher proportion of marriages than in other lands—even of second marriages—goes on the rocks. There is something of the general haste and mobility in all this, just as there is also something of the belief in making the future into the present, taking time by the forelock, squeezing the orange of life dry, before old age or death catch up. It seems illogical, because in the cities and larger towns it seems to bring the catching-up nearer. Or, if it does not do that, it heightens experimentalism of all sorts, accelerates the whirl, intensifies restlessness, increases frustration, and often leads to neuropsychosis. Why, otherwise, was it necessary to persuade people that "life begins at forty"?

Women play a large part in all this. No one should think that laborsaving devices in the home are luxuries. In America, at least in the East and Midwest, they are necessities because domestic service, called "help" in token of equality, is anything from four to ten times as costly as in Europe. It is correspondingly rare. Moreover, as in the factory, a servant can do more in an hour with the aid of far greater capital equipment, of laborsaving devices, than a servant or factory worker in Europe can accomplish. Personal service being relatively rare, and self-service being the rule for more than nine-tenths of Midwest families, the average housewife has much to do. She generally has more space per member of the family than her European cousin at the corresponding standard of living. Laborsaving devices help her to keep the home that model of neatness, cleanliness, and tidiness which it almost invariably is, whenever you walk in, whether in cities, in towns, or on the farm.

She cleans, tidies, and cooks most zealously. She is deservedly and keenly home-proud and a natural-born hostess of infinite charm, kindliness, and consideration. In her home she is as resourceful as her husband in his business or on the farm; and she is as adaptable to unforeseen emergencies—which, in Midwest life at any rate, are many. She is interested, more than he, in more of the ideas and issues that swell the tide of contemporary thought. And she is often more alert, discerning, and discriminating than her overworked and overworking husband.

In the home she puts her husband and children first; loyally, conscientiously, and without question. She is still, deservedly, the heroine of the Midwest saga. She administers the family budget in the home and almost single-handedly brings the children up to adolescence. She is "Mom" to husband and children alike. It is not for nothing that American men, especially midwesterners, retain an unparalleled devotion to "Mom" which colors their inner lives and lasts as long as she lives, or longer. And the obverse of this, of course, is that the men are considered "boys," think of themselves as such, often behave as such, and are called "our boys," "the boys back home," and so on, all their lives. In this respect the region's youthfulness, too, is carried to an extreme; and, as "a boy's best friend is his mother," so are its maternal and feminine aspects carried to an extreme. Nowhere else, in America or outside it, are there so many evidences of man's dependence on, and interest in, women. The women repay it and foster it by great care of their figures and faces, their charm, and their appearance—even if they follow so many well-advertised fashions and ways to secure charm that so many seem standardized.

An unkind American wisecrack says that there are only two depressed classes in America: Negroes—and all white husbands. Just as the Englishman who wears a monocle and has an adenoidal accent is a curiosity in England, and is far more lampooned and caricatured there than he is in America, so the henpecked husband in the Midwest is a figure of fun, a feature of the comic strips, and almost as rare. That's the way it is with folk tales. It is not true, as nearly all Europeans believe, that American women are universally spoiled by their men; any more than it is true, as nearly all Americans believe, that all English wives are domestic slaves, all French wives are betrayed, and all German wives are whipped. There is surprisingly little difference between the status of the housewife and the running of a home in Cedar Rapids and Saint-Quentin, Chicago and Birmingham, Peoria and Mannheim, La Crosse and Bruges, or Cleveland and Budapest—at least for the great majority of housewives. It is out of the exceptions, the abnormal, that we fashion jokes.

But differences there certainly are. In the Midwest the average housewife has more time on her hands, though not much more, than perhaps any other in the world at a correspondingly relative standard of life. Laborsaving devices, well-designed homes, and great public or private services see to that. In that time, like her husband, she is more gregarious, mobile, and curious, more on the trail of some new thing. Yet much of the life of the community devolves upon her shoulders: "drives," reforms, improvements, charities, clubs, forums, discussion groups, cultural activities, diversions, and so on. For all this activity she seems to have a vast store of energy. The result, in the main, is that she has no real, personal spare time at all. It is mortgaged days, weeks, and even months in advance. If it is not, she goes to the telephone to find some other, or others, who are in like case and do not want to be alone, "doing nothing" as they say. In this she scarcely differs, at all, from her husband. She often becomes as nervously worn as he, for her day is exacting, too; and then both of them often seek relaxation of an intense kind outside the home when they are physically and nervously least fitted to do so. Such relaxation tends to become a stimulant or a bromide; and, as with drugs or liquor, the temptation is to increase the dose or the intensity in order to get the relaxing effect. After a time this often puts a strain on marriage.

The well-to-do wives in the cities and larger towns are as small a minority as those who shop in Bond Street or the Rue de la Paix. But the majority of them are far more tense and, apparently, highly strung. Certainly they are more restlessly on the go than the majority of well-to-do women in London, Edinburgh, and Dublin, Bordeaux, Munich, Milan, Amsterdam, Rome, Stockholm, Vienna, and Zurich. This naturally takes more out of their husbands and children than is the case in the great majority of Midwest families. It is in the parties of these women that voices seem more raised, more excited, and more in chorus than anywhere else—except perhaps in Hungary. In this respect there has been a very great change in "society" since 1900 or 1910. The cocktail and bridge party may have much to do with its effect among women. Race or national origin is not responsible for all this; for well-to-do women in Midwest cities show this characteristic whether they are of Anglo-Saxon, Celtic, German, Scandinavian, or other national origins. Well-to-do Jewish wives partake of the same characteristics. It forms the extreme example of that folkway of life which finds caustic portrayal in the pages of the New Yorker and of many American novels and writings. The hecticness and extremism to which it gives rise are not typical. But they are more obvious, just as a few voices raised in the dead of night sound like an army.

In the overwhelming majority of Midwest families "Pop" is not the underdog. He is not driven by his wife to make more and more dollars in order to "keep up with the Joneses." He is quite capable of providing that drive for himself, but not for that reason. He dislikes a back-seat driver in this regard as much as in motoring. He drives himself, unaided, but mainly out of generosity, devotion, and protective foresight; to provide wife and children with a bigger and better life. If, to use the language of some superficial American and foreign writers, he does not rebel at the "tyranny of women and children"; if he is resigned and tamed by the age of forty, it is not because his wife or family make him that way. The economic system and the most fiercely competitive life in the world have done so. He is resigned to that because he has to be. He can be only as successful in life as he can be adaptable. "It's silly to try to buck a trend." It therefore comes most easily to him to be extremely indulgent toward his wife and family. In view of what his wife does for that family, he should be. Although they are individualists, Midwest men put "women and children first." If they seem even more indulgent than women expect, or than some Americans think wise, it is probably because of the prevailing atmosphere of generosity and good nature. And the mixing in this region of so many different national attitudes to home, wife, and children has an effect, too. All these attitudes are very human and lie closest to people's hearts. Their mixture is all the more intense.

Professor Frank Dobie tells of a "sophisticated Frenchman" who thought Americans more preoccupied with sex than any people on earth.[2] To judge superficially by the extremes to which they carry the art of cheesecake, their emphasis on feminine curves in the press and out of it, their invention (or should it be perfection?) of strip-tease, their cult of "pin-up girls," the frequency and intensity of the sex motive in all forms of advertising and entertainment, and the programs of many places of entertainment, that might seem true. Certainly the cities of the Midwest would make it seem so; but equally certainly the smaller towns would disprove it. Yet cities and small-town life are peculiarly linked in responsibility for it. In this, as in so many things, there are a lot of paradoxes. Those who patronize the sellers of "feethy pictures," questionable haunts, and red-light districts anywhere in the world are, more often than not, men who are kicking over traces. But the traces

[2] *A Texan in England* (Boston: Little, Brown & Co., 1945), p. 26.

201

remain, and men nearly always return to them. Life in traces is the only possible social life. If Britishers, Americans, and midwesterners in particular were not at heart and by upbringing puritanical and conventional, they would not get such a kick out of "gay Paree"—nor would they behave so differently there from their conduct at home, nor would the Parisians get such a profit out of them. But the Britishers and Americans go back to Anglo-Saxon respectability, thinking the French immoral.

What every Midwest city, every large town, and even some smaller towns provide for men who want to kick over traces; what often occurs, most unconventionally, during conventions in big cities; what forms the dominant element in smoking-room stories, is not peculiar to America or to the Midwest. "Hypocrisy is the tribute that vice pays to virtue." There is much vice and hypocrisy in the Midwest; but that is because there was, and still is, so much virtue, respectability, and conventionality.

What seems unhealthy to the stranger in the Midwest is the degree to which vice is almost flagrantly organized by syndicates in the cities and towns; the degree to which it becomes entwined with police, politics, and bribery; and the degree to which not a few Midwest men have come to think of indulgence in it as proof of masculinity. This latter idea cannot be, as some suggest, the man's protest against "the tyranny of women"; for it is a very youthful and a general notion all over the world. There was always vice in the towns of the region; but it was not always so organized, so tied in with police and politics, rackets and graft; nor was it then deemed proof of being "the devil of a fellow." There were fights and other forms of physical prowess in which the early midwesterners could prove that. With the organization of vice, however, a certain "teasing" element has entered the picture. This is far from easy on the nerves of jaded or tired businessmen. Long-drawn-out oversuggestion and overstimulation are anything but relaxing. This has even invaded the film, stage, and public prints in subtler guises. The sex motive, simple in mere nudity, easily passes over to license, lasciviousness, and lubricity in many "sequences" or portrayed actions. The Hays office and city fathers can stop nudity; but they cannot always see the cumulative effect of suggestiveness. Again, this is not just midwestern; but in a region of extremes it has had an explosive effect in town and city, farm and family alike. Particularly has it affected the young.

It must, however, be said that street women are more rare in the region than elsewhere; and in profanity among Midwest men of all kinds, expressions of sex are less in evidence than they are in Britain, France,

Spain, Italy, Hungary, and most European countries. Here again is proof of the men's respect for their women and of the social power and influence of women themselves. Vice is kept private. That is its tribute to an all-pervading virtue. There are few street women, but there are "call girls" run by syndicates and "love nests." Vice does not flaunt itself.

Divorce has increased and is still increasing; but, again, this is not peculiarly midwestern and it is almost confined to city dwellers. On the farms and in the more constrained atmosphere of the small towns it is rare indeed. As in other countries, the effect of two world wars within a generation has been to slacken not only the traces of matrimony but also those of all personal and social morality; and to this the countryside and small towns seem comparatively immune. Here, again, the morality and public opinion of city and small town are extremely different. Many state laws, and the reciprocal recognition by states of any legal and bona fide divorce in another state, have put a premium on easy loosening of the marriage tie—to the financial profit of those states, and their lawyers, where very short residential requirements are purposely laid down.[3] But even in a state where the divorce laws are relatively strict—Illinois, for instance—the number of divorces increased tenfold between 1918 and 1938 and doubled between 1938 and 1944. It is increasing at a rate which alarms more than churchmen alone.

In the early 1920's an English author and critic complained that modern society was overvaluing children, aping children, worshiping youth, fearing age, scared of maturity and of responsibility, and behaving like children.[4] He thought it extremely dangerous for democracy, because it would lend to a demand for an all-wise "father" or leader. Well, nowhere are children more valued, prized, and better treated than in the Midwest. Nowhere are parents, and all society, so geared to the life of the young. Nowhere are the names and attributes of "boys" and "girls" so generally used by, or for, so many middle-aged men and women. Yet in no other country or region is divorce more general; and nowhere are the people more staunchly democratic and anti-authoritarian. How are we to reconcile these?

The slick critic talks of modern infantilism; of the bewildered adult trying to return to the comfort of the breast or to the shielding isolation

[3] The secretary of the Nevada state bar, also general manager of a sky ranch, announced in July, 1945, that, owing to rail transport difficulties for civilians, a special private air service would begin from New York and points west to Reno. This is real service. It meets all demands.

[4] Wyndham Lewis, *The Art of Being Ruled* (London: Chatto & Windus, 1924).

of the womb; of escapism from maturity and responsibility, as shown by films, radio, comic strips, and all other bromides which make life seem other than it is; of an *ersatz* life in which all men are heroes, Supermans, or Gables, and all women heroines, Dixie Dugans, or Lamarrs; of the philosophy of "as if"; of a current fairyland and its fairy tales that alone make the shocks, tempo, and monotony of modern life bearable. This sounds very plausible; but, like most plausible judgments, it is shallow and wrong. It refers only to the surface. Beneath it are profound truths that argue otherwise. Moreover, what there is of infantilism is exceptional. It is confined to small groups in cities. Among the great majority, children have to grow up, work, and be adult very young. Especially is this so among the non-Anglo-Saxon groupings of various national origins which are such a large element in the Midwest. It is also true of the farmers' families.

Midwest parents are realists toward their children, as they are realists in so much else. Their own youthful characteristics help them to show a friendly, big-brother, big-sister devotion to children that does not partake of sentimentality. It is too deep for that. Children are still treated as if they were rare; and in the rush and extremism of Midwestern life, with its more frequent wastages and accidents, epidemics and car deaths, this seems natural, despite the outstandingly high survival rate of children. Parents are strict and managerial with children until they are about ten years old. Then they trust their children infinitely more than parents do elsewhere, and at younger ages. They help them to break the law by having the car for themselves and their friends before the children are legally old enough to own a license. They let them stay out very late. It is common, in any large town or city, to find children of both sexes out together until midnight before they are sixteen, and from families in all income brackets.

Parents do not interfere in their children's lives as much as they do elsewhere. Whether it is right or wrong, good or bad, is another matter. It is significant that the parents in a community will never—"well, hardly ever"—put their heads together to lay down common parental rules, so that no child need fear the ridicule of its companions or the chill of isolation from the group. If Johnny or Louise So-and-so's parents let them do something, then "I guess we ought to let Dick and Nancy do it, too." This is evidenced in the children's fashions, their use of the parents' "charge accounts" at the local stores, the hours they keep, and the use of lipstick and other feminine aids by girls of fourteen. It is partly due to the early age of adolescence in the Midwest, which in turn is probably due to climate and to the mixing of so many strains of different national origins. But it is also due to the kindness and sympathy of parents, even if it puts stresses on young shoulders unable to bear it. At least it proves, drastically, whose shoulders will stand it and whose won't. It is rule of thumb, trial and error, which is always recognized as a costly method, if it often pays off.

One reason for all this is the extremely high degree to which the organized social life of children is carried in the schools. Parents have a great say in, and responsibility for, this, not only through their school boards but also through such admirable institutions as the Parent-Teachers' Association. But, in the main, children and young people are encouraged to run their own lives in common. It develops the initiative, competitiveness, and resourcefulness which characterize adult midwesterners, even if it makes the individual scared to go against the group in any way. That is one of the sources of the Midwest's emphasis both on individualism and on collective standardization. It often leads to a paradox.

Though Midwest boys and girls reach adolescence earlier than all European children except those in southern European countries, the girls achieve poise and maturity, both mental and temperamental, much earlier than the boys. A girl of sixteen or seventeen is a young woman in every way, inwardly and outwardly. The boy takes years longer to reach a parallel maturity. He seems to take longer to do so than his fellows in the East, South, or other regions of America, and longer than European boys. Outwardly he has as much, or more, liberty and resourcefulness. Inwardly he has not the poise, judgment, maturity, or ability of self-expression of his sister at the same age. This imposes a severe strain if two young midwesterners marry at or near the same age, as they generally do. The girl is years ahead of the boy in adulthood: more years ahead than her European, eastern, or southern cousin would be. Not only may this explain much of the men's self-consciousness toward, and dependence on, women. It may also explain why the boy is more conscious of "Mom," and why his maturity lags so far behind that of his sister. You have only to be in a roomful of young people at a party in someone's home, see the juniors or seniors in the high schools, or watch young people meeting or talking with others for the first time, to notice the outstanding poise, maturity, and easy self-expression of the girls. Something of this great difference between the female of the species and the male persists throughout life. It does not lessen the masculinity of men. It just makes a wider difference between men and women.

The young of both sexes are thrown together much more than elsewhere, at school and at play. They have more leisure and liberty. They see crude evidences of sex and materialism all around them. They see their parents and other adults in a whirl. They are curious and experimental. Life is uprooted, unstable. How can they be stable? The miracle of youth is that they are as stable as they are. In the big cities and larger towns, and to a less degree out in the countryside, rape by youths of fifteen or sixteen and upward seems astonishingly frequent to a stranger; and the great majority are not Negroes. Differences of national origin, maturity, and morality are many and great. That may be one reason. Another reason for the apparent frequency is the publicity given to such cases. The Midwest is very frank and matter-of-fact. It hides nothing, glosses nothing. Despite the local authorities' rooted opposition to birth control, in deference to the strong religious beliefs of so many Roman Catholics and strict Protestant sects, contraceptives are procurable everywhere. There are more cases of a girl of good family having a "mishap" at fifteen or sixteen, even in smaller communities, than the majority of parents realize. But the young people know all about it: and I mean "all." "Janie Smith's caught it; it was Bill Brown."

Parents are worried and discuss the problems of youth and juvenile delinquency with concern and open-mindedness. But serious cases are exceptional. To see these young people together, with their unparalleled vigor, vivacity, and liberty, makes a visitor from abroad wonder why the exceptions are not more numerous. There is a lot of the show and vocabulary of love taken from the movies, the press, and the radio; yet it is expressed overwhelmingly in puppy love. "Dates" and "going steady," at what to a visitor from abroad seems an incredibly early age, are serious to the young people concerned; but they do not end in mating— not for a long time. They form the earliest natural outlet, in a region of early adolescence, for the romantic vigor of the Midwest. They seem to affect boys' emotional balance and work far more than those of girls. Perhaps the girls, like their mothers, are more matter-of-fact and inwardly less romantic than boys and men. In any case, they mature earlier, and they are surprisingly well able to take care of themselves if the need should arise. That is a handsome tribute to the upbringing of children. The many hushed-up exceptions are the cost of a great gain: the early equality of status and comradeship between the sexes, the early understanding of the opposite sex, and the destruction of what in other regions and countries proves a dangerous myth of mystery about it. And before long two young people can easily marry if they want to and are both prepared to make and run a home. The only surprising result is not

206

the regularity of exceptions among the young but what seems to be a persistent and high degree of sex-consciousness among so many Midwest youths and men, and a corresponding elaboration of their attractiveness and femininity by girls and women. All this early familiarity between the sexes, thinks the visitor, will breed contempt. Quite the contrary: the appetite comes with eating.

Though Midwest parents show unexcelled love for their children, and children for their parents, both of them are surprisingly less demonstrative toward each other in public and in private than in Europe. I say "surprisingly," because, as the people are more emotional, you would expect the contrary. But, when children are grown up, they and their parents are more demonstrative to each other than when the children were younger. This is not true when it comes to babies, to whom everyone accords everything and in whom everyone is passionately interested. But it is true of all children after they are about five or six years of age. The parents *want* their children to grow up. They do not want them to be dependent or what is called "sissy." Pop wants his boy to be tough, to deal with the men and life among which he must live. He wants him to be strong enough to make a good living and to protect a wife and family. So Pop is dreadfully afraid of "sissiness." Mom is far less so and more natural toward the child; which, again, may explain why the Midwest boy goes to Mom rather than to Pop, and why he remains so intimately linked to his mother all his life. It may also explain why his sister gets her poise and maturity, and her great feminine charm, so much earlier. She is a woman; she has to be protected; she employs her arts early on Pop and generally with conspicuous success, as long as Mom is not around. The only peculiarly Midwest feature in all this is the degree to which it is carried.

It seems peculiar to the stranger if his daily paper is thrown onto his lawn (it generally misses the porch, especially in wet weather) by the son of a man whose income is anything from $5,000 to $25,000 a year. The European thinks: why not let the poorer boys earn the money? But the Horatio Alger tradition is strong. All boys must do something menial as if all the parents' incomes were equal, although at home or at play boys enjoy, or suffer, all the differences of their fathers' incomes. Many big businessmen started on a farm or in a factory or with a newpaper route. Undeniably it helps to emphasize equality, resourcefulness, and respect for work. But it also emphasizes inequalities and contrasts, especially when the boy's parents are in a higher income bracket and can give him better education, more advantages, more liberty, and more diversions at all other times than when he is on the paper route or in the factory during a vacation.

As midwesterners marry and have children earlier than most Americans and Europeans, they share more in children's interests and sports on vacation, for both the parents and their children are young. The automobile has been an enormous boon in this respect, too. Camping, canoeing, fishing, hunting, hiking, renting a cabin in the woods—all these testify to the influence of the Old Midwest on the new midwesterners. It comes out very clearly in their sports and vacations. In this, too, it is a case of "women and children first." On an average they get longer vacations. But Pop has his shorter holiday with them, and on vacation—in woods, by lakes, in the many beautiful national parks, and in other regions of America or sometimes even in Canada—midwesterners really relax. They put the tempo of social life far behind them. Rich and not-so-rich alike take their vacation as a family unit until Pop is forty. By then the young folk go off to camp or with other young people and other families, and both Pop and Mom need quieter vacations. The poor cannot do this; but there are few young and poorer parents who cannot get out into the country or to lake shores a day or a few days at a time.

STRESSES AND TOLERANCES

Roman Catholicism was the religion of the first white men in the Midwest. On West Wacker Drive in Chicago there is a bronze plaque which surprises the stranger by telling him that near by was a Jesuit mission to the Miami Indians before 1700. But the pioneering and settling of the region were by Protestants: mainly Scotch-Irish Presbyterians, Congregationalists, and Methodists of the East and Baptists of the South. After 1825, circuit riders and resident ministers alike laid great emphasis on education: especially the Methodists, Congregationalists, and Presbyterians, who by that time had swamped the original Catholics. Many of the first schools, colleges, and universities of the region owe their beginnings to these sects. The strict dogma and doctrine of the Calvinistic and other Protestant sects—whether they came from New England or the South—left their mark on the Old Midwest and on what is left of it today in the smaller towns and on the farms in the "Bible belt." Between 1800 and 1870 large numbers of German and Scandinavian Lutherans and smaller groups of Quakers from Pennsylvania, or of eastern "dissenters" like the Mennonites and Mormons, came into the Midwest. They prepared the way for numbers of alien immigrants to follow and adhere to them. There was a be-

208

wildering variety of religious sects by 1900. But a big change had come over the region and its peoples since the growth of towns and cities. With the alien immigrants, Roman Catholicism restored its original strength and zeal.

On the prairie, or in little scattered communities with few material comforts, the early zealous Protestantism was a real solace, a source of hope and assurance. It was almost the only popular culture for two generations. The people were in the Promised Land. They had only to keep the faith and work hard, and they got milk and honey. As hamlets grew to villages, and towns to cities, resident ministers of the Protestant religion appeared who did not scruple—as in the intolerant and bigoted New England of old—to lay down the rules of all individual and social conduct, to run the community, to fix its educational standards and institutions, and to put the fear of hell, if not of God, into their flock. The evangelical element was the strongest. In it were streaks of Scottish Calvinism, predestination, belief in an "elect of God," and in rewards or penalties in this life for individual conduct. In a climate which was alternately dour or violently extreme, and among great natural disasters, this was understandable.

The folk were extremely superstitious, and the superstitions of many southern and eastern European immigrants were steadily added. That was why they took, and still take, so easily to myths. In the parts where the Old Midwest has been best preserved they are most superstitious today; and there, too, religious extremism and fundamentalism still flourish. This early, strict, and general Protestantism in the Midwest, as in the Europe of the sixteenth and seventeenth centuries or nonconformist Victorian England, was a powerful molder of private capitalism, individualism, and self-help. It found what seemed its logical justification in the people's swift progress from isolated poverty and hardship to ease and wealth, great material opportunities, and great cities.

The cities, as we saw, helped Roman Catholicism to come back with the poor Irish and southern or eastern European immigrants. But the towns and cities also led to a materialism and a modernism which almost strangled the old Protestantism by the 1920's. This materialism, far from threatening Catholicism, swelled its ranks as more and more soul-scarred men and women, wounded in the struggle for life and in its growing tempo, failed to find solace in the old Protestant emphasis on the individual's responsibility before God. They sought beauty, too: a more enduring beauty than that of the movies. They found both in the bosom of Mother Church, its ritual, and the confessional. Those

209

who, for one reason or another could not make that leap, could take to Christian Science, theosophy, yoga, or "some new thing." Whatever they did, they weakened the old Protestanism. It is worth while, and only fair, if we examine this more closely.

The "materializing" of all religions went very far in the Midwest after 1870. Science then seemed to conflict with all religion. It was happening all over the industrialized world; but, as in so much else, it was carried to an extreme in the Midwest. Extremes were more obvious there. They were part of a lifetime's experience. Except in the rural towns and communities, materialism laid its hand on all thought, organized belief, and ritual. So did the new principles of "organization," as though what had proved so wildly successful in business or production must prove so in religion. Churches of nearly every kind became more secular and institutional. Doctrine, theology, and exposition gave way before organization, form, ritual, or social action. Articles of faith became less important. Belief in good works, a "practical" ethic (as it is called) confined to this life, spread widely in all groups of men and in nearly all churches. These are not a stranger's observations; still less are they criticisms. They are those of American and Midwest churchmen, priests and rabbis themselves. They are writ large on the record for anyone who cares to read them. That record is still being written today.

The demand for potted knowledge easily became a demand for potted religion: religion in which laborsaving devices should give the individual what he needed with the least trouble. What he needed was what his forebears had needed: solace and confidence in his rightness. He needed it even more than they in such a complex, rapidly changing life. But he needed it without feeling his own responsibility before God and mankind as keenly as they did. This underlay the drift away from the old Protestant churches into Roman Catholicism, Christian Science, various religions of special revelation, new and strange churches, mystical cults, spiritualism, and outright skepticism. There may have been something of the city dweller's fatigue in this: his bewilderment at the new problems of city life which so often proved intractable. But there is no gainsaying the effect. The great toleration of all beliefs and ideas, which marks this region more than any other in America, gave free rein to new cults and to a great extent prevented any popular excitement over struggles between the old cults and sects. There were anti-Catholic movements, but nothing to compare with the violence of those in the East, except the revived Ku Klux Klan which controlled the state of Indiana—seat of Notre Dame—until late in the

210

1920's. It was more against Jews and Catholics in the Midwest than, as in the South, against Negroes. Its membership rose until in the country as a whole it accounted for one-sixth of the adult population. But, despite much concern and some bitterness, the great transformation of the Midwest went on without convulsions.

The pioneers and settlers had reason to be devout. They saw and marveled at what the Lord could perform through the hands of his elect. It was all wondrous in their eyes. And so, in fact, it was. But there arose generations who knew not Joseph and his brethren. To them, all the marvels seemed part of the order of Nature. These new generations of midwesterners were born among marvels, or they came into the region having already heard of its miracles and miraculous opportunities. They were not very interested in how they had been made, for that belonged to the past. Familiarity bred gratitude out and killed wonder.

Religion always obtains greater devotion where life is a harder struggle: which is why it is stronger today among the masses in the cities of the Midwest, where the Catholics are most numerous, and among farmers, where the old-line Protestantism is at its strongest.

The first wealthy men in the towns were conspicuous. They lived under public scrutiny. They had deep religious beliefs, and, out of real gratitude, they paid much more than a tithe in charity and good works. As their children and grandchildren grew to man's estate, social services ate into the sources of private charity. The fortunate individual's duty to his less fortunate neighbor could be performed by paying taxes. Churches, unendowed by state or federal constitutions and needing to grow with the population, became of necessity more and more concerned with ways of raising funds. It was not altogether a matter of materialism. Many of the people *wanted* religion. Indeed, to a great extent the more hectic and materialistic the life of the city or town became, the more people showed that they needed some kind of spiritual life. But material achievements and machines were setting the pace and driving men. Men had to keep up with them. If you had asked Midwest businessmen whether they still believed that man could not serve God and Mammon, they would probably have agreed; but they would also have apologized for having to give up trying to serve God in any other way than by attendance at church and by paying some of their proceeds over to it. They would have said, as so many say, that they had little time. What were the churches for, anyway? Again, that is not peculiar to the Midwest; but it is marked there.

The result today is that at either extreme of religion—among Roman

211

Catholics, on the one hand, and among fundamentalists, Lutherans, strict Baptists, Seventh-Day Adventists, Jehovah's Witnesses, and similar sects, on the other—there is widespread devoutness and obedience to a moral law. But in the wide space between are a bewildering number of sects, somewhat in spiritual disarray, held together by tradition, cult, good form, and good works, and not quite certain on what doctrinal ground they stand. In the second World War it was among these "midway" sects that most concern was expressed about juvenile delinquency, sexual morality, and so on. The social activities or beliefs of Catholics and extreme evangelicals seem to have more force behind them when the behavior of adults or youth is involved. The sense of vulnerability in the "midway" sects shows itself in acute anxiety over the rate at which Catholicism gains converts. There is more evidence today of religious intolerance than there was in 1914.

The *Christian Century* publishes a special series of eight articles asking whether Roman Catholicism can win America.[5] This reflects Protestant concern at the growth of Catholicism to the biggest single, undivided Christian sect in America, embracing one-sixth of all the people; the richest national Catholic community in the world. In the towns and cities of the Midwest, Americans of Italian, Irish, Polish, and many other origins make it even stronger than it is in the East— despite Boston, Baltimore, Philadelphia, and New York. The religious toleration of the Midwest, on both sides, seems to be wearing a trifle thin. The modernistic evangelists and revivalists stage their rallies for converts with pepped-up music and pep talks, often without a nationally organized church behind them. The Catholics move with the spirit of the times and capture the imagination by celebrations and Holy Name Hours in vast amphitheaters before many thousands of youths and adults alike. The "midway" sects remain in the smaller districts or communities, faithful, instant in good works, but puzzled and disturbed by it all. They are a legacy from the men who made the Midwest. But they are a diminishing minority. Whither are they tending? Even orthodox Jewry finds itself in much the same quandary, with its own "midway" group set between two extremes.

This is what has happened to religion in a region of the most rapid material advancement in history. But what of secular beliefs, tolerances, intolerances, good works, and humanitarianism?

The region from the outset was mainly peopled by "anti-'s": men who were *against* other men, other institutions, other ways of life,

[5] *Christian Century* (Chicago), issues of November 29, 1944, up to and including that of January 17, 1945.

other countries. The East and the South might also be divided between the various groups of people gathered around Boston, New York, Philadelphia, Baltimore, Virginia, South Carolina, and New Orleans; but neither East nor South in 1812, 1860, 1914, 1933, or 1939 was as "anti-" anything as the Midwest—except on slavery. East and South after 1800 were much more "pro-" in life than they were "anti-." They were, again except on slavery, less extreme, less suspicious of other Americans, foreigners, or foreign ideas. They had less toleration among one another than midwesterners: but they had fewer cranks and phobias, too. Midwesterners, on the other hand, were naturally and deliberately pro-Midwest, pro-their-region and pro-themselves. This intensified their feeling of being "set apart." All midwesterners had tasks before them to tax their vast energy to its limits; and that lasted well into this century. Much of it remains, but only among certain groups of midwesterners. Yet the "anti-" psychology remains, spread far more widely among the people than the old spirit of pioneering, building, and enterprise. The "anti-'s" are now more apparent than the "pro-'s." It is partly due to the close-packed and widely different racial, national, and religious groups in the towns and cities. It is also an example of the time lag in people's myths and ways of thought. That is not to say that midwesterners are, or ever were, anti-everything; nor, of course, that easterners or southerners are, or were, pro-everything. It is just a difference, though a big difference, of degree in their attitudes.

For instance, in cultural matters and the life of the mind Boston, New York, Philadelphia, Virginia, and New Orleans looked on the Midwest last century much as ancient Greece looked on new Rome, or as a later Rome looked on new Constantinople. They saw something vast, vigorous, and strange arising; perhaps threatening their older culture and way of life. And in return St. Louis, Chicago, Cincinnati, and other big Midwest cities looked on those of the East or South as republican Rome looked on an older Greece, or as Byzantium looked on an older Rome, Milan, or Ravenna. They saw something decadent, effeminate, cosmopolitan, foreign about them—although Byzantium, St. Louis, and Chicago were composed of all nationalities themselves! It is the same way in which, for so long and so much, the East and South looked to Europe; and as Europe today, like a Western Roman world in disintegration, looks with wonder and no little envy on an all-American Byzantium.

It is this which has given the Midwest so much of its still-continuing, but now unwarranted, sense of inferiority; its chip-on-the-shoulder complex toward the East and South and toward all of Europe.

213

Midwest freedom of speech and general toleration, the making of midwesterners themselves out of new and old nationalities which was going on until 1929, the region's inability to "jell" quickly—all of these naturally produced, and still produce, extremes of tolerance and intolerance, ease and tension, rigid orthodoxy and sheer crankiness, kindliness and phobias, self-assurance and uncertainty, feelings of superiority and of inferiority. These are the marks of a people not yet assimilated to one mode or pattern: a people composed not so much of individualists as of widely differing individuals and of very different segregated groups that behave as individuals.

If there had not been such great tolerance for differences, phobias, crankiness, and ignorance, terrible explosions would have followed fast. Any more rapid and rigid attempt to impose a mode or pattern of life upon all these new peoples would have had the same result—as, in fact, it did in Philadelphia, New York, and other eastern cities in the first half of last century. Hasty in so much, the midwesterners seem to have realized that in mixing and making themselves as a people they had better make haste slowly. They are still mixing and making themselves, though the ingredients were completed by 1929. Accordingly, they are consciously or subconsciously aware that their problems are still different, that they themselves are still different, from others. They allow as much tolerance to intolerance, as much authority to ignorance, as they can; for no one can say for sure what is truth, what will "work," what midwesterners are, or what they are going to be. They are liberal and democratic in this, just as the pioneers were. They are anti-authority, anti-authoritarian, anti-pattern. They will not ape or copy anyone. They let the mixture work and watch "what's cooking." It is cooking fast.

This paradox of tolerance for intolerance in the Midwest results, again, in midwesterners' being greatly misunderstood. The stranger easily sees the intolerance, the ignorance, the phobias. They stick out like sore thumbs. It is much harder, and of course less newsworthy, to see and hear the average, the quiet, the sensible people by whose grace the intolerant flaunt their intolerance. The stranger who goes to meetings addressed by Father Coughlin or the Reverend Gerald L. K. Smith in Detroit, by Mrs. Elizabeth Dilling or Mr. William J. Grace in Chicago, by Mr. Joe McWilliams and by others in Indianapolis, Cincinnati, Fort Wayne, Muncie, Wichita, Hammond, South Bend, or Omaha; the visitor who reads the literature of the Ku Klux Klan, the Gentile League, and others, marvels not at the minority's ignorance of facts, their intolerance and venom. He marvels at the massive wisdom,

214

tolerance, and charity of the majority that can permit this and take it in a stride. He thinks of the recent and present intolerances of Europe and the shape in which they have left it.

True, there is a risk, especially in such mixed cities. True, it is a sign of some social and political, as well as of the individual agitator's, malaise. But to fight bigotry with bigotry is doubly dangerous. The Civil War was a costly proof of that. In a people so mixed, becoming a people with a mode and pattern of life of their own, there comes a time when those very extremisms which have always characterized them, those dissident and discordant elements, find themselves *in extremis*. It is then that they become most extreme, rebellious, vocal, and even a little dangerous. As the Arabic proverb says: "Little dogs yap, but the great caravan passes on." The dogs may upset a camel or two, but you must keep your eyes on the caravan. Much of the intolerance of the Midwest, like the news of its cities' gangsters or crime, gets disproportionate publicity in the press, the movies, and the novel. The dog gets a bad name because of burrs in his tail. Midwesterners do not deny their problems, their cranks, and the phobias of their professional haters. But writers from outside as well as inside the region have publicized them without publicizing the massive common sense and decency of the Midwest.

There is another point. Much of the intolerance and crankiness is sincere. To that extent its advocates are to be pitied. In this long-insulated region of extremes there has always been, and still is, much ignorance of facts. On that ignorance extreme beliefs and prejudices flourish with all the vigor of prairie weeds. Few Chicagoans know what their great public library owes to British generosity after Mrs. O'Leary's cow kicked over the lamp and began the fire of 1871. Few midwesterners know that a rich Englishman founded the Smithsonian Institution. In many polls of public opinion in the Midwest region during the second World War a majority of those answering the questions thought that the Irish Free State was in the war; that Canada was ruled from London; that Finland and Poland existed as independent countries before the first World War; that Finland's debt to the United States was a war, and not a postwar-relief, debt; that Siam was a colony; and so on. Where ignorance of facts is widespread, prejudice easily slips into the seat of reason.

What makes it hard to understand is the great generosity and kindliness of the very people who are prejudiced. Many anti-Semites and advocates of white supremacy are kind, generous, and charitable in all other ways. I rejoice in the continuing friendship of midwesterners in

215

many towns and cities who describe themselves, sincerely if humorously, as anti-British or Anglophobes. No midwesterners were kinder or more generous to me. That is as it should be, but seldom is, everywhere: there is no need to carry your dislike of foreign countries to a dislike of any particular foreigner. Yet I confess it was hard for me, as an Englishman more English by blood than most, to be told so frequently, "Oh, but you, of course, are different; you are not typically British!" The typical British, like the typical midwesterners, prove always in popular prejudice to be the untypical, the exception. To the great mass of average typical people whom we meet, we say, "But, of course, you are not typical." The typical must surely mean the unique. At least it would seem so in the Midwest.

Midwesterners are more aware of their intolerances than other Americans think and than many other Americans are of their own. Their remedy is to stretch tolerance even further. This sets Midwest extremes wider apart than elsewhere. But it also leads to such contrasts with other regions as that between the laudable kindliness of midwesterners to the displaced American-born Japanese (the Nisei) and the treatment accorded to them by many California towns and cities. It is said to have cost the country nearly two hundred million dollars to relocate some 120,000 Japanese residents of California, of whom the great majority were American-born. The cities and towns of the Midwest were the most tolerant and kindly to them.

Racial and other intolerances are now more apparent in the cities and towns of the Midwest than they used to be. It is in them that racial animosity against Negroes pervades as many trade-unions and their members—though not those of the C.I.O.—as it affects employers. It is in these cities that anti-Semitism flourishes. It is in them that agitators have enlisted the aid of the youthful gangs in the slums, with most distressing and sometimes fatal results among Jews and Negroes. It is in them that the greatest superficial likenesses to the beginnings of the Nazi movement in German cities can be seen. The reasons are the same: the Negroes and Jews mainly keep to the towns and cities of the Midwest, where to a large extent they are segregated in their residential areas and economic functions. The two world wars and the great economic developments in the South, especially the extensive installation of new laborsaving machinery in the raising and processing of cotton, tobacco, and paper, have resulted in a vast net emigration of southern Negroes to the towns and cities of the North and Midwest. The idle, ignorant, discontented, lawless, and uprooted flock to agitators and hatemongers as to a Cave of Adullam; and in Midwest cities there are many caves where cave-dwellers can live and operate amid great toler-ance.[6]

If any organized intolerance develops after the second World War as it did after the first—and already there are disturbing signs of it—the Midwest urban communities will have big social problems and per-haps social convulsions. The authorities and leading citizens do not need to be told that. There are now many new committees, conferences, and institutes on racial relations in the Midwest. When the Gardner Cowles Foundation set up a memorial to Wendell Willkie it took the shape of a community center for Negroes in Des Moines. This Midwest tolerance may encourage the bigots, but it also issues in a degree of humility and self-criticism which astonish all who come and stay in the region. Few people can turn themselves inside out and give a verdict upon themselves with as much impartial good nature as many mid-westerners. But you must wait for them to do it. They do not belittle themselves in public.

There are still remnants of the Old Midwest in the people's curiosity, their eagerness to learn and to experience, and their frequently undis-criminating belief in what lecturers, the press, and the radio tell them. Yet, as we saw, skepticism is spreading in the lay field as it is in religion. If knowledge were to succeed to a healthy skepticism, if it were born of that skepticism, the transformation of the Midwest and midwest-erners would go ahead more quickly. But how shall a man get wis-dom and understanding? Only by chastening, says the Old Book. The growth of tolerance and self-criticism in the region during the last ten or twenty years is evidence of much chastening. But midwesterners, like children and all other men, accept chastening only when it is the outcome of their own experience. And their own getting of experience must go on at its own rate.

When President Truman proclaimed Sunday, May 13, 1945, as a day of thanksgiving and prayer after victory in Europe, the following passage appeared in an editorial in a great Chicago newspaper. In very many newspapers throughout the Midwest the same note was struck:

"It is fitting on this Sunday that we invoke a sense of humility, that we seek wisdom and discernment compatible with the complexity of the problems that confront us; that we seek strength without arro-gance; courage without bravado; firmness in the right without bigotry.

"From the evils of ignorance and prejudice and intolerance, O Lord, deliver us.

[6] I Sam. 22:1–2.

217

"If it be Thy will, deliver us from the foe without.

"And from our own apathy and stupidity, O Lord, deliver us as well."[7]

Mere form? The press quoting Scripture? I do not think so. As long as the game goes on, midwesterners will claim they know as many answers as, and probably more than, anyone else. But when there is no more claiming and no more competition, they show a great humility. They recognize limits, especially their own. Realists about so much, they are realists about themselves, too; and if that is not the whole of wisdom, it is a sign of maturity. In the new America which lies ahead, Midwest realism, self-awareness, humility, and self-criticism will count for much more than its self-assurance and intolerance. If the "materializing" of religion has transferred its moral elements to lay life as effectively as this, at least something of what organized religion has lost, the people and America have gained.

AFTER WORKING HOURS

There was never a Midwest leisure class, though Thorstein Veblen, who invented a theory of it, was a son of Wisconsin. There is no leisure class today. The Old South and the East developed men of leisure, patrons of the arts and learning. Many of them, like Henry Adams, lived a life so remote from that of their people that they despaired of America, or went to Europe, like Henry James; just as, more recently, many European artists despaired of Europe and settled in America. In Cincinnati, St. Louis, and many smaller southern cities of the region there are still a few traces of gentle southern influence, but in no other big city of the Midwest. Those who live in the region must work as long as they can. Those who are rich enough not to work leave the Midwest—probably for its good, and certainly for their own. In all Midwest cities and towns there are a few well-to-do people whose enjoyment and cultivation of the rarest and finest pleasures of the mind are as keen as those found anywhere in the world. But they are few.

Much of the relaxation and diversion of the region must therefore be for the many tired or busy men. It means standardization: Mr. Babbitt on Main Street. But it also means that, like other Midwest institutions, the art and culture of the region come from the people, from working people, from the bottom working upward, and not from a narrow social layer at the top. So the culture of the region itself was bound to be rebellious and explosive, breathing frustration, protests, sweat, and corn

[7] *Chicago Daily News*, Friday, May 11, 1945.

218

liquor. From about the middle of last century onward this provoked a great cultural struggle in America.

It began with the Mississippi and Ohio writers, Mark Twain, W. D. Howells, and others; though they "went East." It exploded in Walt Whitman's correspondence and arguments with Emerson; the men of the people against the "elect" of Boston and New York. It was carried on by midwestern realists against eastern stylists and transcendentalists, who were often narrowly linked to European currents and modes: by a whole band of virile, vigorous, and vulgar (in the true sense of the word) Midwest novelists, storytellers, and poets. Writers of the people who were the people, as well as those who described the people's convulsive flexing of their muscles, began to thrust a new image of America under the noses of more delicately minded Americans and of nearly all foreigners. They did not tell of a Promised Land. They told of broken promises, tragic struggles on the land or in mean streets, of nobility amid poverty, of sordidness amid unparalleled wealth, and of the seamy side of life in all groups. They were the vanguard of a new movement.

Theodore Dreiser, from Indiana, told of Chicago and many another Midwest town or city: not stylishly, not even artistically, but with the vigor of the region. Booth Tarkington, another "Hoosier," smoothed over the effects of Dreiser's savage work with the palette knife. Frank Norris took the lid off Chicago's "wheat pit" and off the homes of its wealthiest citizens. Sherwood Anderson of Ohio and Hamlin Garland revealed their Midwest beginnings. So did Sinclair Lewis, who "covered" many Midwest lives, protesting at their standardized pattern. Ring Lardner's and George Ade's sketches mixed comedy and tragedy and all the extremes of midwesterners.

James Whitcomb Riley, Eugene Field, Edgar Lee Masters, Vachel Lindsay, and Carl Sandburg beat out new measures, new verse, generally as virile as it was strange. The seething life of the region's towns and cities, the quieter struggles on the farms and in the rural towns, these were portrayed not as the public preferred to see them, or as myths embodied them, but in terms of the individual's feelings: pride, frustration, resignation, loyalty, defiance, despair, bitter resentment, and revolt. Upton Sinclair and others came into the region as reporters, fascinated by this rawer Midwest life, and told of the stockyards in 1906 and all of its rawness, aspect by aspect. Willa Cather wrote of the pioneer wives and their search for inner horizons to match the width of those on the prairie and the plains. In the period of disillusion after prohibition, amid gangsters and corruption, James T. Farrell wrote the three volumes on young Studs Lonigan and his career in Chicago. Biographers, like Lloyd Lewis, brought out the unrealized richness of Midwest life and history.

The literary life of the Midwest, poetry as well as prose, is extraordinarily luxuriant and tenacious, like prairie vines. Fierce and uneven in quality, it has lost one stem after another. The East or California or the new Southwest plucked them away. This regional culture itself was with equal persistence spurned and rejected by the overwhelming majority of Midwest city dwellers and townsmen. It was as if the writers said to their own people, rich and not-so-rich alike: "This is how you live: now learn of us"; and the people, almost to a man and woman, replied: "No, thank you; we prefer our own myths, our own synthetic fairyland"! The writers and artists tended to leave the region in order to find like minds with which to consort; or, as Norman Douglas said, to "avoid the attrition of vulgar minds." It is a pity for the Midwest that other regions offered more material rewards to the outstanding Midwest authors. And most were human enough to take them, to go where their all-American influence would be greater. But in this way the Midwest stamped much of its life and thought upon the whole of America—more than Americans realize.

Yet many stayed; much goes quietly and steadily on; and today the Midwest has a host of young authors and poets who promise to repeat, in the next generation, what the Midwest school did between 1890 and 1930—but differently. The strange features of this regional culture are its vigor and its quiet persistence in so many different institutions and centers—in Chicago, in many places in Iowa, in the Twin Cities, in Madison, Kansas City, St. Louis, in Ohio and many another locality. It goes on often without anyone in another city of the same state knowing it is there. Local historians and topographers, societies interested in life in the Mississippi Valley, state historical associations, collectors, bibliophiles, private printing presses, bookbinders, music societies, amateur chamber musicians, curators of museums, university students' groups, librarians, and journalists—they form an intellectual leaven which is constantly at work in the Midwest lump. The universities and colleges which still put emphasis on the humanities, often against criticism from businessmen who think them out of date, are actually more up to date than many businessmen and are making more of a contribution to the future stability of Midwest society. The lineal descendant of a banker in Springfield in Lincoln's time, also a banker, now writes, illustrates, and prints his own books on a Washington hand press in the basement of his Springfield home, and collects fine books and the productions of other private presses. Chicago's Caxton Club and its unique Lakeside Press have been continuously exchanging men, books, and ideas with Britain and other lands for nearly half a century, forming a center of fine arts in Chicago and the Midwest as a whole. Typographers and calligraphers in Chicago have been in constant touch with those of the leading European countries since the early days of Gill, Morison, and Edward Johnston in England. The fine bookstores, museums, and libraries of the region testify to the persistence and discrimination of a surprisingly broad stratum (though a minority) of people, old and young, whose interest in the erudite and one or other of the arts is not dictated by modes or critics. Special collections and libraries—for example, the Newberry Library in Chicago or the Nelson collection in Kansas City—have become influential forces in the arts and the life of the mind, the more influential, perhaps, because their work is not considered newsworthy.

Art collectors in the region are many; yet apart from a few names, known to all Americans, painting of as high an order as the region's literature is rare. But anyone who examines the paintings of the children in rural schools and in big cities must be impressed with their imagination, self-expression, and execution. These are children of many different national groups. Their work is full of promise; if they can pursue their medium, the region will be the richer. Architecture is not distinctively midwestern—except for some functional architecture: the grain elevators, some office buildings, the barns and silos of farms, the homes and public buildings of Frank Lloyd Wright, or the libraries and other buildings designed for many towns, universities, and cities.

To a great and encouraging extent, big commercial firms have joined with artists and writers to bring elegance into everyday life: to store windows, displays, signs, exhibits, advertising, printing, paper, packaging, containers, household equipment, and railroad cars. There have been great and frequent changes in all these, and always toward higher levels of artistic form or taste.

Thomas Wolfe left the South but wrote of it and saw all humanity in terms of the folk he best knew. Ben Hecht, Archibald MacLeish, and many another left the Midwest; yet the stamp of the people, of people's hopes and fears, is clear on their work. Here, too, the genius of the place proves inescapable, even if men abandon the family altar. What regions lose, in all lands, the country and mankind gain. So it is with the culture of the Midwest. The region is a rich forcing-bed. Many of its plants are bedded out, blossom, and seed in other fields; but much seed comes back on the wind.

In all this, too, the Midwest paradox is traceable. The artist is peculiarly individualistic, though he tells, sings, or portrays the life of many people. In the region of the greatest individualism and of its opposite, collective standardization, the artist, the most individualistic of rebels, is practically unhonored and unsung. He departs from the average. He won't conform. He depicts the average and the mass of conformists, often in uncomplimentary terms. He reminds comfortable midwesterners of the unpleasantness around them. He tells Wheaton or Barrington about "back of the yards" Chicago. He tells suburbanites outside St. Louis or Kansas City of the riverbank flophouses. He tells the comfortable about the segregated uncomfortable. Whether he is white or colored—the artists' trade-union is in this respect more democratic than most—he tells white workers and employers about the Negro. He tells capital about labor. He tells labor about capital. He tells ministers of religion more about sin and human nature than they care to know. He is a confounded, confounding nuisance. But, as so often elsewhere, he is a vanguard, the herald of a movement that much later gets things done, a voice in a wilderness. Like many a vanguard, he gets shot up.

The comfortable, tolerant, and often intolerant midwesterners may ignore or shoot up their own artists; but they cannot ignore the results. Slowly more and more people are being influenced. Their thirst for something spiritually satisfying, something more than material, is driving them to seek new wellsprings. A growing number, even if still a small minority, of midwesterners in all income brackets in big cities and small towns learn music, follow good music, discuss novels, read criticism, and write "appreciations" for a little group of local friends. It does not matter if much of their curiosity and of their desire for potted knowledge and culture enters into this. At least they want knowledge and culture, to begin with. That is more than many seem to want in other places; and in the Midwest their demands are growing.

Midwest curiosity, credulity, vulgarity, and blatancy have been a long-standing butt of eastern and many other Americans—even of many Midwest artists themselves who despaired of their home folks. (It is human, if silly, to want to reform everything within your own lifetime; often it can only be done that quickly by a dictator—which is probably why "dissidents" and artists become so arbitrary and intolerant that they become dictatorial—and dictators do not agree with the Midwest.) Midwesterners among themselves are frank to recognize their own credulity, blatancy, and vulgarity. They know they are the butt of many arbiters of art and taste in other regions. But, as in so much else, this merely increases their "anti-" feelings, their self-satisfaction, and their determination to go their own way to their own solutions. They are well on that way. They who hustle, won't be hustled. The Englishman is reminded of Browning and the Barretts of Wimpole Street, of the artists who rebelled against the overpowering middle-class vulgarity, narrow-mindedness, and standardization of Victorian England—which ended in the "naughty nineties" and the "anything goes" of our day. In the Midwest, as in so much else, the life of tomorrow is lived parallel with much of the life of last century and behind a superficial standardization. That is the difference.

The desire for wider horizons is one of many evidences of dissatisfaction with "our infantile delusions of roller-bearing ease, moonlight emotion, celluloid romance and instalment-plan living." The standardized pattern of all-American life after working hours itself provokes revolt; and the artists are by no means the only rebels. There are thousands, indeed millions, who refuse to bow the knee to Baal. After all, nothing can pall more thoroughly and quickly than standardization itself; and the restless curiosity of nearly all midwesterners shows their discontent with the standard diversions, even while they pursue them. These diversions are remarkably spectacular; they are nearly all spectacles: sports, games, races, theaters, movies, floor shows, strip-tease; even the streets at night are lighted as if they were the proscenium to life itself, which in a way they are. The imagination of midwesterners is almost universally confined to building or doing material things. They need to be shown something, to touch, taste, and handle it, before they can grasp it. This may explain their attitude to art and intellectual matters, which do not seem realistic. What you can perceive with your five senses is realistic, especially if it pays.

In the region of "show me," showmanship, and ocular demonstration, this emphasis on "lust of the eyes" is natural. Tired businessmen can sit, watch, and presumably relax. But physical and mental fatigue are not the same. Action can be the best relaxation for sedentary workers and weary minds. There seems less action in the diversions of midwesterners than in those of many other Americans. It is surprising because of the energy of the people. The exception is in life on vacation, in the countryside, or on the innumerable golf courses. The whirl from one spectacle to another, and the noise in parties, restaurants, and dance halls, suggest that not enough physical energy is released; that it remains bottled up. In this, midwesterners are surprisingly like Hungarians. They are great athletes when young; they are mighty hunters and fishermen when they want to be; but, also like them, they prefer group life and parties, society and many voices. Like them, too, and

223

unlike the British, they do not care to walk, and they do not believe with Disraeli that "a canter is a cure for anything." They make fun of the English week end, which to a man they believe lasts from Thursday to Tuesday if not Wednesday; but when they themselves take two days off—Saturday and Sunday—they do not take as much physical exercise as the Britisher. The exceptions are those well-to-do midwesterners who form a tiny but extremely cultured minority; who prize privacy; and in whose homes and diversions nothing is lacking. But the vast majority, whether rich or not, are probably nervously weary of hectic but sedentary work or of monotony; and that does not mean they are physically weary—as we learned in the second World War with occupational therapy. It is significant that since 1900 all new dances, jazz, and its offspring, jitterbugging, have been American; and that from the outset more and more physical action has entered into them. They are not midwestern. But their popularity is greater in no other towns and cities of America or of the world.

The region was always one of heavy drinkers: drinkers who could carry their liquor. Drunks used to be more common than in the East. They are so no longer, though midwesterners still seem able to take much liquor aboard and stow it well, without rolling. In the late 1830's, owing to the influence of women, ministers, and many New Englanders, temperance movements began to sweep the Midwest. They were always opposed by immigrants, especially the Irish and Germans. A "grocery" in the Midwest was a liquor store, first and foremost; and state legislatures were greatly occupied with bills and temperance lobbies aimed at "groceries." They still are, today, in the shape of struggles between "wets" and "drys" over local option. Today Evanston in Illinois, adjoining the city limits of Chicago, is the national stronghold of the Women's Christian Temperance Union—which has led to an interesting and regular social mobility across the line between these two communities: "drys" moving into Evanston and "wets" moving out.

The good corn liquor of the South, still preferred south of the Midwest line of southern influence, and Scotch from Scotland, Canada, and the Midwest itself, are understandably popular. The climate has had more to do with this than many imagine. People drink much hard liquor, neat, in very cold climates: Russia, Scandinavia, the Alpine regions, Hungary, and the Balkans. They also drink much of it in very hot climates, too. The Midwest climate varies between that of central Russia in winter and that of Singapore in summer. The pioneers' drinking habits were therefore understandable. Those of midwesterners today, with air-conditioning and central heating, find no such warranty. Their justification must be sought elsewhere: the large number of heavy-drinking European immigrants; the general love of liquor; its action as a drug; the way of life that makes drugs popular; the force and the time lag of habit. But the region which led the national crusade for the "noble experiment" of prohibition, and reaped its worst results in the shape of gangsters and racketeers, again shows signs of a trend toward prohibition in many counties and townships. And not all states went "wet" after the repeal of the Eighteenth Amendment to the American Constitution. One thing should be added: numerous as taverns are throughout the region, as "groceries" and saloons were before them, and numerous as are dice girls, there are extremely few barmaids. Women can and do drink; but women do not serve it to men. In this, again, respect for women is reflected.

On the other hand, taverns and night spots have certainly lessened the old Midwest morality. They may have made the mass of the people more natural, in the sense that they show more of human nature. The drabness of life for the mass of people may have made these places understandable, if not necessary, after 1870. But it is hard—except perhaps for reasons already cited—to understand their numbers in all towns and cities today. They are not like the British "pub," kept by mine host and his lady; or like the French *bistro*; or like the German inn or wine cellar; or like the Spanish *bodega*. "Periodicals," persons who get regularly and periodically drunk, seem to be more common than in other parts of America or in Europe. In many, but not the majority, of the night spots in the big cities there is quite a vocabulary for fleecing a likely customer and rendering him incapable—even if Midwest kindliness will see that he is taken to a hotel (never to his home) in a cab, with the fare paid beforehand. Women will not serve drinks, but they are employed to charm the client into ordering twice and thrice as many as he would need by himself: but then he does not want to be by himself anyway. He or his friends are there precisely not to be alone.

These are not just Midwest characteristics. They are by no means typical of places of entertainment. They are like the few Englishmen, Jews, and Americans who bring discredit on the vast majority of their unoffending fellows. But they certainly are features against which the vigorous and ever present reformist zeal of many Midwest women are directed. It is understandable that so many women, and fewer men, connect all this with drink. But if they think that prohibition will cure it, then they must surely also believe that breaking the thermometer will make the atmosphere cooler. At no time were vice, drunkenness, and lawlessness as acute and widespread as during prohibition. The majority of midwesterners are tolerant in this, too. They do not believe that you can legislate morality or that you can legislate vice, crime, or human frailty out of existence. They are content to leave these things, together with so much else, to the innate good sense of individuals. They are prepared to pay the price, and they do not conceal the price they pay.

Nowhere in America, the land of chance and opportunity, is gambling so much a part of the life of the people as it is in this region. Like a bright scarlet thread, speculation runs through Midwest life from its earliest beginnings: in land, real estate, the wheat "pit," "corners," business, the stock market, prize fights, cock-fighting, horses, card games, "bingo," "the numbers," and down to the numerous and generally illegal slot machines, which are mainly made in, or distributed from, Chicago. Nowhere else in America do you find betting, wagers, and their vocabulary so much a part of common talk. The technical terms of billiards, pool, bridge, and poker are now used in everyday speech, often by people who cannot play them: "behind the eight ball," "an ace in the hole," putting your "cards on the table," "an ace up his sleeve," and the key phrase of all: "Wanna bet?" The general interest in organized sport is almost as much an interest in gambling as in the merits of the contest. Nor does it argue any lack of a sporting instinct. Quite the contrary. It is shared by rich and poor alike, all of whom want excitement as much as, or more than, they want to make "easy money." When the federal government imposed a short ban on horse-racing in the second World War, the gambling syndicates and their clients in the region shifted their operations easily, overnight, to betting on anything imaginable: even the weather. The demand is enormous.

Horse-racing in Europe is certainly as much the sport of the people as "the sport of kings"; but organized gambling is generally restricted to the well-to-do sophisticates who patronize the casino or to competitions. Not so in the Midwest. There, gambling, like liquor, is a revolt from the tedium or intensity of working life; though it is scarcely relaxing to the nerves. In 1944 the legitimate parimutuel turnover of the horse-racing tracks in Illinois almost reached $150,000,000, of which the state got nearly $3,000,000 and the tracks nearly $8,000,000 gross. Yet the parimutuel at these tracks represents only a fraction of the annual turnover in all forms of gambling in the state. Faced with the need for more revenue, cities and states have been urged both to increase their "cut" of legal betting and to legalize more of the illegal betting so that more "cuts" can be obtained. Most midwesterners do not believe you can legislate prudence any more than you can impose sobriety or morality.

As it is, connivance at gambling by some servants and officers of many city governments forms a peculiarly rich source of revenue "on the side," even if it only reaches their own hands. And there have always been a series of notorious links in everyday practice between syndicates for gambling, those for vice, gangsters, racketeers, and a small minority of city or state politicians and other public officers. There is nothing new in that. There are innumerable books, articles, and legal cases describing it. What is new is the extent to which it is being carried and the magnitude of the sums involved. A vested interest in it has been created, perpetuated, and magnified to remarkable proportions. In such circumstances it is hardly surprising that the various syndicates struggle for new territories, stake out claims, contest them, muscle in on others' territories, and resort to murder and arson. True, these odd reincarnations of "frontier bandits" only fight each other. True, they are confined to cities, and only the gambling or vicious public pay their tolls. But the general interest in gambling pays this social price.

The humor of midwesterners is proverbial, laconic, and general. Everyday conversation in the home, on the street, and in business is full of it. There is much of the elemental vigor of the region in it; but it is peculiar. It is not the same as all-American humor. Much American humor today comes from New York, Hollywood, and the radio. It, too, is proverbially laconic; but it is also sophisticated and rather cruel. There is in it an element of Hobbes's "sudden glory that overtaketh a man," especially when he sees a fellow-mortal in a situation in which he would not willingly find himself. That is also part of Midwest humor, but not all of it. Midwesterners can laugh at themselves and their fellows, often like boys. They are as fond of practical jokes as the British. But in the Midwest the exaggeration and boasting of the river-roarers, the pun, and the play on words have survived to this day. So have the pithy expressions of the prairie settlers, in which Lincoln delighted. To the East and the Far West, much of this Midwest brand of humor seems "corny"—a significant term.

Midwesterners are more fond of averages than other Americans. They therefore dislike departures from the average more. So their humor lays great stress upon incongruities, ridiculousness, and abnormality. One feature which illustrates their own lack of sophistication and their matter-of-factness is the almost complete absence of irony and sarcasm. Indeed, it is virtually certain that fine points of irony or sarcasm will not even be perceived. They will be received in dead silence, while an

227

incongruity or the ridiculous will evoke an instant burst of laughter. Those who manage vaudeville on the radio know this well. "You mustn't be clever," they say. Accordingly, there is an enormous amount of humor and laughter in the region: slick in the cities, dry and whimsical in the countryside. But there is not much wit. For that you have to go to a very narrow layer of people in the big cities, the universities, the artists and writers, or outside the region altogether.

Midwest humor is direct. It is of the people. It does not suggest or imply. It hits hard. The art of innuendo, like that of irony, is not understood and is not amusing. It savors too much of someone being too "clever," probably at midwesterners' expense. For the same reasons, the people do not like satire. It makes them more than a little uneasy, unless it is quite obviously aimed away from America altogether. Yet the chief merit and delight of satire, as Swift and Anatole France showed, is to see yourself in what you write and read. At least until now the extreme sensitiveness of midwesterners has made them distrust satire and satirists, including, of course, their own.

The people, particularly the men, find self-expression, fluency, and lucidity in speech hard to achieve. This is bound up with education and the general distrust or depreciation of "cleverness," things cultural, artistic, "impractical," and intellectual. Probably that is why most midwesterners really enjoy going so frequently to hear British lecturers on all sorts of topics, and despite the Englishman's English accent which sounds so affected to midwestern ears.[8] They do not generally agree with what he says. Often they do not get what he is driving at. Often he does not make it plain enough. But they enjoy his fluency of self-expression, even if they distrust it. His mastery of "our sweet English tongue" was one of the chief reasons for Mr. Winston Churchill's extraordinary popularity in America. It was also responsible for the unanimity with which Americans turned on their radios to hear him; midwesterners as much as, if not more than, other Americans. They do not live among people who are used to manipulating the vast English vocabulary to secure those infinite shades of meaning which it permits.

According to the 1940 census, more Americans than in 1920 declared that a non-English language was their basic, familial tongue. Certainly in the cities and larger towns of the Midwest that percentage would be higher than the all-American average. The language and vocabulary of the working people in these cities and towns, of cab-drivers and bell-

[8] It may surprise Americans, and Englishmen, to know that the notorious "B.B.C." accent (British Broadcasting Corporation) and the so-called "Oxford" accent sound immeasurably affected and stilted to *English* ears in America—and to not a few in England.

hops, are very different from those of the East, as they are different from the older Anglo-Saxon of Midwest farmers and rural towns and of the South. The vocabulary is very small; smaller than that of the London Cockney. Speech is very laconic, which is again often mistaken by the stranger for rudeness or abruptness. One phrase, indeed a monosyllable or gesture, serves many purposes. "Sez you," "Oh yeah," "You betcha," and "Okay," brief as they are, become an exhaled "Yeah" with a rising, incredulous inflection, or a crisp "Oke," "Yah," "Y' bet," "Uh-huh," "Fine," or even only a grimace with pursed lips and a nod. Much of all this is European, the Europe of peasants and farmers who are sparing of speech and prodigal of gesture: of Italy and Central Europe. The Irish, whether Scotch-Irish or southern Irish, never lose their great command and beautiful pronunciation of the English tongue, just as more than a thousand years ago they were the masters of Latin. They preserve their brogue. But immigrants and their children who have had not only to learn English but also to translate their own expressions into it as they assimilated the American way of life helped to mold the American tongue of today; and in the Midwest their influence is most apparent.

Of all these immigrants, Germans have had the greatest influence. This is especially evident in the cities and towns of the Midwest. Those who are particularly interested in this process must turn to Mr. H. L. Mencken's brilliant studies of the American language or to the many intriguing dictionaries of that most vigorous form of it: American slang. But in everyday speech very many German expressions have been exactly transliterated into Americanisms. A few examples will suffice.

To work "out of" St. Louis does not mean to work outside that city, as it would in English. It means the exact opposite. It means to work from inside it, as a headquarters, outward. That is one of the German senses of *heraus, hinaus*. The German *noch* or *mal* finds expression as "yet": "I owe you a dollar yet," or "Tell me yet, ..." The use of German floating prepositions is general: "he wants in" or "he wants out" means he wants to get in or out; the colloquial German *er will ein* or *h'rein*. To have an "out" means to have an excuse, alibi, or escape; and "That's out" means out of the question. They are the same as *etwas ist aus* or *hin*. "Out from under" is as pure German as the expressive *von oben herab*. To sit, muscle, cash, or horn "in on" something is another use of German floating prepositions divorced from their verbs; so is to "stop off at," to "lose out on" something, to "rest up," or to be "out on" a limb; so is "Do you want to come with?" To "make with" and to "give with" something are from *geben* and *machen mit*. Okay

229

or all right "by me" is *bei mir;* an Englishman would say "with me." "Leave me" do something is *lass mich doch etwas tun.* The universal plural of "ways" for way—a long "ways" away— is the German suffix *wegs* rather than *weg.* "I see *where* Congress has" done something or other is colloquial German; so is "It stinks." To have a "nice visit with" someone is a literal use of the German *besuchen* or to make a *Besuch bei* someone.

There is something German, too, in the extraordinary lengthening of words: instead of "reaction" you find "reactionism" and quite frequently "reactionaryism"; just as you find "revaluate" taken from "revaluation" instead of the simpler "revalue." It would not be surprising to run across "devaluationize," "devaluationization," or "devaluationism." This lengthening of words and a redundancy in the use of words contrast strangely with the laconic speech of so many midwesterners, especially those on the farms or those of many national origins in the towns and cities. There is in this mixture something of Italian and Scandinavian habits of speech, too. The extraordinary vigor and aptness of American slang are partly due to the need to develop a language of new peoples, by new peoples, for new peoples. Certainly the language of midwesterners is trenchant, apt, descriptive, and alive. There is nothing jaded, stilted, or affected in it. It is always renewing itself. And it has helped to produce a new style in novels, plays, newspapers, and magazines which is as colorful as Elizabethan English seems to us today, though that style probably shocked many an elderly person in Elizabeth's time.

On the other hand, there is a widespread tendency throughout America to employ long euphemisms, to give high-sounding names and titles to simple and ordinary things; and to this, too, midwesterners are not immune. Among people who are proud of calling spades spades, it is intriguing. It has nothing to do with the native languages of immigrants, all of which have simple words for these things. It is peculiarly American; and it is the American of city people, not of the farmers or rural towns. The word "parlor" often replaces "store," as the latter replaced the English "shop": funeral parlor, shoeshine parlor, beauty parlor or salon. But men still go to the barber shop; they, at least, do not visit a "tonsorial parlor," expect in Negro districts.

Clerks become junior executives and assistants. Junior executive assistants to assistant vice-presidents are not infrequent. Typists become stenographers, secretaries, and assistants. A lobbyist suggests lobbyism instead of lobbying; so why not lobbyer? We do not need to ask, anyway, because he is a "legislative representative." That does not mean, as you might suppose, that he is a representative in a legislature, though perhaps the term is warranted, since he often has more influence on representatives in legislatures than they themselves wield, and he certainly gets and uses more money. I like Midwest salesmen. They always say that's what they are, and have not yet dubbed themselves peripatetic turnover promoters, traveling consumption technicians, or perambulatory output distributors. This growing desire for high-sounding euphemisms is partly a protest against the growing classification and standardization, partly ambition. It is also part of the mythology, the fairyland, and fairy tale, which make life seem other than it is. It also reflects American, and particularly midwestern, optimism. It is human and understandable. It is as if roses grew and smelled the same but wanted to be called blossoms of Paradise. "If it makes you feel any better about it, it's okay by me." That is the typical midwesterner's attitude. Realism subscribes to myths; materialism to idealism. No one is fooled. Everyone uses the new formula. Everyone seems happy.

There is no truth in the widespread belief that the Midwest accent and inflection are the most harsh, nasal, drawling, and unpleasant in America. On the contrary, they are softer and less nasal than most. They markedly resemble the West Country accent, inflection, and pronunciation in England. The slowness of speech of Midwest men is often mistaken for a drawl; and on the western limits of the region a drawl does become noticeable. The townsmen speak more quickly than farmers; and on balance the dwellers in the countryside have more of a drawl and a more nasal pronunciation than the townsmen—as men who work in the big, open spaces seem to have, all over the world. But in Midwest towns and cities, particularly in the homes or in quiet places, the Midwest man's voice is soft, quiet, tentative, and pleasant. So is that of Midwest women.

But there is something in the caliber of women's voices in any land, especially when many are raised together in a confined space, that makes you fear they will strike the harmonic note of the building. The Midwest woman is no different from her American sisters and her various cousins abroad. Just as she is more lucid and fluent than her husband, so are her pronunciation and inflection different. Her pronunciation of "day," "fast," "high," "get," "not," "out," and "sorry" differs greatly from her husband's. Her pronunciation of vowels and diphthongs is more nasal than a man's. This is noticeable even among children at high school. It is not the observation of foreigners alone. Many Midwest writers, and other American men and women, have noticed it. Maybe it is a relic from days, not so long ago, when women had to call men and children from fields. That may not be utterly fanciful, for you notice it more in the countryside today, where you also find more of the same quality in the voices of the men.

The Old Midwest was nothing like as lawless as people believe. Frontier society was rough and tough, but its dominant urge was to make settlements, to provide a social framework of law and order for the family, the locality, and private property. As we saw, this framework was quickly established. The dissident, unsettled elements in the Old Midwest quickly left the region, taking most of the frontier characteristics of quarrelsomeness and lawlessness with them. The New Midwest sprang from villages, towns, and cities that already had all the necessary institutions of law and order. "Wild Bill" Hickok (Hitchcock) was born in Illinois and worked on the Illinois-Michigan Canal. But his exploits as a "bad man" were out in the cattle country. Jesse James was another midwesterner. But his adventures were not in the Midwest; they were part of the life of the Plains. So it was with Deadwood Dick, Colorado Charlie, and many others.

The old midwesterners, whose descendants remain in the rural areas, were quarrelsome, fond of horseplay and liquor, and religious. They held human life cheap, but not because they took lives lightly. They didn't. Nature did; and they were nothing if not children of Nature. They were not killers, gangsters, and murderers, even if they killed men in a fight and even if they were given to fighting. Law and order were deeply respected in the Old Midwest. There is no other way to explain the high esteem in which lawyers were held and the frequency with which they were selected as political leaders. In turn, the region was utterly different from the later frontier of the Plains, the bad lands of bad men. It remains today a rural region of law-abiding folk, far less quarrelsome than their forebears.

The cities of the New Midwest, on the other hand, were racked by social problems and lawlessness almost from their beginnings. What was confined to bad men out in the bad lands of the open country beyond the Midwest became largely confined to Midwest cities. The Midwest countryside was in the main settled and orderly. It still is. But from the time that the southern Irish began to come in the 1840's, the immigrant groups flocking to the cities and towns did not always consort well with each other.

Change, violent change, was in the air. Life was held more cheap there than out in the countryside or the smaller towns. These contrasts

232

remain. In the same cities where research, surgery, obstetrics, pediatrics, and health services have immeasurably lengthened life and saved lives, violent deaths seem more common per head than in many other places. In a country and region that place such high values upon their children, death still strikes them down with surprisingly frequent violence. In the last three years before Pearl Harbor, America lost more lives by automobile accidents than in the armed forces in the first three years of the ensuing war. Even the numbers of injured and wounded were comparable. "Anyone can drive a car" seems to be the rule. And many drivers obey it by driving anyhow, despite all rules and regulations.

The region and its people are not placidly uniform. The Midwest was filled, as we have noted, with millions of widely differing peoples within one long lifetime. Many of those people had, and still have, many children. A minority has very few. That makes the average, like many averages in this region of averages, look normal and ordinary. But in fact among the majority of Midwest city dwellers life has teemed so prolifically so recently, and is still so fruitful, that, as in many countries where people are prolific, death does not seem such an "awfully big adventure." People take it in their stride.

Again, though the country, the towns, and the cities developed inside a framework of law and order, it was one of the people's own making, even if its designs were brought from the older America. What the carpenters had made and put together, they could take to pieces or destroy. Politicians, representatives, judges, public officers, police—all these were at first drawn from among a few neighbors by a few neighbors. There was no halo of sanctity about them, no mythology. Even if titles and a vocabulary brought from the East and the Old World were applied to them, those words brought with them no long tradition of awe and respect. Wasn't the sheriff Tom So-and-so, who had played hookey with you? Wasn't the judge John Doe, whose frailties everyone knew? Wasn't the defendant Dick Roe, who, as all could testify, had no really dishonest, vicious, or criminal tendencies? Wasn't the plaintiff rather a nuisance? Who made that law, anyway? And how was it lobbied through the legislature, or council? "Pish! He's a good fellow, and 'twill all be well." Might easily have been me, at that. "Are you all agreed upon your verdict?" Are we? Sure! Not guilty.

If anyone doubts that line of reasoning and the result, let him read Lincoln's cases on Judge Davis' circuit. Let him spend a few days in the courts of Midwest cities today. He will be struck, then as now, by the superficial similarities in legal form, wording, and pleading to those of England. But it is the spirit that giveth life to the law, and the people are as different from the British—and to a smaller extent from those of the colonial society in the East and South which developed the forms and wording of American law—as Hungarians are from Germans, or Hungarian from German law. In a country where, as Bryce noted nearly three-quarters of a century ago, public opinion is the only true sovereign and lawmaker, laws themselves have no more efficacy and command no more respect than popular opinion is prepared to give them. In nothing was that truth more crushingly demonstrated than in the people's defiance of their own Constitution in the days of prohibition. The people are the real judges. They may not always try the cases, but they certainly either apply, or do not apply, the law.

It is only in this sense that midwesterners of the cities today, and even many rural midwesterners, cannot be said to be scrupulously law-abiding. They are certainly not lawless. Few people in the world live under more written and unwritten laws than Americans. There seem to be more lawmaking bodies in America than in most other lands; and that was true even before 1933. Federal, state, municipal, county, village, public agency—all these forms of law make a framework within which the individual must live as a law-abiding citizen. All these lawmaking agencies surround him; and whether he is a businessman or farmer, as soon as he moves from one jurisdiction to another, especially from one state or city to another, he may break laws and regulations of which he is ignorant; and ignorance of the law is no excuse. Many of the differences seem unreasonable to newcomers; and in the Midwest, newcomers are many and frequent. So they break the law.

Any written contract in America will require from half as many to twice or even three times the number of words, compared with those necessary in English, Dutch, German, or French law. Of the making of rules and regulations there is no end. Every "interest" every year is pushing bills through every legislature. The American draws up so many laws in order to have the power of relaxing or applying one or other of them to fit the many different kinds of Americans and their interests. There is a greater need of assimilation of many different peoples to one standard of conduct. You cannot trust so many different people to understand and conform to any loosely defined pattern of behavior. Lobbying, and purely local representation by legislators, are also largely responsible for this. In England, on the other hand, until recently, laws were far more general and far less particular than in America. Another reason is that nearly all Americans distrust appointed public officials. The Midwest from the outset distrusted them—governors, judges, whoever they might be. They feared life-tenure. They feared a power which could not be removed. They still do. That fear was most strongly and often virulently expressed, especially in the Midwest, during the late Franklin D. Roosevelt's successive terms of office.

Democratic as the election of all American judges (except federal judges) may be, however, they are liable to change frequently. They may therefore administer or interpret loosely worded law differently. So the law cannot leave as wide scope to the courts as it can—or could—in England. Again, owing to the multiplicity of courts, competencies, and jurisdictions, a case can be kept merrily going the rounds of one court after another, to the lawyers' deep satisfaction, for years. Juries can be "hung" in so many instances, and no decision may be reached. Retrials are frequent. To an English lawyer the general picture is reminiscent of Old Westminster Hall a century ago, where cases went from law into equity and back again, and from one court into another.

This accounts for the large numbers of lawyers in American life, from the earliest days until now. Thomas Wolfe said that the lawyer was a kind of medicine man to the community. The law was always the easiest stepping-stone for a young man to banking, big business, and politics. It still is. The law school bulks larger in American university life than in Europe. Yet, apart from these temporary reasons for being a lawyer, there was a great and growing need for lawyers of all kinds as written rules and regulations constantly multiplied. No one knows, no one knew before 1933, what he could or could not do until he had hired an attorney. The attorney or legal adviser is not like the family lawyer and family doctor in England: personal friends to whom one has occasional recourse whenever necessary. In America, with its one federal, forty-eight state, and numerous other lawmaking bodies, a retained lawyer is part of the normal costs of any moderate or even small business. He is a businessman himself. His business is not only to know law. That is a minor part of it. It is mainly to know many different sets of laws, how the law is likely to be applied, who applies it, where, in what setting, and in what ways. Many lawyers become real representatives of groups and interests, just as if they had been elected to watch "legislative representatives" or representatives in lawmaking bodies. Here, again, the difference from other countries during this period, and today, is not one of kind but of degree. Yet it is a big difference. It has had a profound effect on public opinion about the law and its administration. And public opinion is a higher court of appeal than the Supreme Court.

I once met a lawyer on the train in Indiana. He told me an illuminating story that illustrates this difference both in the attitude toward the law itself, and in legal procedure. A twenty-year-old soldier of good and modest family—he was a Midwest small-town boy, though not a "Hoosier"—deserted from camp in a Midwest state with three less reputable buddies. They roamed round a part of one state in a stolen car, making their money by robbery with violence at the point of a gun. They were finally caught. The boy's parents were duly informed and asked my traveling acquaintance, the town's leading lawyer, to go to the city in the neighboring state and do what he could for the boy. The father went along, too. The Army turned the boys over to the civil jurisdiction, and they duly came up for separate trials. The father and lawyer first went to the state's attorney and told him of the boy's excellent record. He was impressed and introduced them to the judge shortly before the trial. The judge was sympathetic and said, "Well, don't give us too much of a battle over this, and we'll see what we can do." Accordingly, the case went forward, and the lawyer threw his client on the mercy of the court. The state pressed only three counts against this boy. He was given a moderate sentence.

But then "public opinion" stepped in. One of the two local newspapers, the politics of which were opposed to those of the party that elected the judge, let loose a blast of criticism. Why was this boy not treated as severely as other criminals? Was it because his parents or friends were Utopians instead of Ruritanians? Who put such a judge on the bench? What were the city fathers and the police to do if this sort of thing went on? Was the law to be brought into contempt by those to whom it was intrusted by the people? Was society to be exposed, after a few months of a short sentence had been served, to a repetition of such depredations? Doubtless the governor, belonging to the same party as the judge, would issue a pardon in short order. See to what the citizens are exposed under Utopian misrule! And so on, all in that strain.

In very short order indeed the state's attorney and the police discovered another eight counts against the boy. He was joined with the other boys and was given a minimum stretch of fifteen and a maximum of twenty years. After that, my lawyer friend threw in his hand. He tried to assure the parents that the boy would not come out a hardened criminal and told them to wait until they could present a petition for clemency to the governor. Any appeal would have been fruitless.

That story, with changes and modifications, could be repeated in many city courts in the Midwest. There is much informality, personal and local influence, force of public opinion, politics, and elasticity of procedure. And all these correspond not to what the mass of the citizenry cherish as myths about law and order but to what they really think of many cases as they come up. Each is considered not merely on its merits as a case in law but also as a matter of personal, social, or local expediency. There is more to be said for this attitude than purists, sticklers, and many jurists think. It is flexible, informal, and responsive to opinion. Whether it is theoretically just, whether it nourishes respect for law, lawyers, and the courts, is quite another matter. It was a great and lovable justice of the Supreme Court who said: "The life of the law has not been logic; it has been experience." In Midwest cities the experience is varied and inexhaustible. It has produced its own attitude to law.

Both by very formal and informal procedures, the court takes account not only of the law but also of almost all aspects and circumstances of the case before it. The law is made by politicians. People know who they are. But it is applied by elected judges, who are expected to see justice as well as the law administered. It is yet another case of "checks and balances."

In England if you break the law, there is no help for you. It is the law that is injured, not local society. It does not matter in what kind of court you come up. If the law says thus and so, and the jury say by a majority that you broke it, down you go. The rules of evidence are extremely strict, particularly as to what is or is not admissible. If you are rich, it is certainly easier for you to hire better lawyers and make all due appeals—though even that is not true of serious cases. In many of these, leading counsel have enhanced their legal reputations, and thereby their later earning power, by taking a "poor man's brief."

In nonfederal American, and particularly in Midwest and western, courts public opinion, local considerations, and an extremely wide range of admissible evidence play a much stronger part. And the elected judge reflects public opinion more faithfully than in other regions or countries—even if he cannot reflect all of it, or that of the majority. The variety of courts, treatment, and decisions in America has resulted in a great extension of federal crimes, federal jurisdiction, and federal agencies; for examples, the taking of a woman "for immoral purposes" or a stolen automobile across state lines, kidnaping, and the growth of the famous Federal Bureau of Investigation. But this extension of federal power, as in so much else, is always in conflict with local opinion, local courts, and local lawyers.

Another effect of public opinion has been upon the rules of evidence. That has led many lawyers to be extremely zealous in behalf of the

237

accused. It is a good quality in lawyers. Deeply democratic, with their immense and commendable devotion to personal liberty and habeas corpus, and with their distrust of officials and officers, midwesterners have constantly agreed with more and more liberal interpretations of the rules of evidence in favor of the accused. Maybe there is some trace of a protest against standardization in this, too; of an intense feeling for the individual rather than for the shapeless mass of society. So far has this gone, however, that to many jurists it now seems that the business of the court is to defend criminals from society and not society from criminals.[9]

Other influences, also working in favor of the accused, are not so good for society. For instance, the first reaction of most Midwest city dwellers if they are at the scene of a crime is to get away from it quietly and quickly. They do not want to be involved, for understandable reasons. No one can tell what the criminal's syndicate, gang, or friends will do or threaten to do. No one can be quite sure what the police, who stand to be "shot at" in both senses of the phrase, will think or do.

The reasons for this have to be understood. In many big Midwest cities and larger towns, as in many other such cities the world over, there are "bad lands," localities in which feuds, vendettas, and folk quarrels are not typical of the great mass of the citizenry and are not peaceably settled. The police and other authorities constantly comb this criminal fringe of society. It is a kind of border warfare all the time. Neither the police nor the criminals and suspects are gentle with each other; and often an innocent party suffers. But not in every big city is the intimidation of innocent witnesses carried to the lengths which it reaches in many American cities, those of the Midwest included. And that is due to the organization, the syndication, of crime, vice, gambling, and racketeering.

This is not the place to describe all that, let alone trace its history and development. Many books, legal records, and articles attest its frequency. Yet few people understand the magnitude of the problem facing the authorities. In most cities of the region the comfortable, better-to-do, "right-thinking" citizenry have moved from the center, set up villages or small cities of their own, installed their own police, settled down to a life of complete security, and left the "bad lands" at the center on the hands of the city fathers. Suburbanites criticize the city fathers from comfortable and secure armchairs. Even if they all live in one town, the well-to-do live outside, do not see what goes on

[9] See the illuminating article "Case Dismissed," by Virgil W. Peterson, director of the Chicago Crime Commission, in the *Atlantic*, April, 1945.

at the center, and do not want to see it. They ask only not to be "involved." Yet they complain about the authorities when a crime, or wave of crime, makes their city notorious. In the heart of the cities and in their "bad lands," the gangsters, mobsters, and strong-arm boys carry out their operations. They resort to threats of violence against honest witnesses, their attorneys employ all the complexities of law and procedure, and the authorities are often hamstrung. The drastic code of gangland prevents "singing" or "squealing." And very many cases end in *nolle prosequi*.

Reformers think that if more right-thinking citizens went into politics en masse, if crime-busting were one tithe as popular as prohibition was, the authorities would change and the gangs would change their venue. But they would soon come back, unless the hardworking and decent businessmen and others kept on running the cities on the new lines. Life is short and business is long. It is hard to make an indictment for murder "stick" and then secure a conviction. It will take far longer to root out the gambling and vice syndicates, the rackets, the thugs and the goons who commit so many murders. There were 202 "felonious homicides" in Chicago alone in 1944. In 41 cases no arrest followed. Only half of the cases resulted in trials. A still smaller fraction resulted in the conviction of the accused. And there was only one sentenced to death. Governors are then induced to commute sentences. Many a total sentence of 199 years is completed within 5 or 10.

All of this goes on, too, within narrow limits of variation, in Cleveland, Detroit, Cincinnati, Kansas City, St. Louis, and Indianapolis, and many smaller cities. Lawyers and leading citizens of the highest eminence describe it, in private and not for the record. Citizens know it. The press attests it. Mayors and city officials admit it. But what can they do, beyond giving orders? It is not law or orders that count; it is their execution or enforcement. And that occurs "way down the line."

Cheapness of human life and addiction to violence were not native to America. They were brought in from southern and Slav Europe and from Ireland, by prolific people who lived in tribes and clans and pursued hatreds with zeal and enjoyment. The letting-loose of these people in the rough-and-ready atmosphere of new and growing cities started the trouble. When they all got the vote as citizens and were organized in their wards and dense city localities, it became almost impossible to unscramble the eggs. Local politics inevitably became bound up with the administration of justice, which then became very local indeed. There is not a city of 100,000 souls or more in the Midwest where this problem of violence, cheapness of life, and lawlessness does not raise its

239

head in acute form with fair regularity, and irrespective of the particular political party in power. I have seen an estimate for the cost of murders during the period 1930–40 in the states of Ohio, Michigan, Indiana, and Illinois combined—the core of the Midwest. It seems that, much more than the cost of living and the general price level, the cash cost of procuring a murder rose from an average of about $200 in 1930 to about $800 in 1940. But far more interesting was the estimated risk of detection and of incurring a penalty. That was as follows: detection, 20 to 1 against; trial, 34 to 1 against; conviction, 70 to 1 against; death sentence and execution, 160 to 1 against. Men faced far worse risks of death in the war than that, for far smaller cash rewards.

The Midwest citizen's attitude to all laws, rules, and regulations lies at the back of all this. He forms the mass of public opinion. He is the most individualistic American of all that individualistic people. He hates constraint of all kinds. It is up to his proverbial ingenuity to find a way round, to "get by." He slips an inspector a bill to pass an elevator, boiler, or fire escape as safe. It may be safe, even if it does not conform to a city ordinance; and the wording of that ordinance may have been secured by an "interest" aimed at some other interest or group. He lets his son break the law at an early age by driving the car without a license. The boys and girls grow up in that atmosphere. It may not be serious. It does not seem a crime. But it accumulates and forms a social atmosphere in which "clever," "smart," and "wise" come to have peculiar meanings. The ordinary citizen gets his party precinct captain to talk to the committeemen, to the "ward heelers," or to the ward boss— ominous phrases—to "fix" the summons served on him for leaving his car in an unauthorized place. It is fixed. Citizen and party workers are satisfied. The citizen talks at home or among friends about his or his party man's success. The judge, elected by party votes, may be quite content. Many of the police are not so satisfied. Who's running them? The atmosphere seems natural. No harm seems to have been done to anybody. It was just having a "drag" or a "pull" with someone in the right place.

But great things from little causes grow. Political "protection" has been established. From such small beginnings with small fry it waxes and flourishes into protection for bigger fish who do harm the community and its reputation. What our ordinary citizen and his friends can accomplish, so can people who want contracts or franchises; so can a powerful lobby, a big vested interest, a trade-union and its local branches, or a gambler's syndicate. What Lincoln Steffens described still goes on in the majority of Midwest cities and large towns. But not only criminals and gangsters are thereby indictable. And of all

240

injustices the greatest is to blame the police. They are perhaps more deserving of sympathy than anyone.

In the months of June and July, 1944, police of the Fourth and Fifth police districts of Chicago were reported to have made arrests for gambling, with the following results in the South State Street (Racket) Court:

POLICE OFFICER	ARRESTS	FOUND GUILTY
A	110	2
B	33	2
C	134	1
D	213	6
E	152	3
F	117	2

Two out of every hundred arrests resulted in conviction. And, " in all the guilty cases, the fine was uniformly $10."[10] The enormous majority of cases were dismissed for "lack of evidence" or because "the evidence was not properly obtained." Yet the gambling syndicate's warfare in the city between 1943 and 1945 resulted in the slaying of "Danny" Stanton, Martin "Sonny Boy" Quirk, James "Red" Fawcett (alias Forsyth) a former member of the Capone gang, Morris Margoulis, and many others. Of Fawcett, one of the state's attorney's officers said: "He's been responsible for a murder a year for twenty years." No one brought them to book. They and their competitors settled accounts in traditional fashion. All that the citizens and municipal authorities needed to do was to wait. But meanwhile there were a lot of murders. And few of the murderers were found. The law, its enforcement officers, and its institutions thus come into contempt. The impression spreads among the dissatisfied, the antisocial, and the unassimilated that "crime pays."

Many nice people think it doesn't pay. The trouble in these cities is that crime pays handsomely; so handsomely that many officials, both elected and appointed, and many otherwise normal citizens are attracted into close or more remote association with it. Al Capone's syndicate took $25,000,000 a year from gambling alone; and Al was midwestern enough not to recognize any limitations. He ran many businesses. His money was not just drawn from a few gamblers. If anyone thinks Chicago is unique, let him read the histories of the Birger-Shelton gang warfare in St. Louis and East St. Louis, in which forty people were slain, in which Ku Klux Klansmen were deeply implicated, and in which armor-plated tanks were used by the criminals. Something very like it reared its head again in 1943 and 1944. Let him

[10] *Chicago Daily News*, September 6, 1944.

241

read the records on the slaying of Michigan's state senator Hooper in 1945 because "he did a little talking"; or of the exploits of Pete Licavoli in Detroit, known in 1945 as the "Al Capone of Detroit." Let him read of what went on in Cleveland, Kansas City, St. Paul, and many another Midwest, or, for that matter, American, city: Boston, New York, Philadelphia, Baltimore, New Orleans, Los Angeles, and others. It goes on, in varying degrees, now. Whenever or wherever there is "big money" to be made by organized evasion of the law, it goes on; and naturally it is confined to cities, all over the world. Lawlessness, theft, and black-marketing were more obvious in wartime and postwar Britain than at any time since the days of highwaymen because there were acute shortages and people wanted things badly enough. They were not, however, as violent as in America.

If gangsters die suddenly, their fortunes don't. Their families live on. So crime pays someone, all the time. Even some criminals live on—in beautiful homes in the deep South, or in Illinois, Ohio, Kentucky, Michigan, and California.

Gangsters, mobsters, goons, hoodlums, and their warfare are not confined to the diversions of the people. Some of the worst wars have been, and still are, between rival trade-unions, federations of unions, or local branches into which "emigrants" from gangland have penetrated. (The unions are not always organized from below, by their members.) "Company unions" have been among the most violent. These union wars are as savage as any between the employers' private police, or vigilantes, and strikers. The teamsters' strikes in Chicago in the early 1900's led to the separate formation of "Local 705" in that city and its refusal to continue in the Teamsters' Union of the A.F. of L. It was peculiarly linked to the employers themselves. It kept the A.F. of L. teamsters out of Chicago for a generation by strong-arm methods. One of its leaders "died on Madison St. of buckshot wounds."[11] The great truck strikes in Chicago in 1945 which defied federal authority and necessitated bringing thousands of soldiers into the city to guard and run the trucks were not the work of the A.F. of L., C.I.O., or any other federattion or union, but of the independent "Chicago Truck Drivers' Union" —old "Local 705" in a new dress.

Crime, violence, and lawlessness, however, are localized. I think that ninety-nine out of every hundred persons in Chicago and other big cities have never seen a crime of violence or heard a criminal's shot. In the slums and the quarters into which the poorer workers of so many different racial and national origins are crowded, crimes, especially

[11] Those interested should read Mr. Edwin Lahey's witty account of "Local 705" in the *Chicago Daily News*, May 29, 1945, entitled "Chicago's Andorra."

those of quick temper or coldly premeditated violence, are bound to be more common than in nice residential areas and delightful suburbs. Murder, rape, and robbery with violence accompany gambling, vice, and other raw diversions of human nature—"nature, red in tooth and claw." All are very marked in a few city districts. Unfortunately, these crowded districts have many votes and great political importance. They put the elected officials in power and keep them there. These officials, including judges and the mechanicians of city "machines," think twice about intervening or even prying into the details and personalities of the vote-keeping. The local district boss and party officials are free to make what arrangements they like about local residents, local diversions, local judges, local businesses, local financing of the machine, and what local sources of funds shall be tapped.

The Chicago Crime Commission reported that in one six-month survey of gambling in the various police precincts, nearly half of all arrests were made in the densely crowded Fifth (Wabash Avenue) Police District.[12] But it also showed that in that one district and in that period a quarter of all murders in the city took place, a quarter of all cases of rape, more than a quarter of all cases of aggravated assault, and more than one-sixth of all robberies. While that district on Chicago's Southwest Side houses many Negroes, it contains a majority of white persons in groups of bewilderingly different national origins.

The majority of Chicagoans know no more of this kind of life than they read in their papers. If anyone "respectable" is involved in it, they should not be there at all. They should look after themselves and expect what they get. And if perchance "it" happens to someone on the Near North Side—well, "that's one of the risks of city life." That phrase was quoted to me, spontaneously and sincerely, by one of Chicago's leading lawyers. It was the same man who said: "What can I do? Hell, I haven't got any votes to deliver; and my rich friends and myself can't compete with the financial resources of gangsters and racketeers!"

In fairness to Chicago it must be said that many criminals resort to that city from others in America. Her fame, or notoriety, has been blackened by non-Chicago Americans: not least by Hollywood. And, of all things, to make folk heroes and heroines for the young out of pimps, gangsters, murderers, and their molls was no service to American youth, to Chicago, or to a world that is so prone to judge America by Hollywood's standards. The first real gangsters, accompanied by their goons and hoodlums, were brought into Chicago by tough businessmen and their agents from New York, Boston, Philadelphia, Pittsburgh, and other eastern cities—to break the strikes in the 1890's, in the period

[12] Report to annual meeting, February 15, 1945, and further report summarized in the Chicago Sun, June 11, 1945.

243

between 1900 and 1916, and in the postwar period from 1919 onward. It was only in that latter period that prohibition provided such a rich market, and a savage battleground, for them—as in all American cities.

In this there is something of a moral. Competition and lobbying for "franchises" from governmental bodies have been keen and widespread from the beginnings of towns, cities, public transport, and utilities in the Midwest. The links between elected politicians, elected and appointed public officers, and big-business interests have naturally been close and "affected with" finance from the outset. The states of the new region and the new cities had real estate, rights of way, powers to tax and exempt from taxes, and many other highly valuable concessions to grant in the form of charters or franchises to persons, syndicates, and utilities. Wisely, they made most of these franchises revocable and terminable. Inevitably the consideration offered for them, and for their renewal, was high. If the highest bidder did not always get the franchise, the one who satisfied most of the grantors did. Every one of these franchises was for something badly needed by the citizens. That is what made them pay. Canals, lumber, railroads, streetcars, electricity, gas, coal, highways, municipal supplies, disposal of the dead, standards of quality for milk, delivery and packaging of goods, distribution, parking, access—the list is as long as Don Giovanni's catalogue. The traffic was highly profitable to the business interests; and often, if they wanted traffic at all, they had to pay what it would bear. This led to "corners" as well as to the "cutting of corners"; and, not to put too fine a point on it, to polite and nonviolent blackmail or intimidation.

But what begins with seeming innocence among a few, ends with what is more commonly recognized as guilt among the many. The employer who brings in goons and vigilantes to break a strike lives to see whole unions or "locals" run by goons, the closed shop, the check-off of union dues, and the maintenance of union membership. The first strikers who resorted to violence in one locality live to see big unions run by bosses—like breeding like—who refuse to make accounts of the union's funds to members, refuse to hold annual meetings, and live like princes or gangsters. The big businessman who lobbies a franchise or a discriminatory bill through the city hall, state legislature, or Congress itself, lives to see rules and regulations lobbied through by organized labor. He lives to see "Little Jimmy" Petrillo controlling the musicians of the country and much of the music on the radio; defying a President; and doing it very profitably, for his union treasury at any rate. And all of them see gangsters' syndicates faithfully, if more violently, copying their own violent jurisdictional disputes, muscling in on things greatly needed by both sets of people: liquor, music, gambling,

244

raw and even less raw diversions, and entertainment. There is more than a casual similarity between all these things. It is reminiscent of the old claim-staking and claim-jumping.

The racketeer is the modern bandit or highwayman. He even gives to the poor, as they did. His "ban," like that of a feudal robber baron, falls on whole territories: for instance, the streets in which any given laundry, dairy, or liquor store wants to pick up and deliver. He grants "franchises" for a consideration. He charges what the traffic will bear. He has no legal right to do so. But he has the might, as many an employee and manager in the distributive trades has testified. And few employers who are paying "shakedowns" like to admit it in court. The scarcer the things people want, the greater the opportunity and the wider the scope for rackets. The shortages in the second World War showed that. Many of the goods on the white market came from the black, and no one knew what "corners" by racketeers were affecting the public interest in food, liquor, cigarettes, or anything else legitimate, to say nothing of the real black markets themselves. There was something traditional and familiar about it.

It seems to the stranger a problem of bewildering complexity and scope. But, as in so much, the everyday business of life goes on, the mass of the citizenry do not come into personal contact with it, and society takes it in its stride. There is time to change it all, slowly; in the people's own way and in their own good time. The unpleasantness is almost completely kept from sight, or segregated in small areas. Publicity alone tells the story. The majority of cases in the local courts are fairly, impartially, and efficiently tried. The violence of the criminal does not come near the lives of the overwhelming majority of the people. Those are already signs of improvement. The public conscience is awakened. The press sees to that. Youth has been seriously affected by the general apathy toward lawlessness, and midwesterners will do anything for their young.

They are anxious to solve the problems of their cities, as are their fellows in the other cities and towns of America and foreign lands. The difficulty is to know where to begin: in municipal or state politics, in Congress, in the organization of leisure, in party politics, in the elections of judges decided by party caucuses, in business, in the home and family—where? The encouraging feature is that so few adult citizens think it can be cured by "doing something for the children," or by the churches, or by changing a police chief. It goes deeper than that. It is a problem of city society, of the voters and not just of the candidates, of the citizens themselves. Nice people did not think so when Lincoln Steffens was muckraking. They do now.

245

VI. THE CULT OF THE AVERAGE

TO THE GREAT MAJORITY OF MIDWESTERNERS, HOWEVER AND WHEREVER they live, the education of their children is most important. It arouses much private and public discussion in political circles, in the home, and in many voluntary associations. It is the charter for the equality of children, for which so many immigrants came to the region. The teaching of "the young idea" is not a social institution which "just growed" with Midwest society and is viewed as part of the order of Nature. It is one of those recent man-made institutions which, like much else in the region, is periodically taken out, examined, transformed, and set to work anew. Political changes or voluntary movements see to that, even if the transformations are not as complete as the majority would like them to be.

It is recent; very recent. Public education on any ordered scale in the region is scarcely more than a hundred years old. It was called forth from a busy people mainly by the great efforts of women, New Englanders, ministers, and a few leading citizens. It has had to change vastly and frequently to fit new peoples with new ideas as they populated the region. It has had to assimilate their children and equip them with Americanism. It achieved the widest regional literacy in America before 1914. It has had to keep pace with big changes as the various new forms of transport and the quicker communication of ideas transformed a region of insulated agricultural settlers into one of the greatest industrial regions of the world, if not the greatest. And as they are all still changing, still in the process of "becoming," so is Midwest public education. It is as complex and as varied as the life of the people.

As in many countries a long time ago, and in most today, the main problem of Midwest education was that of teaching the "three R's" to the children of farmers. It was at this stage that many men and women with a little learning, much zeal for the young, and natural teaching ability started rudimentary classes in an attic, a store, a "church," or in their own cabins. Lincoln learned eagerly, arduously, and therefore well from such teachers.[1] But this rudimentary education was unorganized. It was education for the necessarily ignored and ignorant children of a rural, segregated, and hardworking people. When railroads were built and roads were made, waves of immigrants and settlers came both to towns and to country, and then educational institutions multiplied exceedingly. The individual teachers remained, but in little red schoolhouses built for them. These schoolhouses are fresh in the memory of many midwesterners today, and they are still a majority of the schools out in the countryside. They are the monument of the vanishing Old Midwest. But they are still important. The United States Office of Education in 1938 stated that more than half the public-school buildings in America consisted of one room and that most individual teachers were teaching the children through eight grades of study. The problem reflected by these figures is mainly that of the South, Southwest, and Great Plains regions; but in the Old Midwest today it is apparent as soon as you enter purely agricultural counties and townships.

The majority of midwesterners today view problems of the public education of young people up to the age of eighteen under four main headings. These headings correspond to the four main purposes which education of all kinds must serve. First in order of importance, education must assimilate different children from widely differing economic or family backgrounds to "the American way." Whether the school is private or public, in city or town or country, the first aim is to make good American citizens out of widely differing young people. This means that it must iron out disparities, establish an American average to which pupils must conform, and necessarily must also to a substantial degree standardize them. All education does that, everywhere; but in the Midwest there are clear reasons why it must do it to a greater ex-

[1] See Kunigunde Duncan and D. F. Nichols, *Mentor Graham, the Man Who Taught Lincoln* (Chicago: University of Chicago Press, 1944). This book gives a valuable and fascinating account of the beginnings of education in Indiana and Illinois. See also Lloyd Lewis, *John S. Wright, Prophet of the Prairies* (Chicago: Prairie Farmer Publishing Co., 1941).

tent. A Swiss, Swedish, Dutch, French, or British child comes to school in those European countries from a family which is already long and closely assimilated to a national or folk pattern of life and thought. That is not so in most of America; and in the Midwest it is less so than in the East and South. Education is therefore from the outset not just, nor even first, a matter of mere learning; not a matter of "leading forth from" the pupil the capacities he or she may possess. It is more a matter of "putting in" standards of good Americanism and of general knowledge. But as that is by no means all it is in the Midwest, in education we also find extremes, contrasts, paradoxes, problems, and difficulties not found in other regions and lands, or not found to the same extent.

Secondly, education must mold or establish the individual's character and temperament. It must make the pupil self-dependent at the same time as it makes him a "good mixer," a member of the community, and a playing member of the all-American team. It must make him adaptable in a country and region of great differences, extremes, and rapid change. It must also make him resourceful in a region of marked individualism, initiative, and enterprise. Clearly, the task facing the teacher is exacting. He, or more frequently she, must reconcile the accent on individual character with the accent on the average, the pattern, and the community.

Thirdly, education must provide a general, average standard of learning as the young person's start in life—he and she are entitled to it on the basis of equality. The adult citizen, which the pupil will become, will find adaptation, understanding of society, and mixing with his fellows much easier if all of them, when young, share in the same broad pattern and elements of learning. This third aim of education is the most distinctively midwestern. It comes down, in clear and unbroken descent from the earliest days of primitive education in the Old Midwest, tinged with strong feelings of equality and democracy.

Fourthly, and only as far as is compatible with the attainment of these other three aims, education must be selective. It must provide courses in anything for which pupils show a desire or an aptitude. In other words, it must sieve out the pupils who will best profit from a college education, it must spot the able individuals who stand out from the average, and it must give them as much individual tuition or as great an opportunity to become more outstanding as it can afford—but always giving priority to the first three aims.

The midwesterner always distrusted intellectually outstanding people, geniuses of the mind (though not of "practical affairs"), nonconformists in general, and the abnormal. To this extent he showed,

248

and still shows, a remarkable similarity to the Englishman who dislikes things that "are not done." But, unlike most Englishmen, he believed and still believes that all young people, until their majority, have an equal right to a university education and the ability equally to profit from it, even if he knows the results are bound to be unequal. Accordingly, almost as early and as fast as private colleges were founded in the Midwest—mainly by easterners—midwesterners themselves set up state universities. Later, the leading citizens in big cities founded and endowed city colleges which added to the number available to young people. The standards of many of these had to be pitched low, to suit anyone who came to them.

Any student can "work his or her way" through college, if the student wants to. A greater proportion of public high-school students than in any other land, or than in most other regions of America, want a "college education" badly enough to work their way through. Those whose parents are able and willing to pay for them, send them "through college." It is the sacrifice by modest Midwest parents which is made with the least questioning. The extent of that sacrifice is largely unseen, especially by the children; but it is ungrudgingly made in hundreds of thousands of little homes. Thanks to rich benefactors, alumni, or state funds, the universities charge proportionately lower fees than the universities of Europe; but for parents who send their children through college, it is costly. To keep a young person there until he or she is twenty or twenty-one is bound to be so. And that, again, is why so many young people "work their way through."

Yet, to a smaller but still to a large extent, college education is viewed by the majority of midwesterners in much the same way as education in the public schools. The aims are much the same and certainly rank in the same order. The standards are very "practical" in the midwesterner's understanding of that word. The student is there to gain accomplishments that will make of him a worthy citizen. He is there to learn social arts and graces, the common life of sports and games, and the vocabulary of adult life. He is there to acquire knowledge, to take it in. He is there to acquire a training which will prove both practical and profitable in getting his living; to acquire "basic skills." And a minority are there to nourish genius, secure as much individual tuition as they can, enter the tantalizing portals of the life of the mind, and make their own individual contributions to it. Learning is still the "basic skills" or "book-larnin'" that mark the public grade and high schools, as it marked the old midwesterners' idea of education in general.

In school and college alike there is what seems to a European a strange reverence for books and the printed word. It may not be entirely fanciful to ascribe this to the wide extent of illiteracy in the region until one long lifetime ago; and to the reverence for "the Word" and the few men who could read and expound it in those days. Yet it is found all through American educational life. Certainly the heavy dependence of the first Midwest colleges upon religion and churches made their presidents and faculties rather dogmatic. It confined teachers within restraints from which they only began to break free in the 1890's and 1900's. Not all of them are free now. And if they are free from religious restraint, they certainly are not free from political and ideological restraints. But, to whatever it is due, "book-larnin'" seems to bulk inordinately large in Midwest universities—with notable exceptions.

The notable exceptions are famous throughout the world of learning: to name but a few, the University of Chicago, Northwestern University in Evanston, the University of Michigan at Ann Arbor, the University of Wisconsin at Madison, the State University of Iowa at Iowa City, and the University of Minnesota at Minneapolis. The region is equally rich in smaller private or denominational colleges of sound tradition, great learning, and much influence in the humanities: Grinnell[2] and Cornell in Iowa, Lawrence in Wisconsin, Knox in Illinois, Carleton in Minnesota, Oberlin in Ohio, and many others.

But within varying limits it seems to the stranger that the Midwest, and to a smaller extent the American, high school's and college's emphasis is heavily upon *indoctrination* rather than on *education* in the strict Latin meaning of those words; on putting in rather than on bringing out; upon instilling the ideas of others rather than on criticizing them or getting the student to form ideas of his own; upon examinations of the student's absorptive capacity rather than of his originality or exposition; upon assimilation rather than on an independent, critical power to reason and to discriminate. These may seem like hard sayings, and this is not a treatise on education. But these observations are those of the leading educators of America who began and still lead a revolt, much of which borrowed its force and its leading exponents from great and exceptional Midwest colleges and schools. What Harper of the University of Chicago disliked and tried, with success, to change, Hutchins of the same university tries, in different ways, to change today. And there are many such men in the private or state universities of the region now dedicated to the task of reducing emphasis on mass-produced learning, on papers and textbooks and examinations, on grading

---

[2] It was to the Reverend J. B. Grinnell that Horace Greeley in 1853 said, "Go West, young man, go West and grow up with the country."

and "points" and classification systems which treat young minds like sides of beef, counts of yarn, or qualities of tobacco.

In many high schools and colleges the student is graded by credits and marks not on his originality but on knowledge of facts, lectures, and books. Even the examination papers are questionnaires or quizzes by which the student's rank or grade is established. And the teachers are so overworked, giving lectures and grading or marking innumerable papers, that there is little time for individual tuition or seminars. All this results in a standardized pattern of college or high-school education—open to all, the same for all, but hard on teacher and student alike. It is highly significant that the leading universities of the region are famous for their *postgraduate* departments and professors and that only among these can the outstanding graduate, the young man or woman who departs from the average or mass, find the necessary individual tuition, cherishing, and nourishment.

In the main, the best of European high-school and college education aims to *make* the student critical, both of his teacher and of what is being taught. It aims to discover and then develop the original and independent qualities or capacities of the young mind. The only outstanding exceptions were in the universities of the old Germany, in which the professors delivered their lectures, devoted themselves to postgraduate work and research, were a great force in public life, enjoyed high social status, and gave individual tuition to a favored few. American universities were vastly influenced by those of Germany between 1840 and 1900. Much of that influence, despite the revolt against it which began at the close of last century, still remains—particularly in the Midwest.

Clearly, here are the sources of some of those characteristics which we have already noted of the bulk of adult midwesterners: respect for and devotion to the average, a lack of discrimination, a passion for facts, and less ability to manipulate them. Here, once more, is another instance of a Midwest paradox of extremes: emphasis on individualism but also on a standardized average, the greatest tolerance in the world but equally great emphasis on conformity. What is taught as fact from an approved textbook to large classes of different young midwesterners in high schools, with the aim of making them one and indivisible, often ends either by crystallizing prejudices or by creating terrible problems for those university professors who later on try to develop an original, independent, and critical faculty in those same young minds. What the public schools do, many of the best universities, both state and private, have to try to undo. It was the *esprit de corps* which Emerson found and liked in England a century ago. But American educators visiting England since 1918, and especially today, find more striking, and commend more, the individual originality of young Britishers in high schools and universities. And the visitors are not by any means all easterners.

From the outset, midwesterners firmly believed that all human knowledge could be reduced to the level of popular understanding. The forerunner of the "digest" of today, and of the textbooks that tell all about everything, was the Midwest man's and woman's "Companion to Knowledge" of the 1830's to 1860's. It was a thoroughly laudable aim that all knowledge should be "understanded of the people"; and in a society of settlers and small towns largely inhabited by a homogeneous population, it was almost feasible. It did not, however, become feasible when the population changed and became bewilderingly diverse. The average of Americanism to which the children of alien immigrants had to conform naturally suggested an average level of understanding, an average of potted knowledge which should be each child's birthright. But the average had to be lower in terms of knowledge, wider in terms of social accomplishments, behavior, and "basic skills." And, as each child was democratically equal, it followed that the pace of the class should be set within the average pupil's range of ability—often, indeed, within that of the slightly backward pupils, to be on the safe side. The great differences among the children's families and the newness of the Midwest naturally resulted in the deliberate "patterning" of young Americans. The pledge to the flag filled the gap made by the absence of any formal religious instruction or prayers. The teaching of patriotism and what it means to be an American was bound up with the teaching of history from textbooks approved, and even commissioned on well-defined lines, by politicians. The results are not always good for a sound conception of history or of other peoples, or for independent and critical judgment. But they are doubtless good for Americanism. The Midwest has proved that.

The children of alien immigrants, and the immigrants' votes, have altered the content of education to a large extent. It is surprising to a European today to find that most pupils in Midwest high schools and many at college can read, but cannot understand, the great speeches of Calhoun, Webster, Clay, and Douglas. It is doubtful if Midwest schools and colleges today can teach their masterly style and logic; and many midwesterners themselves deplore the passing of the clear simplicity of Lincoln's English, as shown not in his great orations but in his letter to General Hooker. The generation of midwesterners which passed

252

from the scene in the 1920's certainly could comprehend the language of its fathers' day and age. To the pupils in high schools and to many students in college since 1920, that language and the fine logic and reason in those speeches are alien, archaic, and well-nigh incomprehensible. The American, the Americanism, and the American language of today are all very different from those of 1860. They are changing fast; and this is reflected in education.

Whatever schools and colleges may lack in developing an independent critical faculty or originality in their young people, they offset by developing practical and technical skills. The great inventors, industrialists, and businessmen of the region have richly endowed technical institutions, separately or as parts of a university, which are the envy of scientists all over the world. It is in branches of technique that the Midwest boy or girl most easily and naturally achieves self-expression: for in these fields of practical knowledge or skill, formulas or a technical vocabulary are manipulated instead of "abstract ideas." The midwesterners' emphasis on the practical, their insistent query, "Will it work?" and their readiness to try anything once have more than justified themselves in the fields of natural science, medicine, transport, psychology, agriculture, meteorology, and commerce. It is natural that this emphasis should spill over into social studies. It leads not only many businessmen but also many principals, presidents, and professors to believe that departments dedicated to what are misleadingly termed "the social sciences" can be, or should be, as practical, precise, and prophetical as those concerned with the natural sciences. It is natural, too, that they cannot be so practical. But it is also imperative that they should be encouraged in every way to undertake fearless and impartial research. Yet there are still great difficulties for historians, political scientists, economists, and sociologists.

These studies of human society are greatly influenced by currents of contemporary political thought. Principals, presidents, and professors have to tread with extreme delicacy along these dangerous paths, for they have the care of students whose parents have strong political convictions, much distrust of what is called "pure speculation," and a consuming hatred for what is termed "advanced thought" or described as "radicalism." The situation of these teachers in public high schools, and especially in state universities, is not particularly enviable. It accounts for the colorlessness of much that is taught in the social studies. Neutrality must be preserved. In these subjects teaching goes on under limitations and restraints imposed by intolerance or the fear of it. It is just another of the contrasts in the region. The contrast is

253

heightened by the extreme brilliance of achievements in the more "practical" fields of study and research. But it has a bearing on the tendency of many great or promising thinkers and teachers to quit the region and its colleges. The brilliance and originality seem fated, in the main, to be nourished and developed in "practical" studies and skills. The young sense this as quickly as the teachers, and the ship sails forward with a heavy list to one side. The master and his crew do all they can to redress the balance. But it is on the side of the humanities, arts, and social studies that the vessel lacks equipoise.

In all the leading high schools and universities of the region this struggle is going on with characteristic nobility of purpose and vigor. But it would be wrong to say that it is nearly settled, that it is easy, or that the issue is beyond question. And that, too, is not the problem of educators in the Midwest alone. What one can say is that if the outcome is successful there, it will more affect the Midwest way of life, and be more fruitful there, than it will anywhere else in America; and that all Americans will then be astonished at the richness of promise and performance. For the latent talent is boundless.

"THE YOUNG IDEA"

If you turn away from the current disputes between educators in all countries to look at young people themselves, you are greatly encouraged and comforted. Whatever Midwest education's problems may be, whatever it may lack, its results in making good American citizens are great and undeniable. It is natural that midwesterners should want it to be better than it is. But they need not make the best the enemy of the good. The good is all around them.

Midwest boys and girls, young men and women, are more like those of democratic Sweden and Switzerland than any others in Europe. The East of America may still place more of a premium on sheer intellectual and cultural abilities, it may still be the mirror of fashion and mold of form in these fields, but it is in the Midwest schools that you can best study the educational system as it turns out sturdy, convivial, generous, and human young Americans. Not a little of the gallantry and intrepidity of the very young Midwest boys in the second World War is due to their schools and teachers; and a surprisingly large number of those who returned recognized it and went back to the school to tell the teachers so.

For this, the nonintellectual side of the school curriculum and of school life in general is responsible. Whether in a one-room schoolhouse or in the most up-to-date and beautifully appointed schools in the world—and both are numerous in the region—the accent is as much on the young pupils as potential members of the community as it is on what they can be made to absorb, what mental capacities they possess, or what intellectual faculties they can develop. Who dare say, today, in our vexed age, that this is wrong? Humanity has suffered more from frustrated intellectuals than from lowbrows or hearties. The latter are social; the former antisocial.

The pupils are encouraged to run their own social life in their own way and by their own elected nominees. Not all schools, least of all those in the countryside, can afford teachers and facilities to make this social side of school life resemble what it is in the best schools of the region. But in many schools in well-to-do suburban communities, big cities, large towns, and smaller towns, the high-school pupils of both sexes are now social types with a life and lingo of their own. In many high schools I know, I found that the seniors had balloted for the following choices among their number and in each sex: best-looking, most popular, most original, best personality, best dancer, biggest flirt, most bashful, best leader, best athlete, best dressed, funniest laugh, most industrious, most sophisticated, most naïve, blushing beauty, most conceited, biggest show-off, best mannered, most photogenic, most business-like, best natured, teacher's pet, most sportsman-like, biggest eater, wittiest, biggest bluffer, laziest, peppiest, and most likely to succeed. The names were all published in the newspaper edited, managed, and run by the pupils themselves. The average age of seniors in these schools would be a little under seventeen and a half; but among juniors, sophomores, and freshmen a corresponding independence, sense of humor, community spirit, and readiness to give and take as members of the community were as well marked. The emphasis of the young everywhere is on good comradeship; but these lists show a remarkably heavy emphasis on the social achievements and a remarkably light one on anything else. They are typical in that.

Coeducation is responsible for much of this. If it interferes with purely intellectual learning, and if it leads to more sex problems for the young in the cities than out in the country, it results in an enormous net gain. In school hours the constant comradeship between the sexes, the differences of ability, and the scholastic competition between them are all to the good. This is most noticeable out in the country, where the smaller numbers of pupils of both sexes, in groups, form a little nation of their own. They have easy access to sports and open-air games, winter and summer. They work and play together virtually year in,

255

year out. In the towns and cities this comradeship in active relaxation is rarer.

The young people have acute problems of their own. They are generally adept at solving them. But there is now a rift between both teachers and parents, on the one hand, and children on the other, which may grow wider. Already it is causing much concern, and in the Midwest it is particularly obvious. For decades, indeed for generations, children in the Midwest have been taught in school, and often in the home, that their region is the most go-ahead in America and, therefore, in the world; that the past is dead; that the future alone is important, for it is made into today.

While all this is natural enough in the Midwest, it is also natural that it should have the widespread effect of making young people identify their parents with a remote past, as if those parents had been pioneers who cleared the ground for their homes from the forest primeval and shot Indians off it. It has made Midwest youth more impatient of advice and of counsel drawn from both teachers' and parents' experience (they are of almost the same generation) than most of the youth of America— and that, by European standards, is saying a lot. It has probably helped to make them the extraordinarily self-reliant, capable, and resourceful young people they are. But now the social problems of America, nowhere more extreme than in the Midwest, are forcing teachers and parents alike to look around them, to examine their own institutions, the foundations of their beliefs and ideas, and even to look backward to the past.

The young people sense the prevailing confusion of beliefs, the extremes and opposites, the divisions and frictions, but are as impatient as ever of "old-fashioned ideas." Teachers and parents are in a quandary, for they are divided among themselves on great social, political, or economic issues. What are they to tell the young? The parents can make their own decisions what version or what gloss they put upon these issues at home when they talk with the young people or before them. But the teachers and the schools are "on the spot." If a teacher ventures anything like an opinion on any of these issues, or says anything that could be taken as an opinion, he or she may lose a job. The control of education by the immediate locality and its opinion is far stronger in the Midwest than it is almost anywhere else. It is far stronger than the influence of local opinion on law and the enforcement of it. This results not in giving "the young idea" a lead toward clarity but in ignoring or soft-pedaling many vital and interesting questions of the day.

It is noteworthy that the young people debate these questions in clubs and discussion groups which they run for themselves; but to get help and guidance from impartial adults is both rare and difficult. Many American parents and teachers were worried in the second World War about boys of nineteen fighting for their country and others, merely because Uncle Sam told them to. American correspondents abroad testified that many young men had only the vaguest ideas of America's foreign policy, her relationships with other countries including those of South America, and of economics, labor relations, or political institutions in general. This is not isolationism, nor is it due to it. It can be found in the armies of all belligerents in varying degrees. It reflects educational problems. It is the outcome of a public education which makes boys mature early and treats them as men in almost all respects, but agrees in the main not to teach them anything on controversial issues— or to teach it in such a neutral way that no judgment or conclusion can be reached. It forms one of the most vexing of postwar problems. It is one on which the veterans who choose to take their college education after the war will have a profound influence. That influence is already apparent.

Many of the parents' problems do not, however, arise from the teaching curriculum. They arise from the emphasis on social life at school. In no schools is this social life more organized, or better provision for it made, than in many Midwest educational institutions. But it produces problems. The life is that of a mature and adult group with freedoms, codes of behavior, personal relationships, rules of conformity, fashions, and a vocabulary of its own. Parents want their children to mature young, and both parents and teachers do all they can to insure it. The greatest proof of that is the extent of liberty allowed to the young. But that liberty, like all liberty, cannot easily or safely be cut into neat slices and kept in iceboxes, to be brought out at schooltime or for well-defined occasions.

Liberty is the most pervasive of all atmospheres. In many if not most cities and towns of the region the social liberty and self-government of young people at school, which are means to maturity, often become means to revolt; and revolt does not break out at school or college. It breaks out in the home. Social life, when baulked, deteriorates into the rule of gangs among boys and girls. Some of the worst of the juvenile gangs were composed of girls in their teens. More frequently, and less harmfully, it becomes the domination of the group by exclusive cliques, which makes problems for many children and their parents. In the small rural towns the heady wine of personal and group liberty makes young people even more restless, for parental, conventional, and re-

ligious restraints are far greater there. The standardization of all-
American relaxations and diversions by the movies, radio, magazines,
and comic strips affects the young in towns and country alike. Their
chafings against parental control become more acute and frequent.
And naturally this all-pervading atmosphere affects the schoolwork of
many pupils.

Nevertheless, the pattern of good Americanism which the schools
set before their pupils is sound. Like many Midwest characteristics, it
is flexible and adaptable. It can take a lot of beating. Like their parents,
the young people carry a heavy cargo of common sense. They can see
an adult's viewpoint because they are more mature. They are the
freest, most natural, most poised young people in all countries of the
Western world; and that is true from kindergarten or nursery school
through college. No young people anywhere are more attractive. Nowhere else can a grown-up get as much enjoyment from being among
the younger generation. That is an enormous tribute to parents, teachers, and young people alike. Alongside this the costs, the exceptions,
and the problems seem minor and manageable: which is true of so
much in the Midwest.

EDUCATION AND THE ELECTORS

Public education in the Midwest was viewed from the very outset not
only as a right of the people but also as a service to the states and to the
union. It was therefore closely coupled with politics. The Constitution
guaranteed freedom of religion to all, which effectively prevented the
earlier New England conception of education—control by the local
religious community, dominated by one church and parson—from being
impressed upon public education by the new states of the region. Denominational schools and colleges had to be private institutions. The
Northwest Ordinance of 1787 provided the means whereby "schools
and the means of education shall forever be encouraged": the setting-
aside of one section of land, one thirty-sixth of each township, to support, by its proceeds, public education. But to this day public education
is bewilderingly complicated and uneven throughout the region.

The New England system of "local option," local control over public education, is nevertheless most typical in the Midwest. The states
can only provide their superintendents of education with relatively
weak sanctions: for instance, the ability to require educational standards from pupils who want to enter a state university or a state institution of higher education. The assessors of the various counties can, and
do, vary their assessments from which school funds derive. So one

school district may get ten or even a hundred times more money for education *per pupil* than one adjoining; yet the state cannot even-out or standardize either the funds or the teaching in the various school districts. The one section of land set aside for education in the central township of the city of Chicago is in the heart of the Loop, and its annual yield is a fortune; but a few miles out of the city, still in Cook County, there are old, one-room schoolhouses. Whatever is done in the field of public education—whether by the raising of funds, election of officers, appointment of teachers, or setting of standards of teaching —goes back to the people of the local community, the electors. In education they are often as distrustful of the state superintendent as the state is of the federal commissioner of education and his office. Education is the most decentralized of all public institutions in the Midwest. Control of their school or schools is in the hands of the electors of the big city, village, and school district.

This has great advantages and great disadvantages. It is democratic, but it is not equalitarian. A child has to be born in a good village, school district, or city to get good primary education, or his parents have to move to one, which accounts for much of Midwest mobility; or they have to be rich enough to send him to a private school. The wealthier districts get bigger and better schools—and a waiting list for potential residents. The poorer districts cannot afford better schools, so they cannot attract wealthier residents. To help the poorer school districts the federal government may propose subsidies or grants-in-aid to the needy states, but on terms, which means to many of the local citizenry the taking-away of their democratic control of their schools and educational standards. Not always are the "poor districts" in the countryside. In the early 1930's, and before that, big cities went bankrupt and teachers were not paid at all for months, and even more than a year. Yet, as many writers and speakers said in Midwest states when the bill entitled "The Educational Finance Act of 1945" was before the United States Senate Committee on Education and Labor: "Centralized bureaucratic control of the country's school systems would follow inevitably in the wake of federal money." The great disparities and unevennesses between school districts and schools therefore persist. In this, too, the extremes of the region are remarkable. Whatever a poor district does, it cannot make itself rich overnight. Its control of the school can be perfectly democratic and equalitarian within its own boundaries. But it simply cannot give the opportunity to its children which is supposed to be the equal right of all children in the state and country, and which an adjoining school district can give.

259

The inequality of opportunity is, of course, heightened by inequalities of income among parents. The great majority of midwesterners send their young children to the public primary schools of their home district, city, or village. The parents who have comfortable incomes, however, send their boys and girls of high-school age to the large number of private schools in Midwest states. That is not cheap. It costs about $1,250 a year for one pupil, including travel, clothing, fees, and board—whether it is a day or a boarding school. And the really well-to-do send them to eastern, southern, Rocky Mountain, and far western private schools. The average cost in that case would be from about $1,500 to $2,000 a year for each child. Thus, dissatisfaction with public high-school education is widely expressed among well-to-do and comfortably-off parents. There is admitted dissatisfaction with the fewer facilities and standardized training in most public high schools, a demand for more individual tuition in smaller classes, and perhaps—though if so, to a small extent—a desire for more "polish" on the pupil, which the private school certainly applies. The result, however, is to emphasize the extremes and unevenness already noticed. The states and their politicians, the local community, and the majority of its electors emphasize the cult of the average; but a well-to-do, comfortably-off, and substantial minority clearly show that they have the wish and the power to break away from that average.

The United States Federal Commissioner of Public Education, Mr. John Studebaker, was principal of the little public grade school in Mason City, Iowa, in 1913–14. In that city of 27,000 inhabitants, which we described earlier, the elementary and high schools are of course paid for and controlled by the citizens. The city is today well above the average of Midwest, indeed of all American, small cities in the number, equipment, and amenities of its fine public schools. The citizens do not elect but appoint and pay for a municipal superintendent of education who lays down and superintends the observance of educational standards. The state of Iowa's superintendent of public instruction, however, is elected by the people for a term of office which varies with political party fortunes. The only real control which the state of Iowa, through this superintendent, can exert upon education in Mason City is in the state's qualifications for pupils who wish to go to the state university at Iowa City. As these requirements must have reference to a broad, state-wide average, the outstandingly fine public schools of Mason City encounter no difficulties in getting their promising pupils to the university. But the city is properous, and, despite local tussles now and then over funds for education, the schools provide far more for children, and for their parents' taxes, than most in the Midwest. That may explain Mason City pupils' extraordinary success in music, from grade schools through the high schools. (Ten out of eleven years they won the national championship with their high-school band, and many a pupil's necessary "credits" were gained in music.) How different this is from many school districts that cannot afford laboratories, equipment, instruments, teaching of the arts, recreational facilities, and adequately paid teachers! There are a surprising number of such schools that cannot give homework because the schoolbooks cannot be taken home. That does not worry the pupils! But it hampers their progress in competition with their fellows from other schools at the university—if they get there—and later on in life.

But not all funds for public instruction come from public sources. In Ottawa, Kansas, for example, a small city half the size of Mason City, one man led a movement to bring music into the schools. Here, as in many other communities in America, the service clubs, the Chamber of Commerce, and the chief citizens were "sold on the idea." A drive was organized so successfully that the public high school soon had not one, but two, complete and outstandingly good orchestras. Funds were raised for instruments and musical instruction by voluntary effort among the citizens themselves.

Everywhere in the Midwest the stranger encounters great differences in educational standards and facilities; but they are not solely due to lack of funds from public sources. The same sense of community, which makes the local electors cling jealously to their control of their own schools, will also express itself in remarkable communal achievements, private endowments of the local school, "drives" by the Rotary, Lions, Elks, Kiwanis, and other clubs, and organized movements to secure reassessments that will yield more money for public education. The initiative rests with the people whose children go to the local public schools. As most of the parents are, so do most of their children fare.

But there are limits in all democracies to what the electors, of and by themselves, can accomplish. Political party reins are tight in America. The machines are powerful and highly geared. That is more true of the city machines in the Midwest than it is of those elsewhere in America, or than it is of state machines. But the differences are not so very great between political machines anywhere. Public education from the outset was viewed by a minority of politicians and officials—local, municipal, and state—as a source of funds as well as an object of public investment and expenditure. The building of schools, supplies of books and paper and other necessities for scholars, heating, and so on, meant contracts with outside interests. In many cities where machines were highly organized, these outside interests found that they could get the business if they paid something to the insiders for what amounted to a franchise or permit. By itself this amount of graft would not matter much in a rich region which, at any rate until recently, could afford more "overhead" or wastage than almost any other on earth. But in many big and some smaller cities it went farther than that. It invaded and influenced education and educational standards.

There is something, if not much, to be said for graft if it is moderate in percentage, however largely it bulks in the pockets of a few recipients, and if it results in greater efficiency or better wares. Honesty may be the best policy; but, alas, too often in modern democracies the electorate is allowed to choose only between dishonest persons who get things done and honest persons who cannot. For some time in many big cities of the Midwest the different political machines put forward candidates for public office who were admittedly not overparticular in the handling of public funds. But they were efficient builders, and they "got things done"—things that were badly needed. Education was not free from this. The real cost was not what went into a few pockets on the side. It was the debasement of educational standards. It took decades to clean it up. It is not all clean yet.

When a big city's public schools, or even the state colleges and other institutions, have to use poor textbooks and equipment because it suits the interests of public officials and a few specially favored authors and suppliers to make that compulsory, something is more than rotten in the state of public instruction. When teachers have to pass every pupil to please the parents who are voters, down go educational standards and the average level of instruction. Down, also, go the standards and standing of the teachers who will accept and put up with such political dictation in their work. And the people's knowledge of these exceptional but enduring practices has an unfortunate result. It makes them more and more distrustful of state-wide or nation-wide standards and administration of public education. For, they argue, if these glaring exceptions regularly occur in certain big cities which have powerful machines, secret ballots, and all the other apparatus of representative government and party politics, will it not be worse if we forego our local control of the public schools? If the city can compulsorily corner the great market for textbooks, desks, ink, coal, and other educational supplies, how much bigger is the market awaiting the state's or the nation's educational authorities?

Would not state or federal control offer even greater plunder to the small and dishonest minority? Clearly the argument is faulty; but it seems conclusive logic to so many good citizens.

Against this there are encouraging signs to be noted. In many Midwest states there are movements, led by the press, the chief citizens, and the leading private and public educational authorities to "take the schools out of politics," to raise their standards, increase their teachers, reduce the size of classes, and develop individual pupils' own thinking. The Iowa committee for the revision of the state's laws on public instruction recommended in 1944 that the state superintendent of public education should be appointed by a nonpartisan board and not elected. In Iowa and other Midwest states there is a growing demand that the system in New York State be copied—the placing of public instruction under a commissioner and a commission of trustees, called a "university," which administers all institutions of public education.

Until direct local control of public education is reconciled with the need for greater and equal opportunities; until the public schools are "out of politics" or at least out of party politics and the spoils system; until the salaries and tenure of teachers are alike improved and made more secure, less open to abrupt political action, the high ideals and aims of parents, teachers, and pupils will never be realized. It seems likely that these reforms will come first in the state and in the smaller towns, in the widest and the narrowest educational provinces, rather than in the big cities. In the state and the well-to-do small locality the citizens can act on their own initiative and can call upon men and women of great purpose to head the movements. In the big cities such men and women are more rare. They left the city to live in their beautiful suburbs years or decades ago. Their children go to private schools anyway, or to the fine public schools run by the suburban community itself. They have left the city and the proletariat to the city machines.

The teachers themselves have a great part to play. "Teacher" has an enormous influence upon the pupil in the public schools. There are, and have been for many decades, too few men teachers owing to the relatively low salaries offered in most of the public schools of the region. The women teachers have managed to instil a surprising amount of cultural appreciation into their pupils' minds, despite the strict curriculum and the force of local restraints. Generally, the public high schools of the region seem to give more attention and better instruction in the arts than the private schools. But teachers labor against heavy odds. In Midwest private schools the average size of a class is about twelve to twenty pupils. In the public high schools it varies between twenty-five or thirty and fifty or even sixty; and more subjects must be taken by each teacher. Individual tuition in these circumstances is bound to favor the pupils in the private schools. As more and more teachers in the public schools are graduates of universities and teachers' colleges, the standard of teaching itself rises and the burdens upon the teacher are lightened. But the hand of politics is on the teachers' colleges, too. Parents and teachers alike anxiously await reforms in the financing of public education and the leveling-up of standards and opportunities. If these reforms could be quickly carried out, Midwest teachers and young people would need to recognize few limits to natural talent. There is so much of it. No teacher in a Midwest college, whether he is a European or an American, fails to be impressed with the student's eagerness to acquire knowledge, his energy, and his search for discrimination and judgment.

VII. IDEAS, INCORPORATED

LONG BEFORE BRYCE, IN THE 1840's TO BE EXACT, ABRAHAM LINCOLN said that public opinion really ruled the United States. He also said that nowhere did it rule more obviously than in what we now call the Midwest. Yet it was easy to tell what the public opinion of the Old Midwest was. A lawyer on circuit, a candidate for public office, and a circuit rider could easily cover in a few weeks a very wide and accurate sample of all midwesterners. He could talk to a few queer fellows who ran hand presses and called themselves editors, to a few mayors, and to farmers. Everyone spoke the same tongue, used the same vocabulary, conformed to much the same brand of religion or morality, and lived much the same kind of life.

Today it is hard to say what Midwest public opinion is at any time, despite the perfection of the various methods of sampling it by polls. There *is* a majority opinion on any question; but it is made up of the opinions of many different groups, each with different family languages or religions or notions of morality, living in big cities or smaller towns or on farms, and at widely different standards. Consequently, it very quickly changes. It is also largely put into people's minds today and not drawn forth from them after much argument and discussion, as it used to be. Is the answer to a fair and impartially worded question in a poll today what the answerer thinks, or what he has just absorbed from some organ of public opinion and thinks he thinks? What parts do the press, the movie, and the radio play in this process? How much do they standardize, how much do they reflect, Midwest public opinion? And

265

how much does the midwesterner, in turn, affect these organs of public opinion, these "media of public communication"?

Several Midwest characteristics with which we are already familiar are very important here. The people's marked curiosity and demand for the "dope" or "lowdown," for something new or strange; their sense of their local community's importance; their emphasis on the material and the practical; their love of laborsaving devices, short cuts, and potted knowledge; their emphasis on the "sight of the eyes," on pictorial representation; their restlessness—all these are naturally reflected in their newspapers and magazines. Most of them are also reflected on the radio stations. "It saves time to be told."

The newpapers change. The editorials get shorter, more colloquial in style. All the news has to be squeezed onto front pages or into the headlines; so the headline-writer or caption-writer becomes more important than a reporter or editorial writer—and much more influential. Readers dislike "intellectual" headlines; they prefer slangy, snappy, picturesque summaries in the headline; and all reporters are taught to cram the whole story into the first sentence and paragraph, since few read beyond that. Yet the radio scores over the newspapers. The midwesterner used to have great respect for his newspapers. He would say, "I see by the papers that . . . ." and believe it. But today he has not only the sight of his own eyes to contend with. He has also the sounds in his own ears, at home, in the drugstore or restaurant, at the movie, and on the long-distance train. While you can keep a newspaper and re-read it, or check it from a file, you cannot re-hear the radio, replay it, or check what it told you last night or last week. And it is more laborsaving, relaxing, and less thought-provoking to listen to the news on the radio. Instead of turning pages, reading headlines, features, editorials, cartoons, comics, and so on, you just turn a knob and listen. Entertainment, newscasts, commentaries on the news by great names—all these follow each other, and you have no idea that the commentator is really reading an editorial to you, that the entertainment is the comic strip, and that the newscasts are only headlines, after all. To the bold print of the newspaper succeeds the unctuous, intimate, insinuating, healthy, buoyant, and dramatic suavity of the radio announcer, subtly suggesting or not so subtly demanding in the middle of news or serious comment that you get Whoozits' vitamins or Snooks's laxative.

Public opinion is alternately courted and bulldozed. The film plays its part, too. So do the pulp magazines and the growing number of illustrated magazines and technical or nontechnical periodicals. Every

266

device and artifice to appeal to the eye is explored and exploited. *Look*, published in Des Moines, takes Dr. Hayek's *The Road to Serfdom* and gives it to its readers not only in potted form—the *Reader's Digest* did that—but actually in pictographs. Economics is deftly turned into e-comics. Mr. Walt Disney makes his inimitable films to train aerial navigators in meteorology and navigation, just as the public grade and high schools use projectors and other visual aids to suit the children's dependence on the graphic and the visual. The headline- and caption-writers try to catch the eye and form the judgment in less than seven words of 24-point type. The words themselves get telescoped into something less than the old journalese: it is now cablese and headlinese. This method of forming, if not informing, public opinion goes on day and night, particularly in the towns and cities of the Midwest. But it would be wrong to think that it is all planned, conscious, and deliberate; that the publishers or the owners of radio stations and movie-houses can snap their fingers at the public. There *is* a ground swell of public opinion everywhere, even if its force cannot be gauged or its direction foretold.

All that the owners of these channels of public communication can do is to try out one line of argument and presentation or another. They often make costly blunders and lose readers to their competitors, or lose listeners to readers, or vice versa. In doing all this, they are carrying on with public education for most adults. The number of films, comic strips, radio quizzes, and other features that tell the customer something he did not know, and test whether he knows it or not, show how hungry these customers are for facts—even if the facts are quite irrelevant to their lives. "Goethe was (a) a giant in the Bible; (b) a style of medieval architecture; or (c) a German philosopher: which is right?" That kind of question is frequent in high-school or college examinations; but it is just as frequent on the radio or in the newspaper. Moreover, it is not typical of the Midwest, or indeed of America, alone. General knowledge tests, the crossword puzzle, the ponderous British "brains trust," the admirably light American "Information Please" program, and the transatlantic quizzes show that people in many countries like to absorb predigested facts or conclusions. This tempts many an observer, and not a few publishers, radio commentators, and radio managers, to think that the public has no opinion; that it needs only to be bulldozed to believe anything; that "you can fool all of the people some of the time"; and that the public has no memory. I have heard all these things said sincerely, if regretfully, by many a radio station manager, editor, publisher, and commentator in many towns and cities of the Midwest. I have heard them query the value of free public education "if it all ends in this: you ask for knowledge and get a slogan."

Yet many advertisers, advertising agencies, and radio sponsors admit that the effects of their extremism in advertising have been overestimated. The number of radio listeners who cannot remember the sponsor of any show on the air, and who curse the "commercials" and "jingles," is astonishingly large. Thus, a good deal of ballyhoo and advertising builds up "sales resistance" instead of good will. For the two days after President Franklin D. Roosevelt's death, a surprisingly large number of people said that they enjoyed the forty-eight hours' relief from "commercials, jingles, and plugs." When thinking of naïveté, credulity, and standardization in the Midwest, you should therefore also think of individualism, liberty, refusal to stand dictation, and that growth in general skepticism to which we referred earlier. The one breeds the other.

Midwest public opinion, in any group or community at any given moment, naturally shows many characteristic results of education. There is all the young student's eagerness to learn, but there are also deep-seated prejudices which he carries along with him from home, kindergarten, and grade school onward: prejudices which themselves result from lopsided versions of history, lack of instruction in geography and social studies, and inability to employ a discriminating and critical judgment. The Midwest myths, which we have already noted, play a very big part in fashioning public opinion. Almost any idea can be "sold" if it is packaged in one of them. The spontaneous generosity and kindliness, which are the first impulses of the midwesterner, accompany his realistic business sense into any unfamiliar situation. And since public opinion is only partly rational and mainly emotional or sentimental, all the self-confidence, youthful sensitiveness, chip-on-the-shoulder particularism, and egocentricity of midwesterners also go into the mixture. In nothing are the extremes of the people and their region more obvious than in their public opinion and the way it is formed. The Midwest climate of opinion is the result of many extreme kinds of weather. And, like Midwest weather, public opinion is never still. It is always changing. It is almost always unpredictable.

THE PRESS

The power of the press in America is not what it was. Though technically the country today could, for the first time, produce and distribute a national newspaper, it has none. That is probably because no one wants it, and no one wants to try if anyone wants it. The country is still vast and sectional, despite the national radio networks. The press is more sectional, a more faithful reflector of community life, than the radio. In 1936, 1940, and 1944 the overwhelmingly majority, over four-fifths, of American newspapers strongly opposed the re-election of President Roosevelt. In the Midwest the percentage rose to 90! Yet President Roosevelt was consistently re-elected, by the formidable aid of the radio. The reason is that the newspaper, which everywhere in America is only the home-town paper, is more effective in forming public opinion when the issues are local or sectional than when they are national. The greater and more vital the national issue, the less influential the newspaper. That is particularly obvious in the Midwest. On great issues the electorate makes up its mind, and sticks to its decisions, quite apart from the editorial views of the local newspaper editor and publisher and often in flat contradiction to them. And one of the reasons is that only about one in five or six buyers of papers ever reads editorials. Headlines are, as we saw, more important today. And even tinkering with the headlines, or employing the power to suppress news, does not give the few disingenuous papers the power they want.

The Midwest and the marginal belt early in 1945 had over five hundred daily newspapers in the English language for a population of nearly forty millions. England and Wales, with practically the same population, had less than one-sixth of the five hundred and fifty daily papers in the Midwest in 1939. And if you add the twenty-five or thirty Midwest daily newspapers printed in other languages, the difference becomes even more striking. Other singularities of both the daily and weekly press in the region emerge from Table 3.

The daily newspapers in every state have a much larger average circulation than weekly, semiweekly, and triweekly newspapers, but it is hard to say which are more influential in local affairs. In national affairs the daily city newpapers are more influential; they carry more news and comment. Moreover, the city influence is wider than that of its newspapers, for from Chicago and other Midwest cities as well as from New York and the national capital go out vast supplies of clip-sheets and stereo's, known as "boilerplate" matter, which the small town or rural editor gratefully pushes into his paper. This puts the editorial imprint of city writers upon the rural newspapers unknown to their readers. Despite the long-apparent tendency of one city's newspaper owner to gobble up all others in the city, despite the growth in "chains" of papers under one person's or syndicate's ownership, the

269

Midwest is still particularly well served with independent, competitive daily and nondaily newspapers.[1]

Illinois and Ohio are rich in larger towns. They head the list in daily papers. But though they also have a great number of rural towns, the 670 nondaily Illinois papers are almost double those of Ohio, although the two states are nearly equal in population. The more rural states of Iowa, Minnesota, and Missouri show a surprisingly large number of little towns with their own nondaily paper or papers. In over a thousand rural Midwest towns, each with a population between 1,000 and 10,000 souls, you can find well-printed weekly, or twice or thrice weekly, news-

TABLE 3*

DAILY AND OTHER NEWSPAPERS IN EIGHT MIDWEST STATES, 1944

State	Population (in Millions) 1940	All Daily Newspapers	Of Which Foreign-Language Daily Papers	Weekly, Semiweekly, or Triweekly Papers, All Languages
Illinois.......	7.9	106	9	670
Indiana......	3.4	92	....	296
Iowa.........	2.5	43	....	455
Michigan.....	5.3	54	2	351
Minnesota*...	2.8	33	2	428
Missouri......	3.8	53	....	440
Ohio.........	6.9	110	9	369
Wisconsin.....	3.1	44	3	318

* Source: *Ayer's Directory.*

papers, owned by a man, woman, family, or set of friends. They are full of local news and advertising. Many have a national wire-agency franchise. They have circulations in town and in the surrounding countryside ranging from a few hundreds up to five thousand copies or more per issue. These papers are often owned and run "on the side" by a local lawyer or businessman. Often one owner will control quite a number. The noteworthy feature is that they pay. They afford a living to their staff and owners; and they persist.

When one thinks of the small-town Midwest paper, and what can be done with it by a man who sticks to it and to its role in the community, one thinks first and foremost of the late and sadly missed William

[1] For an analysis of these national trends see Oswald G. Villard, *The Disappearing Daily* (New York: Alfred A. Knopf, 1944), and Marshall Field, *Freedom Is More than a Word* (Chicago: University of Chicago Press, 1945).

Allen White of Emporia, Kansas, and of its famous *Gazette*. Yet there are surprisingly many such men and women in the Midwest. Not all have White's style, not all have his lovable qualities and wide sympathies. But all of them have his love of "the little platoon," the local community; and all try with great zeal and success to make their local newspaper something more than a business. Indeed, it is astonishing to the stranger to notice how carefully the farmers and small-town folk really read the local nondaily paper. Each copy is read by many pairs of eyes. In cities many different daily papers are bought, but not one of them is really read by the owner of one pair of eyes. Frequently you find a young man or young woman of great talent and ambition, a graduate from the department of journalism in a Midwest university, acting as editor, living with a local family, gaining little cash but a wealth of experience among the people, and "getting out the paper."

The excellent departments of journalism in many Midwest colleges and universities, each producing their own daily or weekly papers and frequently running their own radio station—the Medill School of Journalism at Northwestern and the schools of journalism at the University of Missouri and the State University of Iowa are outstanding among them—work closely with equally excellent state press associations, with the interstate Inland Daily Press Association, and with many another organization to help owners and editors secure talent or to try out new ideas. The big cities' newspaper owners and editors are tough. They will only consider, in the main, trained and experienced men and women for jobs. But not so out in the small towns. I know many professors of journalism and editors, members of state press associations, who discuss the purchase or staffing of various small-town papers in the state. There are not a few professors of journalism who own their own small-town papers; and all of them have been trained as working journalists or editors.

It is scarcely surprising, therefore, that so many of the region's, and of America's, finest editors, authors, and dramatists began on small-town papers and thus got to know the people of the small community, their life, and their lives. True, these able young people only pass through the smaller communities in their constant movement toward big cities and, finally, out of the Midwest altogether. But from the high-school paper, the professor of journalism and his department at college, and the first desk or table among the type racks near the flat-bed press in a small town, there is a constant procession of extremely able young people. There is a constant recruitment of Midwest journalistic talent at the top in the big cities' newspapers, and a constant freshening of all-

271

American journalism in consequence. Ernie Pyle, who became perhaps the most popular and beloved of war correspondents in the second World War, began life on a farm and began work on the *La Porte* (Indiana) *Herald*. To a stranger who has long had the smell of printer's ink in his nostrils, this is one of the most encouraging features in the Midwest.

The trend toward fewer newspapers has affected small-town papers more than those of cities; but the trend is still plainly visible in cities. The shortage of newsprint and the drafting of young men into the armed services turned very few daily papers into semiweeklies or triweeklies; but it knocked many of the latter out of existence altogether. At the time of the Japanese attack on Pearl Harbor, Minnesota had 502 daily and nondaily papers. But in the next three years that state lost 51 weekly papers alone, and only a single daily paper. Yet the effect of even so typical and drastic a cut in the number of small-town newspapers—and it is abnormally drastic because of the war—is less felt in the particular locality than the disappearance, or absorption by another owner, of a city's daily newspaper. A small-town nondaily paper is bought for small-town news. But the local subscriber also buys the daily paper from the nearest city, in which he finds his national and—to a much smaller extent—international news and comment. If his local nondaily paper goes out of existence, he can always get the daily paper from the nearest city. But the overwhelming bulk of American (and Midwest) cities have only one paper. Of 1,403 cities each with one or more daily newspapers in 1942, there were only 127 each of which had two or more daily newspapers *not* owned or controlled by the same interests.[2]

Thus, on most national and international questions it is the view of the owner-publisher or editor of the big-city newspaper which finds expression and is hailed as American (or regional) public opinion. He seldom goes out to the farmers or talks to the people in the slums or the satellite and suburban communities around the big city. And the great majority of daily papers in the Midwest are not those of big cities. They are those of cities each with less than 100,000 souls, or 50,000 adults. In such cities public opinion can be gauged. It is vocal, quick to react, and not anonymous. The formative centers of public opinion are known to all leading citizens and composed of them: clubs, boards, churches, and so on. The owner-publisher and editor are parts of the life of the community. And although there is generally only one owner who controls the daily paper or papers of such a smaller city, he and

[2] Marshall Field, *op. cit.*, p. 76, gives these and other valuable statistics.

his staff have to keep their ears close to the ground. It is dangerous for their living, social status, circulation, advertising revenue, and much more, if they fly in the face of public opinion. Consequently, the papers of about 550 Midwest cities, each with less than 100,000 and more than 5,000 souls, are generally far more cautiously responsive to the moods and opinions of their readers than the papers of the 26 cities each with 100,000 souls or more.

You notice this difference in many ways. Because the daily papers of the big cities can generally be more courageous and original, they differ more sharply among themselves, reflecting more of their owners' views, and often fly in the face of public opinion. They are less cautious, less afraid to give a lead, less afraid to step out of line. The public of their cities is less homogeneous, less united, more organized in groups; so these papers differ by appealing to different sections of the citizenry.

In Chicago, St. Louis, Columbus, Detroit, Cleveland, Indianapolis, Cincinnati, and Milwaukee there are still competitive daily newspapers. Except on certain subjects which will be mentioned later, these competing papers vie with each other in each city to test public opinion, to form it, and not to wait to see what it may be. In Des Moines, Minneapolis, St. Paul, Kansas City, Omaha, and other big cities, however, there are no competitive daily papers; yet perhaps for just that reason their daily papers are outstanding in quality and in leadership of public opinion. It is neither monopoly, nor the lack of it, therefore, which results in a good daily newspaper in big Midwest cities.

Daily papers which belong to the same owner or chain as those in other cities are found in Chicago, Milwaukee, Indianapolis, Detroit, and many another big city. Yet, in general, perhaps because of the earnest efforts of local editors not to follow one slant or line but to keep each paper responsive to its own community's mood and opinion, in all these cities independent newspapers are in the main better, more original, and do better financially than those that belong to a chain. This is as true of the Hearst papers as it is of any others belonging to chains; and, though there are exceptions, it is broadly true that chains create more problems for their owners and editors than they do profits. The trend to chain ownership in America, as in Britain, is of course not really for profits but for political power: the power to mold rather than to reflect political opinion; the power to make and to break politically.

But, though Midwest or other American observers may deplore it, they can comfort themselves with two thoughts. First, they have greater and freer competition and greater liberty of the press than any other country in the world. Secondly, much as this competition may have been threatened, or this freedom may have been abused, by chains; much as public opinion in consequence may have been bulldozed, the bulldozing does not seem to work successfully—least of all in the Midwest, where the superficial observer might have thought it would. And that is what we noticed in the fields of advertising and radio. The mass of the people won't be bulldozed. They are competent to judge the qualities of a newspaper, whether it is in a small town or a big city, whether it is a monopoly or in competition.

Of course, the extreme unevenness of all things in the Midwest is duly reflected in its newspapers. Nowhere else in America or the world do you find extremes carried to such lengths. But that is natural. It is "of the people." Just as the people's amazing tolerance allows extreme intolerance to be practiced and cultivated by an able and abnormal minority; just as their law and respect for law can stand abnormal lawlessness by a few; so their unparalleled freedom of the press allows abnormalities that seem abuses. But these abnormalities seem louder and more frequent than in fact they are. They may be symptomatic of something in American and Midwest life, but they are not typical.

More serious than any extremism in the Midwest press is not the threat to the freedom of the press coming from *outside* it, but the growth in freedom to *suppress* news or comment or facts. That arises and is exercised *inside* the press, by its owners and editors. Nor is it due to a direct threat from big advertisers, advertising agencies, or group interests among the citizens. It operates as an inhibition, or a censoring myth, in the minds of owners and editors all the time. This is not only a feature of the Midwest press. It is found in all other regions of America, perhaps less in the East; and it is also found in some leading newspapers of the remaining democratic countries. But in certain cases the inhibition becomes a prohibition to print. Rape, personal privacy, murders, corpses—all these are front-paged. But many other things must never be printed. Every Midwest editor I know admits that he has to keep anything and everything unfavorable to Roman Catholics out of the paper; that he cannot comment on, and generally cannot even mention, birth control or the voluntary spacing of children in families; and that the religion of criminals or undesirable persons may not be mentioned. One very friendly editor in Chicago told me that he once said to his staff: "Hell, don't put 'British' in the headlines; 'British' don't sell papers in Chicago; call it 'Allies.'" There, the myth works as an unconscious censor.

To offset this there is a most refreshing and wise liberty in the use of personalities in the Midwest press. American papers, and those of the

Midwest in particular, get "for free" what would cost a newspaper owner $25,000 a week in England in libel suits constantly decided by the jury against the newspaper. The English journalist in the Midwest again finds the atmosphere that of the past, of a Victorian England, of the language of Bagehot, Labouchère, Harmsworth, Blatchford, and Bottomley. It is, for that matter, the air of Springfield in Illinois a century ago when the two papers, one aided by Lincoln, went at each other as vigorously and with as few holds barred as did the two papers of Eatanswill during the election. Midwest papers have run truer to type and tradition than those of England. The Midwest air is certainly fresh after the colorless caution, generalities, and carefully obscure innuendoes of political and other journalism in England.

Hitherto, the laws of libel in England have been constantly tightened by judge and jury alike because of the vast power acquired by a handful of owners in the British daily press. This is in itself a reflection of the British juries' distrust and resentment at the reduction in all well-known and influential daily newpapers to about twenty-five, of which twenty are controlled by six British millionaires or wealthy syndicates. (That should be a warning to ambitious "chain" owners in America.) Judge and jury have fallen over backward in trying to erect defenses for the public. These defenses fix all kinds of inhibitions and restraints upon owners, editors, journalists, authors, distributors, booksellers, and their employees. But in practice they all boil down to damages, "substantial damages," and frequently penal damages. Yet damages of this magnitude put a premium on "gold-digging" and on questionable legal practices: for example, the manufacture of libel suits to "shakedown" a paper. They do not bankrupt British newspapers. And you cannot force the press to publish anything by the fear of damages. All you do is prevent the publication of much that would be salutary in British public or commercial life and lead the public to think that things (and some people) are far better than they are.

As today only twenty-five daily papers in Britain are read by four-fifths of the people, this poses an interesting problem. The American system boldly publishes the worst in American public and private life, makes people so familiar with it that it is taken for granted, and gets little done to improve it. The British system publishes nothing but faint innuendoes and leads everyone to think things are better than they are, so that nothing gets done to improve them, either. Which is better?

The American press, particularly that of Midwest cities, is refreshingly and brutally frank and outspoken. What disfigures it is the same

275

as what disfigures the press in any country of the world where it is still "free": namely, the power to *suppress*.[3] Strange as it may seem to many Americans, despite the far greater concentration of ownership of the press in Britain, there is more suppression or playing-down of news and comment in America than in Britain, in time of peace. For one thing, all British papers have equal access to the news agencies, the wire services. Competitors cannot freeze you out or prevent your acquiring the service—as was the case, until the Supreme Court's judgment in 1945, with the Associated Press services in America. This means that all British papers watch their agency material more carefully than do the smaller American papers, the majority of which are almost wholly composed of it. It also means that they had better print *all* the news and comment on it; or if they don't, their few remaining competitors will, and all of them get much the same agency material. By the same token it means that British editors, again strange to American ears, are more on their toes to make editorial comment. It is nothing to a British editor to stop the presses, write a new editorial, and get them going again at eight, nine, or ten o'clock at night. That does not worry the American editor. Unlike the British press, afternoon papers are more important than morning papers in America; and the morning papers' editorials are written and on sale by seven in the evening. Secondly, few people regularly read editorials in America.

But in other ways, too, it affects the American press. Because they all have much the same basic news, British editors pay far more attention to their features. In America, with a few notable exceptions, features are relegated to the voluminous Sunday issue which exhausts the attention of entire families—if they can spare the time for it. So in America local events give more scope to journalistic enterprise. Knowledge and facts about the world and humanity bulk smaller in the Midwest press. The life of the community gets more faithfully portrayed; but the newspaper profession, even more than the people, exhausts its wits trying to think up some new idea or style. This may well explain, at least in part, the much more experimental, sparkling, and striking style employed in America, particularly in the Midwest.

Characteristically, editors and journalists in the towns and cities of the Midwest carry American methods to extremes. Many of them develop new styles and new methods. They play with their new, youthful language as did the Elizabethans, and often with success. Many of

[3] See the $1,000 *Atlantic* prize article "For a Free Press" in the *Atlantic*, July, 1944, by Mr. Robert Lasch of the *Chicago Sun*, formerly of the *Omaha World Herald*.

them finally follow the usual route of success—away from the Midwest. The older ones remain. Again, Midwest owners, publishers, and editors are overwhelmingly midwesterners. They are therefore consciously or subconsciously sectional, jealous of dictation from Washington, sensitive toward foreigners, and highly individualistic. Any incoming item of news is treated, published, or not published by them in one or other, or indeed all, of these contexts. This aspect of the geographical insulation of the Midwest has to be appreciated. I have heard many an editor grumbling about easterners, the national capital, Congress, and all foreigners—as if they were all alike. "Thailand! Thailand! Where the hell's that? Used to be Siam, eh? Then why the hell alter it? Suppose we were forever changing Illinois or Alaska! That's what's wrong with Persia, or Iraq, or whatever it is now. Used to be a dam' sight easier to run a paper when the biggest headline of the year—two-inch letters—was when the Erie Road paid a dividend!"

This insulation from East and West expresses itself in peculiar ways. For example, all Midwest papers regularly, exhaustively, and editorially discussed the Dumbarton Oaks proposals, prior to the San Francisco Conference of 1945. But none of them, as far as I can tell, published the text of those proposals so that readers would know what the editorials were about. It was left to eastern papers and nondaily periodicals to do so. The same is true of the texts of speeches or important documents: comment first, content afterward; fight first, reason afterward; speak or act first, think afterward. The hangover importance of the old "scoop," when there were no radio chains, is responsible for much of this. It will change. Radio has already changed it. Nothing will change it more than television. That is the bad day ahead for editor and reporter alike.

The cost of such extensive liberty of the press in America, and in the Midwest of such absence of restraint (with the exceptions noted above), is the abuse of it. There is bound to be a certain amount of suppression of the truth, or suggestion of the false, in view of what the owner, publisher, editor, reporter, or rewrite man know to be the paper's "line" or policy. No one but a fool or a moron, or an exceptionally honest man, washes his dirty linen in public. Yet, as in Britain last century, so in the Midwest; when "lobbies" were fewer and less organized to represent vast groups of readers, when advertising was less important in selling a paper, editors and writers used to be far more courageous and outspoken. The Midwest press is, happily, still more outspoken than that of the rest of the country. In particular it still enjoys the inestimable advantage of a large number of live, vigorous, independent newspapers. They are so independent that they are not, in the main, political party organs—to which most of the British press has descended. They cut across party lines, back one candidate or another on his merits, and are ruggedly individualistic. They may not compete in one and the same city. But if they do not, their readers take national periodicals and listen to the competing networks and their commentators on the radio.

There are few papers in American big cities that can equal, still fewer that can outrank, the *Milwaukee Journal, Des Moines Register, Minneapolis Star-Journal, St. Paul Pioneer-Press, Kansas City Star-Times,* or *St. Louis Post-Dispatch* for treatment of news, editorials, features, or other services. And among the smaller cities' papers there are the *Toledo Blade, Peoria Star-Journal-Transcript, Cedar Rapids Gazette, Wisconsin State Journal* at Madison, *Bloomington Pantagraph, Mason City Globe-Gazette, Sheboygan Press, Rock Island Argus, Sioux Falls Argus-Leader, Gary Post-Tribune,* and *Fort Wayne Journal-Gazette:* all on an extremely high journalistic level, yet all of them only a little higher on it than most of their Midwest contemporaries in small cities and towns. There is no "tabloid" in America that can outrank the *Chicago Times* in quality. There are few local papers abroad that can compare with these. I can think only of the old *Dépêche de Toulouse* and the *Frankfurter Zeitung* and of one or two of the old British dailies outside London. Certainly there are extremely few that give fairer, more judicious, and more impartial treatment of the news or comment on it with as good judgment and responsibility of utterance.

Freedom of speech, as we saw, is far greater in the Midwest than elsewhere in America—or the world, I imagine. It is hard to think how it could be more free. So is the freedom of the press. But these two great freedoms have not resulted in that automatic guaranty of truth, beauty, and integrity which John Stuart Mill expected from them. Many midwesterners would like to have a satisfactory explanation of the long continuance of these two freedoms; of the crusades led by noble-minded midwesterners in the press against graft, crime, vice, and rackets; and of the comparative lack of effect on bad politics, bad politicians, crime and vice syndicates, and racketeers. So would I. It often seems that so much freedom and tolerance are possible because of so little law enforcement, respect for law, and restraint; so every person's and every corporation's or syndicate's hide gets thick. Where stronger weapons are available, words break no bones. So people fling them around more, and words end by becoming cheaper and meaningless.

There is a kind of "inflation of words," in the Midwest in particular;

278

and, as with Gresham's Law, the poor money drives out the good. No one worries much about what's printed or said. What's being *done?* It is important to bear this in mind when reading a paper, listening to a speech, or taking part in a discussion in the Midwest. What appears to a stranger to mean something terrific means "small potatoes" to the Midwest reader or listener and is quickly forgotten. Thereby arise many misunderstandings by foreigners—especially Englishmen, who think the Midwest tongue is English—when they read or hear the expression of Midwest views. Self-expression may not be fluent; but it is always forceful. It attracts no attention whatever unless it is pithy and pungent. The attitude to the umpire at the ball game—"Murder the bum!"—is carried over to local, state, and federal politicians and politics, competitors, opponents, and so on. But nobody really means to murder the man. It is not for nothing that the expression to "kill" a story or an idea or a proposition came from America. I have been in many public meetings and private discussions, and even read a good many pamphlets and articles, in which what sounded to me like shockingly strong and unpleasant language was used about a President, his family, members of his cabinet, senators, opponents, Jews, and Negroes. But much of this kind of language in the Midwest is part of a formula or myth. It is necessary in order to get attention. It is expected.

The acute wartime shortage of newsprint and severe reduction in the size of British papers saved British journalism and its style, and a good deal of the English language, from a wordy obscurity. Writers had to think carefully and say what they thought, or what they were told to say, in few words and a clear style. In the Midwest today the press, the radio, and the average citizen have used many adjectives, many superlatives, and many extreme expressions for so long that the majority of non-Anglo-Saxon midwesterners have come to think it is normal peaceable English. Accordingly, when a paper or a speaker rips out invective against some person or group, naming and calling names, the stranger expects to see the object of the attack wither or fold his tent and silently steal away. He is more likely to see the owner of the paper and the object of the attack having a drink together that night in a leading hotel. Ninety per cent of midwesterners do not really believe the extremity of their own extremes. Only the stranger does—and among the strangers are probably a majority of the American people.

Here is one illuminating example. In the second World War American bombers bombed an airfield in southern Italy. The correspondent of a great British paper accompanied the correspondent of a great Midwest paper on the raid. The results on the enemy airfield were reported as follows: The Chicago correspondent reported: "Boy! we left that wop airfield the way Vesuvius left Pompei!" The Englishman reported: "The Italian airfield will, it is estimated, be unusable for at least three weeks." The Chicago style is much more picturesque. But Englishmen and many others think midwesterners are fooled by their own extremism. Quite the contrary. Because it is their own, they are *not* fooled by it. It is the English and the strangers who are fooled. Very few who read the Chicago paper believed the Italian airfield was finished for good and all. But the result was stated according to the accepted formula; and only according to that formula was it accepted. It may result in temporarily misleading the public. Well, their opinions change quickly, and their "forgettory" works equally quickly, anyway. New versions will appear, later. "Make it snappy for the paper," is what the editor will say; but, though the reader enjoys it, he knows the snappiness is synthetic. He knows the comics are not true to life; but it is quite nice to think they are while you read them and for as long as you read them. (It is said that Mr. Henry Ford did not want Little Orphan Annie's dog to be "killed," so he had a telegram sent to the syndicate publishing the comic strip to "save" the pooch. Yet Mr. Ford is a great realist.) It is all part of publicity: the art of giving people not only news and comment but a "kick" with them.

To the stranger it often seems that the "kick," the playing-up of the "home team," the insulation of the Midwest, produce a lack of perspective, inconsistency, or unconscious distortion of the news. After much Midwest criticism of the British for being undemocratic in not having an election in a decade, and after much Midwest self-congratulation on being able to be so democratic in wartime as to hold two elections, it was rather a jolt to find friendly papers and cartoonists in the Midwest lampooning John Bull for going to sleep under the eiderdown labeled "elections"—after a decade! It was also rather a jolt to see so many Midwest papers, which had been almost morbidly sensitive and severely critical of the British press for what they called "interference" in the 1944 American elections, blithely calling on Mr. Churchill to trounce the Labour opposition in England in 1945 and claiming Mr. Churchill and his Conservatives as "the better dogge."

It is surprising how many Midwest newspapermen and citizens firmly believe that American doughboys marched with the British from El Alamein to Tunisia; that American lend-lease was in operation for a year before Hitler attacked Russia in June of 1941; and that radar, the floating concrete harbors for the invasion of France, the gasoline pipeline under the English Channel, the jet airplane, the Bailey bridges,

280

penicillin, and many other wartime inventions or ingenuities were wholly American. An overwhelming majority of midwesterners believe Colonel Charles A. Lindbergh made the first flight across the Atlantic. "There's glory enough for all." The long insulation of the Midwest, its consuming interest in the home team and the boys of the district, are expanded by many of its papers and local radio stations to cover all America; so that everything, to be mentioned, must be American. All nations, all cities, naturally glorify their own sons' doings. But to suppress those of others is something new and ominous. Some British papers did it and gave reasons and excuses—lack of paper, and so on. But in America, and particularly the Midwest, it is hard to understand. It is less understandable in a self-confident country and region, one of such wondrous miracles and with such a bright future, than it is in a small Britain facing a gloomy and highly questionable one.

The American miracles are so many: the building, manning, and leading to victory of the largest navy the world has ever known, all in less than three years; the building of the airplanes, trucks, tanks, and other equipment for an ill-prepared America and a large group of nations besides; the making of synthetic rubber and drugs; the production of the vitally needed foodstuffs and the ships to carry it all; the rushing of twelve million young men, totally devoid of military or naval ideas, into the best-equipped and most mobile armed forces of the world. Surely there is a little glory to spare: to remember those who went ahead?

This, too, will change. Our era is a difficult period to traverse. Only a few Midwest editors and their readers, and only a few British editors and theirs, can adjust their thought and ideas to the "great revolutions of the world" in our day: to the greatness and profundity of the change in the relative positions of the Great Powers of the world. Least of all can those be expected to change and adapt who have been for so long insulated not only from the Great Powers but also from influences in other regions of their own country. Yet the influences have increased, are increasing, and are bound to increase.

STANDARDIZATION OF IDEAS

The all-American standardization is having its effect on Midwest public opinion through all the means of public communication: radio, movies, and, least of all but still noticeably, the papers and periodicals. The average midwesterner today not only buys two or three national weekly or monthly periodicals as well as his two or more local newspapers; he also gets radio every hour of the day without paying a cent for it—directly—though he pays for everything indirectly. He and his family go to the movies probably more than any other Americans at comparable standards of living and certainly more than any non-Americans. The standardizing effect of radio and film upon thought and opinion is more obvious than that of the press. Both radio and film are, in the main, nationally produced and purveyed; but there is no national newspaper. Instead there are the columnists: those whose views are syndicated to anything from twenty-five to two hundred and fifty or more newspapers. Theirs is a steadily growing influence for standardization; as if all papers printed the same editorials. Well, they don't, which prevents complete standardization. Yet the fact that there are many columnists in the same newspaper, often taking opposing views of a question, is no guaranty whatever against standardization. It simply offers the public more, rather than less, standardized and predigested thought.

Thrice as many "pro" and "con" columns in a paper do not help to make readers more impartial or to make them any more competent to decide for themselves. It often adds to confusion. It is bound to add to confusion if education fails to develop critical faculties. But it is not certain that critical faculties have not recently been developed. It may be that the great and recent growth of skepticism in the Midwest about what appears in the press, on the radio, or on the screen is due to impatience with confusion. Certainly that skepticism is most marked among high-school and college students. What, Adam Smith called "the narrow capacity of the human stomach" rebels at too much to digest. The human mind also rebels at too much to digest, whether it is your own or somebody else's mental food. You would expect to find this revolt more clearly marked in the Midwest than elsewhere, for Midwest opinion is more local, sectional, individualistic, and independent. And it does not like the domination of radio and movie by other regions of America. That may also explain why the Midwest press is in the main so apprehensive and distrustful of radio and movie; why its leading owner-publishers are increasing and intensifying their efforts to buy radio stations throughout the region—and, significantly enough, outside; why the Midwest press has been rapidly developing its own local columnists. The Midwest press wants to alter national radio and the movies. It is fighting against national standardization.

The radio—and, in future, television—starts with two strikes on the press. First, the four chief radio networks are national in their competing activities. Secondly, the radio has to serve commercial sponsors, who hope thereby to sell their goods or services to all Americans (and even Canadians) everywhere; rich and poor, Protestant and Catholic, North and South, white and black, Republican and Democrat, employer and employee. They are not selling in the main to a small community of a few thousands or hundreds of thousands. They have therefore to give the highest common factor of interest and entertainment to the greatest mass of the people. Of course, this means that no one and nothing can be allowed to tread on any potential consumer's, or group of consumers', corns. So everything that is said on the air must have not only two sides to it expressed but many, many sides. It must be neutral. It need not be the same person or program that puts all aspects of everything before the listening public; but the alibi must be there. "You object? But you should have been listening at 4:30." It reminds one of the reverend and revered Dr. Cudworth in seventeenth-century England, who tried to confute atheism yet be fair to it. He was too fair. He upset the church by converting many true believers to atheism. So it is with radio. Despite competing networks, the finest and widest variety of entertainment in the world, the best technical equipment, and the best executants, it is the most powerful standardizing medium in America.

Competition has nothing to do with it. There's not a cent's worth of difference between the treatment of a serious subject in the news, or of comment on it, on one network and that on another. Except that the music and entertainment are so much better in America and that "commercials" harangue you every few minutes—important exceptions, both of them—American radio and the British Broadcasting Corporation have about the same effect on people's minds. And that affects the Midwest in much the same way as it affects, say, Lancashire or East Anglia. There is more freedom and responsiveness to what people want in British radio, which is a public utility monopoly, than most Americans realize; more freedom of discussion than on American networks for many subjects. But both face the same problem. If you broaden your denominator too much, the value becomes negligible.

Some of the best radio in America is local; but it is rarer than in Britain, where regional and varying simultaneous programs correspond more closely to local differences and thereby help to prevent standardization. Americans, particularly midwesterners, might profitably ponder why it is that, in a country which so insistently and emphatically aims at individualism and competition, there is more standardization than anywhere else and far less originality of individual expression than one expects. This is most noticeable at the movie-houses and over the air, less noticeable in the press and the printed page. In Britain it is the other way round: the movies and radio show more originality of thought and expression, the press very little. Whatever the reasons, competition, or the degree of competitiveness, is not one.

There are signs that American "movie moguls" and radio experts realize this standardization and lack of originality. It is a pity there are not more informative radio programs in America like the outstandingly conceived and executed "Human Adventure" series. (Incidentally, it is significant that such good dramatization of scientific discovery and progress should have to come to Americans from the Midwest.) For the power of the radio, shortly to be increased by that of television networks, is enormous. Like so much power in the modern world, it is equally capable of evil or of good.

The people themselves and their representatives are beginning to realize this, especially in the shrewd and jealously watchful Midwest. Missouri's new constitution in 1945 extends the 1875 guaranty of complete liberty of expression to radio, movies, and even television as well as to the press. But, be it noted, the inclusion of these new media of public communication also makes them responsible "for all abuses of that liberty." The Illinois legislature in 1945 made radio stations liable to prosecution for criminal libel as well as to other forms of liability. The time of "easy money" in radio, films, and press is coming to an end. The people's rising skepticism is joined with a trace of apprehension about the power of the few owners of these mighty means of communication. It is not altogether fanciful to see in all this, and right at the Midwest core, something of the process in Britain. It began in the first two and three decades of this century with the British press and with the constraints put upon it as it became concentrated in few hands. Midwesterners and other Americans, when lauding competitiveness and individualism, should look to the trend in their newspapers, radio stations, and movies.

How easy, in fact, is it to start a new newspaper, or radio station, or movie company? How easy is it to buy one now existing? And what sort of people can? For what purposes? The British have traveled this road. They may be farther along it. They will admit that their road has not avoided, or safeguarded them from, domination or standardization by a few. The American would reply that the safety of the public lies in numbers—numbers of competitors. But the numbers are falling, falling. We are on different sections of the same broad way. There are more in the Midwest who see that—among owners or employees of organs of public opinion and the public, alike—than in any other region of America. That may be because virtually every newspaper in the region, large and small, has remained in closer touch with the people and the local community than many other American newspapers.

VIII. "WE, THE PEOPLE"

Extremes and paradoxes, restlessness and vigor, emerge with brilliant coloring and much shadow in Midwest politics. Like most social institutions in the region, politics is constantly changing. It shows many similarities and contrasts to, and many differences from, American politics or the politics of other American regions. It is more alive, more lively; but it is taken very seriously, too. It is like a dramatic movie in technicolor rather than a diagram, a comic strip, a photograph, or a blueprint. Politics is the drama of midwesterners, a very political people; and every politician or cog in the machines plays a part. No wonder that bureaucracy and social or economic planning are more unpopular in the Midwest than they are elsewhere in America.

Like the newspapers of the region, politics remains very close to the local community and its people. And, like the people themselves, it resembles Joseph's coat of many colors. There is the political life of the cities, of the towns, of farmers, and of each of the eight states. There is national politics. But, as a by-product of the interplay between all these, there is also a less organized yet obvious influential regional or sectional political feeling: a Midwest political consciousness. This sectional political feeling is less powerful than it was in national politics; but it is keenly felt by midwesterners themselves. In this, their psychological characteristics heighten the sectional feeling. But greater forces than those in the Midwest alone have doomed this sectional feeling to much less significance in the nation than it once had.

American politics and public life bewilder the foreigner unless and until he gives many years to their study. Even then they confuse him. They confuse Americans. Like the politics and public life of France just across the English Channel, those across the Atlantic seem to the Englishman contradictory, tangled, and shapeless. Personalities play more striking roles and enjoy greater influence than in England. They cut across party lines. So do regional and local loyalties. Perhaps the more recent revolutions and civil wars in both France and America reflect this. Clearly, written constitutions and extensively codified laws, rules, and regulations have much to do with it. The vastness of America and the smallness of France would seem to rule out mere size as a factor. Tocqueville felt more at home in the America of the 1830's than Bryce did half a century later. In any case, the guiding principles and methods of American politics remain to a surprising extent what they were less than a century and a half ago, when they were drawn up for four million souls scattered along a straggling seaboard. This constant aim to preserve and apply these political principles and methods to a country that has multiplied its area by twelve, its population by thirty-five, and its capital equipment by thousands within six generations has much to do with it. Contrasts, anomalies, extremes, and unevennesses were inescapable.

The tribute to American political genius is that so many of the original political principles have been respected and preserved, even if political methods have had to be rough and ready and constantly changed. More Americans are now descended from Europeans who immigrated *after the Revolution* than from revolutionary stock—which may account for the emphasis on their origin by the Daughters of the American Revolution. Yet the immigrants and their children, frustrated or balked in the countries of the Old World, became even more ardently "revolutionary" in temper, even more democratic, and often much more radical than the original American revolutionaries. That, too, is a tribute to the all-pervading air of liberty, equality, and fraternity in America. And, as we noted, that air is more pervasive, and all-American problems and characteristics reach greater extremes, in the new and most rapidly developed Midwest.

Let us consider some of the most obvious political features of the Midwest at its noon. First, as with the press of the region, the locality, community, city, or state count for more than the nation, except in the broadest issues of public affairs. This is most noticeable in the northern portion of the Midwest, where local administrative powers are greater.

In the southern portion the states and counties have greater local powers. Yet *all* politics begins locally. Representatives and senators in Congress and those in state legislative assemblies talk very much "for the record"—the phrase is meaningful—but it is the record back home that counts most. They read into the *Congressional Record* all conceivable kinds of printed and written matter from "the folks at home." They take care to send the "boys back home" their remarks, reprinted from the *Record* and mailed free under their congressional frank. (There is no national newspaper, remember.) The representative, either at his state capital or in Washington, must have an eye to his chances of re-election from the day he is elected. He will have to begin campaigning again in less than eighteen months after his election: which in practice means right away. Senators alone enjoy a six-year term. By law all congressmen must live for a good portion of each year in the state or district they represent. They represent, in varying degrees, almost every interest or group in it once they are elected. They constantly receive letters, telegrams, petitions, requests for favors, abuse, and the perpetual attention of lobbyists—I beg pardon, "legislative representatives" of economic and all other interests. That accounts for their great need of secretarial assistance, which the taxpayer provides. All this makes them peculiarly insensitive to any *national* opinion about them. The nation cannot vote for them, and they need not consider what it thinks of them personally, unless they have an eye to the presidency. But it makes them keenly sensitive to local opinion. That is why they have to spend so much time going home to "mend their fences."

That is why, to many a stranger, American national politics and speeches seem full of initiatives doomed to failure, proposals that are demonstrably half-baked, and parochial notions and conceits. The stranger must beware. The overwhelming majority of American representatives are fully aware of all that. But they are representative. They do represent. If the Congress or assembly crushingly vote them down, they do not turn a hair. Why should they? Words are cheap; and their words are not generally their thoughts. They are only the thoughts of some electors. The delegates are only doing their duty "for the record" by having them recorded. In an age that has seen representative government overturned and spat on, and august legislatures turned into rubber stamps, there is much more to say than has been said for the American political system. It produces remarkable representatives who really represent.

We observed earlier that government by public opinion is most marked in the Midwest, where public and local opinion has enormous force. The life of the Midwest, its virtues and its vices, are public property. The power of public opinion is far greater there than that of religion, and greater than it is elsewhere in America. It is, of course, bound up with the influence of locality and with life in communities. It is perhaps a pardonable exaggeration to say that public opinion *is* "the American way" in the Midwest. That is not surprising, because the force of public opinion is always strongest among the middle class, the people who live in the moderate income brackets, all over the world of industrial nations. The aristocrats and the rich, or the poor, snap their fingers at many conventions. The Midwest, more than any single region of America, is distinctively bourgeois in the proper sense of that word. In the main it is a region of comfortably-off, decent-living farmers, businessmen, artisans, and clerical workers living in or near pleasant communities and suburbs. It forms as sound, solid, and respectable a backbone of society as the middle class in Britain. It is as loyal and sensitive to its public opinion, conventions, and myths as the British middle class. It is the width of the extremes on either side of this Midwest middle class that make the whole of Midwest society and its politics seem so different from those of Britain. In other words, the extremes— as always in the Midwest—make the headlines. And that is an all-American characteristic carried to a regional extreme.

Thus, while the rule of public opinion is still almost as marked in Midwest politics as it was in America in Bryce's day, the extremes and paradoxes are now more obvious. To begin with, the Midwest is now, as we saw, mainly an urban region. It is therefore more bourgeois and more class-conscious. Bryce said: "There is no denying that the government of cities is the one conspicuous failure of the United States. . . . . The faults of the state governments are insignificant compared with the extravagance, corruption, and mismanagement which mark the administrations of most of the great cities." In the 1870's and 1880's he was almost wholly concerned with eastern cities.

Today the Midwest is a region of big and small cities, too. It is in the cities that the extremes of an extreme region are most striking. Accordingly, the efficiency and mass production of party politics by machines, which so impressed Bryce, have developed since his day, more than half a century ago, to a much higher degree: especially in the Midwest, where the towns and cities are newer. Public opinion has now less control of the caucuses in city, state, and national politics that run the machines, that run politics and governments. It has less control than it used to have in the Midwest. The onrush of quick communications has not increased—it has lessened—the rule of public opinion. It has not lessened—it has increased—the power of the caucus and the machine.

Therewith, as in Britain though to a smaller extent, the electorate, the public which is supposed to have the opinion that is supposed to rule, has become more skeptical about politics, more apathetic. It has become so, as we saw, about liberty, equality, and fraternity, the freedom of the press, and many another democratic principle or myth. Someone may usefully trace the role of industrialism, cities, and city life in all this. It is significant that these symptoms developed in the Midwest and elsewhere as city life and cities dominated the life of small towns and countryside. It is a symptom that develops with the rise and expansion of a middle class above a "working class." It reached in foreign lands the proportions of a disease in the revolts of the middle class known as fascism and naziism. But neither of them is completely unthinkable *in principle* in Britain or America; at least not to an impartial and unemotional observer; though they probably would not be accompanied *in practice* by the more extreme crudities of the German and Italian disease. To say that is to court violent misunderstanding, like the horrid little boy who exclaimed that the emperor had no clothes on, anyway. But if it needs to be said, it needs even more to be pondered.

In the Midwest, as in Britain, some political frustration and some impatience issued in recent times of crisis in extremism and crackpot ideas—or, rather, ideologies. That is a measure of the all-pervading tolerance and good political sense of the public. But it is also a measure of revolt against demagoguery, machine politics, and domination by caucuses. It is a measure of a widening breach between public opinion and politics, between people and politicians, between the electorate and its representatives. It is the cost of giving up to Party what was meant for Mankind. Because there is only a little smoke, we should not say there is no risk of fire. The warning is there, in all the countries that still cling to representative government. And the Midwest has not been immune. It could not be immune in view of its miraculously quick industrialization and urbanization.

Yet the great mass of the Midwest middle class, like that of Britain, is conservative, tolerant, and imbued with common sense, even if it is politically unimaginative. The Midwest today is the greatest single repository in the world of nineteenth-century liberalism and of the individualism which underlay it. But it is at the same time a region enjoying life in a community to the highest degree. It enjoys a communalism, opposed to communism, that is marked by the strength of communal opinion and conventions. It is marked by life in the public eye; by frankness, publicity, and tolerance; and by a kindly neighborliness. It does not like to recognize the extremes on either side of it. It is therefore insular, like the majority of the British people. Only the extremes on either side of the Midwest middle class can, and do, revolt or break away from it. A few very rich people can afford to be reactionary and intolerant or fly in the face of public opinion. And, revolting against both these few rich reactionaries and against the insular conservatism of the comfortably-off *bourgeoisie* and highly paid artisans, the industrial trade-unions and a handful of intellectuals can afford to be rebellious at the other extreme. But, despite the newness of city life and industrialism in the region, all this is traditional. Probably four-fifths of the immigrants and settlers in the Midwest turned into conservatives and bourgeois men of property within a decade or two. The process and its outcome today are worth some analysis; for, though much is new and changed, much of Midwest politics is old or aging. And that, again, is not peculiar to the region. The Midwest happens to be a fascinating laboratory of political democracy; that is all.

Tradition is perhaps stronger in Midwest politics than in anything else. It seems peculiar to a stranger that in this youthful, curious, and experimental region the bulk of the electorate still belongs to the political party of its parents and grandparents—if the latter were born in America. Midwesterners, young and old, change their religion much more easily than they change their political party. It has been like that now for nearly a century: since the 1850's, to be exact. The British have made a new Socialist party, given it full power, and snuffed out the old Liberals. Not so the Americans, despite Populists and Progressives. The two major parties remain, dividing the field. But the superficial sameness covers a multitude of sectional, class, and other differences. It covers tensions and divisions. The machines of each party break newcomers into "conformists." The newcomers have to enter one party or another; they have to conform, to be assimilated, if they want to get anywhere. That is truly American. Like their party platforms, American party machines maintain themselves by give and take: by giving or promising a little to everybody, and by taking or collecting from everybody. Both party machines promise everything. The Republicans collect a lot from the few. The Democrats also collect a lot, but in smaller contributions from the many. That is British, too.

The differences, tensions, and divisions, however, do change the parties.

Historically, the Democrats were the conservatives. That is why in the 1840's and 1850's most Germans and Scandinavians and many of the Irish were Democrats. All the better-to-do immigrants, and the majority of Roman Catholics even if they were poor, stood on the side of conservatism and tradition: that is, with the Democrats. The German and other liberals and radicals after 1850 were a minority. When the new cities and industries brought in more and poorer immigrants, and the earlier settlers had gained property, the Republicans became the party of business, law, order, and respect for property. Then the Democrats, taking the American poor and the needy of Europe to their political bosom, became (as their enemies said) the party of "rum, Romanism, and rebellion." The Irish were split, as they remain to this day. Most of their men of property are Catholic Republicans, but the great majority of Irish-Americans are not rich; they are Catholic Democrats in the machines of big cities or states. Discontented, ambitious, progressive, or radical elements, either in cities or among farmers, constantly started—and still start—new ideas, new isms, new movements. But, except during Theodore Roosevelt's epoch, these new ideas and movements have generally ended by absorption or affiliation in the Democrat party. And even the Republican Theodore Roosevelt bolted his party, became the "Bull Moose," and went down to defeat in 1912.

Democrats have had an underdog complex since their bitter lesson in the 1850's. Republicans have always shown a selective tenderness to business, high tariffs, individualism, property rights, and proved merit. They have been the traditionalists, the conservatives, the "elect," and have stood for the right to become one of the "elect," for very long. To an Englishman it seems that there are so few real Tory Bourbons and reactionaries among Republicans, and so few real radicals among Democrats, that it is as if all American politics was a regular and disproportionately violent struggle between the two wings of the old Liberal party in England: between Whigs and Radicals—"radical" only in the English sense of that term, meaning nonsocialist, reformist, and progressive. Both American parties manipulate and rejoice in machines, caucuses, and all the arts of demagoguery more than any other parties in the remnants of the democratic world.

Yet after the 1850's both Republicans and Democrats were sectional in their makeup until the 1920's and the great crises of 1929–35. The Republicans drew their main strength from industry and finance in the northeast of the Union and, to a slightly smaller extent, from the Midwest. The Democrats drew theirs from the solid South. The rest of the country was a battlefield to be won. There were many party machines in cities which threw this city or that into one camp or another and, now and then, lost control to the machine of the opposing party. During the epoch of acute party conflict between 1880 and 1912 the Democrats were mainly the "outs"—for which the aftermath of Civil War and the rapid industrialization and prosperity were jointly responsible.

In this period the Midwest, the cradle of Republicanism if not of its finances, produced a galaxy of Republican talent: presidents, members of cabinets, statesmen, and politicians. This was natural. As early as in the 1830's the legislatures of Illinois and of other Midwest states were against federal government, extension of the executive power, and a federal Treasury or banking system. The new Republicanism after 1880 was squarely based upon states' rights, rising tariffs, individualism, and unrestricted private enterprise. It was the first trust-busting of 1890 and the revolt on the prairie, as we saw earlier, that ranged Norris, Murdock, and other progressive Republicans behind Theodore Roosevelt when, like a Bismarck or a Disraeli, he made his convulsive attempts to wean Republican conservatism from "Cannonism" and "standpatism" to a foresighted progressivism and compromise. But even as early as in 1890 the revolt on the prairie was not so much demanding *federal* control of railroads, trusts, and unrestricted private enterprise as control by each state; that is, states' rights. The disappointment of this and other demands for reform from the new Midwest, the Midwest of new urban populations and vulnerable farmers, led the reformist zealots into the Democrat camp and the Democrat forces to their first significant victory in 1912. Yet, by the irony of fate, the Democrat party, after the brief and hectic interlude of postwar boom and Republican governments between 1920 and 1930, had to make the biggest inroad upon sectionalism and states' rights: the New Deal.

With the New Deal all party lines in the Union became blurred, and sectionalism or regionalism was glossed over. The Northeast split between cities and countryside. So did the Midwest. These two regions, twin pillars of the Republican temple, toppled; but it was not long before the king post of the Democrat structure cracked, too. The solid South began politically to liquefy under the New Deal, as its businessmen perceived their community of interest with those of the Midwest and even with "dam' Yankees." Cracks and fissures appeared in Congress and everywhere else, in both parties and in all regions. It was like the terrible decade of the 1850's all over again.

As the New Deal wore on, new alignments became faintly visible. The so-called "working class," the trade-unionists and new industrial unionists of the cities, proved staunchly Democrat. The farmers wavered, backing and filling. The lower middle class went largely Democrat. The comfortably-off middle class and the well-to-do re-

292

mained Republican. Nothing brings out the steady assimilation of the Midwest to the Northeast more clearly than this political transformation between 1880 and the 1930's. It has gone on in other countries; and in most European lands political parties have disappeared in disaster, taking democracy with them. In the 1880's Bryce said that the American two-party system was so democratic, promising, and praiseworthy because neither party owed anything to classes; there was no attitude of class in them. Could anyone say that now?

Since 1920, in the Midwest as elsewhere, most of the poor and the young have been going Democrat. Republicanism, unyielding and rugged, has been unable in the main to hold them. True, both parties no longer rest solidly and foursquare upon their traditional foundations and principles. True, both are split. True, they no longer draw their main strength from different regions or sections of the country. They are more truly national than at any time since 1850. They are both terribly confused between ends and means. (What parties are not today, in the whole wide world?) But in this period the Republican party, like the old Whig party, proved more intransigent, dominated by older men of an older epoch. The results were particularly clear in its birthplace: the Midwest. Today the Democrats have stout citadels in the once solidly Republican core of the Midwest: in its cities and large towns. They have not been so strong there since the 1850's. Despite much havering, a vexatious wartime bureaucracy, and a wartime prosperity, the bulk of Midwest farmers have not returned to the Republican fold in which their normal conservatism kept them after the early 1900's.

Republicanism is widely spread. It is strong and solid among the well-to-do. Then its gets progressively weaker until it becomes weakest among the higher-paid artisans of the A.F. of L. or independent unions. In view of the steadiness of social and political trends in America since 1900, it seems wrong to ascribe, as many old-line Republicans do, the successes of Democrats since 1932—or, to be accurate, since 1912—to movements like those of Eugene Debs or the C.I.O. and its offspring, the Political Action Committee of the industrial unions and their fellow-workers. These are symptoms, manifestations, and results; not causes. The causes lie deeper. Indeed, it is doubtful whether semiskilled and unskilled labor in the big and smaller cities of the Midwest were ever Republican. They have been organized, made politically articulate, and have become Democrat; that's all.

One of the most cogent causes has been the realization that very grave economic, social, and political issues faced the whole of America, and not its sections, regions, states, or cities. It has been the growing awareness that local politics, local methods, and local solutions are not enough, that national solidarity and lobbying mean strength—as Republican businessmen first showed. That is why party politics and politicians have been in such confusion these three decades past. That is why the great struggle between states and federal government which marked the birth of the Constitution and the prelude to the Civil War broke out again with all its old violence of language. That is why so many who hate the extension of federal power, yet realize that the states can no longer solve all problems, are trying to find "regional" solutions, and are advocating "regionalism"—whatever that may mean at a time when everything is more national than ever before. That is why the Midwest has become steadily more assimilated to the East in political life: an assimilation that walks arm in arm with the standardization of these two regions to which we have frequently referred.

For a century and more the Midwest was the political weathercock of the country. It told whence and whither the wind was blowing. With its great voting power, equal to that of the entire East above Mason and Dixon's line, it has long been the decisive element in American politics. What the Midwest decided, generally decided national politics; and the Great Plains region has generally sided with its neighbor, the Midwest. Its impatience with controls and bossism—whether of the Republican Joe Cannon kind or of the Democrat city pattern—has long been shown in many outstanding political leaders who bolted the party or bucked a trend with courage and shrewd foresight. (Someone or something always changes a trend, anyway.) The great transfiguration of American politics in 1912, when the Bull Moose failed and Wilson came to power, was mainly due to Midwest and Great Plains discontent and independence. The great change of 1932 was heralded in the cities and farms of the Midwest. And, of the 82 electoral votes secured by Wendell Willkie in 1940, when Republicans polled an all-time record vote, 68 came from the Midwest and the Great Plains.

Among Republicans, for every Cannon of Illinois or Taft of Ohio, you found a Dolliver; or today you find Stassen or Ball of Minnesota, Hickenlooper of Iowa, Vandenberg of Michigan, and Burton of Ohio. And the Midwest or Great Plains produced the outstanding independents: Norris of Nebraska, the famous La Follette family of Wisconsin, and the Farmer-Labor leaders of Minnesota. This vigor, personal independence of party initiative, and varied coloring in Republican or independent Midwest politics, led many midwesterners—and still lead some Midwest publicists and political leaders—to claim the region as the citadel of Republicanism; the shrine of the only true Republican faith; the hope of the Republican future. So it might have been. So it yet may be. But, before that possibility can be properly judged, it is necessary to look into the recent breaking of many political records.

The late President Franklin D. Roosevelt's unprecedented electoral successes were due to extremely widespread *national*, not sectional or regional, support from many distinctively different groups of the American people. Some gave the Democrats a clear majority vote, others a minority vote. Whether in war or peace, the great bulk of skilled, semi-skilled, and unskilled labor in towns and cities have voted Democrat since 1912—less among skilled, more among unskilled. More members of trade-unions voted Democrat than workers not in unions. In most American cities and towns each with 10,000 souls or more, President Franklin D. Roosevelt had a substantial majority. In towns each with less than 10,000 and on the farms, he had something between a small majority and (in 1936 and again in 1944) a bare minority.[1]

In 1940 the Republicans won ten states, of which only three are in the Midwest: Indiana, Iowa, and Michigan. In 1944 they won twelve states, of which four are in the Midwest: Indiana, Iowa, Ohio, and Wisconsin. Yet both in 1940 and in 1944 the agricultural, less industrialized, and far less urban Great Plains region was more solidly Republican than the Midwest proper. In 1940 it gave Colorado, Kansas, Nebraska, and both Dakotas to the party; and in 1944 there were Colorado, Kansas, Nebraska, North Dakota, South Dakota, and Wyoming. In other words, the citadel of Republicanism has followed Horace Greeley's advice. Not only has it lost its eastern strongholds—except for the loyal remnant of Maine and Vermont—but it has also lost many in its Midwest birthplace. It has gone West, like a discontented pioneer, to the Plains. But it has not gone to the Far West. It has become more of an agricultural and small-town faith, as it was in the beginning. So Maine and Vermont are linked with Kansas, Nebraska, the Dakotas, Colorado, Iowa, and Wyoming; and also with those Midwest states that have many prosperous farms and a disproportionately large number of small towns—Ohio, Indiana, and Wisconsin. Where the big and middling cities are numerous, where industry and organized labor are strongest, the Democrat party wins or the struggle is very close, as it was in 1944 in Indiana, Ohio, and Michigan.

Thus if anyone thinks of Democrat or Republican politics today in terms of American sectionalism alone, he is doomed to confusion. After all, though each state irrespective of its population sends two

[1] See the Gallup poll released March 4, 1945.

senators to the United States Senate, where are "the big battalions" of voters? They decide the composition of the House and the election of a President and government. They are in the East and Midwest; in most of the cities of the country. Sectional influences have lessened. In every election from 1932 onward, the Democrats would have won *even if the solid South had returned a Republican majority in every state.* Democrat success was largely due to the size of its majorities in the thirteen big American cities each with over half a million souls.[2] *Five of the thirteen are in the Midwest,* in five states. Six are in the East, also in five states. The other two are in California. That means the Midwest and East show more political features in common than they show differences; and together they really form one political region of cities and farmers, of urban and rural people.

If you add the votes of these thirteen cities together, you find that their electorate was almost three to two in favor of Democrats; and with the sole exceptions of Ohio (Cleveland and Cincinnati) and Wisconsin (Milwaukee), this overwhelming Democrat vote in the big cities of the country swung their states to the Democrat side. Whoever wins by such a margin in the nation's big cities, almost wins the nation; and what has been proved since 1932 in the thirteen big cities is becoming an increasingly evident trend in the twenty-three cities each with 250,000–500,000 souls.

True, the big cities are overwhelmingly in the East or Midwest. But instead of making party politics sectional, instead of making Republicanism more midwestern, this once again assimilates the Midwest to the East, as we saw when we examined city life and many Midwest institutions. It breaks down sectionalism. Republican strength is as great in the small towns and cities of the East as it is in those of the Midwest. In fact, as we saw, the East has more of them than the Midwest, until you reach the group of really small towns each with less than about 6,000 inhabitants. Indeed, Republicanism is strongest in small towns everywhere in America. Again, Republican strength is greater among farmers and the rural population everywhere, but more so out on the Great Plains and in Maine or Vermont than in the Midwest proper. Any attempt to label the Midwest the citadel of modern Republicanism seems ill founded. Like their opponents, the Republicans have strongholds scattered throughout the country, recruiting their forces from all groups: here more from one, there more from another, but nowhere on a sectional basis.

This invasion of the Republican stronghold by Democrats, and the

[2] The fourteenth city, the national capital, is disfranchised.

recent nationalizing rather than sectionalizing of American politics, is reflected in many other ways. The Democrats' growing strength since the early 1900's has made great inroads among the largest groupings of city and town dwellers, whether those groupings are by income bracket, by race, or by national origin. We have seen the result in the ranks of labor. But Democrats have generally won substantial majorities—equal in percentage to that required in the whole country to win the presidency—among people in the middle and lower middle income brackets. This has been particularly noticeable among the farmers. Democrats have invaded the professions and won the allegiance of professional men in income brackets at or below the average for their profession.

As to racial groups and those by nationality of origin or family language: despite the defection of many Negro leaders and newspapers to the Republicans, despite all the Republicans and their publicity have been able to do, despite the disfranchisement of Negroes and poor whites in many southern states, three-quarters of the Negro voters outside the South still vote Democrat. The Jews seem overwhelmingly Democrat. Americans of Italian, Polish, Bohemian, and other Slav origins are staunchly Democrat. All these groups are strongest in the cities. They are numerous and widely distributed throughout the Midwest. There are signs, too, that the American women, who in 1944 made up the majority of the electorate for the first time, have on balance voted Democrat rather than Republican. Finally, the less well-to-do Irish in cities and towns have stayed Democrat. Among the recognizable groupings of the urban population, only those of German and Scandinavian descent and the well-to-do Irish or Scotch-Irish appear to have remained overwhelmingly and ardently Republican. But even here the division seems still to be one of income brackets and economic functions rather than of blood or national origin.

Despite many striking differences, American politics since 1900, certainly since 1920, has been traveling a road familiar to European democracies. The sectionalism of party politics which marked America—but hardly any European country except Italy and Spain—has diminished and almost died out. Instead, party politics is now as nation-wide in scope as it was until the 1850's, but as it never was thereafter until our own day. Yet, unlike what it was in the epoch which ended in the 1850's, rudimentary class attitudes and class consciousness have come to characterize both American political parties. Machines and caucuses have been tightened and expanded to a nation-wide scale. The average age of politicians and political leaders has correspondingly risen, as the older hands clung longer to the levers. In all this, the Midwest has been more affected than affecting, more of a result than a cause, more the anvil than the hammer.

"LITTLE PLATOONS" IN POLITICS

The Midwest is an amphitheater in which more political contests and tugs-of-war seem to go on than in any other part of America. That is a sign of its political youth, health, and vigor. Its political thought, action, and methods are highly colored by that original difference from the East and South which we noticed earlier: namely, the growth of political life from the bottom upward instead of from the top down. Its approach to politics is therefore necessarily local and sectional.

For the first century of its one hundred and fifty years of life it was developing its own political thought, institutions, and methods. These all arose within a firm framework of Midwest and even of subregional or sub-subregional problems and circumstances. It was bound to be so as long as the chief political problems were the hard facts of building, providing, and financing Midwest communities; organizing them in states, cities, counties, or townships; developing communications; and getting the necessary facilities and amenities of community life set up. All this placed the accent heavily upon local affairs. This adventurous century of construction is the historical background against which current political struggles in the region must be viewed. After all, a midwesterner of seventy today was part of that first century of background when he was born and reared. The atmosphere of Midwest political discussions among men and women over fifty is still thick with local, state, and regional references. Only when you talk to those under fifty, particularly to the young generation of midwesterners born in or after the first World War—those who necessarily have been most influenced by the great national and international events of the last thirty years—can you gauge the great gulf fixed between the older and younger generations. Across this gulf many tugs-of-war in the Midwest, as elsewhere in the world, are now going on.

One tug-of-war to which we gave scant notice in passing is between cities and states, between the urban and rural population. This is really the continuation of a long struggle between the old rural and new urban Midwest. Here, too, history plays a part. The state constitution of Missouri in 1875 was the first in the country to define and set up complete self-government for cities. Until then, either the American city dwellers and their leaders were forced to enter into corrupt and unholy alliances with state legislatures, or the legislatures raided the cities, highjacked them, blackmailed them, and lived off them. The innovation of home rule for cities by Missouri in 1875 was due in great measure to the disproportionately rapid growth of cities in the Midwest. In some Midwest states in the last quarter of last century the city population was three-quarters of that in the state; and, in some, one or two big cities alone accounted for this predominance. That swift urbanization has gone on uninterruptedly, but the cities have had home rule. And that has created another problem today.

The Old Midwest—that of Missouri and the southern portions of Illinois, Indiana, and Ohio where the old southern county unit of local administration predominates—now enjoys a disproportionately large representation in state legislatures. The cities grew very fast until 1930. The rural and small-town people and their state representatives, however, managed to hamstring, block, or postpone constitutional provisions for redrafting the boundaries of congressional districts to correspond with changes in population. Ohio is an arena in which Cleveland in the north tugs against Cincinnati in the south; Columbus, the capital, a big city on its own, rallies Dayton, Akron, Youngstown, and others to its cause; and the farmers all over the state try to get their needs now from one city group and now from another. In Indiana, the northern cities of Fort Wayne, Gary, South Bend, and others are tugging against Evansville and the other cities of the south; the biggest, the state capital of Indianapolis, manipulates all of them; and the farmers can only copy the actions of their fellows in Ohio. In Missouri it is St. Louis in the east against Kansas City in the west, or both against the farmers and rural population. In Michigan, Detroit and its satellite cities make state politics top-heavy. The farmers and small towns dig their heels in and tug against such domination. In Minnesota, Iowa, and Wisconsin the situation is easier, though the actual and potential "drag" of Milwaukee and Minneapolis in their respective states causes much political shuffling and dealing. The problem is most acute in Illinois because of the enormous size of Chicago. It is a revealing story.

Illinois has had no revision of its state electoral districts since 1901, despite the provision in the constitution of 1870 that such boundary lines should be rearranged according to the census every ten years. (Most state constitutions copy the federal rule that in all constitutional issues, as with treaties before the United States Senate, a two-thirds majority is required to make new law.) Today Cook County, the seat of Chicago, with four million souls has more than half the population of Illinois. Yet it has only ten out of Illinois' twenty-six congressmen at Washington. Whenever a bill for congressional or state electoral reapportionment has been introduced into the legislature at Springfield, the "down-staters," both Democrat and Republican, have united in a common local interest to bawl the measure out. And as political representation in the state legislature is on the same principles as that in Congress at Washington, the strength of the "down-staters" cannot be reduced, either.

Characteristically, the famous Democrat machine of Chicago comes to agreement with the state Republican machine at Springfield that they will both call on their members in the state legislature to back a bill for reapportionment. Such a bipartisan deal generally suits particular projects of both Chicago Democrats and Illinois down-state Republicans. "You scratch my back and I'll scratch yours." But what happens then is most interesting. The machines fail to deliver. They cannot keep the boys in line. Down-state Democrats and Republicans alike "buck" their respective machines and bosses. You can lead a horse to water. He may usually drink. But when he won't drink, hell and high water won't make him. So even machines have their limitations in the Midwest. In this case again, their limitations are those of a purely local interest, a subregional solidarity that cuts across party lines and powerfully affects national politics.

In order that reapportionment should not deprive some down-state representatives of their seats in the state legislature at Springfield, Illinois is thus represented top-heavily in the Congress at Washington by rural or small-town congressmen and (if one may use the word) bottom-lightly by those from the big city of Chicago and a few other densely populated areas. In fact, the state is not proportionately represented at all. And that has been more and more evident for forty years.

Take another example. In 1945, also as a result of a bipartisan deal between the Democrat Mayor Kelly of Chicago and Republican Governor Green of Illinois, a resolution backed by both machines was introduced to permit a referendum to the citizens of Illinois in November, 1946, by which they could summon a constitutional convention to revise the constitution of 1870. Thus, the resolution was not to change the constitution. It was to allow the people to say whether they wanted to change it or not. (Missouri, New Jersey, Georgia, and other states had already approved revisions in their constitutions.) Two-thirds of the 153 state representatives then in the Illinois House were, of course, necessary to pass this resolution. It was thrown out on May 1, 1945, because only a majority of 81 voted for it and 65 against it. A two-thirds majority was not obtained. On this occasion the Democrat machine "delivered." It was the Republican machine that failed. The minority imposed its will on the majority and perfectly constitutionally.

300

The president of the Illinois State Federation of Labor (A.F. of L.), the vice-president and executive secretary of the Illinois Manufacturers' Association, and the president of the Illinois Agricultural Association, who also happened to be a big businessman and a representative in Washington of the Farm Bureau, all opposed the resolution and called on their sympathizers and followers at Springfield to resist it. In this case it was not merely local loyalties or subregional allegiances that counted. It was the fear of the probable dominating power of "the big town," Chicago, in Illinois politics. It was fear of Chicago's Democrat machine. It was fear by many associations and lobbies, including the Farm Bureau and the A.F. of L., lest the C.I.O. and the Political Action Committee should dominate Illinois by dominating the Democrat machine in Cook County. But there is much, very much, more than that behind the attitudes of state representatives to particular measures.

The observer from outside at first finds it strange that men who think other countries and peoples undemocratic should so violently refuse to permit their own people to express an opinion whether political changes should be made. The most revealing statements, as reported in the press, are those of the Republican majority leader in the Illinois House of Representatives during the proceedings just described, Representative Reed F. Cutler, from Lewistown, Illinois: "The members of this legislature are the best judges of what should be done..... If you go ahead and waste two years of the people's time and millions of their money on a constitutional convention, the people will just beat hell out of the product as they did in 1922." This is a valuable example of the Midwest conception of politics.

The temporary officials—mayors, governors, and so on—are distrusted, even though they are all elected. They are executives. They may exert too much power. They may put their heads together at the cost of the state, the representative assembly, or the people. The American system of checks and balances against executive power reaches its clearest expression in Midwest politics. The machines of both parties are strong. One may rule the biggest city while the other rules the state. They distribute the spoils and decree appointments and candidates. But, once representatives are elected, they show remarkable independence on many issues, as President Truman did in Missouri when he was judge and, later, senator while the notorious Pendergast machine of Kansas City ran the state in the Democrat interest. Judge Truman, as he then was, came in for some criticism because of his collaboration with that machine. On his own request a grand jury examined his record and pronounced it spotless. Machines may run politics, but they cannot run all politicians. The spirit of a local assembly, like that of both houses at Washington, is one of a club or trade-union. It shows even more *esprit de corps* than most clubs or unions. It may be true, as one observer said of his state representatives, that "some of them have been wrapped up and delivered so many times they resemble a stamp collection." But the majority of local politicians are individuals, and they often revolt.

The great strength of a party machine—the spoils system—is also its greatest weakness. The most powerful boss knows that he cannot continue to be boss without an organization and officers behind him. That means spoils, patronage, and big money. He may buy politicians and he may buy voters. But that is not the problem. It is to make them "stay bought." That necessitates a certain responsiveness to public opinion, or at least to a part of public opinion. The machine must be sure of a majority vote. Even the boss has to compromise, either with his powerful lieutenants who command local votes, or with the public. That is when the weakness appears. To keep his judges in power, he may do a deal with the opposition whereby each party gets an agreed quota of judges. All the judges up for election are then settled beforehand. So neither party goes to an election; the list of judges is approved; and the voters have no say.

Yet the press and the people regularly make things hot—as they certainly have done in Chicago and Illinois over public transport, education, the state constitution, public welfare, and congressional reapportionment for decades. Democrat Chicago wanted municipal transport. That was one reason for the bipartisan deal with the Republican governor and his followers at Springfield in 1945. So the big city had to deliver its machine votes for something required by the opposition at the state capital, in return for their agreeing to pass Chicago's traction bill. The big city "delivers," but something slips up in the legislature. Some group is not not getting enough of the spoils of office. They buck the machine. A bipartisan deal collapses, just as so many deals in politics collapse. The legislature is treated to a terrific barrage of epithets from all kinds of newspapers, supporting both parties.

In an editorial entitled "Legislature Says No!" the *Chicago Daily News* concluded its discussion of the legislature's responsibility to correct discriminations by saying: "Until those abuses are corrected, the democratic process in Illinois remains a grim jest."[3] The *Decatur Herald* commented on this same situation: "Altogether the legislators have done an excellent job of stalling on the two most important issues to

[3] *Chicago Daily News* (Independent Republican), May 3, 1945.

302

come before the 64th general assembly. And they'll do it again so long as the people of the State of Illinois continue to show little or no interest in issues which affect them more intimately than most of them realize."[4] The *Chicago Times* called it "cowardice" and referred to "downstate legislators who once more deliberately have chosen to violate their oaths of office . . . . a disgraceful performance . . . . filled with the carefree, unreasoning spirit of a lynching party. . . . . And that, friends, is not democracy in action."[5] The *Chicago Sun* said: "The people of Illinois have been kicked around for many years, and kicked again this year."[6] You find such strictures in many non-Chicago papers, too.

This is, of course, the language of local politics in the Midwest. The words do not mean as much as they seem to. The editors and the readers know that there is much more to it than just "democracy in action." What has really happened is that a deal between two opposing powerful machines has collapsed. Another deal must be tried. The great strength of party machines in states or cities was built up because that was the only way a two-party system *could* function among a people so largely composed of unassimilated racial and national groups but with equal adult suffrage. It was natural, therefore, that the machines should trade with each other, in order to get done a little of what each wanted. Often a lot got done. The machines, however, ended by running all politics and government.

In a period when federal or state governments did nothing for the poor and needy, when the federal government scarcely touched the citizens of a state or city at all, the party machine—generally that of the Democrats—was firmly based on a goodly proportion of charity. This, too, was natural: for the city bosses in the Midwest, as elsewhere, tended always to be on the side of the underdogs—of whom there were so many, all with votes. Many of the bosses had been underdogs. They knew and lived among their people. So did their ward heelers and precinct captains. The machine was thus, and still is, very much a local affair, very much in contact with the people, and more so than many who write and speak about "the people." True, there was a heavy rake-off for party funds, and the principle of "I give that thou mayest give" was strictly enforced at the polling booths. But as the cities grew, especially in the Midwest, there was nothing but private charity to deal with the sorrows, ignorance, and bewilderment of the poor, who were

[4] *Decatur Herald* (Independent), cited in *Chicago Times*, May 3, 1945.
[5] *Chicago Times* (Democrat), June 15, 1945.
[6] *Chicago Sun* (Democrat), May 2, 1945.

so largely alien immigrants. To the poor, the machine seemed merely governmental. It was paternal: kind but authoritative. It was more democratic than anything to which they had ever been used in Europe. If "no taxation without representation" were sound, why not "no representation without contributions"—especially as representatives themselves were paid by taxpayers? And, after all, what operates in a ward or precinct to aid or relieve voters and their families is what operates as a lobby at the state or national capital to aid economic groups and interests. The important thing to remember is that machines, bossism, and bipartisan deals supplied a real demand. Within the legal, constitutional, or social setting they were the only way politics could operate. They met a real need, when no one and nothing else met it. Whether they meet that need today, whether they ever ought to have met it, whether they meet it as cheaply and efficiently as state and federal authorities, whether the days of the machines are numbered because of new movements and social agencies—these are other questions.[7]

The power of the boss, of the lobby, and of many city or state machines in the Midwest owes a great deal to the public's deep distrust of government, civil service, executives, and elected officials. Parties in power, like officials, come and go; but the machine and its boss or bosses go on forever. So do lobbies. Both lobbies and machines are therefore like watchdogs—in their own interests, of course—but still they perform an obvious political function. A national party has to respect local machines, as these have to respect their own district bosses. There are a lot of lobbies on behalf of a lot of interests, too. They are constantly increasing. To that extent they also represent many elements of public opinion. They "get things done."

From what the all-pervading distrust of officials and executives stems I do not know. Maybe in the Midwest the pioneers inherited much of the old colonial French and British distrust of "the authorities," which men on the spot always feel for the authorities back home. The vast amount of written constitutions, rules, regulations, and elective offices and the frequency of elections eloquently testify to the American, and especially the midwestern, distrust of authority even when it is elected. From the outset of state legislatures in the Midwest—for instance, at the time the legislature of Illinois met at Vandalia when it had less than a thousand inhabitants—machines were built, organized, and operated with the express purpose of controlling or changing the authorities, of

[7] See Harold F. Gosnell, *Machine Politics: Chicago Model* (Chicago: University of Chicago Press, 1937), for an extremely detailed and analytical description of a city machine.

seeing that representatives represented, and of maintaining the party as a lobby and a perpetual organization even if the party was out of power. The discretionary or veto powers of governors were more and more curtailed and reduced to written law. The terms of judges were reduced and made comparable to those of any other elective political office. It was as if, faced with the idealist's demand that justice be done though the heavens fall, realistic midwesterners preferred to keep the heavens up with a little less perfect, a little more political, justice. Parallel to the machines, lobbies were organized to operate on each machine. But it all made public life quickly changeable, malleable, responsive to public opinion.

Moreover—a great blessing in a democracy—if public life proved unresponsive to public opinion, it was bound to become *public* at any rate. And if the voters were prepared to overthrow their respective machines, these could be changed when they did not "deliver." Englishmen know that their officials and authorities are scrupulously honest; perhaps more so than anywhere else. But they must admit, too, that they can often be dense or ineffective for long periods of office; and it is very hard to change them. "Against stupidity the gods themselves struggle in vain!"

The American system offsets the power of the executive, the judge, and the representative by the power and efficiency of the machine or the lobby. Often "the boys" do not stay in line. But often they do. And they are often changed. The Republican Senator Tobey of New Hampshire was very indignant in the Senate in June, 1945, when he discovered what he called "five fat, sleek lobbyists with round bottoms and round heads" sitting outside the chamber and trying to influence the Senate to vote against reciprocal trade agreements and lower tariffs. There was less to be said for his indignation at a long-familiar institution in American politics than for his suggestion that lobbyists should register and publish their employers and salaries. That at least would officially recognize the system as an essential part of the machinery whereby legislative and public opinion interact and are kept in line. And what goes for lobbies might well go for political machines. Or might it?

What lobbies and machines have done, however, notably in the Midwest, is to *increase* the public's distrust of officials, authorities, and politicians; and, as we saw, that distrust never needed much encouragement. This distrust has grown into skepticism. It is strikingly shown by many different polls of public opinion. It has not yet reached the stage of widespread political cynicism. But it is as marked as the growth in other kinds of Midwest skepticism, which we noted earlier and in other contexts. One of the reasons for this is the steady aging of political life, the maintenance in office of aging politicians, the callousness of drivers toward hacks. The public is clearly told by the press who the drivers are and what machines the hacks are pulling. It is also clearly told of the relations between lobbies, lobbyists, machines, and hacks. This has been going on for a very long time in the Midwest, both in city and in state politics. The result, especially in times of national crisis—which means for twenty out of the last thirty years—has been to accelerate the growth of political skepticism and frustration in both parties.

Between 1830 and 1900 the Midwest states produced able, indeed brilliant, political leaders and statesmen. They were very young, often in their twenties or thirties. They were growing up with a youthful region, in young and vigorous communities. They had thirty and often forty years of active political life ahead of them; so they took careful thought in making decisions for the future of their community and themselves. They could be held to account for what they said or did, and they had decades of political life before them in which to live it down. That was also true, to a smaller extent, in Britain and other democracies at that time. But as party machines, caucuses, and lobbies tightened their grip on politics, on the selection of candidates, and on the actions of representatives, something like a hardening of the arteries afflicted politics in all these countries. This has been more and more apparent since 1890: more so in Britain, less in America. It has been most obvious since 1920. In all parties and in all democracies older politicians have been lobbied, caucused, and pensioned into office. They have been made to toe the lines of particular rather than public inter-est—lines drawn outside the legislatures by framers of policy who were not obviously politicians. These older politicians had less time before them. They would not live, anyway, to see all the fruits of their action or inaction. They were amenable and resigned.

It is significant, again, that this process, so obvious in European democracies and even in the East and South of the United States, be-came almost as plain in the newer and more youthful Midwest. It was partly responsible for the growth of Midwest skepticism about politics and politicians of both parties, especially after the first World War. And though that skepticism certainly did not reach the degree of cynicism and frustration that afflicted Britain, France, Germany, and Italy, it steadily grew. It operated to keep many an able young midwesterner out of politics and to give both politics and politicians a bad name. What kind of young man, after all, would agree to be a political "yes-man" or a hack in a Midwest city or state, when he could do better for himself, tax and flex his abilities more, in business? It was a vicious circle. The machines were maintained by their own attendants for increasingly long terms, and the attendants recruited themselves from their own groups. It was the lobbies, and the interests which maintained them, that attracted the young talent.

Yet very recently, and as a result of war, that process has come near to producing its own solution of the problem facing all democracies. From business and the professions, especially from the law and from small beginnings, younger and more able men have gone into Midwest politics: from the associations of the community; from the American Legion, Rotary, trade associations, and trade-unions. This development has heightened the contrast between young and old politicians, intensified the tug-of-war between the generations, and made it more difficult for both party machines in local politics to keep the boys at all, let alone keep them in line. Of all recent political developments in the region, this is the most encouraging. In Minnesota, Iowa, Missouri, and Ohio it is most noticeable. Something like a ferment in both parties has been going on in those states, producing new and vigorous political personalities and party attitudes that have attracted national, and even international, attention. If it has not yet become so apparent in Wisconsin, Illinois, Indiana, and Michigan, that is not to say that the ferment and the struggles in both parties are not also going on there.

This new ferment must not be interpreted as "a blow aimed at machine politics." Machines are, as far as the stranger can judge, indispensable to American party politics. But they may be changed. In fact, that is where shrewd Midwest observers look for the change: namely, in the staffing and the running of the machines. And it is noteworthy that, as so often before in periods of reformist zeal, the first effects of the change are apparent in national and state politics and not in the local affairs of big cities run by the city machines. That is what has already been happening during the period of international crisis since 1939. National and international issues of great gravity have tried men's souls, on the farms, in small towns, and in the smaller cities. Those are the places where the reactions to grave national issues are first and most clearly registered. In the big cities the party machines are more carefully tended. They have to take account of many more groups and interests. They run, and are run, more strictly and precisely. Yet they, too, have felt the new influences and are changing to keep pace with change; for in Midwest politics "change is in the air."

An epoch is coming to an end. It is not just an epoch in the politics of a region. But the region is not trying to move against the current of change. Sensitive, foresighted, and cautiously experimental, midwesterners are going with the stream. They and the stream, too, are likely to travel much more rapidly when over twelve million young veterans of the armed forces—among them a disproportionately large number of midwesterners—come home and are injected into the political blood stream of the nation. That will not be a regional or sectional influence. It will be national, and it will tend to break down the "little platoon" loyalties. This reinvigoration of politics was most refreshingly apparent in the British general election of 1945, the first in a decade. It will certainly be followed by more frequent and larger doses. It may be much more apparent in America in 1946, 1948, and every two years thereafter. The young take a long time to grow old; the old, such a little time to pass away.

INSULATION AND ISOLATION

Insularity of outlook on the world was natural to midwesterners for most of their short history. There was so much of a constructive kind to be done in the region. Communications with the rest of America were poor or mainly for the use of a well-to-do minority. Midwest mobility was largely confined within the region itself until during the last three decades. Politics and politicians stayed close to everyday problems, which were local. Even businessmen were overwhelmingly producing and distributing goods and services for the Midwest and other Americans. The East, the South, and the Far West were left to trade or deal with foreigners. The heavy Midwest emphasis on American myths and on a standardizing, assimilating, educational system resulted in firm beliefs which in some cases became firm prejudices. But they were also responsible for a lack of interest in, and lack of knowledge of, the world beyond America—and even of America and Americans beyond the Midwest. The only costly war in which the Midwest felt deeply involved, until our own day, was all-American: the Civil War; and the South paid for that. The North and Midwest did well out of it, despite their tragic loss of young lives.

Though a few easterners, southerners, and far westerners might realize that the security of the Western Hemisphere, respect for the Monroe Doctrine, and even the safety of the United States depended for a century on Anglo-American good feeling and the British navy, midwesterners and the people of the Great Plains could not be expected to grasp it and, in the main, were not even interested. They were serving America behind tariffs aimed at unknown and unseen for-

308

eigners—tariffs which midwesterners had advocated and supported since the late 1830's. Their material miracles, their fantastic growth, their unparalleled transfiguration of a vast virgin region—all seemed solely due to their own virtues. If many southerners, Yankees, New Yorkers, and millions of alien immigrants had made the Midwest what it was, then it must be because the South, the East, and particularly the benighted countries of Europe offered less to their peoples, were undemocratic, less vigorous and enterprising. Many easterners and southerners could see great differences in Europe, differences between European countries and peoples and their institutions, and a few differences from American institutions that might even be worth copying. Over 99 per cent of midwesterners saw no differences, except in the traits of immigrants. If Irish and Bulgarians, Poles and Italians, Scotch and Germans emigrated to the Midwest, then all of their homelands and institutions must be alike; all must be unenviable; all must be far worse for their remaining inhabitants than the Midwest, otherwise why should so many Europeans come four or five thousand miles to start a new life? And immigrants themselves, though they might still be sentimental over "the old country," thought it benighted, slow, and without a future.

It was hard to describe to midwesterners in the second World War what a blitz was like. After all, it is impossible for anyone to imagine something inconceivable. Imagination's limits are set by the experience and vocabulary (which is part of experience) in which anyone is brought up. Every parent knows the narrow limits of a young child's imagination. Midwesterners were, and to a much smaller extent still are, youthful in this respect, too. Sympathetic, sensitive, and generous to a degree, in the main they could only imagine more as they experienced more of the world beyond their boundaries. That experience has been recent. Much of it has been gained by young Midwest soldiers, sailors, and airmen who saw foreign lands only in the squalor and abnormality of war. Most of it is still to come.

From their very beginnings, therefore, Midwest attitudes to American foreign policy, to foreign affairs, and to foreigners were highly colored by their sympathy and generosity, their own local and sectional concerns, and their own folk myths. More than any other regions of America, the Midwest and Great Plains had taken the discontented and the rebels, the enterprising, the young and the "nonconformists" of many nations and of the older America, and had performed miracles with them. The Constitution itself, made by rebels, prohibited the *federal* government from passing any law diminishing the citizen's freedom to bear arms. That is still significant. Midwesterners developed their own peculiar checks and balances against authority. It was natural for them from the outset to side with the discontented, the individuals who rebelled against authority, and to identify them all over the world, indiscriminately, as the underdogs, the apostles of liberty and freedom— provided, of course, they seemed to offer no threat to the American or the Midwest way of life. If they did that, they were "radicals," and dangerous. If they did not, they were crusaders in shining armor: the Russian, Polish, Italian, and German liberals last century; the Hungarians; the Cubans; the Irish; but not, in this century, the Communists and the Republicans in the Spanish civil war.

Whatever they were, they were foreigners. The sympathy of midwesterners was always expressed in material generosity, at home or in Congress; but midwesterners remained chary of entanglements in foreign policy and particularly of war. They were not imperialistic. Most of them distrusted Theodore Roosevelt's adventurism and "manifest destiny." They were overwhelmingly critical of "dollar diplomacy" and the troubles to which it led in so many Latin-American countries. They identified it with Wall Street and the East, which they always distrusted. More than anything else, they wanted perpetual peace for their country, for peace was the best foundation of prosperity and material progress. In all this they were, again, astonishingly like the Victorian businessmen in Britain. Indeed, they were "little Englanders," where for "England" you can put "Midwest." They were prepared to live and let live. Even if they cheered one side in a foreign contest, they did it safely from the sidelines. "Why can't you leave well alone?" The testy and pathetic query of Lords Melbourne and Aberdeen a century ago was the Midwest motto, too; but for almost a century longer.

That was the general attitude of midwesterners until very recently. But on that broad canvas many significant details made up the general impression. Most important among these were European influences in the region. They were influences, but they had their effect by reaction rather than action, by producing a negative rather than a positive attitude. This was natural, too, among a people who were "anti-" much that was American, but in other regions of America. Until very recently, Europe seemed to most midwesterners the greatest danger to their uninterrupted material progress. It may yet seem so, though that is now more doubtful. The heavy populating of the Midwest, its new cities and towns and even its farms, with so many different European peoples had two great effects.

First, it made these young and new midwesterners, including many immigrants and their children, extremely critical of Europe and its conflicts. If all these Europeans could get on well together in America, why couldn't they at home? Europe was incorrigible. It did not occur to midwesterners that tariffs and little sovereignties in Europe were expressions of the same love of liberty and self-determination that made America great. In Europe, these things seemed silly. The European powers were too small and too old to be able to afford them. Midwesterners had, and still have, little use or respect for small and old things.

Secondly, it strengthened American and former European midwesterners' natural desire to have nothing to do, politically, with a Europe of which they despaired, anyway. Europe must either, it seemed, be an anarchy or an authoritarian New Order, in which case it was a threat and a danger. To hell with Europe; and Europe went there.

Nearly all midwesterners of European origins in the first and second generations naturally tended to look down, patronizingly, upon the country and people of their origin. As we saw, this did not and does not prevent many of them from taking an inordinately keen, active, organized, critical, and sometimes constructive part in the domestic and foreign policies of their European homelands. Indeed, to the foreign observer, they still seem to take a keen and almost un-American part in those affairs. Religions and city machines in the Midwest perpetuate these "national minority groups" (as they are strangely called) and thereby work against the assimilating influences and aims of public education. That is yet another Midwest paradox. Some European countries' authorities, too, wrongly if naturally, work upon the sympathies of these groups.

So one of the Midwest contrasts emerges in the context of foreign policy, too. While there is more freedom and a far higher standard of living for so many European groupings in the Midwest than they could have commanded in their country of origin, they look down on that country while simultaneously they take very definite attitudes toward it: attitudes that play an influential part in American domestic and foreign policy.

Many midwesterners of Polish, Greek, Czech, and other Slav origins, and the Zionist Jews, have long been, and still are, active in this respect. A smaller minority of those of German origin have also been of help to Germany in the past. Those of Scandinavian, British, Italian, and Irish origin are the least active, together with the majority of those of German origin; and these are the "national groups" who least patronize or look down on "the old country." The combination of religious and national loyalties, however, has had the effect of making the great majority of the many midwesterners of German, Irish, and Scandinavian origin strongly opposed to American involvement in what seemed to be merely European wars and of making most of the other groupings "interventionist." While these influences can be clearly traced in all American cities, for obvious reasons they are particularly marked in those of the Midwest and of the Plains. To these influences must be added that of the Midwest Protestant, and particularly the evangelical, churches in which Christian pacifism has been stronger than it was or is elsewhere in America. In this there is an unbroken line of religious idealism and perfectionism which leads right back to the Old Midwest.

The heavy population of Wisconsin, Illinois, Indiana, Michigan, and Ohio by Germans, and the less heavy German element in Minnesota and Missouri, was admittedly the hope of the Kaiser and his advisers in 1914–16 and one of the great hopes of the Nazis after 1933. The country of Czechoslovakia owes its existence as much perhaps to millions of Pittsburghers, Clevelanders, Chicagoans, and citizens of other Midwest or "marginal" cities as to the nation's own leaders in Europe. The Poles of Chicago, Milwaukee, Cleveland, Detroit, and other cities have been, and still are, potent influences upon Polish and American policy. So in their respective settings are Italians, Hungarians, Serbs, Croats, Greeks, Bulgars, and the Baltic peoples. The Irish were extremely potent until recently. Being a melting-pot that has not yet melted its contents, the Midwest has many reasons for fearing, distrusting, and disliking Europe. Conflicts in Europe lead to conflicts, tensions, and even to domestic political uncertainties inside America and inside the Midwest. A mayor, a governor, a senator, a representative— even a President and his cabinet—cannot be sure of their policy, or of their own continuity in power, unless and until they are sure of the reactions and the support of so many disparate "national groups" in America.

A senator from a state, or a representative from a city or district, in which such "national groups" bulk large will be particularly careful of proclaiming his views on foreign policy until he has taken soundings back in the old, familiar channels. He wants to sail into port again. Not all can be as fortunate in their choice of parents as Representative O'Konski of Wisconsin, who can presumably command both Irish and Polish votes. Many congressmen and members of state legislatures represent districts composed almost wholly of one "national group." Their names usually tell the national origin of the group which prevails in their district. Yet theirs is an easier task than that of those who must represent districts composed equally of Americans of Italian and Greek

312

origin, or Polish and Czech, or Hungarian and Croat, or German and Scandinavian, or Irish and Scotch-Irish. The stand taken by Senator Vandenberg of Michigan in 1945 on the United Nations Charter in the United States Senate called for more political courage than most foreign observers, and many Americans, realized. The "Polish vote," as it is still called, is a big hazard in Detroit and Michigan—as it is in other Midwest cities, and as are the votes of "Germans, Italians, Czechs, Jews, Negroes," and so on—all of them Americans.

These various groupings are not "anti-'s" in any regular sense. They just exist, and, as such, politicians must take account of them. Nor, indeed, are American "anti-'s" of non-Anglo-Saxon origin. That impression would be utterly false. For every Nye or Hoffman there are two or three Wheelers, Clarks, Sumners, Busbeys, Days, Reynoldses. Indeed, if one is to judge by names alone (which is dangerous, especially in the Midwest, where so many have been Anglicized), a surprisingly large number of "anti-" leaders and spokesmen boast good old English, Scottish, and Irish names. They are, presumably, the latter-day equivalent of the anti-Catholic, anti-foreign, anti-Irish "Native Americans" of a century ago. And, as such, they will pass. They may be symptomatic in the still largely unassimilated Midwest or Great Plains, but they do not suit the prevailing tolerance of the region.

When some of the countries of origin of these groupings are at each others' throats in Europe, the problem is made more acute. There is nothing quite like it in the world—at least, not in a democracy. Yet the surprising feature to the stranger is that not one member of these "national groups," so excitable and excited over European countries' policies, would ever go back to Europe. Only a very few Germans and Italians (before the days of fascism and nazidom) and a very few British would "go back." And these are the nationalities in America that do not, as a whole, despair of Europe, even today.

This general distrust, fear, and dislike of Europe in the Midwest was most noticeable, of course, before and during American participation in the second World War. The attack on Pearl Harbor was not the work of Europeans. The war against Japan was, perhaps because of that, more popular and seemed more natural to most midwesterners. But to a stranger in the region at the time it seemed that the majority of midwesterners were irked, annoyed, and insulted when Germany, Italy, and their satellites immediately after the attack on Pearl Harbor declared war on the United States, without waiting to see whether the United States would declare war on them. Midwest amour-propre seemed hurt at being forced into war by "the other fellow." But behind this lay the

313

midwesterners' long tradition of peace and prosperity in insulated safety.

For this insulation from the currents of world affairs they did not have to make any obvious contribution until 1941. And again, in this, their attitude had far more to be said for it than that of the Victorian businessmen in Britain or, indeed, of so many of their sons and grandsons in Britain between 1925 and 1939. At least midwesterners and their neighbors on the Great Plains were insulated by vast oceans instead of by a little ditch, and by all the other regions of the United States into the bargain.

This Midwest insulation has been wrongly but widely confused, by foreigners and Americans alike, with isolationism. The Midwest has, again wrongly in my judgment, been described as the most isolationist region of America. At a given moment in the past it may have been.[8] But Midwest and American attitudes change very abruptly; and what is true at one moment in one region is not true the next. Moreover, the Midwest has suffered, as a whole, from much national publicity given to certain organizations and movements the national headquarters of which were, mainly for convenience, in Midwest cities. It has also suffered from a few very vocal organizations and periodicals peculiar to the Midwest but singular in their views or aims.

A study of all kinds of polls of public opinion during the past decade shows practically no difference between the Midwest and the East (New England *plus* Middle Atlantic States) on such questions as joining the League of Nations, voluntarily entering the second World War, the repeal of the "arms embargo," lend-lease, the arming of American merchant ships before the attack on Pearl Harbor, and many other crucial issues of American foreign policy. A few such polls were taken between 1939 and 1942 in American big cities. It may surprise many to know that on the questions of entering the war, lend-lease, and arming merchant ships, Chicago showed virtually the same percentage of opposition (just over 50 per cent) as New York. St. Louis and Detroit combined showed the same percentage as Boston and Philadelphia combined. In 1945 the percentage of those interviewed and in favor of America's joining an organization of United Nations "with teeth and claws" was higher in the Midwest than in the South, and again practically the same as in the East. More significantly, the per-

[8] See the excellent analysis, "The Origins of Middle Western Isolationism," by Ray Allen Billington in the *Political Science Quarterly*, Vol. LX, No. 1 (March, 1945). I do not agree with all of that analysis, which extends also to North and South Dakota, Nebraska, and Kansas. But it is a valuable contribution to the study of Midwest attitudes to foreign policy.

314

centage in favor of international collaboration of all kinds—including military action to stop aggression—moved faster and farther in the Midwest between 1935 and 1945 than it did in any other region of America except (perhaps naturally) the Far West.

Indeed, according to the evidence of these polls, the Great Plains region was more isolationist than the Midwest proper between 1935 and 1942; and the Far West seems to have been more isolationist than any American region up to 1941. If that is so, insulation seems to cause isolationism; but it is insulation from a definite theater of conflict or possible entanglement. When the Japanese menace loomed closer, the Far West became less isolationist; and by 1945 it was more in favor of international collaboration than any other American region.[9]

The Midwest in its relatively short history has been as insulated from the currents of world affairs as the heart of Russia—the center of the biggest land mass in the world. From 1918 until the 1930's, the other Great Powers tried to insulate Russia; and Russia had so much to do at home that she was content to be insulated. Yet, like the Midwest, Russia has been involved, both voluntarily and involuntarily and at an increasing rate, in world affairs. During and after the European phase of the second World War many midwesterners were annoyed and made more than a little fearful by Russian characteristics which, upon close examination, appear very like some Midwest characteristics. For example, Russian insularity; Russian claims to the superiority of their own methods, institutions, and myths; their claims to have won, or done, most in the war; their playing-up of their home team and playing-down of the other fellow's; distrust of foreigners; ignorance of the outside world; emphasis upon material things and bigness; unwillingness to agree on the meanings of certain basic ideas; a great sensitiveness to anything that looks like criticism by foreigners; a great readiness to criticize foreigners. All these are the hallmarks not of isolationism but of the insulation of a vigorous and youthful people.

The Russians have seen terrible wars upon their own beloved ground. They were the first to "scorch" their own earth. Midwesterners, happily, have seen nothing like that since their forebears rooted out the Indians, and that was small in comparison. They have had nothing with which their imagination could possibly compare their moderate and temporary

---

[9] For this purpose I have consulted the Gallup polls; all the polls collated by the National Opinion Research Center at the University of Denver, Colorado; the polls by that Center itself; and many privately conducted polls the results of which I have been privileged to study. All polls have an element of chance in them. All are "short-run" media. But in this case all these independent polls show the same broad results.

material sacrifices of war. For a short season they have had to give up things which their fathers and grandfathers never had, anyway. But they have had to give up the most cherished of all their possessions: their sons.

These they have freely given; no Americans more; and they have given them for a victory that meant life, liberty, and the pursuit of happiness not only to America but also to many nations all over the world. They have given them in faraway countries of whose peoples they knew nothing: Guadalcanal, Tunisia, the Gilberts, Carolines, Marshalls, Okinawa, the American Philippines, Burma, China, and the seven seas, as well as in European lands from which many midwesterners came. It is hard, indeed, to be plucked so rudely and violently from insulation to involvement all over the shrinking globe. It is hard to see the connection between loss of meat or rubber or gasoline or household appliances, the establishment of order far away abroad, the inner peace and prosperity of America, and so many empty places in so many Midwest families.

When all this is considered, the magnitude of the change within a few years is striking. The comparatively few discordant, if strident, voices from the Midwest, the periodic outbursts of foreign-hating chauvinists, are understandable. They are not typically midwestern. They have counterparts of equal stridency in other American regions. Indeed, to a striking extent the centers of intolerance or extreme chauvinism have shifted from the Midwest to the Great Plains and to California. The East itself is not free from intolerance, chauvinism, or dislike of foreigners. The direction and rate of improvement, of movement toward maturity, have been most apparent in the Midwest. It is the few exceptions to this statement which stand out and claim a disproportionate amount of public attention.

What there was of organized, vocal isolationism made its greatest appeal in trying to prevent America from being involved in war—any war. This attempt failed. Failures are not popular in the Midwest. Such isolationism therefore became suspect *as a policy*. You could still hate foreigners, as you could hate your competitor in another Midwest city, the New Deal, Washington, Wall Street, bureaucracy, trade-unions, Jews, Roman Catholics, or teetotalers. But once midwesterners are convinced that a policy will not achieve their purpose—in this case, freedom from war—they scrap it and evolve another. If the other policy means getting on with competitors, organized labor, federal agencies, Jews, Catholics, foreigners—yes, and even communists *outside* the United States—well, then it must be tried. Only the last-ditch minority

316

refuses to try it. And a midwesterner who will not try a new method when an old one has failed is generally regarded as out of date: a terrible criticism. That was clearly manifested in the elections of 1944.

It is all right to try and play one lobby or interest off against another. That is politics, everywhere: even in dictatorships. But to lean too heavily upon isolationism and dislike of foreigners in a region of so many and numerous "national groups" is politically dangerous. The side which leans on tolerance is leaning on what makes the Midwest tick. The great majority of midwesterners know that and vote accordingly— especially in the big cities, where the greatest extremes and differences are found and where the greatest tolerance is needed. You cannot nourish dislike and distrust of foreigners too much without increasing dislike and distrust at home. That is particularly true of the Midwest and its city populations, where so much material for domestic dislike and distrust is lying around.

A note on Midwest Anglophobia should be in order here. It is a fascinating subject which someone, preferably neither an Englishman nor an American, should study. It is not confined to crackpots, though, of course, it finds its most violent expression among them. As we observed earlier, it has a long history in this young region. The English—not the Scotch, Welsh, or Irish—are widely distrusted and disliked in the Midwest not as persons, nor even as a nation, but as a symbol. England to most midwesterners is the giant's castle from which America, and the Midwest, were liberated. England is also the "mother" symbol from which the youth has broken away; so while there is great and widespread respect for the old maternal figure—a respect which quickly bursts forth in unstinted admiration whenever Britain rises to high achievement—at the same time England and English institutions must be panned in order to justify the break. Much of the criticism of things British derives from myth, ignorance, and quick judgment; as does much foreign criticism of things American.

Anglophobia in the Midwest, however, wears many aspects. There is the dislike of England carried to the Midwest by many European nationalities for European reasons and grafted on to the parent-stem of all-American dislike or distrust of the British. There is the Midwest's peculiar dislike and distrust of all cosmopolitans, distrust of the American East, "city slickers," easy manners, fluency, and poise; and that is carried over to Britain too. This is one of the oldest elements in Midwest political life. Over a century ago when the Illinois Whigs voted against Van Buren, they coupled him with "Englishry" because of his cosmo-

317

politan tastes. They cried, "Down with his English carriage, English horses, and English driver!" Yet none of them was English.

The English accent seems clipped and affected to midwesterners. English reserve and diffidence pass for snootiness in a region where American reserve and diffidence would equally be treated as snooty. Fluency or ease of self-expression seems suspiciously like smoothness or glibness. Monarchy, titles, aristocracy, ancient forms of address; all these seem out of date to a people who rightly pride themselves on their youth and up-to-dateness. They do not see among themselves the equivalents of these English institutions. And, of course, they do not see what national purposes are served by the deceptive British habit of conserving forms and formulas but completely changing their contents and functions. Yet they also admire the solidity and stability of British politics and social order. Indeed, they become rather anxious when British social and political life looks unsettled or seems to be going "radical." How, they wonder, can a monarchy and aristocracy go socialist? Well, a colonial society went republican. Was not that admirable?

One of the strangest elements in this attitude to things British is the general Midwest admiration for British politicians and diplomats and their brains. They are almost always viewed as extremely able, outstandingly intelligent, and therefore greatly to be distrusted. Midwesterners are always sure that Uncle Sam's representatives, from President down to office boy, will get the worst of any negotiations in which foreigners, especially Britishers, appear. These wily and able British are supposed by midwesterners to get the best of everything for Britain. This is one of the most striking hangovers from a former epoch. Most British taxpayers, looking back over the twenty years of international diplomacy and negotiations before 1940, would be tempted to weep, draw the veil, and murmur, "The glory has departed." The British people could scarcely have fared worse with any other political leaders, diplomats, or representatives. Midwesterners forget that Mr. Churchill got back into Parliament only with great difficulty after the first World War and was ignored by his own party leaders for eleven years. It is interesting to wonder whether this Midwest attitude will be so marked after the second World War, in which the British were so manifestly weakened and at such a disadvantage in economic and diplomatic discussions.

Clearly much Midwest dislike or distrust of "England" comes from last century when Britain was unassailably powerful and wealthy. What will the Midwest attitude to things British become now that Britain is the most vulnerable of the Great Powers, economically the poorest, the heaviest in debt, the most dependent on other countries for food and work, and with the smallest proportion of young people to build any future? Many midwesterners were inclined to believe that wily British agents got Americans to fight British wars; so they vehemently sought to guard American neutrality. The wheel has come full circle. Britain is now so greatly weakened, America and Russia so strengthened, that the great lines and currents of world power make the once-tight little island look like a little outpost either of Europe or of America. They even make some thinking Britishers desire British neutrality in future. Everyone's attitude is likely to change when Britain's independence of action—or of inaction—becomes less than it has been for centuries.

Midwesterners have not yet caught up with the violent revolutions in world power since 1914. They are proud of America's power. They do not yet realize what it means. Other nations do. Many midwesterners still distrust the British and fear Russia as if the British and Russians had nothing to fear.

What makes foreigners apprehensive about America is an attitude to foreign affairs which is particularly marked in the Midwest. It is part of the youthful self-assurance of the region and the country. It consists of a moral fervor, a crusading sentiment. It is an intense conviction that any and every problem in any place on earth is easily soluble by the simple application of principles of right and wrong, and in very short order. All problems are soluble. All can be solved quickly; that is, within the speaker's lifetime. All methods proposed are either wholly right or wholly wrong, wholly good or wholly bad. Thus, all "empires" are wrong and bad: morally so. They should be abolished and hang the consequences. That they continue at all—indeed, that they continued after 1776—is something like a standing reproach to a nation that successfully rebelled from an empire and to a Midwest that made a new domestic empire by rebelling from the settled ways in the East. Kings and queens are wrong, for the same reason. Titles are wrong. Socialism and communism are wrong. In fact, more seems to be wrong with humanity when it is viewed from the heart of America than when it is seen on its home grounds.

But all this is genuinely and sincerely believed by most midwesterners: more so than perhaps by any other Americans. It is earnestly believed by Midwest liberals; indeed, more ardently by them than by Anglophobes, foreigner-haters, or crackpots. Any Englishman in the Midwest in recent years could understand why Victorian Englishmen seemed unpleasant; why the English were so heartily disliked all over the world; and why everyone, including American visitors, thought them prigs and hypocrites. He was on familiar ground.

319

The stranger is confused when told that the Russians, French, and British are playing power politics by claiming "spheres of interest"; he thinks of the Monroe Doctrine. He is surprised when Russian and Turkish concern over the Dardanelles, or British concern over the Suez Canal, is treated as power politics or imperialism; he thinks of Panama, the Canal Zone, and the way it was obtained. He is baffled when "empire bases" or "colonies" or "oversea possessions" of European countries are criticized; he reads in the same papers and the *Congressional Record* of "minimum" and "legitimate" demands for American overseas bases stretching from Iceland round the Western Hemisphere across the Pacific to the borders of Russia in Asia. He is bewildered by much talk of liberating "dependent peoples" all over the world; he reads that the Filipinos are free but that America will "naturally" or "understandably" have a treaty by which American military bases there will defend both Filipinos and Americans. He is puzzled to find overwhelming support for Communists in Balkan countries and almost everywhere else, where they are treated as "the people" rebelling against tyrants or monarchs; he reads strongly worded criticisms in the same papers about Russia, or about Communists in Britain, the United States, and Latin America. He hears and reads much about imperialism, power politics, the "realism" of other nations, and the unselfish idealism of American policy and business. He tries to square it all. It sounds like England almost a century ago.

It is certainly not hypocrisy, just as it was not hypocrisy in Victorian England. It comes from youthful, naïve, undiscriminating, oversimplified self-confidence. It comes from optimism; from a certainty that anything can be solved permanently, quickly, and easily. It runs the risk of great disappointments and frustration, as the British grandsons of the Victorians can testify. It comes from having been insulated for so long and having achieved miracles in insulation, without needing to consult or get along with anyone but other Americans.

It is not for nothing that Russians and midwesterners today show so many common characteristics in their attitudes to the world. They are both thinking of their past insulation—an insulation now bound to disappear. They know that new inventions have made it disappear, so they are both thinking of a bigger and better insulation comprising much more of the surface of the globe. They are both largely unaware of the way other peoples live. They both have their own models and plans by which, they are sure, mankind would live much more fully and happily, and therefore ought to be made to.

"Now one trouble with our public opinion .... is a combination of

'Messianic complex' with a massive ignorance of the outside world. .... Ours is a 'spatial' psychology..... Now 'space' has failed us and we find ourselves suddenly caught up in totally new and intimate relations with a world that we had always regarded as remote, and of that world we know very little. This has happened at the time when that world is caught in the greatest crisis of all time, the full meaning of which has not yet become fully clear to that world, much less to ourselves .... the thing calls for a new approach in which our 'Messiah' complex gives place to an intelligent recognition of our ignorance of the conditions with which we have to deal. That is the true humility which is the foster-mother of all real knowledge, and we need a good dose of it in our system."[10]

That is a voice from the East of America. It is applicable to all men, everywhere, today. Many will hope for the sake of America and the world that it will be heeded. Midwesterners, of whom it is more true than of other Americans, need to heed it more; for they stand to lose so much, to be so disillusioned and frustrated, if they do not. And that, as all Europe shows, is bad. Happily with all their idealism and perfectionism, which often tends to make the best the enemy of the good, they are realistic, matter-of-fact, self-critical, and adaptable. If they were not, Americans and many others might view their future more gloomily.

[10] The late Thomas F. Woodlock in the Wall Street Journal, January 10, 1945.

IX. AFTERNOON

We have not come through centuries, caste, heroisms, fables, to halt in this land today.—WHITMAN TO EMERSON (August, 1856).

BEFORE WE GO TO SPECULATING IN FUTURES, LET US SEE WITH WHAT WE have to speculate. Let us begin with a trial balance. The future of the Midwest is bound to be much more closely linked to the future of America than the region was to America's past. The Midwest began from scratch. It developed along lines laid down in the main by its own people, and it deeply influenced all-American history. That period, the two epochs of the Old and the New Midwests, really came to an end in 1929. That year marked the high noon of the Midwest.

In the great experiments and wars of the last decade and a half mid-westerners have conserved—as all peoples do after events have moved ahead—many of their noontime characteristics. But all America, and even countries overseas, have been influencing and conditioning the region and are increasingly bound to do so. In its turn the Midwest has been influencing the East and other regions of America by its ideas, its experiments, and many of its people.

Meanwhile the world has been undergoing violent convulsions in so-called peacetime and in war, under the impact of strange ideas, ex-periments, and methods. All of them have been applied in, and need for successful application, bigger laboratories than a region or even the greatest nation. As far as we can see into the future, their application will have ever wider effects. Nothing can ever be as localized in its effect

322

as it once was. The "locality" has been extended to take in vast regions of the earth's surface and many nations. That means, of course, wider areas of standardization in which ever quickening communications result in ever quickening reactions: roughly the same kind of reactions everywhere at roughly the same moment. That is a threat to regional characteristics and peculiarities.

Because of all this during the last ten or fifteen years the American consciousness has become more national, more nation-wide, more of a pattern than ever before. It has been made more nearly all-American. It is not yet complete, and it has not been achieved without local friction, tension, resentment, and revolt. But the big tides in both domestic and foreign affairs have swept across the country and overwhelmed many a local singularity or regional particularism. Many of the problems faced long ago by industrialized nations in the Old World have reared their heads for the first time in America since 1929. Even if the proposed solutions are naturally more American than European, the effects on so highly industrialized a people are much the same. This is particularly obvious in American opinion on world affairs and American foreign policy.

The immense economic and military power of America is as impressive and bewildering to Americans as it is to foreigners. It is so new and strange. The change in America's role in world affairs has been so great, so violent, and so abrupt since 1914 that neither the Americans' own adaptation to it, nor that of the rest of the world, could be fast and full enough. Two world wars within a generation have knocked three empires off the map of the world, made a vast new Russian empire, created a dozen new sovereign nations, knocked half a dozen out of existence again, made America the greatest financial creditor in history—virtually the only one, on balance, in the world—reduced Britain to the status of a debtor for the first time in centuries, thrown the entire Orient and half the world's population into social chaos, and upended all our notions of money, capital, work, time, space, communications, strategy, and defense. On the shrinking canvas of world affairs futuristic pictures have been drawn with violent strokes and in glaring colors.

The great British commonwealth of nations straggling all over the seven seas and safeguarded for more than a century by the biggest navy in the world (for which only a few million taxpayers in Britain paid) is now mainly composed of independent British nations. But the forty-seven million souls in the British isles are more vulnerable in Europe alone than at any time since 1066. They are impoverished; debtors to foreigners; unable to eat, be clothed, or housed without exports; unable to export without first importing food and raw materials; unable to sustain their people even on drab levels of subsistence without vexatious rules, regulations, and controls; and now gravely overpopulated relative to their natural resources and to the proportion of young and vigorous people in their entire population. How much for defenses and for manning them can they afford in the future?

On the old terrain of the land and in the new element of the air, Russia and America are the dominating world powers. At sea, especially with her new naval air arm, America rules the waves. New forces of economic, strategic, and political attraction are at work, tugging many so-called sovereign and independent nations into new and strange orbits.

Providence is more than ever on the side of "the big battalions," but they are new and strange battalions. No one knows whither they will be led or who will lead them. No one really knows whither they want to go. For the first time in history, world power is probably equally divided, but on sharply distinct continental lines: America in the Western Hemisphere; Russia in Europe and most of Asia. Between them come the oceans and many smaller powers who live by the sea. Yet America and Russia do not *need* much of transoceanic trade. That makes the continental division seem more, rather than less, disturbing in the long run. As fast as inventions shrink the globe, they also divide its chief natural areas and their peoples. And ideologies, which seep across oceans and frontiers, also help to prolong divisions, tensions, annoyances, differences, and conflicts.

To make matters worse by making them more uncertain, new inventions threaten to do away even with the new weapons that won this war; to annihilate more space; to make hay of the strategic, logistic, economic, and other principles upon which strategy and power are still founded. New sources of energy, as potent for peace as for war, for good as for evil, for welfare as for power politics, have been discovered. Neither great nor small nations, neither liberals nor reactionaries, neither communists nor capitalists, neither bureaucrats nor increasingly unfree individuals, can be sure what all this will provoke in national and international affairs. They only know that whatever happens will happen quickly. It is not just a question, as it was after 1918, of old hands at the old helm. It is one of old and new hands at the new helms of strange vessels, driven by unfamiliar engines on uncharted courses with untried crews. If it is a time to try men's souls, it is at least intensely exciting. It is so exciting that curiosity and experimentalism among the young vie with the natural conservatism of the middle-aged and the old, who would like a quieter life after so many upsets in three decades. All of this has deeply affected the whole of America.

Since 1929 the Midwest has been wide open to such influences. It has become, as we saw, increasingly and now almost completely dovetailed with the East to form that industrial North of the United States which the Civil War made inevitable. Like the East, it has its rural and farming population. But they are bound in the future, as in the past, to bulk ever smaller in the region as a whole, to loom less significant in the scheme of things economic and political, like the farmers of the East long ago. This new North, with nineteen of the forty-eight states, already accounts for over two-thirds of the country's domestic market, over three-quarters of its industrial capacity, and just under three-fifths of its people. Almost every modern method, device, facility, or invention has been working to bring about this integration of East and Midwest. Now they are working faster and more furiously than ever.

The radio brings instantaneous news or comment and helps to create instantaneous and standardized reactions. The press, still local or regional, offsets its editorial views with nationally syndicated features and columnists for whose writings it accepts no responsibility and for whose accuracy it does not vouch. Newspaper chains and the increasing importance of the national capital and the Washington bureau break down the local or regional characteristics of the press. The teletypesetter, teleprinter, and wirephoto make chain publication—and even a nation-wide newspaper—easier to run, as the New York Times proved with its wirephoto edition at the San Francisco Conference in 1945. The new television networks promise to expand this ever widening orbit of standardization and still further to break down localism and regionalism. Easier travel and mobility, which made the Midwest, bid fair to unmake its sectionalism. Chicago became an intercontinental airport and port of entry in 1945. The long-overdue equalization of freight rates on American railroads in that same year promised to integrate even the South with the Midwest up the great central valley and river basin of the United States—thus belatedly making the Illinois Central Railroad the two-way street which its founders before the Civil War planned, and which that war and its aftermath prevented. Increasing leisure and use of airways, railroads, and highways will rapidly increase this standardization.

In the economic field the organization of industry and of unions goes rapidly ahead. No antitrust laws can prevent the flow and exchange of new ideas and methods in industry by industry, just as they cannot prevent lobbies. The concentration of firms into big industrial units, and even into units going outside the bounds of one industry, has been going on for decades in America: mainly between the East and Midwest. That, too, cannot be stopped by laws. Despite the nation-wide dispersal of defense plants capable of conversion to civil uses, the Midwest has increased its share of America's industrial capacity during the war. The country's geography and communications cannot change the importance of connections between East and West, the central hub of the Midwest itself, or the unity of production and distribution.

The fillip to southern industry by the equalization of railroad freight rates cannot overcome these overwhelming natural advantages, though it will aid the South. The old financial domination of the country by Wall Street has disappeared, just as that of Boston yielded to New York a century ago. Today Washington and Wall Street, like the Treasury and the Bank of England in Britain, form a kind of hybrid plant; but in America the Midwest, unlike Scotland or the British provinces, is as important in the self-financing of industry and trade as the East is in providing finance. Industry, commerce, finance, distribution—all of these are wider in scope in the combined East and Midwest than purely local or regional institutions. Indeed, in many industries, initiative now comes from the Midwest and affects the East as well as the nation. These economic trends are naturally paralleled by the activities of trade-unions which tend more and more to become less local, less regional, and more national in scope and organization. It all breaks down the earlier sectionalism of the Midwest.

Even the Midwest farm lobby, which used to be the most united and most politically powerful in Washington, has lost ground; for American farming as a whole now suffers more from specialization and technical differences. Accordingly, the Grange and the Farm Bureau, representing mainly the well-to-do farmers, have differed with each other on many policies; and both are opposed by the smaller farmers' and tenant farmers' National Union. Technical and other differences in American farming have changed the old agricultural sectionalism of the country and have resulted in new alignments: alignments by form of tenure, size of farm, crops raised, and the many different economic interests of American farmers. Therewith, the old radicalism of the prairie and the Northwest—the western portions of the Midwest and the eastern parts of the Great Plains—has lost its united front and much of its political power. Consequently, sectionalism among Midwest farmers has greatly diminished. What is true of the trade-unions is also true of farm organizations, industrialists, and trade associations: they become more and more national in scope, organization, and activity.

The industrialization of the Midwest, which made its towns and cities and populated them, cannot stop; nor can they. Although city populations in America as a whole seem to have been halted in 1930, perhaps reflecting the halt to immigration, it has only been temporary in the Midwest. The census of 1940 shows that. The second World War snatched young men and women from the farms at a faster rate and in greater numbers than was normal. Not all of the survivors will go back. Not all who want to can, for many reasons. The most mechanized agriculture in the world has been mechanized more rapidly than ever before, and after the war it promises to be even more swiftly mechanized.

Add to this the natural, long-run trend of young people from the farms and rural areas to the towns and cities, and the inevitable result must be a further growth in urbanization and urban life. This may be slightly offset by the further growth of suburban and satellite communities—which, however, are still urban. Moreover, as in the first World War, many Negroes and white workers who came into the Midwest will not go back to their native regions. That means, in turn, a growth of the cities' problems: slums, central overcrowding, derelict areas, delinquent properties, a further fall in city revenues, a contrary increase in public demands on city treasuries, the evacuation of cities by more and more factories, social and racial tensions, labor troubles, and problems of public health, transport, and education.

These urban problems are not peculiarly midwestern. They disfigure city life all over the world. But the important thing to remember in this context is that in any further urbanization of the Midwest the region must inevitably become less sectional in outlook. The more urban life the region has, proportionate to its rural life, the more like easterners must its urban dwellers become. Here, too, the cities and towns that made the New Midwest bid fair to unmake its old sectionalism, as they, their industries, and their trades combine more and more closely with those of the East to make the new industrial and distributive North of the country.

The war has given a powerful impetus to this combination, for it has located or expanded far more productive capacity in Midwest towns and cities than in those of the East. The greatest continuous region of industrial production and urbanization in the world, only a hundred miles deep on the average, now runs from a little north of Milwaukee through Chicago, round Lake Michigan, across to Detroit and as far

327

as Buffalo in the north and Pittsburgh in the south. That is where the greatest absolute expansion of American industrial capacity of all kinds has occurred. It certainly creates enormous problems of reconversion to civil uses, of "displaced persons," of potential unemployment, and of state and municipal administration.

The farms of the Midwest, or of any other American region, cannot absorb more than a small fraction of returning veterans; and the immigration of workers from other regions into this great industrial, urban belt has been very large. The pent-up demand for civilian goods, foregone during the war, will keep much of the Midwest, its cities and towns and their factories, busy for some years until the backlog of demand is satisfied and production has to be based on maintenance and *net* new demand. In that period of transition, uneasy as it will be, the main problems will not emerge into the light of day. They will be masked, unrecognized. The life of cities and towns will go on. Their expansion will to a great extent be maintained and "carried." A large number of women war workers and older hands will retire in favor of returning veterans.

But when that period is over, and the normal "maintenance" demand and exploitation of *net* new markets return, the big problem of industrial cities will emerge in naked ugliness. That problem is likely to be most acute in the Midwest. Meanwhile industry itself will have linked the life of these Midwest cities still more closely with that of eastern cities; so the solutions to the problem of northern industry and urbanization in America are more likely to be *national* in origin and scope than local, regional, or sectional. If you standardize the problem, you have to standardize and generalize the solution, too.

As we have seen, the decisive trends in national politics since the 1900's have been those of cities and towns. The new North, composed of East and Midwest, has the overwhelming majority of them. As Midwest and East have become more and more united and standardized since the 1920's, the main lines of politics have become increasingly identical in both regions. In both they have followed the course of the majorities in the cities. Indeed, all the unifying and standardizing factors already mentioned have had their effect on national politics. They have had it in struggles for the allegiance of the bulk of the city populations. In fact, politics became really national, nation-wide in appeal and in organization after 1920 and for the first time since the 1850's. The expansion of lobbies, trade associations, and trade-unions on a nation-wide scale and the breakdown of the farmers' sectional strength only hastened all this.

328

Similarly, entirely new notions of American foreign policy; the violent alterations in the world outside which revolutionized America's position in it, willy-nilly; and the consequently rapid overhauling of American strategy, defenses, war production, and location of strategic industries—all these resulted in breaking down sectionalism and regionalism, unifying East and Midwest, and more closely dovetailing transport and communications in the great industrial North on which America so heavily depends.

In the life of the mind, public education, and the arts, national rather than regional notions have impressed themselves on the minds of educators, artists, and intellectuals. Experiments are, of course, still localized: among educators in Massachusetts as in Illinois or Wisconsin; among artists and intellectuals in Greenwich Village or mid-Manhattan as on Chicago's South Side or in Streeterville, in small Missouri and Ohio towns or out in Iowa and Minnesota. Yet the reactions come on a nation-wide scale, almost simultaneously. There is no medium of public communication today which is not going to work more instantaneously and on a nation-wide scale in the very near future. That simply means more mobility, standardization, and nation-wide distribution of ideas.

As in everything else, it does *not* mean that the Midwest "succumbs to eastern influences." As in industry, trade associations, trade-unions, and farm lobbies, so in education, ideas, and the arts, it may equally mean that the East succumbs to Midwest influences. As the Midwest still has more youthful characteristics and vigor, it will probably end by standardizing more of the East on Midwest patterns than of the Midwest on eastern models. The Midwest may not make as many inventions in ideas as it does in material things, but in both ideas and material things it experiments, adapts, and exploits more powerfully and more exhaustively than any other region in America. And the one who makes most experiments, models, and adaptations is most likely to be the one from whose designs the dies and jigs are made. So northern standardization, in the end, may well bear a greater resemblance to Midwest models than to those of the East.

Finally, it is barely one American generation since mass immigration into America, and particularly into the Midwest, was stopped by Congress. By 1970—twenty-five years hence—it will be two American generations since that epoch-making, and epoch-ending, decision was taken. Within one generation of 1929 the greatest melting-pot in the world will have fused much of its original ingredients. That process has been obvious these ten years past. But it will have gone immeasurably farther in two whole generations, by the time America celebrates the bicentenary of Independence.

As this Midwest crucible at last really melts its existing contents, without new ingredients, it must pour them into molds. These molds have become more and more of an all-American pattern during the last couple of decades; in fact, since 1920. But their shape has been increasingly standardized since 1930 and 1940. All the other standardizing and integrating factors have inevitably influenced the home, the family, the way of life, the diversions, the ideas, and the thought-patterns of midwesterners and easterners alike—and of many other Americans besides. Because of the time lag in generations, because young fathers and mothers live to be old grandparents, much of the Old Midwest sectionalism and its characteristics will remain, just as the Scotch remain particularly Scottish in a long-unified Britain. But the old sectional features will disappear at an accelerating pace.

America is so young and new, the Midwest particularly so, and new inventions and communications are capable of such immediate and extensive application in the East and Midwest, that characteristics become old and are swamped by the new more quickly than they are anywhere else. Moreover, the Midwest puts a special and particularly heavy premium on the new, anyway, for the sake of its novelty alone. Thus, in the next two or three decades the new North will produce its own American type, fused of Midwest and eastern elements, pursuing a way of life which is itself undergoing new kinds of standardization but on practically uniform lines. There will be "pockets" which this process affects little, if at all—the rural areas of the Midwest and the rural towns—but in the new North they will become what the rural people of Maine, Vermont, upper New York State, Pennsylvania, and the Chesapeake tidewater lands are to the East today.

Against all this unification and standardization there will be individual rebels, just as some midwesterners have always revolted from the increasing complexity and standardization of life. Some will be reactionaries who hate change, loathe the increasing paper work and bureaucracy which a vast area of standardization necessitates, and detest the inevitable social, political, and legal accompaniments of it. They will want all the benefits of big markets and none of the costs. There will also be their counterparts at the other extreme: those who turn "radical" because of the rigidity of such a complex and standardized system, who want to destroy and build anew, as if you could easily do that to as delicate and vulnerable a piece of apparatus as the new northern economic, political, and social unit. And, if you did, your new system would have to be even more rigid. Raucous and strident voices will be raised at both extremes.

But the process lies, as much as anything can ever lie, in the logic of history. There can be no stopping it. The majority of midwesterners in their towns and cities begin to realize it now. They will fully recognize it very shortly. And to what they recognize as inevitable they are the quickest to adapt.

PROBLEMS AND PEOPLE

Midwesterners face a future with the same perplexities and anxieties that vex other Americans and many other peoples, but with greater confidence. No one can yet say if the confidence is justified, or if it is just a traditional and out-of-date self-assurance, like that of Victorian England. One of their greatest contrasts and paradoxes is still obvious. It is their new standardization and "conformity" in a region made great by "nonconformists," rebels, and singular individuals. Will the new standardization, the junction of East and Midwest, and the Midwest's own heavy emphasis upon "a prairie sameness" in basic skills and technical education—to the exclusion of a more rounded and mature education—hasten and complete the uniformity of the new North? Will they make out of midwesterners uniform and typical northerners? Or will the region's initiative, enterprise, vigor, and curiosity produce a new type of individual, not just a human unit?

These questions vex all industrial and urban peoples in differing degrees; but they are most insistent in the Midwest. There, the problems of industrial civilization, of democracy, of mass production in economics as well as in politics and social affairs, are most apparent. There are two vast national laboratories of social experiment in the world today: Russia and America. America depends overwhelmingly on the new North. Can the American vastness reconcile its new and greater scale of operations with respect for the individual and his freedoms? Can it prevent the crushing uniformity of bureaucracy and petty minds? Can it develop the rich variety of the creative spirit in the individual man? If it can develop curiosity, initiative, and variety, it will succeed. But to do so, it must somehow offset the killing effects of the new standardization. It must stop the creative human intelligence from being canned or cast in molds along with the material means of living. If it can do that, it can point the way ahead for the remaining vexed democracies of the world. If it cannot, it seems bound for social and political convulsions.

Some American observers, scared of the threats in this new standardization and vastness of operations, have flown to a new concept of "regionalism" as a solution. Fearing the inevitably national scale of federal powers and agencies, trade associations, industrial concentration, and trade-unions, they think they can shield and nourish individual freedoms and creative intelligence in half-a-dozen regions of America with a sponsored cultural life of their own.

I think this is natural, but it is doomed to frustration. The tide of events is flowing against it and has been since the dawn of American history. Creative intelligence can be helped and trained; but, as far as we know, the aptitude for it is born in a child, and not all children have even that. Where and how it is born is not a matter of locality or parentage. All our institutions can do is to provide environments and facilities for proving its existence and improving it, calling it forth in all its richness, and making the very best of what each child brings into the world. Now that is a job which cannot be carried on behind a shield, in some locality or other. No one can say where, or from whom, rebels and geniuses will be born. Look at Beethoven's or Lincoln's parents!

The trend is toward wider and bigger fields of social activity. If our new problems are ever to be solved, we shall need brains matching these wider fields and familiar with them: men and women who have not been shielded or brought up to believe in a separate dream-world or "cloud-cuckoo-land." We shall need mature, rounded, human minds that see life steadily and see it whole. We shall need minds that can look both before and after; that are not keyed to short-run operations; that see the material needs and possibilities alongside those that are nonmaterial. You are more likely to get those minds by accepting and participating in the Spirit of the Age, the *Zeitgeist*, the movement and trend of the times, the minds of the men who get things done, and by working in them and upon them, than by bucking them and standing aloof. It is just the latter error which so many intellectuals of the last thirty years in all our democracies have committed, with disastrous results to their society and themselves.

If eastern and midwestern millionaires or big businessmen, vexed by political and social portents, could take time to think more than two or three years ahead, they would heavily endow institutions for the liberal arts, the humanities, and other nonmaterial fields of mental training and inquiry. That would open up new horizons before people, lessen the crushing weight of standardization and monotony, enrich the increasing leisure of the majority, strengthen individualism, develop a critical faculty, and diminish the risks of mass hysteria, radicalism, and

332

crank worship. Is not that what many of their grandfathers did? That earlier effort was later ignored, and the human spirit began to revolt.

This sounds like advocacy of "bromide" or "opiates for the people." If these things are bromide or opiate, then the people will get worse ones anyway—but in synthetic form, in rawer and larger doses, and from dubious peddlers. That is one outstanding problem before the new urban, industrial society of the northern United States.

But it is not just a problem of towns and cities, even if it is most acute there. The new North, like France and French North Africa, has one big natural advantage, even in adversity. It may have a surplus of industrial capacity, but it also has a surplus of agricultural production. It has a reservoir of solid and dependable farmers, who have to look both before and after or go bankrupt. It can recruit itself from their children. It can feed and equip itself and others. It is the greatest regional or national reservoir of both industrial and agricultural skills in the world. In both agriculture and industry, output per man-hour is between twice and four times what it is in any other industrial country. Yet, as in those other countries, there is a real social tussle between agriculture and industry, a continuous and embittered tug-of-war between city and rural area, urban workers and farmers.

No one outside Russia knows what feelings or stresses exist between Russian city workers and agricultural workers, between town and country. Yet Russia is the only social laboratory with which the new North of the United States and its eighty million souls can be compared. Russia may be too vast, too ordered, too standardized from the top downward for such a tug-of-war to have developed; though I suspect it exists and is masked. If, as we assumed, the drift to the towns continues in the new American North, and particularly in the Midwest, what is to be done for the remnant of the Old East and the Old Midwest in the rural areas?

The undeniable goodnesses of the rural town and the so-called farming "community" will tend to become ever more narrowing in their effect. Already, what do these rural towns offer to the very few of their own boys or girls who go to college and actually want to go back and "do something" for the home town? Few Americans know the number of personal tragedies experienced by those few who "made good" and then tried to go back and do good or share good with the home folk. This problem is bound to get worse if the small rural town is dying and knows it is.

Yet the land remains, and it is rich. It will have to be increasingly conserved by state and federal action. Iowa has one-quarter of all the

Grade I farm land in the United States, and three-quarters of it lie within the short space of two hundred and fifty miles from the state capital. Is the farming of most of the richest land in America to depend on federal subsidy taken from urban taxpayers? Are the farmers and their workers and rural neighbors, who account for a third of the people of the new North, to face a future of guaranteed prices—a kind of belated "kickback" in return for the cities' exploitation of the farmers for three generations behind the American tariff?

This is no wartime or postwar problem of the short run. It raised its head in the 1880's and 1890's, in 1920, and again in the 1930's. The New Deal's Agricultural Adjustment Act and "triple-A program" weaned farmers from their old prairie radicalism to the Democrat party, the party which is also most dependent on the masses of urban workers. Then the war brought a more "natural" prosperity to the farms, while it exceedingly multiplied bureaucratic vexations. Which way will the farmer look now?

When world-wide communications are resumed with greater speed and carrying capacity, when the scorched earth bears again in Europe and the Far East—as it always does very quickly, and as it may do with greater abundance in response to new methods—what lies before agricultural America? Before the second World War the world was plagued with so-called surpluses which were controlled, or destroyed, or put into "ever-normal granaries" in one country after another at the urban taxpayers' expense. America was not immune to that, either. Indeed, she suffered greatly from surpluses. May she not suffer even more in the relatively near future? And will she not suffer more deeply if, as is certain, American agriculture goes even faster and farther along the road of mechanization, laborsaving, and the raising of yields? These possibilities are going to affect the Midwest farm, farm land, farmers, and farm votes more than any others except those on the neighboring Great Plains. And indirectly, of course, the effects are going to be felt in towns and cities as the labor which is "saved" on the farms drifts to them. They are also going to be felt in national politics: the politics of both parties.

Social and economic revolutions of this kind, and on this scale, make the old-line politics of Republicans and Democrats look sadly out of date. Indeed, whether they tackle the problems of farmers or those of city workers, can Republicans or Democrats in fact attempt very different solutions? The labels and methods may differ. The principles and the costs seem likely to be the same.

Then there is the problem of the big and smaller cities. Even here, the few big cities tend to get bigger, to take more of the surrounding smaller cities and towns into their economic orbit. As they grow, the problems at their center multiply while the suburbs and satellite communities escape them. The increasing size of marketing areas tends to increase the few big cities and arrest or lessen the influence of smaller cities and towns. In turn this vitally affects state and national politics, magnifying local political tensions and tugs-of-war.

States and big cities have developed remarkable plans for the few immediate postwar years. Most of them depend partly on their own revenues and party on federal funds for these projects. The plans drawn up by St. Louis are a model of foresight and self-help; Chicago, Cincinnati, Kansas City, Cleveland, and others are not far behind. Detroit faces more grievous problems of reconversion and "displaced persons." But all big cities, and to a smaller extent states, realize that the problems of the future—both immediately after the war and for all foreseeable time—cannot be locally or even regionally solved. As with agriculture, the federal power must help to finance public works, communications, housing projects, airports, and schools. That means more federal control and to some extent more spoils; closer connections between national and state or city political machines; and the breaking-down of localism or sectionalism.

The problem of the cities is the problem of industry and distribution, of mass employment, mass unemployment, mass production, and mass politics. It is also, to an increasing extent, the problem of leisure. The Midwest and East, the great reservoir of skills, have developed all these to a point at which skills themselves become less and less important—even in agriculture and in politics. I have been on farms where one man and many machines sowed five hundred acres in less than two weeks. I have been in factories where one man in a tower ran all the operations of a whole bay that employed eighty men in 1926. The region with the greatest capital equipment per worker in the world, and consequently the greatest output per man-hour, is bound to produce the greatest demand for leisure among those employed and the greatest demand for security of employment in order to be sure of enjoyable leisure. No one wants the enforced leisure of a pauperized minority—which we call unemployment.

As skills decline in importance among the mass of operatives, the more essential skill of foremen and managers becomes rarer and more precious. Once upon a time any man of ability could rise to become a foreman, manager, or employer on his own account. There are greater masses of workers today; and fewer who can rise far or quickly. Maybe the rapid growth of industrial unionism reflects the attempt of the operatives, especially the artisans, to get economic significance and power—the equivalent of that social significance which so many dwellers in small communities get by "joining things"; clubs, groupings, orders, and so on. They get leisure and good wages. What can they do, what do they do, with both? That takes us back, circlewise, to the lack of opportunities *outside* the economic sphere. Yet if these opportunities existed and the will to use them were developed, the effect on the social, political, and economic order would be highly beneficial. Thus economics and production cannot safely be insulated from nonmaterial life, any more than intellectual affairs can be insulated from economics and material things.

Can the increase of leisure be organized to select the ablest workers for higher positions? Can this take the place of the old apprenticeship system, now doomed by the assembly line and mass production? Will management be the first to see that its own long-run interests necessitate such an attempt? As the political power of mass politics at Washington and in the states carves out more and more of the field of what was purely private enterprise, and adjudges it to be "affected with the public interest," management obtains a remarkable opportunity to develop new influence and powers. The process has already gone very far in railroads, public utilities, radio, the production and distribution of food, labor relations, air lines, and interstate commerce in general. It has even begun in the collecting and dissemination of news to the press. Even the lobbies of the biggest interests, those of capital and of labor alike, have become *national*; and the use of the word "public" in public relations is significant. There is a problem of the people, who make the mass of the public; and it increasingly demands consideration. Public relations is not enough. It is only a bromide.

As the economic machinery of the new North is further developed and integrated, so it becomes more delicate and complex. A depression that used to spread slowly from the East across America, taking weeks in its passage, now breaks out like a prairie thunderstorm, suddenly and simultaneously. Bigger and bigger cities, bigger "big business," more rapid communications, more intricate connections, more and more capital equipment and processes—all these spell the greater dependence of wider regions and more people upon more delicate economic machinery. One jolt, and the country's social, economic, and even political machinery goes out of gear. Regionalism, localism, and the old-fashioned rugged form of individualism are fighting a forlorn rear-guard action against all this. It is scale that counts; and more and

336

more of the new North is bound to operate on a national scale in the future.

See what is happening in many Midwest towns and cities already. Many smaller cities are dependent on one or two industries or factories, which in turn become increasingly dependent on bigger and wider industrial concerns overlapping all regional boundaries. The increasing vulnerability of a few local concerns increases the social and political vulnerability of an entire city. South Bend, Kenosha, Fort Wayne, Dayton, Cedar Rapids; the list can be indefinitely extended, especially in Ohio, Indiana, Michigan, and northern Illinois. But a similar list can be made in Massachusetts, Connecticut, New York, New Jersey, Pennsylvania, Delaware, and the north of West Virginia.

True, there is an optimum size for, and a limit to, the economies of mass production. The assembly line becomes very costly in overhead, management, and foremen. Many small plants can produce at lower unit costs for a given local market than many larger concerns which tap the national market as a whole. Quick adaptability remains a great economic asset. But, again, the trend is clearly toward wider regions of distribution and operation; and that is bound to affect the Midwest and East and their cities more than any other regions or cities of America. Foreign trade will become more important to American industry than ever before, once the postwar backlog of domestic demand is satisfied, and once production programs are on a "maintenance" basis. That in itself will work great changes in the new northern region of the country.

Other changes are in the air. The older, southern portions of Ohio, Indiana, and Illinois, and perhaps all Missouri, are likely to be drawn closer economically to the northern industrial belt of the South: particularly to Kentucky, Tennessee, Arkansas, and Oklahoma. The proposed Missouri Valley Authority would give an impetus to any such movement. There are interesting examples of the problems thus raised in the southern Illinois oilfield near Salem and Centralia.

There, in a big oilfield developed among farm lands within the last ten years, populations have doubled. "Foreign" oil workers, mechanics, and oil-machinery suppliers from Texas, Oklahoma, and other non-Midwest states have flooded in. The Old Midwest towns of a few thousands of souls and their amenities have not been able to cope with all the new social and political problems. Old strata of the local population rub shoulders with the new, who are now just as numerous. Great strains and stresses are thus placed on existing institutions, local authorities, and even on traditions, customs, and ways of life.

Round the "marginal belt" of the Midwest this is now going on more

337

than ever before—just as, in their day, the discontented Illinoisans, Iowans, and other midwesterners left the region and took their problems and ways of life to California, the new Northwest, or the Great Plains. In the foreseeable future there may not be as much mobility within the inner core of the Midwest as there used to be, but around its margin there is likely to be much more. And that equally holds true of the southern fringe of the East. Therewith the new North as a whole will increasingly affect the life of the nearer South, the new Southwest, and the Great Plains.

More than ever is this likely to happen as it becomes the national factory and assembly plant, taking in from the other regions and sending out toward them. It will be long before the new Southwest and Great Plains, beyond the marginal fringe of the Midwest, gain substantial industries of their own. Even the industries of the Far West, because of geography, railroads, and the location of markets, are likely to be limited for decades to come and to face relatively more vexatious problems of reconversion than the bigger industries of the East and Midwest. Other regions can have *assembly units*; but production, assembly, and distribution on a national scale must for all foreseeable time be more cheaply and efficiently acomplished in the new North of the country. And that, again, means a national consciousness in the entire North and the disappearance of Midwest sectionalism.

The passing of the Old Midwest last century accompanied the miraculous industrialization of the region. That had already happened, too, in the East as the new men and new cities of industry, trade, and finance swamped the colonial society of the states from New England down to Maryland. A little later, the original agrarian society of the Midwest went down in its turn before the advance of industry, cities, and urban workers—despite revolts on the prairie. If the growing-pains of the Constitution had ended in dissolution, if the Civil War had ended in a compromise or a southern victory, the Union might have become two or more different nations with lives and economic systems of their own. Happily this did not occur. But the inevitable result was the concentration of economic power, population, and control in the East and Midwest. If you want to find the clearest traces of the old America today, you must take to the hills, to the Great Plains, and to the new Southwest. The East and Midwest have been, are being, and must continue to be industrialized. They have already undergone much of "the managerial revolution."

So great and so rapid has the change been that few recognize its implications. Most people still use the slogans or catchwords of a

338

generation ago: "bosses," "bankers," "capitalists," "communists," and so on. Bankers no longer "control" industry. Nor do "bosses"; at least, not the bosses whose names are known. They are themselves almost as controlled as the organized workers. Governments, federal and local, have had to draft codes and blueprints according to which, and only within the framework of which, any economic decisions both by labor and by capital can be made. There is very little freedom of private enterprise left. "I do not argue; I merely state the fact."

The Midwest is still confused and bewildered because of the speed with which all these changes have occurred, and because so many businessmen and workers who are still active can remember how recently all this was utterly different. Moreover, the Midwest still has a large number of small businesses employing up to two hundred workers—though their employers, too, risen from the ranks of workers, have to take their decisions within the same framework of governmental rules and regulations. Yet in terms of total output the Midwest has passed the Rubicon, like the East. Its *big* businesses take the effective economic decisions. Its urban society is now composed overwhelmingly of bourgeois and artisans. Uniformity, grading, standardization, status— all these seem to have seeped over from industry into the industrial society of the towns and cities, just as they first did in the East. And now the uniformity of both regions' economic and social systems is fusing the whole of the North into one material.

It is not to the familiar, traditional, and older voices of the Midwest that one must listen today to gain encouragement as one scrutinizes the Midwest prospect. It is to those of younger men, men in their thirties, forties, and early fifties, men who have proved in war their ability to make managerial revolutions on their own—at which all the world gasped. The future lies with these men: with their realism tempered with their Midwest romanticism of newness and experiment; with their adaptability, vigor, imagination, and fair-mindedness; with their ability, far more necessary today and in the future, to place the human alongside the material and trim the material to fit—not vice versa.

They may fail through not being human enough. But they show every sign of knowing the risks and being prepared to "do a job." I think they will more powerfully affect the East, and so the whole North, than those of the East will affect them. That is perhaps how the Midwest can best be said to have reached its prime.

If the Midwest is hastening toward an afternoon of wider uniformity, it carries many brakes and safeguards taken from its own past. Big business and trade-unions are spreading standardization, but they bump into bewildering diversities of individuals and individualism in the Midwest. Like many another movement, they are affected by them. So much is clear in the clash of unions and their jurisdictions in the region, in the rugged individualism of small producers, in the strength of the Republican party in the region, and in the independence shown by local Democrat machines. Independence and a sturdy respect for the individual, despite the urge to conform, mean that the changes in the afternoon cannot be as quick as those of the forenoon and noontime.

Like the British, midwesterners are mongrels and enjoy the mongrel's powers of resistance: resistance to anything. Unlike the British, whose mongrelness is old, theirs is new; and they need time to settle the vigorous mongrel strain. That will take another generation. As it passes, the changes will come about more quickly. The diversities of racial and national origin that now mark the region will become less obvious and less important.

The accent is still on youth in this youthful region; but, just as the wild and radical Midwest became rapidly conservative and "conformist," so is it likely to put less emphasis on youthful qualities merely because they are youthful, and more on sober maturity. In a critical era, and amid social and economic apparatus of increasing delicacy, that also is a safeguard. It may be severely tested, especially in cities, by the organized young veterans of the second World War. But that is a national problem; and Midwest cities can stand a good deal of testing. They have stood it from their recent beginnings.

It is the Midwest accent upon the individual that will prove the greatest asset of the region. It will profoundly influence the two national parties and their policies. It has done so already. As the new North of nineteen states becomes increasingly uniform, this Midwest emphasis on the individual, his qualities, capacities, and freedom, is likely to color the attitude of the whole—thus coloring all-American politics and policies—rather than to become extinguished. In our mass-conscious day and age, that is very important.

Dr. Hayek in *The Road to Serfdom* thinks that the United States may retain more individual freedom than any other land.[1] The Midwest

[1] Friedrich A. Hayek, *The Road to Serfdom* (Chicago: University of Chicago Press, 1944).

is the greatest repository of individualism and of respect for the individual in America, which means in the world. The grandfather of a middle-aged Englishman—not only of a rich Englishman but also of an artisan or a clerical worker—would think his grandson in 1939, and far more so today, almost a serf; a kind of peon; bound hand and foot to boards, rules, regulations, and red tape, if not to the soil or to a particular job. This process has gone rapidly ahead in America, but it is recent. It really began only a couple of decades ago. Compared with the life of an Englishman, an American's life is still one of individual liberty and pursuit of happiness.

In all of Europe, including Britain, the idea and ideal of the nation, the collectivity, the social whole, has become the yardstick of all action. It is the noblest of ideals. But as a political, economic, and administrative idea being translated into everyday practice, it is as arbitrary and dogmatic as the idea of "the economic man" laid down by economists a century ago. America may be bound to travel the same path, as she generally has in social legislation, about a generation behind the leading European countries. But meanwhile she has most of that period to watch, to sit out, to afford her traditionally large percentage of waste, to learn, to adapt, and to compromise. She can profit by others' mistakes, of which there are already many.

It may not be easy. It may mean some violence, which is not new in America. It may mean unconcern with the rest of the world—though only for a season. The American social laboratory is still insulated and virtually self-sufficient. Of all countries, she has the greatest chance to reconcile the claims of the individual human being with those of modern society as a whole, the One with the Many, the unit with the mass. Mobility, opportunity, the individual worker's or consumer's width of choice, the four freedoms, standards of living—all these are far greater in America than they are anywhere else on earth. What is more, they will probably become relatively greater, owing not so much to what America does as to what other peoples do, or have to do, to get a living at all.

Naturally it is on this favored nation, and on the most favored and the most American region in it, that so many anxious eyes are fixed. In the next critical decade or two, the Midwest emphasis upon tolerance, compromise, "what works," and adaptation is likely to overwhelm its relatively small manifestations of intolerance and reaction. If that is so, the Midwest has the equipment and the chance to make an enormously important contribution to the East, and thus to the constructive thinking of the new North, of America as a whole, and of free men

341

and representative governments everywhere. If the Midwest does not want to do that, if it does not do it, it will be false to its own nature and to the great past that made so great a present.

The world beyond America does not appreciate America's own anxieties. American national uniformity does not arise, as in Europe, from below and from a long past. It is overlaid upon diversities, tensions, struggles, and stresses which must continue for at least another generation. Some will continue, unsolved, though diminished, for many generations. (What is the "solution" to the Negro problem?) But American social and political institutions and methods are elastic. That is an asset. It means, of course, less certainty, less predictability than in other lands. For example, some labor unions go bourgeois and join the Republicans; others remain with the Democrats; others wander "in the middle mist," throwing their allegiance now here and now there. Politics in turn are fluid. We have noted many examples of revolt from traditional or familiar alignments in American regions, among businessmen, and among farmers. The views, desires, and votes of twelve million organized young veterans of the armed forces are an unknown quantity; and American politicians, like others, eagerly angle for the support of unknown quantities. What has been happening to Midwest sectionalism has also been affecting political and economic thinking: the barriers, even those of party, are going down.

Most midwesterners, quick to see it last century, again see that some new unifying moral and political, indeed moral-political, force is needed in the life of their country. There are signs of restless search for it on all sides. People know that it must now be national. The restless vigor and divine discontent of the Midwest enter very strongly into this. Desire for some new thing, curiosity, practical idealism, urge to build: these familiar features are also intensifying the search. Even the reactionary strength of the small minority at least shows the midwesterner's attachment to ideals—in this case, those of the past.

Midwesterners are now more on the move, more restless, probably more vigorous, and therefore more dangerous if balked or frustrated, than ever. Their great energies are as yet divided, as their minds and loyalties are confused. In this confusion they are not singular. They are only singular in the wealth of assets with which they can solve their problems. The solutions do not depend on a sufficiency of material means. America has enough and to spare. They depend only on the ability of men and minds to measure up to the problems. An optimistic people, should they be pessimistic now?

We have seen many popular ideas about the Midwest and midwesterners exploded. It is no longer the "cradle of Republicanism." It is not mainly agricultural or rural. It is not pioneer-minded, imbued with a sense of the pioneers' equality, and with their radicalism. It is no more isolationist, foreigner-hating, or insular than other regions, and less than some. It is not undereducated, a region of "hicks," lacking a culture of its own, unproductive of the graces of life and uncreative in the arts. It does not hold the South and the East together in a great American pyramid. It is not a region of little business against the big business of other regions; nor is it one of small towns and cities against the big cities of other sections. It is no longer so distinct in its differences from the East; indeed, it is fusing with the East. Its distinctive characteristics are not those of its cities or towns, its business, or its farming—though you find differences everywhere if you look hard enough. Its distinctive characteristics are those of its richly varied peoples, their neighborliness, their tolerance and conformity to one broad way of life, whatever they do for a living. These people and their ways have gradually been changing, becoming more like those of the East.

They will change progressively faster as the years go by. But the change is not that of dying. As a snake sheds an outworn skin, this change gives new life. It is the change of growth—growth that in its turn affects and even changes others. In that sense it is creative and influential. It may well be decisive in American affairs, as it often was. If it is, it must now be influential, even decisive, in the affairs of the world.

Humanity, the world of men and their nations, is infinitely diverse. So is the Midwest, which is a microcosm. What the Midwest took from other Americans and from all Europeans it can give back, in our day or in that of our children and children's children, changed by its own alchemy into something immeasurably and unrecognizably greater. There is something of destiny, of the natural law of compensation, in that thought. All who love their fellow-men will rejoice to see it realized.